High Endeavours

The Life and Legend
of Robin Smith

JIMMY CRUICKSHANK

CANONGATE

Edinburgh · New York · Melbourne

First published in Great Britain in 2005 by
Canongate Books Ltd, 14 High Street,
Edinburgh EH1 1TE

This paperback edition first published by Canongate Books in 2006

1

Various publishers and individuals have generously given permission
to use extracts from their work; all contributors are noted in the
Acknowledgements on p.328. Every effort has been made to contact
copyright holders of the extracts used in this volume, however, the
publisher will be happy to rectify any errors or
omissions in future editions.

British Library Cataloguing-in-Publication Data
A catalogue record for this book is available on
request from the British Library

1 84195 831 X (10-digit ISBN)
978 1 84195 831 6 (13-digit ISBN)

Typeset by Palimpsest Book Production Ltd,
Grangemouth, Stirlingshire
Printed and bound in Great Britain by
Creative Print & Design (Wales) Ltd, Ebbw Vale

www.canongate.net

CONTENTS

THE BIG EARTH

The Hyperborean, bottle-clutched by drunken floes
And drowning in the race of the wind, and
Gray
All's blueless – but greens
That float a mile above the sky
sky uncoloured,
And moster-wheel mile below the black.
Seen, not awfully,
But as a jigsaw puzzle,
Glossy down-side up,
And flat upon a tray
black,
infinite,
in no place.

Plum in mouth, and
Pollen nostrils
Paint-box ten by two by point two,
Pocket 'Lear',

And all us
ripe and thick and sweet as multi-sunsets
Steep as Styx and
Deep as Hell.

– Robin Smith, 1955

INTRODUCTION

The *Daily Express* said of Robin Smith when news of his death came through in 1962: 'He was a legend by the time he was twenty. He was to climbing what Stirling Moss is to Le Mans, Jim Baxter to Ibrox, Piggott to Newmarket.' Robin and Wilfrid Noyce had fallen 4000 feet on a high profile, joint British–Soviet expedition to the Pamir mountains in southeastern USSR as the Cold War between East and West was reaching a crescendo.

A Philosophy graduate of exceptional talent, about to embark on doctoral studies at University College London, Robin was only twenty-three when he died. The loss of one of such vitality was shocking. It was hard to believe that he was dead. However, this account is principally about the drive and verve of youth, about achievement, and fun – a Celebration of Youth. Robin's own sense of humour was renowned.

Testimony to Robin's diverse achievements in his short life comes from many sources. 'Possibly the most outstanding mountaineer in the long and varied history of the Scottish Mountaineering Club', its journal recorded. Academically too he shone, to the extent that one of his former lecturers says that his technical brilliance in mathematical logic deserves a tribute, not merely a mention. In the field of climbing literature, his innovatively 'beat' articles have had a profound influence ever since, attributed by Chris Bonington in *The Climbers: A History of Mountaineering* (1992) to his 'laconic yet vivid writing style'.

The 1950s saw the start of the great move to the mountains as settings for popular recreation at a time when respect for convention was in decline and youth was discovering a voice of its own. Robin was both rascal and rebel. Paradoxically for one now looked back on as the 'James Dean of mountaineering', however, he was invited into the folds of Establishment-inclined bodies with remarkable consistency.

By 1959, at the age of twenty, Robin's reputation as a mountaineer had already spread abroad after a fine series of Alpine climbs, including the first British ascent of the Walker Spur, the climb then second only in reputation to the Eiger. In Britain, in characteristic tatty gear, his pioneering efforts produced climbs as hard as any at the time and invariably more elegant in concept. In inimitable bold style he claimed more than forty new summer and winter ascents, several of which are now considered classics. This waif-like youngster, in whom a trace of vulnerability always lingered, went on to rank at the highest level in one of the toughest of sports, and was described as 'without a doubt the hardest man this side of the Border' to Sir John (later to become Lord) Hunt, leader of the fateful expedition to the Pamirs, as names were being put forward at selection stage.

Robin was a complex being and, well as I knew him at certain stages of his life, I am on my own unable to portray his nature adequately. I was one of his classmates at secondary school and his climbing partner for the last two of those years, but I have had to call on the help of others from as far afield as Russia, Italy, France, America and Canada. His exceptional personality is thus depicted by those who knew him, via biographical tales based on experiences in his company. Part One describes his background and developing passion and talent for climbing; Part Two illustrates his life as a university student and his ever more ambitious climbs; and in Part Three the focus is on the expedition in which he achieved, so young, the accolade of joining Britain's eminent climbers in the Pamirs – and lost his life. Throughout, I quote extensively from Robin's own diaries and letters, as well as the accounts of those who knew him and those who climbed with him. Part Two is made up largely of chapters contributed by a long list of Robin's friends and climbing colleagues, and in the Acknowledgements on p. 328 I thank all the individuals who have so generously supported me.

Here, then, is the story of Robin Smith. It might inspire some to take to the mountains. It might influence others to keep well away.

PART ONE

AN APPRENTICE NO MORE: 1938–58

1

EARLY DAYS

Born into India's expatriate British community in 1938, Robin Smith was to find his young life turned upside-down at the end of the Second World War.

In 1937 his parents, Mary and Ben Smith, and infant elder brother had emigrated from Scotland to Calcutta, where his father took up an appointment as a naval architect. Robin was born there on August 30th the following year. He first set foot in Scotland shortly before his eighth birthday in the summer of 1946, when his parents, in line with customs of the day, brought their children – Charlie, Robin and Marion – to Britain for their education. But for the dangers of sailing to Britain during wartime, this phase of childhood would have arisen two years earlier for Robin. Generally children arrived for schooling at the age of six, never to return abroad.

After a tour of Scotland, which included visits to relations in Edinburgh and Arrochar, where he met his paternal grandmother, Robin and his brother were taken to Crieff in Perthshire for schooling at Morrison's Academy. He was just eight, Charlie ten. Marion, aged six, became a boarder at an Edinburgh school prior to her parents' return to India. The boys were to board at 'Dunvegan' in Murray Drive, the house in which 'Bee' (Elizabeth) MacNeill and her mother looked after children for thirty years. Asked if she could remember one by the name of Robin Smith whom she had looked after between 1946 and 1950, the octogenarian's response was remarkably animated considering almost half a century had since passed:

> I can recall all my boys in some way or another but Robin is particu-
> larly memorable. He was a most lovable wee boy, sensitive, friendly but
> happy on his own or in the little dream world which he liked. He was
> very untidy too, didn't care how he looked or what other boys thought
> of him, and did things and reacted unlike any other boys. What I
> remember most distinctly about him, though, was his lovely big smile
> and the poetry and beautiful essays he wrote with so much imagination.

2

By the time Robin arrived in Crieff, the kindly Bee had become known to the children as 'Beebee' in preference to the formal Miss MacNeill which some parents expected. She had been looking after children since 1939 following the outbreak of war when children were evacuated from areas thought to be at risk from bombing. Before long Crieff was inundated with youngsters, including Bee's own sister's two sons.

While Robin was still a toddler in India, such was the inflow to the little town that children could only go to school for half days, some in the morning, the others in the afternoon. They had plenty of freedom and access to the open air on their own or with friends and there were hardly any cars to worry about. On the other hand, until air travel became readily available in the 1950s, parental visits from India were limited to once every three years in view of the duration of the journey by boat. Bee well remembers that the infrequency of those visits could make life difficult for children and parents alike.

Life as a boarder was certainly very different from that experienced by those brought up at home by their own parents, no more so than during school holidays, when those whose parents lived abroad went to stay at special holiday homes. On such occasions Bee looked after Robin's white mice, which she allowed him to keep in the shed. At the Christmas break one year Robin and Charlie both contracted measles and were returned to her lest they start an epidemic at the home. Bee was confident that the children were happy in her house, and at school for that matter, but ventured that 'it was a strange way of life for them and you never really know what goes through a child's mind'.

After two years Charlie was old enough to go to senior school in Edinburgh and a boy called Norman took his place. Robin and he became good friends, Bee was reminded of an episode when Norman left his coat at school and she asked Robin to bring it home:

> He came back with a big grin on his face wearing both coats and looking like goodness-knows-what. I asked him if the other boys were not laughing at him and he said 'yes', but I could see from his grin that he couldn't care twopence. His little eccentricities made us laugh, in the gentle way you do with a child whose nature captures your imagination. Without a doubt he was one of my mother's favourites, and of mine too for that matter.

Often at weekends Bee took them for bike rides, or for walks along the river, into the hills, or to the local reservoir. Robin always liked to walk beside her. In the summer they had picnics, sometimes by the River Earn, where the boys fished for minnows and went swimming. Robin started the habit of smearing blaeberries (bilberries) onto his face, a prank other boys found fun in copying. 'On seeing his purple-stained face my mother always said to him, "Robin, what *have* you been doing?" He would laugh and I think her pretended shock just encouraged him', recalls Bee, who also read stories to the children while they sat at her feet, engrossed and out of mischief's way. It struck her how much Robin loved books.

Robin left Morrison's in 1950 to start at George Watson's Boys' College, Edinburgh – where Robin and I first met shortly after his twelfth birthday. One of Scotland's top schools, founded in 1738, Watson's is primarily a school for day pupils, though there are a limited number of boarders – in the 1950s about 100 out of a total of some 1500 boys. Boarders lived in groups of between ten and twenty-five in separate houses, each run by a schoolmaster. State grants subsidised 90 per cent of the fees.

The picture of an exceedingly ill-at-ease newcomer remains vivid to me to this day – slightly dishevelled, head inclined slightly to one side, and big-eyed twitchy glances swivelling nervously between teacher, class and floor. Nonetheless, something about him was intriguing, particularly when, during the Scripture lessons of a former army padre once based in India, they would reminisce about mongooses, cobras and other exotic topics. Made welcome into our loose-knit multi-fringed gang, Robin gradually blended in with wary caution.

Robin's sister Marion, looking back on having spent four years at a school 50 miles away from her brother, recalls that she hardly saw him as a child: 'Charles and I found this way of life difficult, and Robin too perhaps, though he seemed more accepting and adaptable.' Even after Robin moved to Watson's in Edinburgh, Marion saw her brothers only on Sundays as they walked to church under supervision from boarding houses up opposite sides of Colinton Road: 'We never spoke on those occasions, but a silent acknowledgement would take place.' During this period Robin's aunt effectively acted *in loco parentis* to her nephews and niece. Her son, Peter Lothian, was also at Watson's.

His clearest memories of Robin are of his occasional visits for Sunday lunch after climbing practice on the city's Salisbury Crags – sometimes 'fingers only', which impressed him.

For more than three years Robin was one of about twenty boys in a House run by Physical Education teacher, Peter Fleming, at 85 Colinton Road – as Sandy Bannerman, then one of Robin's fellow boarders and now a solicitor in his home town of Hawick, recalls:

> The first memory I have of Robin – and I find it difficult to remember him as Robin and not as 'Eb' – was his arrival at the Boarding House, or 'Bughut' as we called it. In fact, I remember seeing his black, tin cabin-trunk before I ever saw Robin. Painted along it was the name 'Ebenezer Smith' and we were all eager to meet the poor unfortunate who had been christened Ebenezer, then somewhat disappointed to learn that 'Ebenezer' was his father's name, not his own. We were soon introduced to the newcomer, who had a slightly waif-like appearance with a shock of unruly brown hair, slightly protruding ears, large eyes and legs which were not entirely straight. Everyone in the Bughut was given a nickname and Robin, thanks to the name on the trunk, became forever known in the school as 'Eb'.
>
> The Bughut was run with a rod of iron by an infamous PE instructor who rejoiced in the name of 'Butch' – short for 'Butcher'. Mrs Fleming was our matron and far easier than Butch for us to cope with, but I think she started to find Robin quite a handful, especially when Butch was not around to wield authority. Everything had to be done strictly according to his instructions and anyone stepping out of line was severely dealt with, by the use of a gym shoe across the backside, for however many strokes the 'offence' merited.

Fleming was a daunting character. In the gym the shoe was his constant companion. The contrast between him and the sweet gentle Bee MacNeill of Crieff can hardly be imagined. When Robin's aunt phoned the boarding house, she much preferred to speak to Mrs Fleming rather than 'the dreaded Butcher'. Other calls were not welcome and Archie Hendry, a French teacher at the school, who was later to become Robin's climbing mentor, bemoans that even a teacher could not contact a pupil by telephone 'at that place'. However, the Bughut boys were soon to discover that Robin too had an iron will and could hold authority in disregard. Sandy Bannerman again:

He frequently crossed swords with Butch. I remember one occasion when they eyeballed each other from about six inches, with Butch requiring Eb to follow a course of action that Eb did not think either fair or reasonable. You will be in no doubt as to who won eventually, but not many of us would have had the temerity to stand up to Butch or question his instructions. Eb was, however, that sort of person, a bit of a rebel!

Everyone from the Bughut attended church on Sundays, though most were not very keen and several used to read newspapers or comics and suck Pandrops, much to the annoyance of nearby church elders. At weekends, unless the weather was very bad, the boarders were put outside after lunch until tea-time to amuse themselves. In the early days a popular game was 'British Bulldog' in which one team would be the hunters while the other would try to get back to a protected base. Robin became very adept at hiding up the larger trees. Of course, the others quickly caught on to this but it struck Bannerman that, when he did make his rush for base, it took a good tackle to bring him to ground.

It was generally felt that Robin's bandy legs also helped make him very elusive on the rugby field, where the boys considered him a keen competitor, strong in the tackle and fearless. Donald Scott, who had already gained ten rugby caps for Scotland as a threequarter was then a young PE teacher and his recollections of Robin as a rugby player are still clear in his mind:

> He played with complete gusto, tremendous effort, but with little in the way of team work. His was an individual approach. Like a spirited Shetland pony he would take off at the opposition where they were strongest and by sheer effort and startling changes of direction attempt to pierce their defence. He seemed happiest when the odds were greatest. This individuality ran constantly through Robin's school life. It meant that he never made a 1st XV player but his worth as a member of the 2nd XV was extraordinary.
>
> Traditionally boarders were the most unkempt of players and, if they couldn't find their own infrequently washed kit, simply wore other people's. Robin seemed to have developed this into an art form!

As it happened, Hendry's attention was first attracted to Robin on the rugby field when he (Hendry) was acting as referee. Two bodies were locked together on the ground although the ball was in touch. As he moved to separate them, a player explained: 'That's Eb, sir, he never lets go!' Hendry does not remember Robin having any obvious sporting gifts – 'just determined enthusiasm'.

Robin developed a reputation in the Bughut for not needing to put in the painstaking homework and dedication required by others for academic progress. 'When he cared, he would pass with flying colours,' recalls Bannerman, who can still visualise Robin in action 'with his elbow on the table, his right hand (I seem to remember he was left-handed) through a mop of somewhat untidy unruly hair, scribbling away at great speed.' Robin's old school report card supports that anecdotal assessment – his academic record improved each year from twenty-eighth place in the first year to fifth in his final year.

* * *

Robin's interest in mountains started at an early stage of secondary schooling, when he climbed Braeriach in the Cairngorms on a family holiday at the age of eleven in 1950, and Cairngorm itself the following year. He climbed Sgòran Dubh and Ben Macdhui when he was thirteen and Cairn Toul and the Angel's Peak a year later, in August 1953.

Then, in April 1954, five months before his sixteenth birthday, he claimed Scotland's highest mountain, Ben Nevis at 4406 ft, on a three-week cycling holiday with me and another classmate, staying at youth hostels. His bike was an old gearless rusty heavy wreck, but he resolutely refused to borrow a better one even though we both had flash racers. However, it soon became clear that his mind-over-matter attitude was not enough and, after some bickering on the first day, he told us that we would just have to go at his pace. Left with no choice unless we were to desert him, we went woefully slowly, but still got the occasional rocket for speeding. His clapped-out machine finally broke down at Kingussie, where he decided to spend a few days on his own in nearby hills before returning to Edinburgh by train.

It was during our stay at the Glen Nevis hostel that we climbed Ben Nevis – in shorts and gym shoes and without a compass, Alan Mathieson, the third lad, reminds me. There was deep snow high up and, though we had occasional spectacular views through clearings in the mist, it must have been a fluke, he suggests, that we did not disappear over the cliffs near the top when we suddenly discovered ourselves alarmingly close to the edge.

The family holiday that summer was in a rented house at Achmelvich, Sutherland, when Robin climbed Suilven, Stac Pollaidh and Torridon's Bheinn Alligin. Both Suilven and Stac Pollaidh, two of Scotland's most remarkable hills, fail to exceed 3000 ft, the essential criterion for classification in Sir Hector Munro's popular list of Scottish peaks worthy of consideration as separate mountains. Robin thought it most unfair that such fine mountains should attract no more than limited recognition and admiration, for the contrived reason that they failed to match up to this arbitrary standard. Suilven was particularly special to him and he was often at pains, as if a supporter of the underdog, to promote the worth of smaller mountains. Naturally, Marion was there during those holidays:

> Those were the times when I got to know my two brothers. Our mother was a keen hill-walker and Robin and I would climb a mountain with her while our older brother went fishing with our father. I used to resent being dragged up yet another mountain, but would feel a sense of achievement at the end of the day when we were down again. Of course, Robin was in his element.

Robin's mother Mary Smith, née Reid, an Honours graduate in English at Edinburgh University, was one of five children of an Edinburgh family. One of Robin's female contemporaries looks back on her as a most impressive woman, independent, free-thinking, and quite liberated – the sort of woman who would always attract attention. According to cousin Peter Lothian, she and his mother (a doctor) were particularly close, outnumbered as they were by three brothers, and sharing non-religious views within an otherwise church-orientated family. Their father was a Church of Scotland minister who had once served in Calcutta, and two of the three brothers were also ministers.

Robin's own father's roots lay in Arrochar, where his Highland-drover forebears had eventually settled. The son of a journalist, he was to die in 1956 at the age of fifty-seven, so Robin saw little of him. Mrs Smith lived until 1987, when she died at the age of eighty-one after living the latter part of her life in Dollar, Clackmannanshire, with her elder son Charlie and his family. Charlie, a naval architect like his father, outlived his mother by only four years, dying at the age of fifty-five. Marion gained an Arts degree at Edinburgh University and later a degree in Music, which she now teaches. Charlie and Marion each had a son followed by three daughters; Charlie's son, the first of the eight to be born, is called Robin after his uncle.

Holiday visits from India by Robin's parents back in the 1950s, never more so than on family picnics, have also stuck in the mind of Alan Reid, Robin's older cousin and another Church of Scotland minister. He remembers his aunt as graceful, girlish, shy and intelligently humorous, compensating for the gravitas of his uncle who, even so, exuded nothing but kindness towards his nephews. It always struck Reid that, in a family of three ministers (five if one goes back a generation), the Smith side of the family was refreshingly agnostic and positively sceptical about the orthodox truths of religion. He still has hazy recollections of embarrassment at family gatherings when training for the ministry, due to too much shoptalk and in-language, and of Robin, Charlie and their father observing in critical silence.

Reid conjectures that he perhaps understood Robin intuitively by also being the younger son of a Reid parent. He can now see that their elder brothers shared a quiet, strong, responsible outlook:

> I was free to be quixotic, irresponsible, experimental and frivolous and so, I think, was Robin. The flashes of encounter with him are so vivid, indelible. The grin was always there, the eyes bright with intelligent humour, the cheeks rosy with health, the mouth wide and generous. The forehead was high but not haughty, ill-concealed by an untameable mop of brown hair, plastered down on state occasions. But the eyes have it. I can't remember anyone looking at me so directly, quizzically, challengingly. It was as if he were immediately prepared to take seriously that which might conceivably be of worth in what you said: the rest could be instantly discarded.

Reid has described that particular look rather well.

2

FIRST SCRAMBLES, FIRST HOPES

By September 1954 Robin had been attending school in Edinburgh for four years and classes were about to start for his penultimate year of study. He had just returned from another family holiday at Achmelvich in Sutherland, where adventures on coastal rocks represented his first contact with what could be called real climbing. I was there for a few of those days, after cycling from Edinburgh to stay at the youth hostel in the village, and the start of our climbing partnership inadvertently originated in this tiniest of backwaters, where sand and rock consort with Gulf Stream tides. 'Beginning of understanding with Jimmy', Robin noted in his retrospective record of the time,[1] whilst 'dreams of Split Rock' reflected his aspirations towards Achmelvich's toughest climbing challenge, a giant block of rock that had broken away from the mainland after prolonged undermining by the sea.

The following month his climbing career got properly under way with the help of Archie Hendry: 'Salisbury Crags with Archie. First time on a rope followed by visits in which I worked out the routes for myself. Sometimes Jimmy too.' A month later Archie and climber-solicitor George Ritchie took Robin to Glencoe where at Lagangarbh he had the thrill of staying in a climbing hut for the first time and 'climbed Lagangarbh Chimney and Sphinx. First time away, intro-duction to the climbing world. First of superiority complex? "Robin", not "Smith" to Archie. Good weather conditions, fine day on Bidean. First mountaineered Munro. Brocken spectre.'

Looking back to an era that precedes today's relationship between teachers and pupils, Hendry can still recall that day on Buachaille Etive Mòr in November 1954 when Robin climbed his first ever mountain rock route:

> The school discouraged climbing with pupils, but Robin was launched and became a regular visitor to the Lagangarbh hut. With a fresh-faced youthful companion, he appeared so often and asked politely and diffi-dently 'May I climb?' Somehow the appellation 'sir' disappeared and

the apprenticeship was under way. His initiation into climbing reminded me of my own beginnings – I too had imposed myself on an experienced climber, and then borrowed his books.

Hendry, now entrapped as Robin's climbing mentor, had been a top-class climber until he damaged a knee in his early twenties. Another of Robin's former classmates, Kenny Allan, comments:

> With his Triumph '650' Thunderbird and his motorcycle leathers Archie Hendry was quite different from normal teachers who arrived at school in raincoats by tram. Sometimes we managed to take advantage of his passion for mountaineering by getting him to concentrate on climbing stories rather than the likes of French verbs. I don't know how it came about, but one Friday in class Robin and Jimmy were making arrangements to go away for a weekend's climbing. The rest of us watched them go off into a new world . . .

Rock outcrops around Edinburgh, however, particularly Salisbury Crags, also figured a lot in Robin's early days, as he strove to immerse himself in the world of climbing. The Crags are a crescent of volcanic cliffs more than half a mile in length and up to 120 ft high in places, dominating a large part of the capital and forming the foreground to Arthur's Seat, the city's mini Ben. Although climbing on them was illegal they were a popular training ground for the city's climbers. Tales of the dangers of being caught climbing on the Crags abound, but Robin and I used to meet there regularly, converging by bike from different sides of the city. He had to have a partner and I couldn't bring myself to let him down. We used an old hemp rope that Hendry no longer needed and had instructed us in class how to use. Robin would ferret out a route, often on his own and, if it was not too hard, climb it solo before it was my turn, usually unroped too. On difficult lines, we gave each other top ropes, certainly for first goes. Most routes did not exceed 30 or 40 ft, but they were good practice and, as a consequence, a few months later our first mountain routes were not to seem as hard as we had imagined. The Pentland Hills on the southern edge of the city also came to appeal to Robin, though usually more for open space and exercise than for climbing.

His first taste of winter climbing was to come at the age of sixteen, during the Christmas holidays of 1954, at Glenmore Lodge in the

Cairngorms. His diary records 'a hard day on and above Fiacaill' where he overheard some favourable discussion of himself. 'First and only day on skis, got on well. Liked it – why no more?'

* * *

Back in Edinburgh, however, the long-standing conflict between Robin and Butch Fleming was coming to a head at the boarding house, common knowledge to staff and pupils alike. PE teacher Donald Scott again:

> Although I did not have first-hand knowledge of Robin in the context of boarding houses, I could well imagine that the necessary discipline and routine required in such an environment would not be to his liking. His was a free spirit and this was not an atmosphere in which he would be content to drift along. Ideally, Robin should have been 'fostered out' to an understanding family which would have recognised his needs and allowed him to stretch his wings. His intellect ensured that he did not struggle with his studies and although he, like other boarders, took an active part in school life he must have felt constrained by the rules of the game.

Certainly, Robin got a kick out of bucking the system, as when he used to leave the Bughut by the attic dormitory window after 'lights out', go climbing on Salisbury Crags by moonlight, and return in the early hours while Butch remained unaware. But the level of ill-feeling between Robin and Butch continued to escalate.

The climax came after Robin returned to the Bughut one Sunday evening from an outing to the Crags a few minutes late and Butch started picking on him, going on to prod him on the shoulder as he did so. Robin responded by slowly, disdainfully brushing away the finger-tainted mark from his garment with the back of his fingers. Butch was not used to any expression of contempt. Harsh words flew in both directions and some jostling ensued, but to this day it is unclear if Robin was booted out or left his 'hell-hole' of his own volition. At any rate, in unchaining his shackles he became a bit of a hero figure.

Fortuitously, his mother was back in Edinburgh, albeit with his terminally ill father. This doubtless made Robin's exit from the Bughut easier, but he still had to spend another eighteen months at school during which time the sympathetic environment of a boarding house run by mathematics teacher, Willie Clark, at 10 Morningside Place became his base for climbing activities whilst he remained at Watson's.

Robin now set about getting us both organised. He already had most of his own gear, which included Vibram-soled boots and an old, but fine, ice-axe that once belonged to an aunt, and directed me to Millets, specialists in the ex-army equipment much favoured by a generation of post-war climbers. My shopping list included a pair of soldier's boots and three types of nails[2] that I hammered in on my mother's coal bunker according to Robin's instructions.

Then, in January 1955, he got a new rope . . . 'first use of it with Jimmy on nasty ice in Pentlands'. Robin was particularly proud of this new 100-ft length of nylon, the height of technology at the time, explaining that it was not only stronger than Archie's old hemp rope but also lighter, less bulky, had more stretchiness in the event of a fall and, further, did not absorb water to become heavy in wet weather. The frozen waterfall on Logan Burn lay a few miles from suburban Colinton, across rolling hills: four to six inches of snow, a still, blue sky, freezing – a perfect winter's day for Robin's very first ice-pitch. We roped up and off he went, slowly, cannily, chopping away but, after a short distance, he had to turn back. After a rest, off he went again, but it was tricky and, when it became clear that a fall onto the ice-covered boulders below would be a serious matter, defeat and final retreat had to be accepted. As we headed home, we wondered how he might have fared in my nailed boots. Not too bad for a first go on ice, we thought, though on passing back through Colinton with axes and rope we were taunted as poseurs by two girls. Still, we didn't let that bother us, and the day concluded on a further high note: 'Hitched back – first time. Good day.'

A month later, and shy though he was, Robin plucked up the courage to go on a JMCS (Junior Mountaineering Club of Scotland) meet to Glencoe. 'Frightful in bus going there! Very young – sixteen – and feeling others felt me very little,' he recalled. 'Excellent conditions – starry walk to Clashgour – Tee shirts enough on iced Munros. I lasted the pace well, probably impressed people with keenness.' It was on that outing that he first met someone who was to become a regular climbing partner for a short spell two years later. That was club secretary Jim Clarkson, of whom he wrote: 'Though officially on "other side" of fence, felt sympathy partly 'cos he did with me . . . good lad, kindred spirit.' Desperate to impress and be accepted, Robin seemed often to be received by older climbers with an air of macho unfriendliness, though Clarkson always treated him decently. Some club members, asserting independence after the constraints of National Service, looked on the older Clarkson as a figure of authority, whilst his being English, it's a shame to say, didn't help. Robin had to make up his mind about who to side with, and his decision that Clarkson was a 'good lad' was consistent with his tendency to respond warmly to the older person who extended consideration.

There soon followed his 'first visit to Arrochar – hostel by train after tentative efforts at hitching'. It was now March and Robin was once more in the hills, having again set off on his own: 'A bod takes me to the caves on Sat. afternoon, leads me up and down, but sees that I can show him how to climb. On Sunday I set off in ignorance to find the Cobbler thro' mist & gale & snow. Magnificently gain backbone of South Peak, deem it wise to go back as no compass. Scaring views thro' mist, gen stuff chancing it on hard steep snow-rock traversing, one or two needs to brake . . . hard men on bus back unconvinced of my exploits.'

During the Easter holidays of 1955, shortly after Robin's morale had been perked up by a 'gladdening long friendly chat with Archie', we set off on our first expedition. Hitching was to be our normal means of transport, the starting point being at the Maybury on Edinburgh's western extremity where the road forked: straight ahead to Glasgow, or right, through the centre of Scotland via Stirling, Callander and Crianlarich, direct to the heart of climbing country. The latter was the ideal way, but with less than one tenth of the number of cars on the roads that there are today, traffic was always light, so we usually gave it a miss. On our first big trip we stuck together – 'frantic stuff via Glasgow' – but thereafter tended to hitch separately. Glasgow was a difficult place to negotiate, but we learned to get to Argyle Street for a Number 9 tram as it headed northwards via Clydebank to Dalmuir, on the edge of the conurbation. Men returning from work, many via the pub, were intrigued to see lads with great rucksacks and climbing gear. They gave us their chat, usually insisted on paying our fares, and we enjoyed some good laughs together.

At 3843 ft, Ben More above Crianlarich is an apparently innocuous mountain, cone-shaped with only one gully of limited snow-climbing potential, a wide scour on its west side. The gully was to be our first objective. Cloud level was about 1500 ft above us and, as we climbed, the wind became stronger. With the drop in temperature, our wet anoraks and trousers froze, rather helpfully making them windproof. Higher up, by now in cloud, the wind grew significantly, becoming strong enough to make progress difficult. Robin had forgotten his gloves, but my hands were fine, so I lent him mine. Before long we suddenly found ourselves unable to stand in the ferocious wind and driving snow, being forced to crawl east with the wind towards the mountain's lee where we knew that a descent would be hazard-free. From there we were quickly back down on the road, where the rain was moderate, the wind light – just as when we set off. Back in the Crianlarich hostel Robin rather grudgingly undid the buttons and laces that my well-chilled fingers could not manage. Never again were we to experience such extreme conditions together.

After that 'very hardy but unsuccessful assault on Ben More (goggles and all – we virtually do it but no)', Ben Lui, six miles up the glen, near Tyndrum, was the next target, this time from a base camp where we initiated the tent and Primus, part of Robin's newly acquired cache of gear that had set him back a grand total of £30. Although Robin's assessment of the steep east-facing Central Gully was that it had been 'dead easy', it was our first real snow climb. That said, the snow was soggy and up to our calves even at summit level, avalanche conditions perhaps, but Robin wasn't certain – he would read further on the subject back in Edinburgh. The absence of a cornice to tunnel through was a disappointment, though he did admit to finding the mountain 'a good Munro'. The walk-out, which involved wading across the River Lochy in the dark, proved to be a 'long gen evening over pathless path and bog and river to close on Dalmally. Jimmy near shattered.'

Having visited Oban for provisions and after a night at the hostel, we planned to spend three or four days heading north, notching up the ten or so Munros to the east of Etive's loch and glen as we went. However, after several days of foul weather camped in a soggy wood by the Noe with no more than an abortive attempt on Cruachan to our credit, we were forced to abandon that part of the expedition for the comfort of Crianlarich youth hostel – but not without a 'burn-up'.

Robin's burn-ups, I should explain, were to become a character-istic ingredient of our expeditions to the hills. The source of some good rows, they invariably started without prior discussion and were usually uphill. I used to tell him that it was a bit like starting a race without giving athletes advance notice of the event, though on the one occa-sion I did recklessly threaten to do the same to him some day to see how he would like it, he rather relished the idea. My normal reaction was to try to talk him out of it, or to get him to defer doing it until I was sufficiently psyched up, but I soon came to recognise all that as a waste of time. When Robin was 50 yards or so ahead, the abusive comments – a feature of this transitional phase – were converted on my part into a wrath that compelled me to step on it, determined to match his pace so that, when he stopped, I could make the point (flawed tactics that spurred him on even more). After an argument, however, neither of us nursed grievances and whatever was said was quickly forgotten.

After some 'dance and adventures etc around Crianlarich' (a sort-of-ceilidh attended mainly by auntie-type ladies), we went by thumb to Glencoe where Robin managed his first true lead on rock, Lagangarbh Chimney, though 'horrible slime, fierce winds and gusts proved it to be desperatish' despite Archie Hendry having led him up it only six months previously. Fortunately the weather did improve as the day progressed, allowing fleeting views from the top of the Buachaille until darkness and flitting clouds started closing in. Hard climbers, as Robin knew, often descended rock routes unroped, and we soon found ourselves semi-stranded on the west flank of a ridge after veering off-line. However, unroped leaps across narrow chasms retrieved the position, the sensation of exposure thankfully diminished by our hardly being able to see to the bottom.

Following that 'chancy descent of Curved Ridge' to find the tent adrift, we were invited to spend the night in the SMC (Scottish Mountaineering Club) Hut at Lagangarbh. It was there that we were often to bump into the renowned Jimmy Marshall. He and Archie Hendry were regular climbing partners and godlike creatures to us. Marshall was ten years older than Robin, Hendry twenty.

In the morning we made a 'weak-hearted attempt on Chasm North Wall' before leaving for the youth hostel at the bottom end of the glen, Robin 'hungry for info'. Older climbers recommended Pyramid – 'dead easy'. The highlight of our stay in Glencoe was to follow when Crack Climb became Robin's first true multi-pitch route – an important step forward. Then a traverse of Aonagh Eagach, the ridge on Glencoe's north side, produced a 'Pleasant Disappointment, but 2 Munros', while back on the south side again we climbed Central Gully on Bidean nam Bian, at 3766 ft the highest peak in the area.

Near Bidean's summit there was a long field of frozen snow down which we practised glissading. Robin had read up on this, but we found that the recommended method of controlling your speed, by pressing the spike of the ice-axe shaft into the snow behind you, made it difficult to get up any real pace. It was a lot more fun to scoot down fast, like a skier, and fall onto your side for an emergency-stop by forcing the pick end of the axe head into the frozen snow. This went fine until Robin hit a soft spot, went head over heels and dropped his axe. I happened to have gone down this section first and was watching. It was quite spectacular. Then as I fumbled to release my axe from my wrist (Robin's, like many axes, did not have a wristband), he wriggled and twisted, somehow managing to get into a feet-first position – just in time to snatch my axe as he shot past, enabling him to brake to a halt alarmingly close to the start of a boulder field.

* * *

While these adventures were taking place on the hills, early consideration had already started at school about prefects for the following year although decisions would not be announced until early June. A school magazine at the time noted several of Robin's characteristics split between good and bad: couldn't-care-less attitude, scathing wit, equestrian physique, irresponsibility, obstinacy, untidiness and reading the lesson in the hall at morning assembly (a nerve-racking experience). The article was intended to amuse. There is no doubt that Robin looked, and was, a bit shambolic. Donald Scott, the young PE teacher, remembers him as a 'young man carelessly clad scuttling along late for class or other appointment, a lock of hair unruly as ever and his head slightly lowered to one side'. On the other hand, he was clever, though he did have that rebel streak in him. Nonetheless, he was to become a prefect in his final year, 1955–56, much to Hendry's surprise.

It is generally agreed that a major influencing factor in that appointment was his winning the school's mock election, a victory that must also have boosted his self-awareness and confidence – a key factor during his formative years. Voting took place on the evening of the General Election of May 26th, 1955, following which Anthony Eden took over as Prime Minister from Winston Churchill. Howard Andrew, a former classmate:

> Robin confided in me his idea to poke fun at the school literati by introducing an anarchic contribution to the Literary Society's mock election, to him a rather po-faced, earnest activity. He wanted, he said, to highlight the futility of partisan party politics. 'But is the alternative not just chaos?' I asked. Robin grabbed the word 'chaos', repeating it with a mixture of venom and mischief. 'We could be the Scottish Chaoserians', he mused and, with a typical leap of lateral thinking, changed the pronunciation of 'Chaos' to 'Choss' to rhyme with 'Chaucer' whose work we had recently been studying.

Robin then thought up the impressive-sounding chant 'Choss! Choss! Choss!' and invented a pseudo-Nazi salute in which fingers drooped loosely from the raised arm to resemble a cow's udder. 'Like most revolutionaries, the Scottish Chaoserians started modestly', a report in a school magazine said. 'Suddenly, terrifyingly, it caught on. Within hours dozens of boys were exchanging the Choss salute. The party leader, "Eb" Smith, was chaired each day to the shelters, followed by a fanatical mob of drooping-fingered, howling supporters.' As the week progressed Robin took to wearing the scarf and beret of a nearby girls' school as an electioneering gimmick.

David Steel, now Lord Steel of Aikwood and Presiding Officer of the Scottish Parliament, then one of Robin's fellow boarders at Willie Clark's but a supporter of another candidate, recalls that particular election: 'I can recall Eb standing on top of the old air-raid shelters at Tipperlinn playing fields, haranguing the mob in a gloriously disorganised and entertaining manner, which won him the votes.' However, Robin's supporters' methods were rather crude, as the school magazine reminds us: 'Urged on by the Great Leader, they would bear down on all dissenters in tight formation. Success of Choss field manoeuvres depended almost solely on brute strength and numbers.'

There was speculation that Robin might have no easy task in the debating hall, where voters would at least be safe. After one candidate condemned Choss as mass hypnotism it was Robin's turn to speak, which he did wearing the scarves of, not just one, but four girls' schools as pandemonium broke loose. His speech, thought to contain less material of value than the others, nonetheless sparked heated exchanges, the report continued: 'In a hoarse-voiced harangue, Smith played on the emotions of the electors and would have convinced an unbiased observer that he, Smith, disliked the VIth Form, Boarding Houses and the Combined Cadet Force. So he opposed Tyranny? Amid the ensuing uproar, the only question of note was from a brave IIIrd Former who asked why, if "Eb" opposed Tyranny, he enticed his party to fanatical mob violence out of doors. This query brought the house down . . .'

After the noise of battle had rolled away, it was declared that Robin had won 118 of the 246 votes cast, the runner-up gaining just 45. Donald Scott considers that fifth-form victory as perhaps Robin's greatest achievement at school, concluding that 'as one who loved to tilt against authority he knew well how to extract a response from his listeners. I never saw the like again during the thirty years I taught at the school after Robin left.'

Climbing, however, was continuing apace for the victorious electioneer. Already he had met with success in leading parties of other sorts (mainly myself) on the dissimilar challenges of rock, snow and ice but, as the summer of 1955 approached, it was rock climbing that was getting into full swing. A few days after the mock election, the sixteen-year-old Robin returned to Arrochar where he bivvied in the caves and met up again with the Glaswegians he had met in March, noting that he 'can still climb what they can't'. Even so, another attempt to get to the top of the Cobbler failed. His next outing was to the Trilleachan Slabs, on the north side of Loch Etive where he would 'first meet Jimmy Marshall, re-meet his crude friend, do good climb, see Len Lovat worried, do what Ian Haig can't. Hear of Dalness Chasms. Break a bit more ice. Still v. much small boy.'

As we headed off together in June, Robin continued to stick in, always keeping his ear to the ground, and we had 'a gt weekend at

Glencoe. I arrive after good hitching on Friday evening. Jimmy already there, beat off up mountain, inspect Hangman's – Birth of a desire? or just weaning? – Romp up Shackle. Tho' my boots lousy I was on gt form. Archie was there. We meet that telling silence, refusal to show "impressed" touch of incredulity as before, after Lagangarbh Chimney lead, but much more so. Jimmy bivvied on top of Buachaille – sort of did us down!'

We were climbing late in the day on a perfect midsummer evening and decided to go to the top for what had to be an idyllic mountain sunset. And so it was – still, mild and beautiful, as we sat relaxing until around midnight when, with daylight effectively gone, it was time to go down. Robin's move towards the cliffs prompted me to ask where he was going – Curved Ridge, unroped, was his plan. Now, we had only just recently had a bad experience there, so I suggested playing it safe by going down the path, though that too could be dicey at night if you were to take a premature turn off the main ridge. It soon became clear that Robin was not prepared to go via the path, nor I via the cliffs. Somehow, the idea was mooted that I should stay on the summit overnight and, as part of this amicable compromise, Robin left his anorak for my legs in case it got cold. A few hours later I descended to the morning of the long faces where we recognised the risks of separating like that, although Robin, satisfied with his solo descent in the dark and abetted by the way-out worth of my bivvy, did not find it too difficult coming to terms with our disgrace. 'Next day – Agag's Groove. Easy, I said – not so good(!). We have a fine bathe.' Despite that 'Easy, I said' faux pas, Robin's confidence was helped by a 'further breaking of ice with Archie', and he was obviously beginning to feel comfortable on harder climbs.

Immediately after school broke up in July, Robin spent a fortnight in Norway with his family, a visit that inspired the poem which is this biography's epigraph. Back home, he and Alan Mathieson, who had been with us on Nevis at Easter the previous year, went on another cycling trip, this time to the Isle of Arran. On a fine summer's day Robin climbed Goat Fell (Arran's highest peak, at 2866 ft), Cir Mhor (the island's sharpest top) and A' Chir. 'Little did I know,' Mathieson recalls, 'that he had more than just Goat Fell mapped out in his mind as we walked up the easy ascent from Brodick. This was meant as a walk and we had no rope, so when it started to get hairy on leaving the summit I turned back.' The Arran ridges certainly have tricky, exposed spots and it is hardly surprising that Mathieson's lasting memory is of 'some day out'. Then Robin made his way up north, more ascents – as bonny as any in Scotland – under his belt, and he and I met up 'chancily outside Glen Nevis YH, fine weather, camp high up glen at bridge, terrific pool etc. Next day: Terrific weather, pad round by YH to mid-way loch, bathe, down and along cliff, book open. Tower Ridge by Douglas Direct, first use of Krab, shambles.'

A late start, an unrushed pace with rests in the sunny weather, a swim, then a prolonged stop for lunch, meant a late arrival at the rocks. Blaeberries were growing at the lunch spot, I remember. Robin talked of the conditions they prefer, when they fruit etc – all part of mountain heritage, he thought. To him there was more to mountaineering than just climbing. He was a person of many moods, though not moody in the conventional sense. At one extreme he could be obscure, difficult to fathom, near uncommunicative – if disturbed in a contemplative frame of mind, for example – at another, the ultimate ball of fire. When excited he could now and then appear a little odd to those who did not know him. I didn't like that. Nor did I like it when a hint of a mean streak – at odds with his fundamental nature – occasionally showed if his excitement happened to coincide with one of his 'scathing' moods. But on this day, not unusually, he was at ease with himself, at ease with the world, gentle, funny, talkative. The highlight of the day in practical terms, however, was the new karabiner. We chatted about its potential use and, as one was hardly enough, decided first to try it as a runner to protect Robin's leads. All in all, it was a memorable outing – 'long day ended in chancy descent' – but we managed not to flirt too intimately with the perils of Five Finger Gully, that serial life-taker on the Glen Nevis side of the mountain.

The following day we moved to Glencoe, climbing Clachaig Gully in the afternoon. Later, at the hostel, we met a number of people we were to team up with for a few days. 'Funny English blokes (pot holers), Glaswegian Pat and 2 English girls,' Robin described them. 'We go to Archer Ridge and Rowan Tree Wall – rock wettish, but went very well. Pat in trouble. First time I had led a party of 4. From Aonach Dubh the others went down Dinnertime Buttress. Jimmy and I, rugged, on to Stob Corrie nan Lochan – up Church Door Buttress

. . . a wee bit desperate. I want to finish with Deep Cut Chimney, but Jimmy wouldn't.'

I had had enough for one day, a day in which, on the approach to Aonach Dubh that morning, Robin had gone into supercharged burn-up mode. Pat and the other lad were not fit enough to match the pace and fell a long way behind. When Pat taxed me that evening about why Robin had done it, I would have felt most disloyal if I had divulged the sort of thing I would say to Robin on our own. Pat reckoned that his trouble on the hill that morning had been caused not just by the burn-up but by not being allowed a reasonable rest after he caught up. As leader on the second rope, he got into difficulties on the exposed penultimate pitch of Archer Ridge – totally stuck. Robin meanwhile had just finished the final pitch, with me at the belay beneath him. The outcome was that Robin unroped, tied a loop on the end, threw it down to me and I lowered it to Pat who found relief resting on it before tying on and completing the pitch. After the fourth man was up on the stance, it fell to me to lead the crux pitch myself. All meat and drink for Robin above us.

His reference to the next day – 'Jimmy saw to the girls' – could perhaps be mischievously misconstrued but the truth is that with the chance of a break from climbing I did no more than agree to take them up Bidean. Robin, with any number of substitutes, went off with Pat, and we all met on the top after they had climbed a 'nasty, tough chimney which had defeated us at Easter'. The presence of the girls – real townies (Londoners), but plucky though now tired – prevented the more arduous descent via Lost Valley, and Robin wondered if this was the 'origin of [my] views on women/climbing? (à la EUMC !)'. I don't know about that, but I do remember that the one I rather liked preferred a blinkin' hillwalker.

A couple of days later Robin stepped up the pace even further by leading the Buachaille's Grooved Arête, a 'Severe' which was a grade harder than anything previously attempted.[3] By then it was time to have another crack at one of the mountains closest to his heart: 'Then I pack off home, or rather to Lochgoilhead. On first day there – quite perfect ! – I drag brother Charles, weak but willing, up Slacks. I climbed magnificently: Charles much impressed. First time after 3 assaults & failures to summit of the Cobbler.' He had finally done it!

Even at this early stage of his climbing career Robin was regularly covering great distances in his quest for new and increasingly difficult climbs. Of course, all this cost very little, as travelling by thumb and camping were free, while charges for youngsters at youth hostels were near nominal.

As getting lifts was usually easy too, Skye (via Edinburgh) was to be the climax of the holidays that summer. Having hitched there separately, we met up again at the Glen Brittle youth hostel after Robin had covered the last eight miles on a 'terrific night walk from Sligachan'. Ever since he first involved me in his climbing dream, the island's Gabbro Rock had been a regular topic of discussion: rough, jagged, coarse as sandpaper, tough on skin, marvellous for adhesion. Now we were about to try it!

> Day 1: We pad up to Sron na Ciche. Eastern Buttress – excellent climb, we make good time. On to Sgurr Alasdair on the ridge. Day 2: Cioch Direct. 4 very good guys above. Good descent with 2 others. Day 3: Cioch West – nasty day. Day 4: A day on boulders, damn all else.
>
> Day 5. Good day – ('Hard Severe'!) Mallory's Climb. Fine impression of exploration of gt face, a long climb through mist and rain, though by then hardened to it. Then round to Corrie na Grunddha for White Slab, but it was nasty. We problemed instead. This was golden age.

After Skye, Robin headed off to rejoin his family, who were now holidaying in Sutherland. It was here, on the rocks of Achmelvich bay as little as a year ago, that his 'first scrambles, first hopes' had signalled the birth of his lifelong fascination with climbing. This year he even had the necessary skills to climb Split Rock, though at a price, for in managing this, a pattern was set for a long series of hopes and ambitions that would each one day come to be looked back on as 'the end of a dream'.

Already at this early stage of his climbing career, Robin's skills were beginning to impress, although Archie Hendry was starting to express reservations about getting too involved in Robin's mountaineering aspirations. Jimmy Marshall:

> Robin's intense enthusiasm was just too strong for Archie to rebuff and before long we were teasing him about some of Robin's more daring exploits which, to say the least, seemed hazardous. Of course, we did

not then know what the lad had in him. There really did seem a chance that his activities might, if anything went wrong before he could amass enough experience, land his name on the sad list of mountain fatalities. Amongst friends we used to joke and conjecture about his chances of survival and teased Archie about what he had let himself in for with Robin as a protégé. How, for example, would he explain things away back at school? Archie's nonchalant retort on one occasion, 'Boys are expendable', caused great mirth, but it didn't take long to detect Robin's out-of-the-ordinary talent and the feeling of fear for his future was soon replaced – but not yet – by relaxed speculation at just how much he would be able to achieve.

3

UPPING THE GRADE

Now regarded as showing early signs of talent as a climber, Robin was also finding that his progress at school had not gone unnoticed. In September 1955 he returned for his final year not just as a prefect but as captain of one of the school's four houses. Such a rise to recognition would have been unthinkable as little as six months previously, and Howard Andrew, a former classmate, was as surprised as anyone with the transformation:

> I wonder whether his mischievous idea at the 1955 mock election crystallised into reality faster than he expected. It certainly forced Robin into a prominent position to which he would not have normally aspired and he almost certainly became a prefect on the strength of that. In the rest of his school activities he seemed to shun positions of authority. For example he joined the school Scout Troop, a very un-Smithlike institution, but only on his own terms – he didn't present himself for any of the (to him) trivial 'badges', but did participate enthusiastically in games with no intrusive rules. And of course he didn't become a Patrol leader.

However, nothing was now more elemental than climbing for Robin, who was getting to appreciate Archie Hendry more and more whilst warming to his disclosures that other climbers had been talking about him. Nevertheless, as evenings grew shorter and autumn rains started, trips to the mountains were infrequent:

> October: Weekend at Glencoe. Cold, bit slimy but dry. Archie, George Ritchie, Jimmy Marshall and gang all up. Attempt on Red Slab, foiled by wet. We camped, I think. On Satan's Slit, we spent a long time looking for traverse, found it OK but missed the crux, finished on January Jigsaw. Watched Jimmy Marshall romp down Shackle.
> November: Celebrating first year of climbing, nasty weekend in Arrochar. Nasty camp site, nasty dog and nasty man. Recess Route, cold and damp, didn't hugely impress. Centre Peak by Variations then, after much persuasion, nasty Nimlin's Direct – Jimmy in rubbers found it easier than me. Harrowing moment. Good finish.

Then 'Damn all till Christmas' when he went to Glenmore Lodge again rather than stay in Edinburgh with his mother and his father, whose health was failing fast. It was there that he met up with some of the Creagh Dhu Mountaineering Club,[1] a group of climbers united in the anti-establishment traditions of a club founded in 1930s Glasgow during an era of poverty, unemployment and slums. The hills and climbing were wondrous escapes from deprivation for the founders. A number of the country's leading mountaineers were amongst its members at the time that Robin's career was getting under way. Membership continued to be by invitation only, based as much on personality as on climbing skills. Even in the 1950s, with work again available in the shipyards and factories, a weekend of glorious release into the wilds for the typical Creagh Dhu climber started with a mad dash from the work gates – men with the same needs as Robin, and for similar reasons perhaps, though from greatly contrasting backgrounds. Listening to their chat, Robin's competitive instinct found a new outlet and, although beaten in a 'race' up Bynack, he twice managed to win others on Macdhui. Tom Paul, however, was clearly stronger than him, notably on pull-ups. 'Right then I made the tacit vow,' Robin wrote. 'My arms, fingers would just have to get stronger.'

When he returned to school, 'to more blethers with Archie', a full twelve months had passed since his move to Willie Clark's boarding house, where he had settled in well. To Clark, Robin was 'just like any other boarder'. In his nineties when this was written, and ever a relaxed, kindly man he retained warm memories of someone whose keenness on climbing is hard to forget:

> At No. 10, a detached three-storey building, the interior of the study and the external drain pipes attracted his attention. Climbs to the roof via a drain pipe were undertaken – unauthorised of course – and Robin once demonstrated in the study how to move along and up a vertical wall using the picture rail and pieces of furniture for hand- and footholds. A shelf fixed to the wall and used for books and school bags was an obvious target to demonstrate how to negotiate an overhang. Unfortunately the shelf was unable to support the combined weight, so books, bags, shelf and Robin all finished up on the floor!

The first mountaineering of 1956 was in February on a JMCS outing to Glencoe: 'Attempt on Arch Gully – first real ice climb, got on well as far as halfway up first crux, hadn't nerve to rush it, could have finished if blasteds hadn't arrived – annoying to find that I wasn't [as good] on ice as I was on rock. However had good sport continuing. Archie later in a confab reassured me that they hadn't got up either.' Robin again enjoyed the company of club secretary Jim Clarkson and discovered that university lecturer Derek Leaver too was friendly.

He was desperate for opportunities to tackle winter climbs, but that was easier said than done. A month later, however, we went off to Nevis, again on the JMCS bus. 'Conditions on the ball. Slug up by starlight to campsite. We went well, arrived 2nd?' Robin noted, explaining how we came to be so incredibly sweaty before settling in for the coldest night of the millennium. Our objective, Gardyloo Gully, is a long snow couloir that becomes very steep as the gully narrows towards the top. Just below the top is an ice pitch, about 50 ft long that year and a serious undertaking for us. Robin, to his disgust, could not manage it, so we decided to stay put until four figures some distance down reached us. We wondered if they would be cocky, do-you-down belittlers, the type that really bothered Robin. But we were lucky. The quartet, kind and considerate, climbed through before throwing down a rope: 'Could hardly be hauled up as a sack; and fifth man! Taught us a thing or two, good thing altogether – I still have to dispel the Ice bogey. Have snow and ice golden age ahead. However, on top sun drove away nastiness and very pleasant descent with number of bods.'[2]

Though without a doubt we had experienced a spectacular day on a serious route, to date Robin had achieved little on snow and ice and another winter was almost over. What with rugby, limited daylight and lack of transport, he had relatively few opportunities for winter climbing. Tackling that 'Ice bogey' would now have to wait a further year.

However, spring was in the offing and another major expedition got under way during the Easter holidays when we 'got landed at Crianlarich, so had excellent day up Y Gully to top of Cruach Ardrain, Ben Tulaichean, Stob Garbh, Stobinian and Ben More. Terrific lift to Kingshouse then another to Lagangarbh. Still morning, so up Buachaille. Up Crowberry Direct for first time. Down Agag's Groove (calamity with small pack containing camera, boots etc!)' The descent was briefly interrupted while we 'debated' how in the first place the sack came to whizz past my ear in all too vivid an illustration of what a fall would mean. Careless tugging down of loose rope, or big clumsy feet? Whichever, my mother's Brownie camera was a goner by the time we went on to tackle 'Red Slab (V. good, found it hard, played ass over Jimmy's belay, impressed Falkirk crowd, put one over the Glaswegian schoolboys, who were hard. Our hardest climb to date [Very Severe]). Down Crowberry Direct, astonished the boys of Falkirk. Making up for Gardyloo! Saw Glasgow boys on Fracture. First real sense of rivalry – I hadn't entered the second world of hard competitive climbing in the know, hadn't considered serious comparison, saw them as a source of info, not rivalry.'[3]

Ardgour, our next port of call, on the west side of Loch Linnhe near the head of which lies Fort William, had long held a fascination for Robin. With it being just a little inaccessible, he thought that good new routes could be picked up there. After stocking up in the town we crossed the loch on the Corran Ferry, caught a bus towards Garbh Bheinn and set up camp beside the burn: 'Next day good. Attempt at a route on Lower Pinnacle, South Face. Very attracted by line, quite hopeful still that I could get up it and that it would be an excellent V.S. route. Perhaps not yet climbed. After interesting chaos we shambled down, interesting traverse to Great Ridge – excellent climb, done without rope.' Robin had seen what was to become his first hard new route a year later. Next day the weather broke and low cloud shrouded the mountain when we reached the rocks. Climbing wasn't on, but, rather than waste the day, Robin proposed that we hone up on abseiling, a technique neither of us had used on the hill, though Robin had recently worked out how at low level. He selected a suitable point about 30 ft up the face and gave a quick demonstration. When he reappeared I knew it was my turn, but with my instructor's will-he-do-it-or-will-he-flunk-it grin for motivation, success was assured, encouraging us to carry on practising until content that we had acquired another mountaineering skill.

Once again, when forced to retreat, we made for a youth hostel, this time to Glencoe, where the weather was slow to improve. Nonetheless we 'battered up Clachaig Gully in nails, rain, cold and nastiness' with Robin attempting to get me to lead it from start to finish, though only until I precluded a fall by jumping off Jericho Wall. I lost both a nail and the lead, Robin quipped. Later, when I refused to join him on an unroped descent, he climbed back down the gully after claiming that he would be quicker than me by the path.

This rotten spell of weather was making Robin untypically depressed: 'Jimmy, good lad, all for sticking it out – "good weather sure to come". I wanted back – why?? – not really to work.' It was as if he was homesick, and he did return south to Edinburgh, although a few days later we met as arranged at Lagangarbh where he made a self-confessedly half-hearted attempt on the Buachaille's Raven's Gully.

Of course, it was not all downbeat, particularly on the day we stood on the top of Bidean where Robin wondered just how quickly we could make the descent. He had even done the decent thing by discussing it in advance. So, after he checked his watch, we set off, running and skidding down the top snows, then glissading at speed down the long snow slope where we had practised the year before. The snows cleared just as the path starts along the edge of the gully – Mother Nature had intended the time to be good. Down this, in front of me, Robin moved at frenetic speed, leaping, skipping, changing feet in anticipation of footholds, arms flying for balance, axe in one hand, rope bouncing on his shoulder. A final dash over almost level ground brought us to the road and we collapsed on the heather verge. Robin, official timekeeper, examined his watch, pondered, looked again to ensure no arithmetical mishap, then announced '34 minutes' – this through a wide, satisfied grin from a flushed face glistening with sweat. We stripped off a little and lay back to cool down, trying our best to be unassuming in our moment of glory. Difficult to beat, mark you. Just the right conditions. Who could do the bit by the gully faster? And that glissade! Yes. It must be a record . . . definitely!

Later that month, on April 27th, 1956, his father died of cancer in Edinburgh and I could now understand the reasons for Robin's display of despondency and half-heartedness a couple of weeks earlier. I don't know if he knew how close to death his father was when he paid that visit to Edinburgh from Glencoe. Maybe he just kept it close to his chest. All I know is that he was very out of sorts, otherwise I would not have hung around at Glencoe waiting for him.

Willie Clark, the teacher in charge of Robin's Bughut, remembers that Robin was particularly upset at not being allowed to go to the funeral. Mrs Smith, dismissive of ceremonies, funerals included, had decided that it would be inappropriate for her two younger children to attend. Marion, Robin's sister, was not quite fifteen at the time: 'My father's death was just before Robin's university bursary exams, in which, as a result possibly, he did badly.' That and widowhood were blows to their mother financially as she had three children to support, Charlie at Glasgow University, Robin and Marion still at school.

By this stage, Robin was restless if he did not get away climbing at weekends, with or without me, and teamed up occasionally with Johnnie, one of the Bughut lads. David Steel, Robin's fellow boarder, remembers him at this period:

> Robin Smith was both truly scholarly and grossly untidy, with a wonderful sense of humour. Knowing that he was already an avid mountaineer I used to tease him, telling him I could not see the attraction of the sport. So he challenged me to come with him. Early one morning, we crept out of the boarding house and made our way to Salisbury Crags, in theory before the park wardens were on duty. With a rope tied round his waist, he scrambled up the sheer rock face like a monkey. He did in fact have very powerful long arms and strong fingers. He paid out the rope, the other end of which was attached to me, having given me five minutes' instruction on the lower face. Then he bade me make the ascent . . . but to a total novice, finding the cracks for finger and toe holds was nerve-racking. I began to understand the thrill of the sport, if not to enthuse about it. Eb shouted instructions from above, and I made it almost to the top when we were spotted by a park patrol. The last few feet were covered at remarkable speed, and we fled the scene of the crime!

Robin meanwhile had learned that some high-flyers were using Woolworth's gym shoes on hard rock routes, and we too – especially me – found that the thin, flexible soles of these 'rubbers' really did give much better adhesion. By this time descent via hard routes had become one of Robin's bents, no more so than on the Buachaille, where much of our climbing was done on the Rannoch Wall, a near vertical face forming one side of Crowberry Ridge. Several routes thread up the ridge, including the Severe Crowberry Direct that the likes of Jimmy Marshall regularly came down unroped. So then must we, despite its level of difficulty and exposure. Even before rubbers came our way, Robin was scooting down it like a monkey and, while my own pace in nails had improved, I had to settle for a sensible balance. Nobody likes appearing incompetent, yet the consequences of a minor misjudgement were all too obvious. Then Robin's masterstroke, Woolies' rubbers, suddenly improved both my speed and, it struck me, my chances of reaching a ripe old age.

Up to that stage our equipment had been pretty basic and Archie Hendry asked Robin if he would like a pair of Austrian Kletterschühe. As my nails were already a bit worn, we thought we would make a better-balanced team if I instead were to buy these lightweight, flexible, rubber-soled boots. (A few weeks later, Archie produced another pair which Robin bought for himself and, though we always preferred rubbers on hard routes, we did look more stylish.) A second karabiner and sling also came Robin's way, meaning that we could now use one for my belays while the other protected his leads. Of course, harder pitches often did not have placements suitable for slings as running belays, committing Robin to long leads unprotected other than by me – though thanks to Robin's briefings about what good seconds should do in the event of a fall by a leader, I had a routine tucked up my sleeve for such an eventuality. While he was flying through the air, it would be my job to pull in the momentary slack behind my back with deft arm movements in order to shorten the effective length of the fall. Robin did make a point of warning me not to be over-enthusiastic in taking in the slack, as failure to have a tight grip at the crucial moment would result in his being dropped and in my hands suffering searing burns as the rope zipped through. He cited a gory instance.

With summer fast approaching, the final addition to our collection of gear was a piton, though lack of a hammer, it has to be said, restricted its functionality – not that that mattered too much as Robin himself had already concluded that he loathed the idea of the artificiality such objects introduced. Anyway, Glencoe beckoned and at the end of May mid-term was with us. 'Hitched up solo on Friday,' Robin recalled. 'Spent evening going up Lagangarbh Chimney, down Lagangarbh Buttress East Face, up Staircase Buttress, down North Buttress, inspecting Hangman's, Raven's Gully and Gallows. Saturday: after quandary, off up Buachaille Beag after hell of a shattering gully.

Fine wind, pelt along ridge to bag a new Munro. Then at a whoop down to Lairig Gartain and up Buachaille Mòr. Right along to a broad gully, which down went I to meet Jimmy shortly at tent. V. pleased at form in bashing up and down.' I did not get there until the evening after playing cricket in Glasgow, having taken my climbing gear on the team bus in order to hitchhike straight to the hills after the match. A busy weekend lay ahead for us. He added:

> Sunday: Off to be hard on Buachaille – Archie, Jimmy Marshall and George Ritchie there. We did Route 1 (?), down Crowberry. On the way we suddenly met Jimmy Marshall belayed above Fracture, Archie thrashing below. Funny! We dithered, considered Raven's, tried Fracture – got beat by cold, not wet, before a large audience. Spent v. pleasant evening in hut.
>
> Monday: Straight up Fracture, nae bother at a'. We tried Bottleneck half-heartedly: gave up – not beaten – because of slime. So Slanting Groove, then my 'passion' at work: magneted to Hangman's, up crux easily but chaos and ripped seat rubbed at nasty crack move. Fracture over again. Disgusting descent! Then home.

Robin was now starting to seek out the hardest climbs in a serious way. As they grew harder, so guidance to me from above (from Robin that is) became more frequent. These were exciting moments when Robin would brace himself in case one of my lunges should fail. Either way, he couldn't lose – fun if I made it, fun if I were to miss – but luck for me could not continue indefinitely, and I did not fancy the idea of hanging in space, hundreds of feet from the ground. Primal instincts, I confess, reduced me to thumbing furtively through guidebooks for easier routes not yet tackled in the hope that they might somehow appeal to Robin. One way or another, 'Jimmy was about up the creek as a climbing partner – always cricketing.'

Robin, though stumped by my tie to the team as vice-captain, but still pleased if either the team or I did well, took this inconvenience in his stride and scouted around for other partners, sometimes at Salisbury Crags: 'After a very pleasant morning Donald Mill proposed the Lakes – I was hooked, lined and sinkered on a twinkle of a fly. Saturday: On Birkness Combe, Grey Crag. Donald harrowed on Harrow Wall and above. I was harrowed but got up Slabs West, very chancy on wet rock. Then to top of ridge, beetled along in wind and rain. Sunday: Over to Pillar Rock. Up Old North – excellent. Shambles near Nose. Then down Old West, attempt Rib and Slab, wet, terrific stuff. Donald not so keen. I tried solo: too hard, I lacked confidence, slipped round side and beat off up New West – high exposure, not hard. I was much impressed by Rib and Slab. Then hell ride in torrents, frozen stiff, fog like fungus, wretched till back in Edinburgh.' (A weekend also memorable to Mill for his detour up an easy gully to give Robin a top rope on Nose!)[4]

Now darting here, there and everywhere at weekends, Robin followed the Lakeland trip with 'a magnificent, magnificent Sunday on Ben A'an, one of my best climbing days ever. Nothing fantastically hard . . . but Great Sport'. Another Sunday was spent locally on Caerketton followed by 'a long walk to Habbie's Howe where I enjoyed my first shandy – and first real tour of the Pentlands'. Then, taking advantage of the good fortune that Mill had a motorbike, he went north to Glencoe where Hangman's on the Buachaille was the highlight: 'I get up – frantically just! Desperate move in middle, where I got stuck at half-term; rest quite easy – crux a pad.'

It was around this time that I arrived at school to be told by a rather sheepish Robin that he had had a fall somewhere in the Lake District where, apart from bruising, his only injury was a small cut on the back of a hand for which a plaster was enough. Nonetheless, it was an incident serious enough to remind Jimmy Marshall how Robin 'could have been taken out at a very early stage without a fair degree of luck'.

As the weekends came and went, Robin was pleased to discover that Arrochar was hitch-hikeable with a start from Edinburgh as late as six o'clock. As Donald and bike were not available he 'took hitches to Tarbet and padded up to the campsite. Jim [Clarkson] and I on Sunday beat off up Cobbler; fine but very windy, restricted. Blown about on Punster's – excellent, overhanging recess! Chimney Arête, sort of, Cat Crawl. Then to South Peak: I soloed quick up Ardgartan Wall, then we did Ardgartan Arête. First real idea of the build-up of Cobbler, the magnificence thereof.' He truly loved that mountain, perhaps influenced by the knowledge that his father was raised in Arrochar, which lies at its foot, and that his mother had reached the Cobbler's summit. It was even an Arrochar connection that brought his parents together, when his father was contacted to tell the then Mary Reid, visiting her father in Calcutta, that her friend from Arrochar had died in childbirth.

Then suddenly, out of the blue, doom and disaster afflicted Robin, who wailed, 'I bust my wrist, summer, progress, the lot!' Arriving at school, I found him with arm in plaster from elbow to knuckles in a less than happy frame of mind. As a volunteer in the erection of the school's Sports' Day 'Obstacle Race' course, he was part of a group who found an alternative use for one of the obstacles. The official idea was that competitors climb a 5-ft barred gate, hurry along a plank supported by another gate, and jump off at the other end as they sped on their way. However, it also provided a fine setting for a jousting competition, and Robin duly managed to get the better of several opponents, though of the last by such a fine margin that he was badly off balance as the opponent was dispatched. The ensuing fall onto grass resulted in a broken wrist bone, making us muse of Pyrrhic victories and the irony of his recent injury-free bounce down that Lakeland crag.

As I extended sympathy, the awareness crept into my mind that our summer expedition was scheduled as a blitz on the hardest climbs of Glencoe, Nevis and Skye. Now, it would be dishonest to pretend that I was looking forward to this trip with anything other than trepidation and, as a great feeling of guilt swept over me at the thought that Robin's broken bone might have come to the rescue, I put it to him, in suitably disappointed tones, that the accident appeared to have put an end to our plans. Not a bit of it! As he moved into manipulative mode, he cheered up, venturing that the trip was still on with me leading the rock climbs and it including an as-yet-unspecified but spectacular long-distance hike. He made the hike part sound appealing and conceded that the standard of climbs would have to be lower than previously planned. I would be happy on 'Very Difficult' grades – Robin said 'Severes', maybe harder. We settled on 'Mild Severe', though I felt uneasy with his conviction that the grades of Skye climbs were overstated and that we should wait to see how we were getting on when we got there.

Circumstances, however, if not ideally from Robin's perspective, had contrived to expand his list of accomplishments – as coach of a tug-of-war team, the performance witnessed by Donald Scott: 'Prevented by injury from participating himself on sports' day, Robin set out to dominate his house team and, with complete ignorance of the techniques of this complex sport, by sheer enthusiasm and willpower shared in their success.' A school magazine stated that it was 'unlikely that any of the victorious tug-of-war team will ever forget Eb's vocal encouragement', and added further general compliments about his influence.

Despite his fundamentally bolshie and anti-Establishment nature, Robin had taken his responsibilities as a prefect and house captain seriously. And he did them well, a contributing factor no doubt being the personality of his housemaster, Donald Doull, to whom he related well. However, those assessing Robin from school photographs could easily be misled, as Scott points out:

> The prefects' photograph of a demure-looking Robin in no way portrays the character of what was a complex young man. This was one of the few moments when conformity could have been uppermost in Robin's mind – perhaps occasioned by his recognition that his elevation to the post of prefect was a valued and worthwhile achievement.

So understandably, not just paradoxically, Robin adjusted to the role into which he had been thrust, and even came to be talked about in terms of leadership qualities. On the verge of leaving school, however, he was still undeniably shy, even nervous, away from the school environment. Further, modelled by experiences under the 'aegis' of Butcher Fleming, he was, we suspect, wary of the idea of leadership because of a concern for its possible association with control and authority. His former classmate, Howard Andrew, who went on to take up climbing at university, suggests that Robin's nature did not change in this regard:

> His disinclination to accept posts of authority continued after school, even though he was to become secretary of the university mountaineering club at an early stage. That was Robin seeking involvement, not authority, at the heart of the club and his election to the SMC committee a few years later was, from what I have heard, the result of pressure from friends. He was destined to play a prominent role within climbing groups through the force of his personality, his enthusiasm and the uninvited near-reverence shown by others towards him as a

climber of renown, but he preferred, it seemed, to exert influence without being the focal figure.

Such then was the individual that Watson's was about to entrust to university in the outside world – though not before he had taken me to a public library to pore over maps in search of ideas for our hike of hikes. An obvious line stretching north from Ardgour for about 60 miles, most of it over rough country that would rarely if ever have felt the foot of man, suddenly caught our eye.

4

CRACKS OF DOOM

So, it was agreed. The big hike would be preceded by climbing in Glencoe and followed by further climbing on Skye. But first we were to go camping to Arran and, immediately school broke up towards the end of July 1956, we borrowed a ridge tent from the Scouts before setting off with a couple of other classmates.[1]

Up Glen Rosa, past the last farm building, the perfect camping spot offered itself on a small, lush, flat, green site by the bend in the river. The bank was well eaten into, but risks seemed minimal. And so it was for two nights until, on the third day, the weather broke. The rain intensified whilst we were at a dance in Brodick and we had to walk home in it. About 3 a.m. the water started coming in and we had to throw our gear onto higher ground to save it from being washed away. Soon it was sodden. In the morning a child gathering eggs found us sheltering in a barn, our largely naked bodies covered by potato sacks for warmth. Her mother kindly fed us and helped us sort ourselves out. The next day, on stepping off the ferry, we got back to Edinburgh with the help of just two lifts, the second on the back of an open lorry as the sun shone. The real business, however, did not get under way until the following week when Robin and I met below the Buachaille, in Glencoe – both of us a little wiser in the ways of nature, he now used to, if not happy about, the plaster cast protecting that cracked wrist:

> Bugged up Agag's.[2] Jimmy led the lot, climbing well after initial trep-
> idation. Down to Lagangarbh for evening, met Bob Grieve and son,
> Len Lovat, some Glaswegian and a Manchesterish man – Marshall
> called him 'Foony'. Best evening's discussion I have heard. Next day
> Shackle. I was in a crap mood, desperate! Jimmy romped up! However
> I recovered and led the last tier. My arm was getting suppler, the plaster
> weaker. Spent the evening talking to 'Foony'. These 2 nights trans-
> ported me. I was carried to the world of Eiger and mountain hut,
> Morsely & Bourdillon, Brown and Whillans, Central Buttress & Étriers

– I swallowed and gulped! Boston knew personally, had climbed with, perhaps the finest mountaineers in the world. My ambitions fired, soared. Could I . . . ? Couldn't I . . . ?

From Lagangarbh we moved to the hostel for a couple of days before setting out on the big hike via Fort William to stock up on provisions. Our packs were so heavy that out of curiosity we diverted to the railway station to weigh them before setting off via the 'ferry at Corran . . . to Glen Gour, sketched map, great packs: stoured up magnificent country to magnificent camp site. Finest situation I have been in of the kind! Deer and fish and all!' That was no more than a two-hour walk into the hills, at Lochan na Beinne Bàine, yet the sole of one of Robin's Vibrams was already starting to separate from its upper when his 'perfectly fitting boot gave. I, ass, threw them into the loch.' The offending boot was dispatched with a hearty over-arm lob, but it had not hit the water before he sheepishly looked at me for reassurance that he had done the right thing. He hadn't. The other, not much good on its own, went as well after which we watched, entranced, as ripples slowly defiled the lochan's glassy surface. He too would now be walking in Kletterschühe.

The following day a lunchtime swim in Lochan Dubh came as a welcome relief before we tramped nearly 1000 steep feet up and over a ridge to avoid a lengthy detour on what was, Robin reflected, a 'fine, sunny, bit of cloud, long magnificent day. Genuine cross-country trek, halfway bathe, route shambles, glimpses of Loch Shiel, deer sanctuary. Pathless, sun beating, packs now old seamen, now not a feather, colours laugh flinging.' Back down to lower levels, Robin went into burn-up mode at the start of a long gradual incline. The ritualistic pattern of behaviour reserved for such situations may not have been memorable but for blisters brought about by my own defective boot. He refused to stop to allow me to apply a plaster (in his sack!) – if anything upping the pace, which channelled my anger into a determination to catch him up, even if blood had to spurt forth. Then, perhaps fortunately, the sole broke away and I shouted the news to Robin, who deemed it a deserving enough cause to pull up. 'Songs belched on last lap,' Robin somehow remembered of our approach to Glenfinnan. 'Wuthering Heightsish farm, only growling dogs & darkness. Beat on to nasty campsite; chat with porter, recommended to station for bed. Our boots had gone! Blast! So Jimmy to Fort Bill, I to Skye.'

Sadly, it had become clear that the hike would have to be curtailed. It would have taken us across 40 miles or so of pathless mountains, glens and rivers north via the head of Loch Hourn to Shiel Bridge, well on the road to Skye. Without doubt Fort William had a cobbler, though not necessarily Mallaig, which now lay in the right direction, as Skye had suddenly become our immediate objective. Since Robin's boots had not gone as badly as mine, he would head that way on his own the following day.

It was at Glenfinnan that evening, I remember, that Robin got his comeuppance for having been such a little rat to me on the walk. As usual when our paths diverged, gear and food were allocated between us to allow each to be as self-reliant as possible, and to have to carry equal weight. A routine had evolved for this contingency. Articles were split into pairs and a coin tossed for each pairing, the first toss always for the tent on the one hand or the Primus and rope on the other – the tent and Primus functional items, the rope dead weight. There were rules as to what the claimant of the tin opener and Primus was entitled,. matches and candles required special consideration, and so on. Always there was an aura of excitement and drama, and never before had the event taken place on such a grand scale.

The first coin was spun. I won and, as the weather looked settled, chose the Primus and rope. I won the next toss, the next, and then the next – such a sequence naturally starting to become a bit much for Robin. To further aggravate his disquiet, I went on to win the next, and then the next where one of the items at stake was a jar of peanut butter. Now we both knew that Robin was addicted to the stuff whereas I couldn't stand it. He couldn't contain his frustration at this atrocious run of bad luck and, as he muttered, I fell back on my rucksack, creased with laughter. I sat back up, stroked my chin as you do with any difficult decision, and questioned if I should perhaps give peanut butter another try, just managing to get this out in calm collected style before collapsing again. Robin, unable to contain his fury, unleashed the sort of sermonising that would have been a credit to any fire-and-brimstone minister, spouting off about decency, morality, fairness, humility, insisting that I for sure had never heard of them. I then managed to rise onto an elbow to put it to him that his long run of bad luck was perhaps some form of divine judgement for his lack of consideration towards me during the walk. That set him off again, the trigger for another collapse on my part. However, his humour was soon to improve, due in part to my unduly generous change of heart about his much-favoured peanut butter.

Next day Robin reached Mallaig from Glenfinnan after fine walks and scrambles on worthy, undervalued non-Munros to the south of Lochailort, experiencing a 'chos lift, chos camp and chossily mended boots' as he went. He reached Skye via an 'absurd steamer to Kyle', and we met up at Sligachan as planned, I fresh from Fort William after spending the night in an unlocked gatekeeper's hut at the entrance to a hydro-electric scheme under construction in the middle of nowhere. Having spotted it just as it seemed I would have to sleep in the open, I was instead pampered with the luxuries of an electric fire and an armchair while the slope of the desk allowed the Primus to stand exactly level for cooking with two of the three legs extended. Bliss! For me at least, but not for Robin whose 'b.bts. have gone again – Jimmy met me only to find my 2nd pair bust. We whipped straight to Portree, watched local drunks dance, but an old grump refused to mend them. So the only thing is to beat up the Cuillin not only with arm in plaster but also in gym shoes. Now gazing at Sgurr Nan Gillean, waiting for a lift to Glen Brittle.'

The imminence of more rock leads was making me more than a little nervous, but leading was part of the deal. One particular day, climbing from a camp above Glen Brittle House, became memorable for both of us. 'Very fine and up Cioch Direct,' Robin wrote. 'I couldn't lead crux: Jimmy OK, then chancy traverse. I was by then as good as Jimmy, then I cooked the lead on VS Crack of Doom. Jimmy led first bit well – pleased with self. I suspect he was scared of crux. V. pleasant interesting lead in plaster.'

It may be that Robin took a loyal decision to leave my reputation unsullied, for his jottings of our activities on the Crack of Doom differ from my own recollections. The Crack of Doom is a fine long (700-ft), exposed climb though not quite, according to Robin, one that justified inclusion in the hardest category. That was an opinion I had been fearing as he would automatically reckon that it was up to me to lead it, and I knew that refusal was out of the question in view of his subtle mélange of arm-twisting techniques. The strain had got to me, but I was very aware that 'today' was the last of the expedition and the thought was passing through my mind that I should maybe make it my last as a climber. I didn't know how I would tell Robin, but concern on that could be deferred.

Progress on the Crack of Doom was good. Then, just below the crux, or perhaps it was the crux, the route took me to the left edge of a steep wall across which led an extremely narrow 15-ft horizontal fault back into the right-angle of the crack. But, by using the outside edge of the left foot and the inside of the right, it might just be possible to 'walk' across it. There were no handholds, but the wall seemed just, only just, sufficiently inclined to permit that. Very delicate stuff, and almost certainly off-route. Twenty-five feet below, Robin's face and now filthy plastered arm were picked out by the sun, and it was a long way down past him. It turned out to be as delicate as I had imagined, but each invasive surge of fear was repelled, then supplanted – as I inched across – by an all-engulfing glow of calmness and control, a sensation not lost more than forty years on.

I had held myself together. I was still 'here'. Then up came Robin. The following pitch also led out onto the exposed wall but could be evaded by scuttering up behind large chockstones. I took this dishonourable option, and the ensuing abuse from Robin, who, after unroping, instructed me to pull the rope up, then throw it back down to him. In a passing reference to his success with an arm in plaster, he said the pitch had been easy, leaving me with the thought that I should maybe have taken it on. On the other hand, I was unsure if he meant it, even though he had come up quickly. In any case, the crag's steepness and difficulty were soon to lessen, and it had struck me that any further high-risk moves could well be confined to that pitch with its convenient escape route . . . perhaps forever. It suited me fine that Robin wanted to take over the lead:

> Then beat over Sgurr Alasdair and the 'Bad Step', along ridge, magnificent cloud-thro' views, stupendous sunset. After all, I was by now the gen leader. Romped up Inaccessible Pinnacle unroped, but Jimmy liked rope down. Then beat down ridge and over bog, strike camp, to youth

hostel. God knows what they thought to see us, dishevelled, after 10 p.m. with rope, great packs, my arm in plaster! How I wished they could find out without show from me!

The descent was most casual as the sun set over the Outer Isles and it was only further down the hill that we realised we were pressed for time to reach the hostel before it closed. Before leaving the ridge, one of my boots again came apart and the pair was buried under a rock to great mumblings, in which Robin joined, unaware that it would be thirty-six years before one of us was to find out that Kletterschühe should have been reserved exclusively for rockwork. Consequently, we were both in rubbers when we reached the hostel, where I became a little nervous lest Robin's level of excitement might give the game away about how he was thinking. I didn't want others to overhear his whispers as we waited to be booked in. Mark you, but for a feeling that I was a bit of a fraud after flunking a pitch and being on the verge of packing in climbing, I too would have liked people to know what we had been doing. But we're maybe all a bit like that when it comes to the 'recognition factor'.

I felt great unease at casting Robin aside, leaving him with no alternative but to scour the country alone even more than before, crag-crawling and hostel-whoring for seconds, with no one to share his dreams, once again the waif. In the end, I never disclosed to him directly that I had chucked climbing. Rather, I became unavailable due to other sports he knew I would not drop. But he would manage just fine without me in the holiday-abundant atmosphere of Edinburgh University. For me, retirement from the climbing scene was inevitable – after all, I was getting on for seventeen and a half. As retribution by the gods of the mountains, however, I was sentenced to spend five years in an accountant's garret, compared with which the thought of the very hardest climb, unroped, on wet rock, with split boots, in the dark, became progressively less daunting than the final steps into the garret itself.

Looking back to when we left Skye, Robin noted a minor compliment followed by the observation that I was 'not cut out for greatness in mountaineering. Next day our paths there parted. Never since have I climbed with Jimmy. He was a good lad, we understood each other . . .'

We did, even though it's true that he could drive me mad. But you couldn't not like Robin. Knowing now of his reputation in top climbing circles, it is flattering to think that in his own fair hand are the words, 'I was by then as good as Jimmy' – the sort of story to tell your grandchildren, as they say. And I'll maybe leave out the little bit about his arm being in plaster.

5

NOWT DOING

Robin was soon raring to go again after hitching back to Edinburgh from the family holiday at Achmelvich, where he had headed when we parted on leaving Skye. He was now eighteen, having celebrated his birthday in Achmelvich on August 30th (1956). Impatient to test out his wrist on a big route now that he had hacked off the plaster cast with a penknife, all he lacked was a partner:

> Jimmy puts off, 'Och, well, you see, I says.' Donald working. Macauley not on 'phone, so off solo to Arrochar in search of a kindred or a sucker. Looked in at youth hostel, nothing doing so up nasty dripping path. 2 days of retreat before drip columns. Nasty, nasty howf. Not a bod seen. Fine nail problem climbs, especially one I now have in repertoire – perfection of a climb for nails. Hammered down to Arrochar to get out of muck, hitched to hostel with musical Yanks, looked for a sucker since there was clearly no kindred.
>
> Nowt doing, so dithered, hitched to Buachaille but no one at the Lagangarbh hut, so off to Bidean. Up Lost Valley, inspected Gearr Aonach, did very Joe Brownish climb on a boulder, good lunch, beat off up Beinn Fhada (both tops), then nan Lochan, then Amphitheatre – shattering ascent of shattered Central Ridge with heavy pack. Down to B Buttress, shambling about there, chancing it, then hammer down Dinnertime – first time – in darkness. Back to the youth hostel for usual all-impressing moment: late entry, strong dark silent man, ropes and boots, obviously hard.

This search for partners eventually took Robin to Nevis, where, with hardly three weeks left before he was due to start university, two came his way: Ted Wise and Ian Douglas. Their second climb, the Crack on Càrn Dearg, had a sinister reputation. It was not often climbed, partly because it was difficult for all but the best, and partly because of unpleasant, mucky sections. Robin himself takes up the story:[1]

> In the morning the three of us climbed Route 1 on Nevis. This was Ian's third climb, he had climbed a Difficult, a Very Difficult and now

44

a Severe, and so we thought we should go and climb a Very Severe. Down and round the corner we came to the foot of Raeburn's Buttress. A long scramble leads to a sudden steep buttress which falls back and narrows to a shattered arête running up to the summit plateau, and the buttress in the middle is the bit that gives the trouble. There, the other routes sneak round the side, as the front of the buttress is too steep, but the Crack goes up the front. From below the climb looks deceptively easy; the first pitch just looks steep, and the rest vertical.

There are four main pitches, a wall leading to the base of the Crack and three crack pitches. You think all is well, you will scramble up to the base of the Crack and if it looks nasty come down; the wall looks like 80 ft of 3-ft steps, but the wall is a winking monster. You rush off upwards, but as you rush you feel the wall swing smoothly up through 30 degrees, and then you aren't rushing any more but are strung up on nasty little overhangs topped by littlersloping ledges with the odd little crack in the back which will take a few fingers once you scrape out the mud and the ooze and the moss. At 50 ft you fix a wretched runner, which at least gives Ted something to do, for you are feeling him muttering up the rope, and then you climb another 30 ft to reach the stance, which slopes at round about 30 degrees and you look for a belay. You throw off several boulders, big ones, until there are only small ones left, and then you get fed up and hope you've thrown off all the loose ones and take a belay on a small one.

Then you are Ted, and you climb up quicker because you know the way to go, but you find it just as nasty and the rope doesn't go straight up but is squint (or bent?) and if you let go you're in for a swing but you don't let go. You reach the stance but there's no room for two, so you find some more boulders to the right, big ones, and you squat on top of the biggest and probably the loosest.

And then you are both Ian and depressed. This wall has depressed all three of you, but now the first two are on top and don't want to come down, the third is at the bottom and doesn't want to climb up. Anyway it is getting on and the first two have been slow and there is hardly time for a party of three to get up. You take a step or two, prod the rock here and there, take a step or two down, untie and elect to watch. You aren't surprised that there follows a chaos of ropes. This is sometimes found with Smith around, and here, standing on sloping slime and balancing boulders, with two ropes and a thumbnail belay, they take some time to swop stances. The first Crack pitch is 50 ft long and is really a chimney. It overhangs and is undercut and the entry is

45

rotten, and so it is awkward to enter, but the rest is all right and they get up it all right; then they go to the right and seem to hang around on the overhanging wall, but they will tell you later that a ledge runs right for 10 ft from the top of the chimney and they dig out a belay down the back of a block on the right.

And now they are thus. Wise is tied to the right end of the ledge. Smith stands 10 ft left. The ledge is 2 or 3 ft wide, slopes, is heaped with rubble, cuts out of the overhanging wall in profile like the centre stroke of a streak of lightning. The wall below them cuts back under them, above it hangs over them thrusting them outwards. The Crack swings up and over to the left from the left edge of the ledge. For 20 ft it overhangs, overhanging walls on either side, but then the left wall falls back as a steep slant, while the right wall still overhangs and hides the rest of the crack from Smith and Wise on the ledge to the right. From the bottom you can see that the crack continues in the corner between the slab and the overhang, and once they are on the slab the crux will be past, but by now the light is going, you can hardly see them, and so the rest of the story is my own unbiased version. It took me about five grunting attempts, blowing myself up to jam in the crack, wriggling up and hissing down, deflated, until at last I could twist up and over the final bulge and get on to the slab on the left. The way was now clear to the third and last overhang 50 ft above, the crack was still steep, but the holds were great and good. I went up 20 ft or so, and tied on to a belay, but it wasn't a very good one. I went a bit higher and took a better belay; then I hauled up our spare food and clothes in the rucksack; then Ted joined the two ropes and tied on to the lower one, so that I had a great pile of slack to pull in; and this was all to the good.

By now Ted had been crouched on the ledge for a long cold time, and his stomach was sinking with the sun, but he came straight away, and from my belay I could see vertically down the crack, and through the overhang, and I made out bits of Ted blocking the light as he climbed to the left, then I saw his head coming up from under the overhang, and then he had wrapped himself over the bulge, and his hands were above the bulge, one hand in the crack, and one hand on the slab, he was very nearly there with only one more move to make, but there he came off. He was on a tight rope, but with the stretch of the nylon he went down about 2 ft and swung away from the overhang. His fingers were too tired to pull him back, he was hanging on the rope, slowly spinning, with nothing below him for about 150 ft but a few slight bulges near the bottom. Now I hadn't a clue as to what was going on, he shouted to be lowered, so I just lowered away, chortling the while. He told me later that the ledge he had started from was too far to the right, he was wanting to pendulum in to a smaller ledge sticking out of the overhang 30 ft below, so he began to swing himself towards and away from the face, but when he first reached the rock he was above the ledge, as he swung away, I was lowering him past it, and when he swung in again he was too low down. A little lower he swung into something else, but it wasn't much good and he was spinning round and before he could land he had pendulumed back and further down into space. Halfway down the angle eased a bit, and from there the face was just a little less than vertical and Ted went spiralling down here and there brushing a bulge until at last he landed on the easy rocks at the foot of the first pitch.

So Ian and Ted were safe at the bottom, they were all right Jack but I was not.[2] I couldn't climb down and I wasn't going to abseil, because we might have lost our ropes and I didn't like abseils. They offered to go away around by the Castle Ridge to the summit plateau, then down the arête of Raeburn's Buttress to give me a top rope on 20 ft of overhang, but that would have taken a month, already they could see me only when I moved as a darker blur against the darkness, and those last 20 ft didn't look so bad. The face was a great leaning overhang, but the Crack cut up through the middle looking deep enough and wide enough to let me get right inside and wriggle safely up. I told them below, it would go quite easily; they could go back to the hut and I'd join them in a couple of hours.

So they beetled off and I pulled up our 220 ft of rope and draped it in a shambles round my neck, then with the rucksack on my back I climbed up to the foot of the overhang. Just there, there was a good ledge, going left, and I thought, this is a good thing because I can stand on it while I look at the overhang. But the overhang didn't look so good now, it looked as though it might not be deep enough to climb as a straight chimney. Moreover, my arms were getting fed-up and my stomach and back were all cramped after lowering and laughing at Ted. I tried the first few feet, then came down and dumped the ropes and the rucksack on the ledge, then tried them again and came down. I tied on to one end of the rope and allowed enough slack to reach the top of the pitch, then I tied the rest of the rope and the rucksack together in a bundle so that I could pull them up after me when I got up.

The Crack was at first about a foot wide, which was wide enough, and although it started shallow it soon cut back deeply enough to let me get right inside, but just before the end of the overhang the recess was blocked by a roof. So from under the roof I had to wriggle sideways to the edge of the Crack, and leaning out, fumble for the guidebook's good holds over the overhang, then swing out of the Crack and swarm over the top. When I reached the roof at wriggle level I was facing the right wall of the Crack. Just at head level throughout the wriggle the Crack was too narrow to let my head turn, it had to face sideways, either into the recess or out towards space. I set off on the wriggle, at first facing the recess, but I went too high and my head got stuck, so I came back and I thought, if I face the recess then I can't see where I'm going. I set off again, facing space, and I got to the end of the wriggle and finished up leaning out of the Crack. From here I began to fumble and before long I found the good holds, but I thought, rot the guidebook, these are obviously poor. I had no qualms about the swing, it was just that having swung I might not make the swarm, and I might not manage to swing back, and around this time I looked down through my feet and I was looking straight over the overlay below and if it had not been so dark I would have looked straight down to the bottom of the climb, and I shrank up into the Crack like a scared slug's horns. Then I began to reverse the wriggle, but I was still facing space and I soon got stuck and I thought, like this I can't find my footholds. So I wriggled out again to the edge of the Crack and I leaned away out and I turned my head, then I came back along the wriggle facing the recess and this time I got to the back of the Crack. From here I had just to go down about 18 ft but going down in my state was still quite hard. I struggled and hung and scraped and finally jumped to the left and landed on the ledge that was to be a good thing because it was going to let me look at the overhang.

There I sat for a while and blew and waited for a bit of strength, and I knew it must be getting very late. The sun was way down on the other side of the Ben and had see-sawed the shadows from the Allt a' Mhuillin up the screes of Càrn Mòr Dearg to cover up the redness. I cursed and stamped about a bit and then went back to the Crack, which was really rather stupid because already it was so dark I could hardly see the holds. I got up the Crack to wriggle level, but only just, and I wedged myself away up in the back and refused to wriggle out, and couldn't see how to get down. I had already been getting resigned to a night on the ledge, but unless I could find my way down I would have to pass the night trying to stay stuck in an overhanging crack.

All was well, however, and with a lot of luck and a fiendish scrabbling I finally got back to the ledge before I had fallen off, and by then
it was sure that I wasn't going to get any further, but relative to an
overhanging crack it seemed a very desirable sort of place. The ledge
was about 8 ft long and only slightly sloping. The right end was quite
a bit higher than the left, and so I had to lie with my head at the right
end, but unfortunately this was also the narrow end; the left was about
1? ft wide but the right end was less than a foot. Below the ledge the
face went down for about 20 ft as the sort of steep slab that you can
just about sit on without any holds, and then it heeled over into the
overhangs. There was a thick moss growing all over the ledge and the
slab, and I thought, this will be a good thing because it will be soft to
lie on. Then I opened the rucksack and I found a spare anorak and
jersey of Ted's and a jersey of my own. I pulled a jersey over my trousers
and put the rest on in the normal fashion; then I found chocolate and
raisins and an orange, and so I was really having it easy. I threaded a
sling behind a chockstone in the Crack above my head, and I tied on
to one end of the rope and threaded it through the karabiner in the
sling and fixed it as a belay. Then I bundled up the rest of the rope as
a pillow, and put my feet in the rucksack as all the best books recommend, and lay on my back all buckled up on the ledge. The belay could
have stopped me from falling right off but still I couldn't relax because
then my head slipped off the narrow end of the ledge. So I fixed the
belay rope from my waist under my left arm to come out at my left
shoulder and from there to the chockstone. My left hand could keep it
taut between my shoulder and the chockstone, and so my head could
lean out against the rope which kept it from slipping off the ledge. In
this position and after a fashion I was able to relax, and so for an hour
or two, but the night was very clear and I began to get cold, and only
then it occurred to me that I could make more use of the moss than as
a mattress. I tore away great lumps of moss and earth from the ledge,
and when I had scraped it clean I started scraping the slab below as far
down as I could scrape. Then I arranged myself on the ledge again and
piled all the vegetation on top and beat it into a great mud pie that
covered me all but my head and I passed the rest of the night in compar-
ative warmth.

Sometimes I dozed a little, and now and again I bawled at the night
with great bursts of skiffle all about a worried man and long-lost John
and Stewball and the like until the stars began to disappear and a vague
sort of lightness began to come up from behind the back of Càrn Mòr

Dearg. Then it was all red with sunrise and I could see everything clearly and I realised that it would be a good thing to extricate myself before search parties began to appear. I threw off the moss and scraped off some of the filth that stuck to me. I stamped about and beat myself for warmth and arranged the ropes and the rucksack and then struggled up the Crack to the roof and wriggled out to the edge. But everything was cold and I was stiff and I dithered about for a long time until I heard distant shoutings from below. I looked around and I saw four figures coming up from the CIC to pick up my body from the foot of the climb. I shouted back but they could not see me in the Crack, and so, glad of an excuse to go down, I struggled back to the ledge and waved things till they saw me. As they came a little nearer our shouting became a little more intelligible, but still we could hardly understand each other and it was only when I saw them making for Castle Ridge that I realised they were coming round to rescue me. With horrid visions of top ropes and tight ropes and ignominy and the like, I felt the need to do something to save the situation, but then as I was bullying myself to go back and wriggle in the nasty overhang, I noticed below me, 20 ft lower down the Crack from the ledge, a line of weakness crossing the face to the right. It had been too dark to see it the night before, but now it looked very promising. I left everything on the ledge and went down to have a look. I traversed well out to the right and it was not at all hard, and from there it was easy to go right round the bulge and back to the Crack above the stupid overhang that had stopped me for so long. By now the rescue party was well up Castle Ridge. I bawled to them to stop and so they stopped to see what I was up to. I went back to the ledge to gather all the gear around me, then down and out along the easy traverse and up and round to the top of the overhang. The rest was simple and I scrambled up the Crack till it disappeared at the terrace below the final arête of the buttress. The arête looked very good in the sun, but I thought I should get down as soon as I could, as my rescuers were coming down and across to the foot of the rocks. I found a narrow shelf cutting down across the right wall and into the corrie between Raeburn's Buttress and the Castle Ridge. I rushed along this to the tumble of slabs in the corrie and I slithered down these in a great haste and a great shambles of ropes and rucksack and coated with filth and moss to make my peace on the screes at the foot of the rocks.

6

STUDIOUS CLIMBERS

Robin's reputation as a climber was already a topical issue by the time he started university shortly after those exploits on the Crack. On the one hand, a school of older climbers questioned the wisdom of being on the same mountain as him lest they get caught up in a desperate rescue mission or worse, but Jimmy Marshall thought otherwise. Rather, he looked on that recent escape as an omen that Robin was going to 'make it', and looked forward to what Robin might be capable of achieving as a mountaineer.

During his five years at Edinburgh University between 1956 and 1961, Robin took an Honours degree in Mental Philosophy.[1] Upon entering university, he joined the Edinburgh University Mountaineering Club (EUMC), going on to became the editor of its journal. His sporting and social life quickly came to revolve around the club's activities. Meanwhile, he remained a member of the Junior Mountaineering Club of Scotland, through which aspirant members of the national body (the SMC) almost inevitably passed. Robin was elected to the SMC in October 1958, at the age of twenty.

University meets were held regularly throughout the year, and many of Robin's first ascents in fact came to be done with club members. Throughout that period he lived with his mother and sister in Comiston, a south Edinburgh suburb, whilst his brother was studying naval architecture at Glasgow University. The house at 12 Comiston Springs Avenue was the first conventional home the children had known since leaving India ten years previously.

Now that I had packed in climbing for cricket (and rugby), Robin turned for partners to other former schoolmates, also students like himself. Having dragooned four or five in all, he proceeded to carry them along in a wake of enthusiasm that quickly dispelled their initial feelings of half-heartedness. Amongst them was Kenny Allan, to whom Robin had always seemed different – part of the crowd, but an individualist, and never really one of the gang. So it was that Allan came to find himself dodging parkies (park wardens) with Robin at Salisbury Crags on Sundays, being instructed to lean out, not to use knees and discovering the difference between a hand jam and a jug handle. Before long all were sharing in the pleasure and excitement of the hills. Kenny Allan:

> As time went by Robin tended to spend more time with hard climbers, but the long university holidays still allowed him plenty of time to spend with us lesser mortals. Always he was leader, never happier than when carrying a big pack, moving fast over long distances and showing us how unfit we were. Or we could be climbing happily on the Cobbler when Robin, a man of instant decisions, would decide we should go off immediately to Nevis. It would take the combined weight of three personalities to convince him that joint ownership of equipment gave us a say in these decisions. In a one-to-one situation Robin always won, or made life miserable for the other person. He did not believe in democracy unless the majority agreed with him. He didn't believe in smoking either, and even though you couldn't see across the tent for candle smoke and paraffin fumes, the 'bucking fuggers' were required to smoke with heads stuck outside the tent.
>
> His powers of persuasion and iron willpower became more obvious the older he got. I remember going out of the tent in a storm in Glencoe to get water for the mince. Robin was supposed to have brought the torch but had forgotten. I fell about 4 ft into the burn, but Robin's main concern was whether or not I had lost any mince, and I was not allowed back in the tent with wet clothes – consequently, I ended up removing them in the wind and rain outside. Looking back, I must have been soft, but Robin had convinced the others that this was a good idea. He could sometimes be outrageous, but we had known him for years and this didn't bother us.

Vic Burton – another former classmate, and now an orthopaedic surgeon – was also there when Allan fell with the mince. At university Burton met Robin occasionally in the Old Quad Common Room, one of the few areas where there was a cross-fertilisation between the Arts and Medical Faculties. There Robin would attempt to introduce Burton to his subject, arguing that material things did not necessarily exist as objects. Robin was concerned that we all made assumptions that influenced our human activity without rational proof. It was perhaps this approach, Burton suggests, that enabled Robin to conjure up holds in rock which were not apparent to anyone else.

Tangible evidence of this conjuring was demonstrated in Ardgour where he and Robin headed in spring 1957 to fulfil an ambition nursed by Robin since he'd been there with me a year previously. They approached the climb from a camp at the foot of Garbh Bheinn. Burton managed the first pitch without problems, then spent the next two hours with water trickling down his neck, as Robin searched above for a way past the overhang. The running commentary on progress eventually climaxed with a triumphant yell, the prelude to an impressive display of strength from Robin in managing to pull his partner's 'hypothermic-stiff body' up the rest of the climb. It was Robin's *first* first ascent, one he finally christened 'Blockhead' and described as 'a fine steep climb, with several small running belays'. (The current guidebook talks of a difficult and serious route.[2])

The following month, in the latter half of May, the club held a meet in Arran, camping by the waterfall in Glen Rosa. On the Monday, on Cir Mhor, Robin shared an ascent with seven others including four girls – one of whom, Janet Holt, had never been on rock before. From the beginning there was a note of mystery about the expedition. Nobody quite seemed to know where they were going, or, if they did, they were singularly unwilling to divulge plans. However, all followed in different stages of ignorance and good faith, and made their way upwards via Prospero's Prelude to the foot of a very large, wet and rather alarming-looking rockface. Above lay Labyrinth Direct, a strenuous Severe, not made any easier by the high wind and recent deluge. Janet Holt:[3]

With repeated assurances that it was easy, wasn't far, and wouldn't take long, we began to climb. The first pitch was up a cold slimy green chimney. Robin and Donald [Mill] went first and found a belay on a small grassy ledge about 100 ft up. As the ledge was obviously too small for us all, I followed up the next pitch. It was 100 ft of dirty vegetatious rock and I remember my horror on reaching the top to find that the only way on was by way of a 50-ft traverse, which wandered over a sheer rockface to the left, and which, to my inexperienced eyes, looked completely devoid of handholds and utter suicide. Wishing myself anywhere but where I was, I watched while Robin and Donald made their way along the narrow ledge and up the crest of the 15-ft corner at the end. By this time several people had arrived on the ledge and after a somewhat lurid discussion as to just how we would swing when we came off, I began edging my way gingerly along that handholdless crack. Arriving somehow at the corner, I half-climbed and was half-hauled over the crest to the next stance. One by one, the others followed with varying displays of speed and agility.

While Robin explored the next pitch, the labyrinth itself – a narrow crack blocked by five or six chockstones – the rest of us, feeling very wet and cold, sat and watched the mist trailing down the glen towards us. Seeing Robin's legs disappear over the first chockstone and vanish into a small dark hole, I lost faith finally in the continual assurances that the worst was over and felt sure that far from being over, it could surely have scarcely begun.

The first chockstone was climbed from the outside and then somehow, leaving one's legs to look after themselves, one wormed one's way into yet another wet, dark and very narrow chimney. With pushes from beneath and pulls from above, with the aid of knees and back and a few words of encouragement, the less experienced of us somehow reached the daylight at the top. The rest climbed.

I don't remember much about the next two pitches, except that at the end of the second we were faced with what surely must be quite the most ominous pitch of all. A large, wet and quite impossible-looking finger layback gave way to twin cracks, which ran round the face and to the left to the top of the climb. Robin eventually disappeared over the slabs above. Below, we heard the last person emerging from the labyrinth and, spread out on various grass ledges between the two small pitches, we waited patiently.

After what seemed like hours, Robin appeared triumphantly on a peak above us. I don't know if anyone really climbed that layback. All I remember for myself was a shoulder or a head underneath, a tug from above, flying through space, landing on the twin cracks and crawling up the final few feet.

Way down below on the far side of the gully another used match was tossed out from the shelter of an overhanging boulder followed by a waft of smoke that soon dissolved in the gusting wind. Huddled up at the back of his safe haven, out of the cold damp air funnelling up from below, a pipe-smoking bespectacled old man had been taking advantage of five and a half hours' free entertainment from a foot-a-minute epic that had climaxed in showbiz style with Janet's first ascent on rock. Although a little frail at this stage of his life, the club's seventy-five-year-old honorary president was a renowned Alpinist of the 1920s and 1930s, known particularly for classic new routes on the Brenva face of Mont Blanc. Thomas Graham Brown, a Fellow of the Royal Society for many years and also of its inner circle, the Royal Society Club, had returned to live in his native Edinburgh from Cardiff, where he was Professor of Physiology until 1947. He was first nominated the climbing club's honorary president in 1950. His academic and Alpine accomplishments, along with his disposition, were the basis for the esteem in which Robin and the other Edinburgh climbers held him.[4]

Graham Brown was no run-of-the-mill septuagenarian. He liked participating in club meets wherever possible, climbing respectably difficult routes, sleeping in draughty tents and accepting rides on the back of motorbikes. Prior to one Arran meet Brown contracted shingles for which his doctor told him to rest up for a couple of months. However, a second opinion advised six weeks rest only, so he concluded that further consultations could be sought to further diminish the period and, on this premise, attended the meet as arranged – good therapy, apparently, as his shingles soon disappeared without complications. Jimmy Marshall adds:

> He was a great old boy with a mischievous twinkle in his eye. He loved the rendezvous in pubs or at his place, where discussions could extend through the night on big Alpine lines, old and new, of which he had such extensive knowledge. He in turn took great pride in the young bloods' endeavours, delighting in their successes or their sometimes more interesting failures. There was total empathy on both sides of the relationship. As I see it, those discussions and the general ambience of G.B.'s study must have contributed significantly to Robin's developing interest in the power and potency of the written word.

Before he returned to Edinburgh from Cardiff, Brown was already a little bit different, eccentric even. After retirement he continued to occupy his old laboratory, a large room filled with stocks of books, periodicals and papers, some of them physiological, most of them Alpine. Behind all this, and out of sight, were his camp bed and other belongings.

In Edinburgh he lived in the city's West End, in a splendid Georgian flat at 20 Manor Place surrounded by old newspapers, half-burnt pipe dottle, cake wrappers, empty tins of tobacco and general untidiness. Generously he let out the unoccupied part of the flat to a group of Robin's friends, free with no strings attached, and the whole of the basement area, including a vast cupboard, soon became inhabited by the more unruly end of the EUMC, their possessions strewn around. Brian Wakefield was the pioneer:

> It was through Robin that I came to know Graham so well and shall never forget my first visit. Manor Place was a very posh area, very Edinburgh, if you see what I mean, full of professional offices and the like, but No. 20 was the exception.
>
> The whole flat was covered in a *very thick* layer of dust – particularly the carpets. Cobwebs were everywhere. The stairway leading down to the floor we were to occupy had obviously never been used since Graham had taken over the place. He had installed himself in a vast room over-looking the weed-infested garden at the back and there was a 'footpath' from this room to the front door. Another track led through the dust to the toilet and from there to his bedroom, where he slept in a sleeping bag.
>
> Graham spent his time reading and writing in front of an electric fire trying to light a marvellously curly briar pipe that would have been the envy of Sherlock Holmes or some other such sleuth – a bing of used Swan matches (well over a foot high and growing) testifying to the time spent on this particular task. We wondered how he never set fire to the place, which he almost did one day when we caught him frying an egg while using an egg-timer!

In his younger days Brown had been competitive, determined and, according to some of his Alpine Club colleagues, a difficult person. His 'scientific' approach to mountaineering as a younger man appears alien to that of the young Robin. But there was no friction between them, owing perhaps to the absence of rivalry between those of such dissimilar age groups, and to the elderly Brown having mellowed. Also, they had much in common: a desire for new routes, a keen sense of humour, and a well-honed intellect.

After rounding off the long weekend in Arran with what he described as 'a fine little mouthful to follow the South Ridge' – the first free ascent of the Rosetta Stone, a 30-ft boulder problem near the top of Cir Mhor – Robin returned to Edinburgh where he was appointed club secretary. That was just two months before he and Dougal Haston were to meet for the first time.

To the general public, Haston is certainly the best-known climber to have come out of the university club. Less than two years younger than Robin, he was killed at the age of thirty-six in an avalanche while skiing in Switzerland, where he had taken over the running of the International School of Mountaineering after John Harlin's death on the Eiger. Perhaps influenced by Robin, he also studied Philosophy, although he didn't complete his degree. Haston is best remembered for his part in putting up the Harlin Direttissima on the north face of the Eiger in the winter of 1966, the first ascent of Annapurna's south face with Don Whillans in 1970 and that of the southwest face of Everest with Doug Scott in 1975. A memorial stone stands in his honour outside the post office in Currie (now part of Edinburgh, on its southwest fringe), where he was born and brought up.

When he first met Robin in the summer of 1957, Haston was very much a novice. His first trip to the mountains had been in July of the previous year, when he climbed Glencoe's Bidean nam Bian with friends Stenhouse, McDonald and Patey – the 'Currie Boys', as they came to be known. It was another nine months, however, before any actual rock-climbing was attempted, and this only with an experienced leader. In May 1957, Haston and his future regular climbing partner, James 'Eley' Moriarty (also from Currie), were taken up Serpentine, a beginners' route on which they learnt the rudiments of ropework and the use of the karabiner from Jimmy Marshall's brother, Ronnie. Several other climbs followed, under the guidance of Jim Clarkson, until, on June 15th, Haston and Stenhouse climbed Greig's Ledge alone on the Buachaille's Crowberry Ridge, Glencoe. Whilst just another route suitable for beginners, it had special significance for Haston: 'This was a great experience for us – namely our first solo rock climb.'[5]

Continuing his learning process with experienced climbers, Haston wrote of an unroped ascent of Observatory Ridge on Ben Nevis with Clarkson three weeks later: 'Some pitches were quite difficult and exposed but we managed to surmount them.' Of the descent via Tower Ridge later that day, he added: 'Three hundred ft from the top, one finds a deep cleft between the Great Tower and the ridge proper – this is called Tower Gap. At this point we stopped to rope up, as crossing the gap is quite difficult and certainly very exposed.'

That, then, was the sum total of Haston's experience when he and Robin met by chance on July 21st below Buachaille Etive Mòr. It was there that Robin suggested that Haston and his friends join him on Revelation, a climb staggeringly harder than anything the Currie Boys had attempted. Jimmy Stenhouse also took up the challenge. As it turned out, Robin had only 80 ft of rope but splitting the second pitch into two and getting Stenhouse to untie further up, so that it was possible to protect Haston on the traverse below the crux, he ensured that all went well. The climb took five hours, mainly because of trouble with the rope, belays and slimy rock, but left Haston enthralled. However, the reactions of others were quite different, as he recalled in his biography: 'Delighted with ourselves, we were amazed in our naivety to see the jealous mind in action for the first time. "Madmen", "You could have been killed", "What would you have done if we had had to come and rescue you?", "No congratulations".'

Of course, some climbers did think that Robin took undue risks with inexperienced climbers. Certainly, he was not too bothered about the standard of a partner's climbing ability, although the sudden upping of difficulty clearly did Haston no harm. That first meeting with the Currie Boys was necessarily brief, however, as Robin had to leave the following day to meet others in Arrochar, with a view to working at the nearby hydro-electric scheme on Loch Long. Kenny Allan recalls that their idea had been 'to get in a week's climbing before starting work. But Robin straight away met an experienced climber who was about to go off to the Alps and that was the end of all thought of work for him. Money didn't seem to matter in the least to him when there was an opportunity to climb, even though he was as skint as the rest of us and would stay short of cash during the coming year.'

They all thought Robin daft because the income meant their being able to afford a motorbike or pints of beer in the coming term. To them, Robin was completely unmaterialistic and, whereas they looked on themselves as having a balanced view of life, happy to have the hills as an escape or as another interest, they did not share his extreme passion for climbing. His love of the mountains was now an obsession.

7

ALPINE AND CURRIE SEASONING

It was towards the end of July 1957 that Robin's Alpine career got under way. He and Jim Clarkson had climbed together regularly since Robin started university, so Clarkson was not short of first-hand knowledge of the intrinsic perils in their partnership, as we know from references in his diary to bouts of trepidation, bivouacs in furious gales, arguments about tactics, moonlit winter ascents, great hikes, apprehension about not finishing before darkness, endless waits at belays and cutting steps off a mountain in an icy hurricane. Despite all that, he described one particularly incident-packed outing as 'the best weekend for a long time'. Innovatively, at Easter on Esk Buttress, Borrowdale in the Lake District, rather than refuse protection to Robin on Great Central – 'I felt unequal to it and refused to try it' – Clarkson climbed Bower's Route, an adjacent easier route, and protected him on long leads from there. That same day he even helped in the rescue of a sheep stuck on a narrow ledge, it all ending well with Robin on a top rope carrying the beast to safety. And, rather stoically, Clarkson had come to accept that 'the lot of a "second" on an ice climb is always unpleasant'.

Most climbers in those days, including Robin, regarded Chamonix's now defunct Biolay campsite as their Alpine base. Another focal point was the Bar National, the only bar where British climbers were really welcome. Steve Read of Nottingham Climbers' Club, who first met Robin in Chamonix and was to climb with him in the Dolomites two years later, explains:

> The campsite and the Bar National were so well used due to the weather.
> Many a week or two could pass when the peaks were hidden by cloud
> and it was raining in town and probably snowing 'up there' on the big
> rock routes. When I first arrived in Chamonix, the Austrian Walter
> Phillip and his partner, Riccardo Blach, had been waiting *six weeks* for
> a route to get into condition. When it was like that climbers just mooched
> around town, with little more than visits to the swimming pool and
> occasional fights with local youths to relieve the monotony.

As is usual in most sports, there was more climbing done in the bar than on the hills. It's where you met everybody, found climbing partners, boasted of your latest near miss, drank too much beer and made a lot of noise. It had atmosphere. It also had a table football machine and one of those new television things, with some kind of animated pop singer doing a jive and singing some catchy tune that everyone started humming around the campsite.

The British were unpopular in town because they were the scruffiest people about and kept the campsite squalid. I overheard a local saying the English lived like pigs, and he was right. Amongst the British, the Scots were reckoned to be the scruffiest of the lot, and the biggest freeloaders! But maybe I am just another 'slimy Sassenach', which is one description I heard of the English by a Scot! There was always a kind of rivalry between the two communities. I must say, though, that I never heard Robin express any extreme views on the subject.

For three years prior to this, Read had been an engineering foundry apprentice, but increasingly became disillusioned with the restrictions of the life, whilst yearning more and more for the excitement he found in climbing and mountaineering: rather like Robin but without extended student holidays. So he left the apprenticeship, went to Chamonix intent on spending as long as possible in the Alps, and still vividly remembers his excitement when the immense granite needles above the town first came into view. Read had been inspired by Herman Buhl's classic book *Nanga Parbat Pilgrimage* and Gaston Rebuffat's *Starlight and Storm*, especially the descriptions of north faces of the Alps, which he believes Robin had also read. Now Robin had come to see for himself. Jim Clarkson describes their arrival:

> We arrived in Chamonix on a dull, cold morning, and it looked like another bad season. Breakfast at the Hotel Chamonix, then shopping, including buying equipment for Robin. This took longer than expected and it was late afternoon before we started up. The original plan had been to go to the Requin Hut, but now there was only time to go to Montenvers. This pleased Robin as he wanted to do the NW face of the M.[1] Stayed in the Jortrin, but only I paid, which made the price reasonable!
>
> On Monday [July 29th], we started fairly late, about seven, and two hours later reached the face. The morning was fine and sunny, but fairly cool and the face seemed very fierce and grim. The route went up an

almost vertical dièdre, and the first pitch was iced, with a little trickle of
icy water running down. Robin took a very long time here, and I kept
hoping he wouldn't get up, but after an hour or so he did. While on this
bit, two English bods from Chester, Ben [Lyon] and Brian [Thompson],
arrived and started up the climb behind us. By now clouds had rolled
up and we were in damp cold mist. In fact, just like a fairly poor day on
the British hills. The second pitch was a chimney of IV, still quite hard,
to a tiny platform. Then a horrible thrutch up a crack behind a flake. I
failed to climb this and had to ascend on prussik slings. The next pitch
was artificial, and Robin took a long time even to get halfway up. By
now it was mid afternoon and we were only a third of the way up the
face. The other two had already abandoned the climb, and I felt hellish
with nerves. After a long argument I persuaded Robin to pack it in, and
we descended to the top of the Poteau by abseil. Then, in pulling down
the rope, it jammed. So Robin had to go up again, on prussik slings, to
get it organised. The rest of the descent by abseil was uneventful. I was
jolly glad to get off such a fierce face, and trudge back to Montenvers.

Such, then, was Robin's first ever Alpine attempt, on the northwest
face of the Aiguille de l'M, the lowest peak in the Chamonix Aiguilles.
On the following afternoon Clarkson and he walked up to the Requin
Hut, and on the Wednesday headed for the Mayer-Dibona route on
the Dent du Requin after meeting Brian Thompson and Ben Lyon
again at the hut. They too had decided on that climb. Brian Thompson:

> I was keen to do the climb as my wife Jean and I had turned back on
> it the previous September after losing the way, and spent the night in
> a snow cave on the way down (our third wedding anniversary!!).
>
>   Almost a year later here I was with Ben ploughing through the soft
> snow leading to the gully at the start of the route when we were passed
> by Robin storming past on his own. He uncoiled his rope at the start
> of the rock and shouted down to the older man, still well behind us,
> to hurry up. By this stratagem they were first on the route!

Jim Clarkson:

> Started about 4 a.m. In just under an hour, we reached the first rock
> pitch in the approach couloir, a smooth slab on the left. Robin found it
> hard and I found it harder, though I expect I have led things as hard
> at home. Then on up the snow. Two more rock pitches, a short chimney,
> a route up a slab on the left to avoid chockstones, then easy rocks and

out onto the sunshine of the ridge. The next section was technically easy but, with a lot of slushy snow on the ledges, it was hard work, and on this bit we moved solo. Presently it steepened and we roped up again, eventually moving left of the crest of the ridge. There was some doubt as to the position of the route here, and Brian and Ben who were ahead were in some difficulty. After some while we decided to move back, and tried another route. This involved a strenuous thrutching crack, then easier rocks took us to the ridge again, here incredibly exposed with sensational views down the north face.

Ben Lyon:

We kept with them all day, until the route went out leftwards onto a face, and was difficult to follow. Robin had gone way off route and was having to retrace his steps. Brian was leading us and found the way up. By this time Robin had calmed down, accepted the offer of tying onto our rope, and we finished as a foursome.

Jim Clarkson:

We reached the summit at 4 p.m. – twelve hours of climbing, a long time. The descent started with a sensational abseil down the Chimenée Founteic, which was really an almost vertical dièdre. Then easy ledges across to the shoulder. Below this, bad snow and sleet down to the glacier and lots of big crevasses to wind round. Arrived down at the hut after 8 p.m., and the optimistic plan to cross to the Envers des Aiguilles that evening was out of the question.

Ben Lyon:

Looking back, it was very clear that Robin was the impetuous young 'pusher' and that the much older Clarkson was engaged in a largely futile battle to restrain him from what he saw as recklessness.

A couple of days later, when we had got to know each other a bit, Robin and Brian decided to do a route on the Grépon, whilst Jim and I wanted to do something a bit less stressful, and I fancied being the leader on a more modest route. In the event, we did the NE ridge of the M.

Brian Thompson:

The classic Mer de Glace face of the Grépon was our target. I remember Robin insisting that he lead the famous Knubel Crack. It didn't matter to me who led what and I've little memory of the route. However, Robin did duly lead the crack and we were on the summit in good time, though the descent by the Nantillons glacier was a little fraught due to the soft snow.

Jim Clarkson:

On Saturday [August 3rd], Robin and I made a very late rise and spent the morning in idleness at Montenvers. At mid-afternoon, we started the walk to the Col du Géant [en route to Italy]. Went tremendously well to the Requin Hut, where we rested a while. At 5.30 p.m. we carried on. At the Géant icefall we put on crampons and got through easily. Above, there were miles of fairly crevassed glacier: much further than it really looked. We met a couple of descending parties who were amazed to see us going up so late! Really it was a pretty sensible idea, for the snow was now freezing up. The sunset was incredibly beautiful, with pink light on the Verte, red on the Dent du Géant, and the Aiguilles silhouetted black. Also, we saw the Brenva face for the first time. The last rise to the col seemed a very long way but, at nine o'clock, we reached the new Toriso, and there was rock-and-roll music blaring out. From the terrace outside, we looked across to the Aiguille Noire. What a contrast! Then, we went down to the old hut, and indulged in a hut meal. It was much too late to think of going down to Courmayeur that night: the lights were many thousands of feet below us. So, we slept at the hut.

On Sunday we went down to Courmayeur [in Italy itself]. However, down there the heat was incredible. We stayed at the Edelweiss at La Palud. After dumping our gear we wandered into Courmayeur. Robin was hoping to find Gordon Burns to try some harder routes.

On Monday, again, the heat was remarkable, and the thought of plodding up to the hut was just too much. Robin wanted to start for the Noire, but I felt stale, and could not conceive of wanting to climb again! So, Robin set out on his own for the Noire, just after midday. He would do the South Ridge solo! On Tuesday morning it was dull and raining, but I thought it would take more than a shower of rain to put off Robin.

Nevertheless, Robin was forced to turn back, though not before encountering Donald Mill, who was descending and nearly 'stood on a tousled head with a large grin underneath'. Amazed to find Robin back again at the Edelweiss that evening, Clarkson suddenly found himself helping with plans for an assault on the ridge that Robin had just abandoned:

On Wednesday [August 7th] the weather was better, quite good in fact, and in the afternoon Robin and I went to do the Noire [south ridge of the Aiguille Noire de Peuterey]. Our plan was to climb as high as possible that evening and if possible to reach the Pointe Welzenbach which is the first peak on the ridge (and well up it). The ridge looked very friendly and attractive, not nearly so fierce as I had imagined. The first 1500 ft of climbing is quite easy, though a bit loose, and we did this unroped, except at one place which I found difficult. After what seemed a very long way, we came to the place which the guidebook calls the beginning of the difficulties. Immediately the rock became excellent, and the climbing was mostly about hard V. Diff. At one point Robin took a shoulder, and I climbed on loops of rope: strenuous. The weather was now very threatening, with a big thunderstorm to the SW. It was getting dark too, and at this stage I viewed a well-sheltered platform 15 ft below the ridge. Just as we reached it, the rain started pouring down. There was no question of continuing: this would be our bivouac. I quickly put on my duvet and got into my polythene bag. It was amazingly comfortable apart from the condensation. The storm was a big one with forked lightning right overhead and heavy rain and hailstones. At one stage we were lying in a pile of hailstones. The storm went away, then came back again. And there was intermittent rain all night. Still, I slept quite well, evidently. Bivouacs aren't such unpleasant affairs!

I woke about 4.30 a.m. and found it coming light. There was still a lot of cloud and rain about, and we were just about at mist level. Presently, Robin stirred, and we found that he had stuck his feet through his polythene bag and his sleeping bag was soaked. We had breakfast, an affair of bread, raisins and lumps of sugar, for we had no stove. Heavy rain continued on and off, and for a long time we were uncertain whether to continue. Robin said we should go on, and I thought it unwise though I did not particularly want to go down yet. Eventually Robin won the argument, and we started on even though it was still raining a bit! The rocks were very cold and unpleasant, and three pitches up it was sleeting and hailing. Then, the rain left off. There were sunny intervals and gradually the rocks dried off. There remained a strong SW–W wind, though. To the Welzenbach wasn't so very difficult. Then, a very steep abseil down to the gap, about 90 ft. The next tower, Pte. Bredel, was perhaps the most difficult at a very steep and smooth step, climbed by a shallow dièdre, with a fair number of pitons . . . then another difficult pitch on the left of the ridge before easier climbing.

The descent to the next gap was easy. The Cinquième Tour was also difficult, its dicey pitch being the Grand Dièdre . . . The last peak of difficulty was Pointe Bich. The descent beyond was by abseil, though it could be climbed down quite easily. It was now almost night, with a very icy west gale. In the gap at the top of the Noire there are two huge *gendarmes*, and we found a good sheltered ledge below these on the east for our second bivouac. This was a much colder night, and I didn't get much sleep.

On Friday morning the rocks were covered with verglace, which made the scramble to the summit quite tricky. The view from the top was incredibly wild, with mist forming like smoke from the ridges of the Aiguilles Noire and Blanche. The Innominata face of Mont Blanc was mostly in mist, but the sight of high red pillars dusted with powdered snow and streaked with ice, rising up into the clouds, made it perhaps the wildest scene I had ever seen.

After the Noire we had a rest day. The weather in Courmayeur was perfect – fine and sunny – but up above there was a big wind blowing a plume of snow off Mont Blanc right onto the Brenva face. Not a good omen, for we wanted to do one of the Brenva climbs next.

Sunday [August 11th] was the day for our ascent to the Fourche Bivouac, but from early on the weather looked poor. Plans were modified to an ascent to the Triolet hut, then we decided just to recross the Col du Géant to Chamonix, where there are some lower climbs. I set off for the Torino at teatime, Robin saying he would follow, but he did not turn up that night and I found myself short of food. So, I had to go begging from some Swiss!

On Monday morning, it was snowing hard! Robin turned up quite soon and, after eating, we started down to Chamonix. On the col itself the weather was hellish, with a huge wet blizzard that you could hardly face into. Crevasses were hard to see too, and on the top part of the descent Robin, who was in front, fell into quite a few small ones. Soon, the snow became less and we came into sleet and rain. The rest of the descent to the Requin Hut was uneventful if trying and unpleasant.

At the hut we heard that an English party of three were missing on the Requin, and one of them was called Derek. Could it be Derek Leaver? Surely not. The guardian of the hut had written them off: '*Les trois, ils sont morts.*' Just as we were preparing to leave, the three came down the hill, and Derek Leaver was among them. They had been late finishing the Mayer-Dibonna, and had been benighted just below the summit – in that hellish night! Still, they were safe and sound. I had decided that the weather was hopeless and planned to leave for home that night. Robin stayed on with Derek and I took the night train for Paris and home.[2]

In the event, Robin's further climbing was limited to an ascent of just one minor route, the west face of the Pointe Albert with Gunn Clark in foul weather. Whilst today's Alpinists would not rate any of his 1957 climbs as exceptional, the south ridge of the Noire and, to a lesser extent, the Mer de Glace face of the Grépon, were long and far from straightforward. At any rate, Robin, not yet nineteen and without previous experience of high mountains, had cut his Alpine teeth.

* * *

On returning to Scotland, Robin was soon active again, this time on Sgurr nan Eag on Skye, where he was responsible for a couple of new rock routes (Chasm Left Edge and Ladders). By the time winter came round, he was still climbing with his usual intensity, making the first winter ascent of Cuneiform Buttress on Buachaille Etive Mòr with university lecturer Derek Leaver. The new year of 1958 saw several very hard winter ascents, notably Crowberry Ridge Direct, on the same mountain, and perhaps the most impressive of all, Eagle Ridge on Lochnagar in the Cairngorms.

Since Tom Patey's first ascent of that Lochnagar gem in 1953 there had been few pretenders for a repeat. In those days the old Loch End bothy on the shores of Loch Muick was still in use, and it was from there that Robin set out with Doug Dingwall. Later, with the pair not back and the evening wearing on, the university lads back at the hut were facing up to thoughts of a rescue. 'Then about midnight,' David Hughes remembers, 'Robin appeared, linked by frozen rope to Doug after a full retreat down the ridge which is now a Grade V. The weather had forced them to turn back less than 50 ft from the top without torches (at least ones that worked) and they had climbed down in the pitch dark.'

As winter drew to a close, Robin teamed up with Haston again, this time for an extended week in north Wales at Easter 1958. The weather was cold with occasional snow showers, according to Les Brown who was there at the time as part of a strong English party. Robin and Haston had been watching them on Cemetery Gates, one of the most prized routes on Dinas Cromlech, following which both parties abseiled down Cenotaph Corner. Brown puts Robin's visit into perspective, 'At that time the English climbing scene was in thrall to Joe Brown and Don Whillans while one or two of us were tentatively carrying out repeats of their climbs. Then out of the northern mists appeared Robin who set about systematically and tenaciously repeating many of their "classics".'

This was in fact Robin's second Easter visit to Wales, and he was returning to territory where he already had twenty ascents under his belt. Now a man with a mission, he – along with Haston – duly ticked off, one by one, many of the best-known test pieces of the day. Bellevue Bastion, Central Route and Scars Climb on Tryfan, Rowantree Slabs on Idwal, Lot's Groove and Lot's Wife on Glyder Fach, and Ivy Sepulchre and Jericho Wall on Dinas Cromlech all fell one after the other, followed by Sickle, Brant Direct and Kaisergebirge Wall on Clogwyn y Grochan, and Hangover and Diagonal Route on Dinas Mot. Then, on April 8th, they finally turned their attention to their two main objectives, Dougal Haston believing that:

> Cemetery Gates is the most awe-inspiring route in the pass. As I sat and watched Robin going up the first 90-ft pitch I wondered how the hang I was going to be able to follow. At last he managed to struggle up and the come-on call came floating down. But on starting the climb I found the sheer airiness of the crack made the climbing a pleasure. The crux of the climb comes at the very top of the crack and involves a funny finger layback. I made this quickly and then flopped onto the ledge above. After some belaying mix-ups, Robin quickly polished off the last pitch. On coming up I found it enjoyable and, of course, exposed.

After this success they went up to Cyrn Las to try Subsidiary Grooves but were caught out by nightfall on the second pitch and had to abseil off in the darkness. Overall, however, the day was a great triumph, for, in that era of improvised protection and rudimentary equipment, the unrelenting verticality of Cemetery Gates that dominates the whole crag made it a very serious proposition. It was a climb repeated by none but a small group of élite climbers, the only route to surpass it in mythical status being the beckoning corner to its left. Next day they set off up the hill; Haston recorded:

> The Cenotaph is considered to be one of the hardest routes in the British Isles, if not the hardest. Once again I was in for a long wait but this was livened from time to time when I had to hold Robin on a doubled rope to allow him to rest and put on a runner or hammer in a piton. When coming up I ran into difficulties at the first crux, which is only 20 ft above the deck. It provided me with the hardest move I have ever made on a climb. It involves a direct pull on a finger jam. After this the crack continued on its strenuous way but with no difficulties comparable to the first crux. In about an hour and a half I arrived at the niche which is only 10 ft from the top of the climb but which the leader needs two pitons to get out of. It is a horribly twisted position and I had to remain there for about half an hour knocking out pitons while Robin sat 10 ft above and laughed himself silly.

Robin's was the seventh ascent of Cenotaph Corner, the second by a Scottish party, though the climb did take more than six hours. Robin explained this away to Geoff Oliver by saying that he could have climbed much faster but did not want to upset the locals! A month later Oliver witnessed Robin in action in the English Lake District during an 'audacious border raid' on Scafell that resulted in two good bold new routes – Leverage and Chartreuse. Those further ascents had the effect of reinforcing Robin's growing reputation south of the border where stories about him are still bandied about. Les Brown:

> On North Crag Eliminate on Castle Rock of Triermain, Robin was stopped for a long time on the crux gangway, working out the moves with his usual tenacity, when Pat Walsh of Glasgow's Creagh Dhu arrived at the foot of the crag and threatened to tell Joe Brown that Robin had failed on a 'Wee English boulder problem', whereupon Robin committed himself and launched up the crux moves!

Following that ascent of Cenotaph, Haston separated from Robin to do some leading of his own, a sign that he had started to spread his wings. However, the pair's accomplishments that week can be looked back on as having laid the foundations for a partnership that was to see numerous celebrated adventures both at home and abroad, even if it would sometimes be a little shaky. As a duo they even seemed destined to rival that legendary English tandem of Joe Brown and Don Whillans. Commenting on the natural synergy that existed between Robin and Haston (and his Currie friends), Jimmy Marshall writes:

> Wild, irreverent bundles of raw energy, the Currie Boys were intrigued by Robin who took them on to hard climbs in outrageous conditions – he with his bauchly boots, they hopelessly equipped but armed with blind faith in his ability. They willingly endured this *baptism by fire* from which they quickly acquired core values already assumed by Robin for himself. This association was very good for both parties. Though only sixteen or seventeen the Currie Boys were 'worldly wise', frequently drank themselves legless, bopped, jived and chased the lassies. They accepted no one at face value and distrusted authority, especially if it wore an old face. Robin, no doubt analysing this phenomenon, delighted in their company.

Whilst it is true that Haston was still a relative rookie in April 1958, Robin's own climbing apprenticeship can safely be said to have terminated then, following such demanding leads on those Welsh routes. More importantly, it signalled the birth of a new Robin – a fact underlined by the disappearance of the schoolboy appellation 'Eb' and its replacement from Currie with something less Watsonian. The metamorphosis to adulthood was complete. 'Wheech' was about to be let loose on the world of mountaineering.

PART TWO

TALES OF ADVENTURE AND SMITH THE MAN:
1958–60

8

SCHOLARLY REFLECTIONS

It was not just on climbers that Robin left his mark. At Edinburgh University during his third year of study in 1958–59, notably, he formed friendships with two of his lecturers in the Department of Philosophy.

Willie Stewart was completing his second stint there after a gap of two years at McGill, Montreal, as a visiting professor. Most of Robin's classes were given by Stewart himself, although his course in Logic and Metaphysics was the responsibility of Stewart's twenty-seven-year-old assistant, Gordon Greig. Stewart, in his early forties at the time, wrote a number of letters to Robin:

4 Learmonth Terrace
Edinburgh 4
20:v:59

My Dear Robin,

All joking apart, I *want* your Leibniz essay – and in reasonable time! My reason for writing to say so is that I have just been going over my mark record to see, in the first place, how people stand in relation to each other – up to the final essay mark – and, in the second place, whether the standard (at the upper end of the scale) justifies me in asking the Professor to award a class medal and the Hutchison Stirling Prize.

As things stand at the moment, you haven't a great deal of competition for the top place – but you *do* have some; consequently I want an essay from you – and, to be blunt, I want a good one, *and* I want it in time for me to present it to Professor Ritchie.

As you well enough know, I have the greatest sympathy with people who have temperamental difficulties about philosophising to order or producing things for an arbitrary deadline, but on the other hand, since you *have* done better than anyone else (with one possible exception) in my class since I returned here, I don't want you to mess the thing up either by handing in something impossibly late, or inadequate, or (by the way) too 'wild' (i.e. wayward). So even if your heart *is* in the high lands and not in the Universe of the Monads, do get down to it and deliver *by the end of next week*. You can perfectly well do it in that time (and also forgive the pedagogical peremptoriness of the tone). In fairness to the other (two) possible candidates I shall have to give them the same warning.

If you can't be good, be prudent.

Yours sincerely,

W F M Stewart.

PS: The contents of this letter, tho' obviously quite proper, are equally obviously, quite private.

Robin did win the medal, but Greig felt that he had 'never met anyone so talented with so little taste for academic spoils. I got the impression that he was pleased for Willie's being pleased that he had got the medal.' Although Robin forged friendships with both lecturers, his relationship with Stewart was by far the more relaxed. Unlike his conversations with Greig, theirs were in no way vigorously focused, a drawback now being, Stewart found, when I discussed Robin with him, that he was unable to recall much by way of detail – 'just a misty memory of sodden amiability'. With hindsight, Stewart suggested that the style of that 1959 letter might have arisen from 'Robin's ability to attract Guardian Angels and what that said about him'.

There were other letters and Christmas cards from Stewart, entrusting Robin with confidences, giving guidance as the need arose, exchanging banter. On June 7th, 1959, when forwarding documentation in recognition of Robin having gained first place and thus the medal, he put Robin on his guard: 'I suppose I should warn you not to let it go to your head; but the remaining hazards and exigencies of the course will, no doubt, render you sober enough without any heavy advice from me.' A month later, on July 8th, he told Robin he was emigrating to Canada:

My Dear Robin,

I take it you are no longer among the hops and oast-houses of Kent, but are probably somewhere upon the mountains in Morven or Appin. There is a certain amount of news, some of which may not please you. Gordon, for one thing, has got himself a lectureship in Logic in St Andrews.

I myself am sailing for Canada on the 9th of September on the *Ivernia* out of Southampton. The University of New Brunswick is in need of a Professor and Head of the Department of Philosophy to develop and expand (in the words of the President) the teaching of Philosophy which has, for some years, not been in too healthy a state.

Ritchie's successor is not yet publicly announced; but, from what information I have and, having your interests very much at heart, I would recommend you to close your Hume (and Logic books) and open your Hegel; or, if not your Hegel, then a book called *Nature, Mind and Modern Science* by a Mr Errol E. Harris from South Africa. There may be more to Colonial (or Kaffir) Hegelianism than I have found, and you may discover it. The best (if bleak) advice I can give you is to conform to the dispensation sufficiently to get a decent degree. Thereafter, if you wish to resume the study of Philosophy in some other place, you will at least be in a position to get in. Gordon will do his best to guide you about the possibilities (pity you can't transfer to St Andrews).[1] The person who will probably succeed me is a very good man and I shall commend you to his care.

As will be obvious, this is a private letter, and none of the contents re the Department – other than my own departure, which is already known – is for quotation.

I hope you have had a good time, have earned enough, and are in one piece. Write, or, if you are in Edinburgh between 10th August and 8th September, ring me up.

Yours ever,

W F M Stewart

Stewart's final note to Robin was dated January 6th 1962 from Fredericton, New Brunswick:

My Dear Robin,

I was very glad to have your letter. I liked your egg-shaped angels. (I like you too also.) Of course I shall support you in anything you apply for. London is a good idea, and I agree that you are unlikely ever to be very happy in mucking Oxbridge. If London, why not St Andrews? Gordon has now moved there permanently, but there's no good my inviting you here – much as I should like to have you – as there isn't a bleedin' mountain within 3000 miles. Ben Nevis is, in fact, nearer to Fredericton than the Rockies are. The world is rather badly arranged. I wonder who you'll land with and what write on. Gellner is still, I think, in LSE. That might cheer things up.

Write again. Meanwhile,

Love,

Willie

It would be interesting to get Stewart's reactions all these years later, I thought, and in 1993 I eventually traced him to Calgary:

Dear Jimmy,

As you will remember, when the first phone call got through about Robin, I had no difficulty in relating to what you were saying even though more than thirty years had passed. However, I have one unavoidable limitation that I have to remark on – I am now seventy-six years of age and I suspect that my memory is no less capricious than it is in most elderly people. But I will do my best.

I read my initial 1959 letter to Robin with great interest; what surprised me most was how 'bossy' it was. I would like to believe it was not the tone of voice I often used with students, and certainly not with very good ones like Robin. Generally speaking, I found his temperament, wayward as it was, very congenial and in those more relaxed days, there weren't so many absolute 'deadlines' to meet. In this case, I can only excuse myself to myself by noting there was some urgency of a *practical* kind, and my obvious uneasiness that he might not respond to it perhaps, as you suggest, reflects a trait that his sister noted.

What made Robin fascinating was that he showed, in my view, a very rare sort of combination of quite remarkable physical prowess with a quite remarkable intellectual capacity of a pretty rarefied sort. About his physical prowess I have to speak with care. I was never myself athletic and never ever thought of climbing or doing anything more strenuous than walking across a moor. I certainly heard a lot about him from other people. In particular, I had heard from a younger colleague in another department, who was greatly interested in the climbing scene, that he had met Robin, that he was a noteworthy character now in first-year Philosophy, that he proposed to enter the second year (my class) and that I should look out for him. With that warning in advance, it did not take me long to identify what was indeed a very singular character. About his general philosophical ability, I think I was a fair enough judge, tho' in the case of his chosen specialism, I would defer to Gordon Greig.

There were, I am glad to say, both on his side and mine, some more sociable traits that didn't have much to do with either climbing or philosophy and which occasionally emerged in the basement of a howff somewhere near the end of Queen Street, where a good deal of Danish lager (which I was sold on at the time) got consumed, and it is in that sort of atmosphere, quite free of competitiveness or consideration of

75

this sort of talent or that, that Robin's sheer likeableness could shine so captivatingly.

But, generally, the point arising out of my letters is that, as I hope is obvious, I had Robin's interests very much at heart, and I knew that the academic world would always be a hazardous place for him and I was trying to guard him from some particular *kinds* of danger – eg he and I agreed (which originally surprised Gordon) that Oxbridge was not for him because in both places aspirants were required to 'swim with the stream' and that, for someone like Robin, would never have done.

I was in fact in Edinburgh when I heard what had happened in the Pamirs, but I didn't know any member of his family to whom I could write. In any event, I had to return to Fredericton the next day or the day after. The first thing I found waiting for me was an outsize picture postcard from Robin with, on the picture side, the familiar aggressive profile of Vladimir Lenin against the equally familiar streaming red banner and, on verso, a spidery scrawl saying that he was having fun and learning something about Marxist orthodoxy; which I took to be a joke with intent to tease me.

Naturally I no longer regard any of my letters as 'private' ... Whether Robin regarded me as a father figure is difficult to say. All I can say is that we came to 'empathise' in some peculiar way.

So, you can see, the impression of Robin as someone I liked and admired is perhaps remarkable only in that it is deep and long-lasting.

With regards. Yours sincerely,

Willie Stewart

Willie Stewart retired as Professor Emeritus at Calgary in 1983. He died on November 10th, 1995, aged seventy-seven. Of his self-confessed rise to respectability as a central figure of the academic establishment, he commented that 'Willie when young would not have suffered much of himself when old.' Might Robin have been saying the same of himself by now?

ROBIN AS STUDENT

For further insight into Robin's academic aptitude and personality, Gordon Greig, his lecturer in Logic and Metaphysics at Edinburgh University in 1958–59, has contributed to this biography. Of the trio which he, senior lecturer Willie Stewart and Robin formed, Greig suspects that Stewart and he himself may have fallen into roles predesigned – and then sustained – by their charge. Here is an abridged version of his recollections:

> From my Edinburgh teaching days I can recall only a handful of students' names. Robin alone I remember, vividly and in detail. We were drinking chums and sometimes wandering loonies. I shall try to convey something of his panache, his shrewd intellect and roguish manner. These may come through via my selected, sometimes selective, memory of conversations and events that took place in 1958–1959. Sadly I knew Robin for that one year only. We shared many attitudes, some common antipathies. I liked him a lot and I trust this shines through my narrative.
>
> Within our trio, Willie was the Sage and Guru, I the nuts and bolts Technician, Robin the serio-complaisant dedicated Novice. Perhaps his self mockery early that academic year was designed to keep us guessing or to persuade us that he was to be no uncomplicated convert. Perhaps it was a fall-back strategy in the event of any future waxings or wanings of 'dedication'. It says a lot for his charm and subtle suasion that we were inveigled into this charade. Willie talked of matters initially more close to Robin's heart – the Great Ideas, Progress, Civilisation, the Nature of Man's Nature and the like. I taught him the dirty dialectical tricks of the trade in the guise of Logic but had my stabs at Uplift also. Together we sophisticated him out of his philosophical babyhood and saw his original studied pose of enigmatic detachment become utterly ruined by his own behaviour.
>
> Robin basked in Willie's company, enjoying the outpourings from the store of wit and wisdom of a figure whose shining eminence put him above the hurly-burly as a true Old Man of the Mountain. At any rate Willie was the Wise, I the merely Clever. I was as one whose skills

Robin might shortly hope to emulate. Academically Robin and I became close kin. Terrier-like, we worried the same set of specifics endlessly, so recall is relatively easy. Yet I knew little about Robin in the conventional sense – of his birth, education or family. We were not into the graces of polite conversation. Practically every moment of a one-on-one was dedicated to listening, learning, arguing on the one hand, teaching and preaching on the other – shop or near shop-talk always. I was a conscientious neophyte honing my teaching skills and Robin was hard-headed enough to think – 'time spent, a'thing learnt'.

Inter-Honours Logic that autumn of 1958 was to be my first professional assignment. I had just completed two years' National Service prior to which my teaching had been limited to some part-time tutoring at Cambridge. In those days there was no talk of teaching university teachers to teach. One was thrown in the deep end and the students were left to drown. Only seven years younger than myself, Robin was about to become my first student as once I had been Willie's.

I was more than mildly uneasy for a variety of good reasons and my unease was not helped by Robin. His was a disturbing presence. His fixed stare, alternated with moody distraction, promised trouble and challenge. Of course I then knew nothing of the man behind the manner. Later, when I taxed him on his past demeanour, he replied that he had been wondering whether, since my course was required, he would have to 'chuck the whole philosophy thing'. So much for liking at first meeting. Had I but known I was ripe for Robin's disapproval. In my debut I must have seemed formal, pompous, arrogant. His initial reaction was guarded at best. He was ever determined never to appear cowed, apprehensive or gratuitously deferential. *Incipiently prickly and latently aggressive* was my overriding early impression. At any rate in that first week of lectures our 'friendship' rode the knife's edge.

At this early stage in our relationship I had no inkling that Robin had an eminent reputation in climbing circles, and certainly not that climbing was his consuming passion. Willie Stewart and I were hosting an inaugural ice-breaking Inter-Hons. party. Robin arrived late, cheeks flaming, tousled, somehow redolent of the wet and wild. As a concession to some perceived courtesy he wore a tie (!) and a jacket. The jacket could not have been bettered had it been bedded in a bog. He had been climbing in Glencoe and proffered some climbing problem as an excuse for his lateness. Our conversation soon hit stony ground. Robin would not accept that any one could get into difficulties coming down nearby Sgòrr à Chaolais on Beinn à Bheithir, an incident still vivid in my mind, mark you. 'You couldnt! There's no climbing there! Nobody could ever get into trouble there!! Nobody ever goes there . . . ever!!' he finally contended, this said with a brutal violence matching the name of the mountain. I either didn't know anything about 'climbing' or misused the word or both. His antipathy towards me seemed confirmed. After the usual miracle of the malt, however, confrontation dissipated and at one point Robin agreed that views from these tops could be very fine. So Robin *had* been there? Maybe so – 'but a very long time ago!' He could, reconstructing his past, just remember a Moderate. I heard him say something unflattering along the lines of '. . . like walking up the Mound' [an Edinburgh street].

I have referred to this conversation not merely because it may have signalled the beginnings of our friendship. More importantly, it shows how Robin's virtues sometimes came ungently wrapped. He had little time for social humbuggery, none at the expense of honesty. Sadly one wonders, whether some never got past Robin's rough edges, and occasional gaucheries, to discover his charm and sympathetic, intelligent self.

Robin's technical brilliance in mathematical logic was unsuspected by many, known by few, and perhaps appreciated by none save myself. His proof-working over theorems and metatheorems was impeccable, never failing a perfect mark. His moves were quick, sure and intuitive, fired by a fine, creative imagination. Robin discovered a deep, quiet content in our tidily packaged perfections. However, I feared for him in the allied, but to us alien, 'discipline' of Moral Philosophy. His intellectual fastidiousness could not stomach the mess of imprecision that passed for the delineation of the Right and the Good. But Ethics was obligatory, as a rock in the way and more than just a rock, a looming threat also, since the Moral Philosophers determined 40 per cent of the Honours' final marks. Moral Philosophy was our great shared intellectual antipathy and I confess to having abetted his iconoclasm. Robin was forcibly struck by the conspicuous triviality of classroom Ethics, the irrelevance of it all, the forced hothouse dilemmas, seeming all the more blatant and pretentious after weekends of survival on our winter mountains. I tried, without much zeal, appeals to prudence and expediences. I doubted their efficacy. When a mood or a cause came upon him he could be thrawn and, when pushed, uncompromising. His reaction to Ethics was overdetermined by so much. The bruised rebel in him distrusted the fustian; the individualist shied from the mandatory universal norms; the positivist shunned the transcendent, other wordly absolutes; pre-eminently, the serious thinker in him deplored the clever-silliness of the minute moralisers – of the *'dare-I-eat-a-peach?'* school of fussy prissiness. I remember our christening it thus, inspired by Eliot's Prufrock and the Duty-driven Pietistic Kant.

Strangely, given his club journalising, Robin seemed loath to commit thought to paper under the loose constraints of a term essay. The probable diagnosis, later partially confirmed, was that he was a procrastinating perfectionist. His essays, once to hand, were markedly idiosyncratic in form and content and, where the subject matter permitted, decidedly offbeat. Like many academics in the more 'airy-faerey' disciplines I encouraged my students, especially the brightest, to think for themselves and not merely return my own stuff, no matter how well-digested. This can be a dangerous prescription and Robin made the dangers evident. An ingredient in the mix was his desire to shock and test the limits of his instructors' tolerance as he paraded his heresies. Exotic end products were but tenuously tied to the topics set. However, it was the quality of the performances that was critical and this was utterly first-rate. His determined striving for intellectual independence and his creative attempts at originality led him into strange byways (Stewart's 'wild' and 'wayward'). Re-reading his climbing articles I realise how sore a trial philosophy-writing must have been for Robin – a thoroughbred wordsmith pulling in the shafts. Had he been steeped in such as MacDiarmid and Joyce? He had all the quintessential flow of the Celtic 'fringe' and the ready, quirky scholarship.

Philosophically Robin and I were set on being crassly radical, doctrinaire Positivists arraigned with Hume against Superstition and the Absolute Idealists.[1] These latter, and their archetype Hegel, Robin had suffered in other courses. He abjured high-flying Hegelian Idealism with its highfalutin', obscurantist rhetoric much as he disliked mountain-talk's being clapped in purple prose. As a Positivist, Robin could rationally, respectably reject what he instinctively distrusted. Critics decried it as a young man's philosophy as if this detracted from its appeal and power. At any rate it meshed but well with Robin's *values* and *attitudes*. Positivism, for us, had a rare affinity with climbing – the *direttissima* par excellence, great clean natural line with an ambitious sweep, the point-blank, blanket refusal to tolerate easy exits into intellectual rubbish.

Like other Positivists of that period we envisioned a greater role for Logic. Our formal truths stood as solid granite outcrops amid the shifting rubble of philosophical opinings. Early in that heady term of high conceit, we wanted the clarity of Logic set as the archetypical language for all Philosophy. Whitehead, Russell's early collaborator in Logic, had doubts about this programme, and thus, about the relevance of Logic to Philosophy. Clarity, he said, was not enough: 'Seek Clarity and distrust it!' Russell's waspish retort – 'Why should he say that? He never found it!' – pleased Robin, but doubts had been engendered.

Robin admired Russell among contemporary thinkers – there was his towering contribution to Modern Logic in its infancy, his biting dry fire wit, his savaging of complacent conformings. But what perhaps appealed most to Robin was Russell's portrayal of the conflicting strains within himself, he who sought and lauded disciplined precision while being an incurable, 'inconsolable' romantic. In 1944 Russell wrote that he had 'always ardently desired to find some justification for the emotions inspired by certain things that seemed to stand outside human life and to deserve feelings of awe. I am thinking in part of very obvious things, such as the starry heavens and a stormy sea on a rocky coast; in part of the vastness of the scientific universe, both in space and time, as compared to the life of mankind; in part of the edifice of impersonal truth, especially truth which, like that of mathematics, does not merely describe the world that happens to exist.'

To the 'starry heavens', 'stormy sea', 'rocky coast', add 'beetling craggy cliffs' and 'soaring pinnacles of rock and ice' and you have Robin neat in a nutshell. I think, in this connection, of the Nietzschean crack, apt for Robin, 'You must have Chaos within you to create a Dancing Star.' Robin's 'wild and wayward' had its roots in such. From time to time he needed to project his inner states and invest them with more enduring significance.

Partying with others, *shop-talk* seemed antisocial, so we mostly rambled on about climbing and climbing literature. One conversation remains fixed in the memory. I was recalling reading Colin ('Cloggy') Kirkus' book for the novice climber with his tips for indoor climbing. Kirkus had suggested constructing obstacles, strategically placing Doulton dogs on the edges of the ledges, and, generally, upping the grade. I outlined my ideal – a composite of many samples of Highland hotel Gothic. Robin enlarged on the possibilities of the substantial free-standing wardrobes with their wide-swinging doors, of the sudden moves required to avoid nippit fingers. The wardrobes, the tallboys and the generous sills would permit a complete room traverse. If the traverse were too easy we could omit or re-position some furniture. I already had a private rule about touch-for-balance 'holds', having had an unfortunate experience with my own suburban picture rails. Picture rails were to be treated as rotten rock and not abused. But Robin did not share my bourgeois sense of property and thought all holds were on. We christened the ideal 'Loch Awe', after the hotel I had most recently visited.

Later, the memory of 'Loch Awe' not yet dimmed, we found ourselves at a party in seemingly solid, late Victorian surroundings. The drink was vile but potent. When we reached the 'Wine's in, Wit's out' stage Robin murmured 'Loch Awe' and soon was spread-eagled moving up, silhouetted sloth-like on the wall. Fuelled by Votrix, others followed. Suddenly there was a crack, a crash and a wrenching squealing from the direction of the lavatory. The elderly cistern, a high-on-the-wall pull-chain job had given way; four ragged dry dooks, like rotten teeth, pointed at the ceiling. The pipe that squealed stood twisted and uncrowned. Bowl shards gleamed whitely at our feet. There was no attempt to assign responsibility. Robin declined comment although he must have been near or on the scene of the crime. Merely one cryptic crack directed at myself. "It was just like *your* picture rails."

At the dry, fusty formal get-togethers Robin's presence had to be more subtly stated. He had a trick, in a falling silence, of rising from the lotus with a supple simian grace in one fluid motion, no upper body movement, nor hand nor arm assists, to slouch with studied gawkiness, preternaturally solemn, towards the canapes and tea, returning bearing his supplies, then again his sinuous genie-glide, now in a controlled descent, despite the well-filled cup on wobbly saucer, to resume his gnomic version of the teatime Buddha. A few repeats – Robin never passed on free food – sufficed to foster dawning appreciation. Some feebly essayed minor uprisings in faltering emulation but all these were utterly furtive; each had become a solipsist on being reacquainted with his body and its powers. Nothing of course was said; the talk was all of Paradox. Robin, when next we met, wondered if the party paradoxes had been resolved in the faculty post-mortem. I replied that they had not been even mentioned; all the talk had been of kinetics, of rival take-off sites (floor *vs* hassock *vs* chair), great personal athletic prowess buried alas in the unverifiable past. Robin was hugely satisfied – impact made with no vainglory.

Stewart and I tended to parade our geese as the swans they sometimes were for others' adulation and urged Robin to grace the philosophical Haldane Society with his presence; he should be seen, seen to be listening, even to be listened to. Robin, good side uppermost, agreed to visit. He must have adjourned some meeting in a climbers' howff. A radiant smile, teetering to grin, to us his 'sponsors', a conspiratorial unmanly giggling that ill became him and his bevy of hijacked hardmen, then a somewhat early exit and return to howff. And he had the nerve to ask how he had done! He did revisit 'The Society' occasionally, after this inauspicious introduction. Robin was a bonnie dialectician and should have 'fought aye the foremost' but his shyness was often shy of curing and he tended to snipe from the flanks. Sometimes with his peers, supposing me out of range, he could be more expansive, growing dominant in debate and coming nigh to lecture mode. When he saw that I might have overheard he suffered profound embarrassment. I do not believe he found the idea of lecturing *per se* repellant. Rather I think he feared I thought him swanking.

Sometimes our *shop-talk* strayed to the fringes, mountain-talk intruding obliquely. For us the Humean family of Faculties – Memory, Imagination, Reason and Emotion could be best appreciated against a backdrop of mountains. We supposed a soloing, free-climbing novice would be more at ease in a Moderate gully than on an exposed yet Easy buttress. In this instance, Memory, with no relevant experience, has to be discounted. Was this then a clinical case of Reason being overcome by fearful Imaginings? Suppose we came to the aid of Reason and let the novice 'know' the relative gradings. Would this new knowledge guarantee a more just *appreciation* – a word furtively flitting 'twixt *Reason* and *Emotion*? Might he accord some validity to the gradings, but merely abstractly, intellectually, failing thereby to refashion his feelings, passively waiting for these to be refashioned by further events and his evolving nature? Were, despite all, his fearful imaginings to persist, we might dub him 'acrophobe' – a victim of his irrational fears. But in what cases were fears rational, or, for that matter appreciations just or gradings valid? Rational, or more normal, fears occasioned, for example, by the crossing and recrossing of avalanche-prone areas took us more to the core of Hume's philosophy.

Inherent unpredictability was not intellectually incoherent; rationalist theories to the contrary were as tottery as elderly seracs. The world was not necessarily rationally ordered as the Absolute Idealists maintained. It was not required that all phenomena be predictable, that the class of all relevant variables be closed. Hume's example was Weather, ours all that Weather might induce. How often snow or scree was found to be stable when it looked otherwise; how often one had liked, or not liked, the 'look' of something and taken this look as a guide? Hunch or a hope? Could a serac look safe as an unhefted load looks heavy? Which seracs would stand, which fall? All our lives, in all their aspects, said Hume, were governed by surreptitious reliance on unprovable assumptions – subliminal animal inductions. Was Robin's 'reliance' on the look of the terrain rational, irrational or somewhere in between. Reason or Instinct? It was easy to become absorbed in Robin's mix of mountain and philosophy.

In examinations a one-sided conversation was Robin's ideal, the examiner put at *his* ease, for example, by reminders of shared experiences – '. . . . just like last week in Bobby's Bar when *you* said . . . ', or, '. . . you know that I know the outlines of Hume's theory . . .'! Being chattily companionable in a logic paper, properly a scribble of squiggles, wasn't easy but he gave it his best shot with a sentential calculus system abbreviated as 'R.S.1' (Rosser's System 1). Robin cawed indecently about this harbinger and in the examination peppered his paper with 'R.S.1', taking time, and also care, in case I was obtuse, to write in full 'R.S. will be Number One'. In the philosophy papers he had more scope for knavish tricks. His most effective was kin to that by which Mark Anthony beguiled the mob. Robin's variant ran along the lines of 'I thought of doing Question 3 and, again, of doing Question 4 but, arguably, these questions are not properly distinct; behold the complex intricacies of the detailed tracery of theories, both assumptive and subsumptive, that unites them. The status of these theories must first be questioned and thus we have a new, more worthy, *Question 3.5.*'

I didn't wish to probe his devious strategizings. In our always ongoing intellectual games of move and countermove it would have seemed beyond the pale overtly to dissect and analyse and thus to seek advantage. Nor did I wish to slow or clog the turning-churnings of his busy mind. However I was nettled by this unique upturn in gamesmanship and his perverse singularity and asked if Russell's favourite Biblical injunction was his own. Robin, surprised that Russell had one, and, nonplussed, had none to offer. 'Thou shalt not follow a Great Multitude to do a Great Wrong,' I said, appreciating the massive Calvinistic undertow. 'First part's good,' said Robin.

Towards the end of the academic year Robin broached the possibility of an academic career. In those days there were but few openings for career climbers and making a living while living for climbing was always a problem in a more conventional occupation. Had there been such openings Stewart and myself are utterly convinced that Robin would have made climbing his career. In Mathematical Logic, my rather narrow specialism, Robin was more than competent, he could be brilliant. Initially this gave me qualms. Philosophy and Logic do not always

call for similar skills. Logic, kin to Mathematics, often deeply calcula-
tional, often see-it-soon and get-it-right; Philosophy more diffuse,
discursive even literary. Sometimes they come together in the same
person, sometimes not. I very much wanted Robin to do well in all the
branches of that hotchpotch we call 'philosophy' and wished that he
would take nothing for granted because of his brilliance in Logic.
However Robin's later handling of Hume settled such qualms. He could
fashion a career in Philosophy even if denied a chance to strut his logical
stuff. At worst he would be as a rock gymnast on an easy snow climb.
Such a career had other attractions. He appreciated the non 9–5
mentality and envied my seeming freedom from authority. As we went
into the pros and cons one theme became dominant. Robin enquired
about workloads, lecture preparation time, research time. Eventually it
came to me. He was pondering the time that might be available for
extended climbs and expeditions.

People with very great talent, such as Robin, may get by with little
industry, working just as hard as they need to attain a relatively modest
goal – in Robin's case access to higher study. His time was so crammed
with his mountain obsession and the need to satisfy his thrill addictions
so strong that he wasn't, could not be, consistently hard-working. But
he could raise his industry level which, when matched with his considerable talents, let him make the grade. Perhaps he worked, as is alleged,
in his final year, though it is hard fully to reconcile that with his gaining
a Second Class Honours degree, not the First that was clearly within
his capabilities.

As Robin's teacher, what I most vividly recall was a self-inflicted
midterm marathon examination. This incident more completely than
any other clarifies my vision of him. The subject matter was logistic
systems. The first part, on philosophy of logic, was to be completed in
one and a half hours. The second part required metatheorem proofs
and several theorem demonstrations. For those innocent of logic,
demonstrations are proofs that cannot cite theorems as premises; they
can be extremely long and tedious affairs. In order to separate super-
sheep from genius-goats I suggested 'do as many as you can in the
allotted time'. Robin (of course!) asked if I could complete the paper
in ninety minutes. I said I could. Pressed, I confessed that I *might* be
pushed for time but thought not. It was not just facility with the techniques of logic that was required; there was the sheer oxymoronically
rapid drudgery. It required concentration, stamina, mental toughness.
I should not have used those words. To Robin it seemed like a chal-

lenge. What I might do with difficulty could not be done by them. It should not be expected of them. Could they have more time? Robin had considerable persuasive powers; his peers agreed. How long then? 'As long as you like.' His, in the nicest possible way, was a wily soul. He had adroitly transformed my token democracy into near Robinocracy. Books could be used in the exam. Finally there was an implicit promise of a pie and pint in Rutherford's at the close.

Robin, with battered rucksack bulging with a logic library, was well settled in by 2 pm. At 3.30 Part 1 was handed in. At 5.00, the erst allotted time, there was some shuffling. Nobody left. It would be too public an admission of defeat. Around 5.30 some made motions of retreat. By 6.00 all had departed save Robin. He stretched, walked about a bit and then sat down looking radically mischievous, with a cocky cheeky grin. He delved into his rucksack for a more than adequate pie and pint substitute. He was in for the long haul and well prepared. I began to mark others' Logic papers thinking this sight of me-as-judge rather than me-as-victim would rattle him. He might never have noticed. I finished the Part I papers including his. My slim volume of chess problems was soon exhausted. University regulations required me to invigilate. Also, I rationalised, a servitor might try to turf him out were I not there. So I stayed. But it had gone far beyond rules and expediences. It was now seen for what it had been all along – a matter of honour. Robin was not just being, typically, the Imp of the Perverse. He believed he could complete the paper, *given time*.

At 10.05 he said 'they're closed'. In the far off fifties less generous licensing laws showed scant regard for aspiring late night tipplers. Around 10.30 he announced that he was finished, or rather that his paper was. There was a small expression of concern – did the last demonstration require seventy seven steps? It did. He said since it was all finished he was off to Salisbury Crags for a stretch. It has been difficult, fully forty five years on, to forget that complex look on his face. Friendliness yes, but also a badly concealed gloating gleam in his eye, a roguish quirky smile as he took off from the fug with his rolling piratical gait into the wintry air . . .

Three years later, in February 1962 during a 'year out', Robin accepted an offer from University College London – 'for admission to this College in October to read for a PhD degree in Philosophy. The minimum length of your course here will be 2 years.'

10

SPIRIT OF ADVENTURE

Whilst we can perhaps recognise the element of danger when Robin
scaled Edinburgh's Castle Rock[1] carrying an umbrella during Charities
Week,[2] or in his solo descent of the Buachaille's Agag's Groove in
wellies with a bland 'Excuse me' to ascending aspirants, it may come
as a surprise that social gatherings could also be potentially hazardous.
Sheila Samuelson, one of Robin's fellow climbers, explains:

> Early on in my university career I was asked to vacate my premises
> after a party attended by Robin and his band! If you invited them, they
> would begin the evening by 'doing the routes', swarming all over the
> building inside and out like a troupe of monkeys, careless of shifting
> drainpipes and cracking cornices.
>
> In Robin, at least, the simian strain was palpable. His back could
> bend like a rubber gnome's. His legs allowed a good view of the land-
> scape beyond them, as through a gothic arch. His hands hung down
> beside his knees. We used to say that Robin could scratch his ankles
> without bending down. His balance was incredible. He would stand
> nonchalantly on one foot on a minute toe hold far up a rock face, hands
> in pockets to warm them, meanwhile rubbing the other foot up and
> down the back of his leg to ease an itch.

Sheila enquired if her twenty-first birthday party could be held at the
flat of David Hughes, another EUMC member. The four sharing it
managed to get their long-suffering landlord's approval, the only
provisos being, Hughes recalls, that:

> Spirits were banned, noise must be reduced after midnight and, if
> anyone stayed overnight, they must not leave in the morning until the
> neighbours had left for kirk. It was, after all, Morningside!
>
> It turned out to be a good party, mainly climbers, all in high spirits,
> with lots of food and beer and wine. But later in the evening we suffered
> an invasion of junior doctors who had brought the forbidden spirits.
> When they ultimately came to leave, Robin insisted on waving them
> goodbye from the kitchen, where he found the window difficult to

open. In fact, it was screwed permanently shut after winter gale damage, but Robin soon solved the problem by removing the lot – frame, glass and all – and throwing it into the garden below where it disintegrated on the stone path. And the landlord didn't even wake up! (Next day we had a whip-round for our contrite reveller.)

Around that time Robin had what seemed to be a very promising relationship with an American girl by the name of June. 'A lovely girl with black hair and eyes and a peculiarly transatlantic grace,' is Sheila's memory of her. 'For a time Robin became quite normally human. Eschewing the uncompromising precipices he usually frequented he took her climbing on feasible rocks and refrained altogether from impish tricks.' Generally Robin appeared to avoid serious involvement with the opposite sex, perhaps because he saw an attachment as detrimental to his single-minded dedication to the mountains. He could show initial interest, then shy off, though not with June Hamilton, whose diary has helped her clear the cobwebs from memories of her year in Edinburgh:

> Wading through some painful prose written at the time with the purest of twenty-year-old intentions, hazy memories and faces of those associated with the EUMC in the fall of 1960 did come back into focus, along with an overwhelming sense of how painfully young we were then.
>
> Descriptive words like 'fascinating' and 'inscrutable' crop up in my journal entries about Robin. He frightened me. He definitely was not what I was used to in my protected private-school environment up to that point. His social graces were non-existent and he didn't give a damn. His mind went way beyond mine (but he wasn't looking for a soulmate). I was a novice of the first order in climbing ability, philosophical discourse and human relations, at all of which Robin was a master.

Robin sought June out in the Common Room and, in a short intense three-month period, they climbed together (pure terror for her on one occasion in a gully on the Buachaille), talked endlessly, drank quarts of beer and whisky, shared bothies with other mountaineers and, in general, glimpsed one another's very different lives with curiosity and awe. Their friendship faded away after the Christmas vacation, however, while Robin's quest for the ultimate mountain continued apace. Within six months of her return to the States, she became engaged to her childhood sweetheart, whom Robin had wanted to murder in fine style, and 'had taken great pleasure in describing just how, for my benefit'!

Sheila Samuelson well remembers a weekend spent with Robin and June, rounded off by a most sociable pub crawl back to Edinburgh:

> You could do that sort of thing in those days. Nobody, including the police, thought of drinking and driving as being particularly incompatible. Robin was on tremendous form, obliging us by singing 'I am a Mole and I Live in a Hole', which was his party piece, dropping his voice into his boots on the chorus line and rolling huge, brown eyes. Robin could charm the wild creatures from the forests if he wanted to. (Generally he didn't.)

Robin seemed at ease with women unless he was conscious of the gaze of others – in the same way that he seemed to suffer profound embarrassment if he thought that his lecturer might be overhearing his arguments as he debated philosophy with other students. When it came to those of the opposite sex who might make suitable partners, however, Dougal Haston has suggested that things were different. As the 'with it' Currie Boys viewed matters, Robin failed to match up to their own polished style:

> His intelligence as an Honours Philosophy student was at the time beyond that of his constant companions, Eley the engineer, Stenhouse the apprentice draughtsman, and myself the schoolboy and eventual student; but in practical experience of life, he was a long way behind us, who were three years his junior.[3] In a discussion on Kant or Hume, he left us with blank faces; at a party we would leave him in the corner while we went after the girls. The advantages of co-ed.

Andrew Wightman's views do not differ much from Haston's: 'While, for some of his street-smart friends, "chatting up" girls was second nature, for Robin it was a skill he never mastered. Meeting new girls at dances or parties tended to be a non-starter.' Wightman recalls being with Robin in a house in Glencoe with another friend, some Glasgow climbers and the friend's girlfriend. A lovely girl, and kind too, not only did she give them tea but insisted that Robin remove his breeches so that she could stitch a tear. 'Robin was smitten for weeks. He had the misfortune to fall instantly for some girls he met!' recalls Wightman. However, it is as one of Robin's regular climbing partners that Wightman now looks back to times they spent together both on and off the hill:

> Inching home through the London commuter traffic I hear on the radio a rather serious discussion on the life and social impact of the '60s singer, Roy Orbison. Never mind the vicissitudes of his life, his voice has me on the first floor at 369 High Street – the Scottish Mountaineering Club rooms in the heart of Edinburgh's Old Town, commandeered for a party, the windows open to the spring night, and one of Orbison's hit songs, 'Only the Lonely', blasting into the street. Any passer-by inquisitive enough to investigate is liable to be treated in a medieval fashion consistent with the area's turbulent history. Hard cases are rejected with jeers and insults, or physically, depending on how they react. Some don't take too kindly to this and return with reinforcements but there is only room for one abreast at the top of the twisting narrow stair and they are easily repelled. At the heart of it, with a big grin and pudding-bowl haircut, diverting only to restart Roy Orbison, Robin gyrates between the beer stocks in the kitchen, the fun at the door, and the girls and the dancing in the main room.

The late 1950s and early 1960s were times of change within the Scottish Mountaineering Club, and a small group of young iconoclasts had started to represent a new order. Robin Smith, Dougal Haston, Eley Moriarty, Ronnie Marshall and Jimmy Stenhouse were at its core. A few, particularly Jimmy Marshall, bridged the gap, encouraging the newcomers and providing leadership. There were inevitable clashes between the old guard and the young radicals. It was in this atmosphere, as a schoolboy trying to break into climbing, that I met Robin. Although I went on to climb with him regularly, some of my most vivid memories are not of climbing, perhaps unsurprisingly as those in our climbing circle also moved as a loosely knit social group.

During that period Robin was an ardent supporter of the university club, which had skill in depth and was looked upon as one of the best clubs in the country. It became an integral part of the Scottish climbing scene and Robin, by his presence alone, raised the standards of every member by at least one grade. At the weekly lunchtime meet in the Deacon Brodie's pub Robin was somewhat self-effacing, and never held court, but was undeniably the focal point. It wasn't that Robin went out of his way to provide leadership – nothing would have been more out of character. He did it by his presence, almost by a process of osmosis.

On the other hand, he was a dangerous man to model a student career on. Coming from a school with no tradition of self-disciplined study, I assumed that everyone got into the common room for lunch and passed away the afternoon talking, drinking, climbing – anything but study. The first exams were, for me, like running into a brick wall. If Robin ever did any studying it must have been in short, very short, bursts. In his final year one of his class friends approached me, asking me to use any influence I might have to persuade Robin to come to a tutorial, or even to a lecture! Once, when he was searching through his pockets for money – and considering how short money was, Robin was somewhat cavalier in how he kept it stuffed randomly into jacket and trouser pockets – a letter demanding an essay fell out. The frustration of the sender leapt out of the page, although amusingly put. Submission date was of course already well past, but Robin appeared unconcerned.

Perhaps Salisbury Crags were too conveniently located. You could walk there from the university and all too often we did that to the detriment of both academic progress and shoes. Robin's class showed through clearly of course. Where people struggled up difficult routes in their PAs [tight-fitting rubber-soled climbing shoes named after their creator, Pierre Allain], he would make it look terribly easy as he shuffled up in suedes, but without ever any hint of superiority or showing off. But the Crags can't take all the blame.

After a weekend away, when Graham Tiso had to drive back to Edinburgh to open up his Rodney Street climbing shop, for example, he first dropped off Robin and myself at the top of the Aviemore ski road as we would be missing nothing more than lectures. On that beautiful, cold, clear night we walked over the plateau to the Shelter Stone to dislodge the resident fox that must have moved out minutes before we arrived. The smell was overpowering. By morning, unfortunately, the cloud had closed in and as wet snow fell we headed back up onto the plateau en route for Aviemore. There was a white-out on top and I shudder now with embarrassment at how rarely we carried a compass, relying instead on very fallible instincts. Two hours after setting out we realised we were lost, eventually coming across footprints which we followed until twigging to the fact that they were our own. Back we went to the edge of the plateau and lined ourselves up with what we reckoned was the general direction of Aviemore. I walked ahead to the 30-yard limit of visibility and laid my ice-axe in line pointing back to Robin. Robin then walked by me into the mist for his 30 yards. Sometimes when we lost each other in the swirling mist the leader would retreat back to the shouts. It was hit or miss stuff in daylight but as the gloom of late afternoon took over we began to think of having to spend a night out on the plateau. Even Robin looked relieved when we stumbled in the darkness into the ski tow. Lectures, however, still seemed a dull option and that night we hitched a lift over to Laggan where we slept in a cow byre that Robin knew of. The animals had the straw, we had the concrete, and it was uncharacteristically a pleasure getting up in the morning.

Off we set on General Wade's road over the Corrieyairack with the sun shining and spring in the air. As we began to climb it clouded over and soon we were walking in thick mist through soft snow which eventually became thigh deep. You could only break trail for about 100 yards and following wasn't much easier. As we crossed the top of the pass we were hardly moving. Night fell and the heavens opened as we dropped down through silver birches towards Fort Augustus. We shared a filthy animal shelter with some cows and in the morning hitch-hiked over to Kintail where Norman Tennent had the hotel. There we walked the ridges, climbed with him on local outcrops and slept in his barn. At the end of one long day we came down to the Glen Licht bothy to find that someone had left bacon. For allowing hunger to overcome any vestige of decency, we were made to pay a heavy price in pain and dignity when the expected two-hour walk back to the hotel took five and left us too exhausted to move the next day.

With spring in the air Robin decided he wanted a haircut. His hair-style seemed simple enough but the scissors were either poor or I needed some practice. Whatever, the result caused a short-term coolness in our relationship. But it was time we went back to being students, so off we set, hitching separately until a pickup truck pulled up beside me at Crianlarich. Robin, comfortable in the warm fug of the cab, simply grinned when the driver indicated that I could ride in the back. The journey home was rather like the Fort Augustus animal shelter left open to the ravages of a biting, 50-mile-an-hour, non-stop gale. In Edinburgh a grinning Smith helped me straighten my frozen limbs from the foetal position.

Memories of being with Robin have a photographic clarity, like travelling to Carnmore late at night in Graham's car, the sky in the west faintly aglow, the heather on fire to the north, while Robin sits in the back bellowing out, for the umpteenth time, the few lines he knows of 'Blueberry Hill' . . . In Glencoe we are lambs to the slaughter at the hands of the Creagh Dhu as John MacLean throws dice by the light of a Tilley lamp and Jimmy Gardiner is crooning 'Luck be my Lady

Tonight'. She may be for some, but not for us . . . On the girdle traverse on Aonach Dubh which Robin wants to complete in a day, we run out of time in the best tradition. A late start and slow progress on virgin territory: a classic day out. Some outings have a competitive edge in them and this time it is running – running blindly down the mountain in the dark. Robin disappears over a small cliff and I follow lemming-like, but hardly a moment is lost thanks to bones made of India rubber . . . On the East Buttress of Bheinn Eighe, Robin is without his PA's, forcing us to swap boots each time we lead through. Making my way up the upper reaches of the cliff, with daylight gone, I can't work where to go. Finally I make myself heard over his singing and he tells me from 80 ft above to launch out on a hidden hand traverse. For me following, easy, but what sixth sense has told Robin? And how many would make that sort of move in the dark? Then the inevitable race down the mountain, without a doubt the most dangerous part of the day! But Boggle was born.[4]

Robin might have had holes in his breeches and the toes of his boots, he might have forgotten his anorak but, on the mountains themselves, he was the ultimate virtuoso. He was at one with them. They were his natural habitat. Once I overheard someone say rather pretentiously that reading Proust as a student had been the greatest influence on his life. It would be exaggerating to claim that my answer would be Robin Smith, but the strength of his character, his determination and his dedication do affect me to this day.

I was working in Kent when Robin was killed in the Pamirs. It was Madge, one of the supervisors, who told me that he was dead but she had no need to speak. She knew Robin from previous summers and was moving purposely towards me. I knew as soon as she caught my eye that the friend who had taught me so much, and with whom I had shared risks and caroused, was no more. A postcard from Robin making arrangements to meet in Chamonix arrived from Moscow a few days later.

We had all, Robin included, guffawed at the sentimentality of the quote at the end of Gervasutti's biography: 'The Gods take those that they love.'

11

YO-YO

My God, it was steep – and that was the path, or what would have
been the path, if there had been a path. I had never been to the north
face before; I had climbed a number of routes on the east face and on
the traditional parts of the west face, but here never . . .

David Hughes was often to be witness to displays of Robin's audacity
on that 'path' and, for that matter, on the Aonach Dubh cliff to which
it led, in May 1958 and May 1959. Robin – 'just a mate we thought of
as a good climber' – had another new line in his sights. A Yorkshire-
born engineering student at the time and later a director of a manu-
facturing company back in his native county, Hughes recounts the
making of Yo-Yo, a climb now long considered a 'classic':

Robin was a great one for burning off seconds. During my time at
Edinburgh he never seemed to climb regularly with any particular
person, but cast his eye over what was available. So I have never been
quite sure why I was selected. It may have been that I had a reasonable
amount of gear and was willing to be led. Ambitious I was not. I simply
enjoyed the mountain environment – as I still do. Ambitious, no.

We camped at the head of Glencoe and scrounged a lift down the
glen on Derek Leaver's Norton – a favourite means of transport, three
up not unknown. Those of course were the days you could leave your
belongings with security at almost any roadside or campsite, sure that
it would still be there when you came back. *O tempora, O mores!*

We sorted out the gear, such as it was – about a dozen slings of
varying size and vintage, half a dozen or so steel karabiners, two or
three pegs and a hammer, but no harnesses. A tatty collection.
Chouinard and chrome moly were light years away. I can't remember
what Robin had on his feet, certainly nothing technical, but I had big
boots, rigid-soled, full shank, not at all bendy. It was obvious that Robin
had either been up for a look, or had an extremely accurate report of
where his route was, because he went straight to it early that afternoon.

With the rock overhanging in two planes and the ground almost overhanging as well, there was a lot of 'what if' discussion about coming

off. We needed to protect even the first bit because the ground fell away very steeply to the left and the landing would have been nasty from little more than a few feet up. The rock was reasonably dry and the bit in Ken Wilson's book *Hard Rock* about Robin wiping the rock with a towel must have been an apocryphal bit of thought transference from elsewhere. After a couple of hours trying to rig some runners and fiddling with jammed knots, off he went. We were tied onto two 120-ft hawser-laid, full-weight, having-seen-much-better-days 'Viking' ropes.

After a time Robin reached an abandoned 'Stubai' hammer hanging from a peg (I still have it, though it's broken). It had been left by Don Whillans after an earlier attempt in very wet conditions, so here we were, heading in the steps of the great as we shuffled with our bits of tat into the long dièdre. That's where I learned all about the jammed knot runner: great for protection but it usually knackers the slings, mainly mine in this case. Robin led it quite quickly until he reached what is now the stance at the top of the first pitch, but our pitch 2.

He then brought me up and because this pitch is in a corner I was not too conscious of the exposure. This was the big layback, which I loved, because in those days I was twice as strong and half the weight. I couldn't jam any better then than now but I could layback move after move between reasonable bridging rest points – perhaps, for me, the best pitch ever. And so I landed beside a grimacing Smith belayed on a peg slotted behind a flaky thing. No hammer required, it was loose, but tension on it from below stopped it from falling out. By that time it was getting dark. We looked at the next pitch, but did nothing about it, and decided to escape up a long, rising, fairly exposed (about 4c), featureless, leftward-trending ramp which eventually led to – the anything but – Pleasant Terrace. I fled up it into the gloom, runnerless. Then we headed back down to the glen, collected the sacks and made for the pub. It was shut.

Halfway we had got, so Robin made a few notes and claimed Halfway as a new route in the climbing journals. Today it is Yo-Yo's first pitch, plus our escape traverse.

We left it to mature for a year. Nowadays that would have opened the door to a multitude of suitors for the whole route, but, because I had been on the first part, Robin asked me to go with him to finish it. It seems to have been accepted then that the same party kept at it. A gentlemen's agreement! In the meantime he had done Shibboleth with much trumpeting from the *Daily Record* and the like, so I was very pleased to be asked to go again even if our little cliff on the north face of Aonach Dubh was not considered of great moment. This time we got serious, sorted out the gear beforehand and camped in the Coe below the cliff itself. As ever – my tent, stove, pots, gear, grub, cooking and – as ever – his enthusiasm.

When we got to the start, Robin had remembered how to protect it and was up to the Whillans' stance in no time – he had liberated a pair of PAs, but the ropes were the same. He anchored one of them for me to climb up and belayed me on the other, much quicker and easier than those fancy Jumar mechanical gadgets behind which seconds now make effortless progress up big-wall climbs abroad. The second pitch was also quicker, again because he knew it, and soon we were viewing the prospect.

The same peg still rocked in the same slot, so I tied on and sat on my heels below it to keep it in tension. I was glad to have rigid boots because the outside edge of my left foot was on a hold about an inch and a half wide, with the right tucked underneath me as I sat on it. My feet could not have survived that torture in modern rock boots. I cowered under the sailcloth, armour-plate hood of my Black's anorak while Robin cleared the next pitch. For five hours I was bombarded with a vast collection of moss, mud, grass, birds' nests, assorted shittite (rock of a Scottish variety) and other unmentionable rubbish from an increasing height at an increasing velocity.[1] The mind goes blank under these circumstances, but I did eventually realise that, as usual, the light was beginning to go. The sun sank over Ardgour, nasty black clouds were gathering round us, and then the lightning started *below* us . . .

So down he climbed. I wonder how many have reversed that pitch taking all the protection out on the way. Having removed every jammed runner he arrived back down and looked at me.

'Can you tie ropes together?'

'Yes, why?'

'I think we'd better ab off.'

At least I think he said 'ab'! So, with two ropes tied and hung round this still-loose peg, I drew the short straw and vanished slowly into the glen. He worked on the basis that, if the rope, the peg or my knots failed, he could always climb off. Bright lad, that! Then he bit the bullet and, still quite terrified of my knots and the lousy peg, slowly rotated around the lay of the rope to ground, feet out from the cliff. We coiled the ropes and rushed off. And the pub was shut again.

It rained on the Sunday, but the pubs were always shut on Sundays, so on the Monday morning we staggered back up that interminable hill. None of the chockstones had fallen out of the chimney, which was all nice and clean and, before I knew it, I was once again squatting by the rickety peg. But the bombardment was minimal, all clear from the last time, and soon the third pitch was over. Wilson's *Hard Rock* describes this pitch well:

> The corner is climbed with difficulty for 40 ft. At this point the crack widens into an overhanging chimney, jammed with rattling chockstones round which the climber entwines his arms as he lunges out and up over the prow, with nothing but thin air between his feet and the screes below.

I had not failed to notice the exposure, and was lunging like a good 'un, I can tell you! The last bit up to Pleasant Terrace must have been an anticlimax, though, as I've never really remembered much of it and find it difficult to equate with the book. Anyway, we terraced pleasantly about teatime and scrambled down the hill. After all the uppings and downings, there could only be one name for it.[2] Then we went to the pub and it was *open*.

12

CLIMBING – THEN, NOW, WHY

The more improbable the situation and the greater the demands made on [the climber], the more sweetly the blood flows later in release from all that tension. The possibility of danger serves merely to sharpen his awareness and control . . . Unlike routine life, where mistakes can usually be recouped and some kind of compromise patched up, your actions, for however brief a period, are deadly serious.

A. Alvarez, *The Savage God: A Study of Suicide*

Much has changed in climbing since Robin's day and a new grading system for rock climbs has helped measure the difficulty and athletic demands of routes. The highest Scottish grade in Robin's time was VS (Very Severe). For further information climbers were dependent on what they could see of the climb from the foot of the cliff, on the reputation of the first ascent team, and on word of mouth. A HVS (Hard Very Severe) grade was introduced in the late 1960s, while today the overall difficulty of a climb harder than that is conveyed by an open series of grades starting at E1 (the letter 'E' signifying 'Extreme', levels of difficulty increasing numerically). The gymnastic demands of pitches are also precisely graded now, alphanumerically using letters 'a' to 'c' only, from 4a (easiest) to 7c (hardest), the difficulty of the hardest pitch becoming part of a route's overall grade. Robin's Shibboleth, for example, is rated E2 5c. (There is a note on climbing grades in Appendix I.)

In Robin's time, limitations in equipment meant that major routes harder than E2 were not feasible. The breakthrough from E2 to E3 was a quantum jump which, apart from a one-off E3 on the untypical Trilleachan Slabs in Glen Etive in 1968, did not materialise until 1976. Even so, that advancement and further improvements were dependent on more than just better equipment and clothing. Attitudes changed. The use of chalk to remove sweat from hands and improve borderline holds, and minute pre-inspection from a top rope, had started, although it was other activities that came to be frowned upon more. Cleaning potential routes by abseil and practising moves on a top rope are, some would say, cheating. Exercising to develop specific muscles and access to indoor climbing walls also became part of the new scene.

These practices allowed standards to be extended to E5. In 1986, E6 became attainable, but only on routes with permanently fixed bolts enabling protection where none was previously possible. This contentious activity is frowned upon on Scottish mountains but is commonly employed in continental Europe. There followed conventional, often high-risk, E6 climbs. Since then, as boundaries have been pushed out and safety margins squeezed to maintain the thrill of climbing for top performers, standards have edged up to E10.

As absolute and average climbing standards rocketed, improvements in equipment and its associated protection have profoundly altered the rock-climbing experience. John Inglis, an able climber with an interest in the history of mountaineering, whose own name was to be added to the list of mountain fatalities at the age of thirty-one in 1994, reckoned that 'setting off up a climb with modern gear and armed with precise details of the barriers ahead is less of a leap into the unknown than the equivalent trip in Smith's time'.[1]

In any era, however, one has to distinguish between pioneers and those repeating climbs, and today's gym-honed trailblazers do from time to time push themselves to extremes of danger. That said, they invariably perform the sort of feats Robin could barely have imagined, at far less risk.

Improved footwear became a crucial factor, though Robin's generation had already started to feel the benefits of technology. Around 1957 PAs appeared from across the Channel, allowing tiny ripples on rock to be exploited as friction holds. Robin, however, did not always use PAs, as Jimmy Marshall explains:

> The ethos of the time was avoidance of excessive technical aid, that is to achieve one's objective without recourse to overly sophisticated clothing or gear, a doctrine in which Robin became an undoubted master. One expression of this was his choice of footwear for, whilst we were all won over to PAs, he never evinced much concern about what was on his feet and regularly wore much-battered, lightweight walking boots, even on some of his most significant new routes.

Today, high-friction 'sticky' rubber boots are impregnated with resins which allow purchase on steep rock totally devoid of holds. Specialist footwear now exists for smearing, edging, limestone, gritstone and competition-climbing.

Protection in rock-climbing has also advanced substantially. Running belays (or runners) consisted in the 1950s mainly of short loops of rope threaded round rock spikes and chockstones. Thinner, less robust runners, held in place with sticky tape, were all that was available for small protrusions. However, the placing of a small stone or the knot of a looped rope – the 'jammed knot' – into a crack as a substitute chock had become common practice. Pitons were used sparingly for belays, even on new ground, and always with a definite reluctance, at least in the mountains. Today there is abundant protection from sophisticated wired wedges of all shapes and sizes, let alone the intricately engineered alloy camming devices – 'Friends' – which adjust to fit almost any crack or slot. Various widths of very strong nylon tapes that loop easily over very small protrusions are now in use as runners, while ropes and karabiners too are stronger, lighter and better designed. Further, sit-harnesses and safety helmets remove much of the bite from the twin hazards of falling off and rockfalls.

For winter climbs on snow and ice, a grading system comparable to that for rock routes was introduced in the 1960s. A Roman numeral indicates the overall standard of the climb, while an ordinary number is appended for the severity of the hardest pitch (see Appendix I). But changes in winter climbing techniques have been so fundamental that, following the advent of the dropped-pick ice tool – enabling the climber to 'hook on' – and the universally adopted technique of front-pointing on steep ice in the early 1970s, Robin's routes are rarely repeated in the manner of the original ascents.

Those innovations immediately dispensed with the prodigious effort required to hack holds out of ice and have allowed exploration of longer, steeper pitches – far less strenuously too than in the days when overcoming a steep ice pitch might involve hours of exhausting step-cutting with a single straight-pick axe. Traverses then were particularly arduous as separate holds had to be cut for both hands and feet. Ice-piton protection also was primitive compared with today's high-tech titanium ice-screws, and improvements in clothing – lightweight waterproof breathable fabric and plastic-shelled boots – have further cushioned winter climbing. Of course, winter conditions are always unpredictable, and some of today's routes, such as ascents of massive icicles, are, to say the least, 'hairy'. Even so, Yvon Chouinard, the original developer of the curved ice-pick, now somewhat wryly questions the wisdom of having produced a tool so efficient that 'your grandmother could climb vertical ice on her first day out'. The impact made by Robin on modern mountaineering, without access to modern tools, was expressed by John Inglis in these terms:

> The enduring appeal of Robin Smith's brief brilliant career owes much to his legacy of fine Scottish first ascents, in both summer and winter. Any ambitious modern climber who may know nothing of Smith, his articles, or escapades, just cannot avoid the striking quality of many of his climbs. Stated simply, most major Scottish climbing grounds explored during the late 1950s boast a 'Robin Smith Route', usually following a compelling, often inescapable, central feature, and frequently giving the best climb on the cliff. The most famous rock climbs, such as Shibboleth, YoYo, The Bat and The Needle all fit this description, and were recognised as classics the moment they were recorded. Remarkably, Robin's hardest winter route, the Tower Face of the Comb on Nevis, still merits a very respectable grading amongst modern climbs.

* * *

It must be difficult for anyone who has never climbed to understand just how frightening climbing can be. Nor can the non-climber appreciate just how much mental control climbers have to call upon to hold themselves together. Fear, or rather one's ability to master it, either addicts a climber to the sport or ultimately forces him or her to stop. It is an essential part of the buzz of climbing. Addicts, like Robin, press themselves to climb more and more difficult routes, their fulfilment peaking on ensuing adrenalin rushes. Familiarity derived from experience can allay the feeling of fear, of course, but there will always be those who have to curtail their ambitions or drop out.

Although climbing has long been a very different sport from when Robin climbed, some things have not changed much. A few still climb solo close to the limits of their abilities, and risks are still as consider-able as ever on the very big mountains, where the one-in-ten chance of serious mishap invariably means death. Weather, never totally predictable anywhere, continues to play a disproportionately impor-tant role in that environment.

An ambition to explore is still at the heart of the matter for the more adventurous, a desire to set foot where man has never been before. Communion with nature ranks high with some climbers, as it did with Robin, some restrict themselves to mountain walking, and companionship is a factor for others. Moreover, the thrill experienced by moderate climbers as they 'up the grade' is surely no less than ever.

13

RASH ENOUGH TO BREAK A LEG

'SEVEN INCHES FROM DEATH' shouted the inch-high block
letters on the front page of the *Daily Record* of Monday, June 16th,
1958. 'Hurt Youth Saved on Mountain' ran the subheading,
announcing that Andrew Fraser, Robin's climbing partner, would live
to climb another day following an incident that predated organised
mountain rescue teams. Many consider Shibboleth, the new route
Robin put up that day on Buachaille Etive Mòr's Slime Wall in
Glencoe, as his finest, whilst the events surrounding medical student
Fraser's fall added an element of spice to its reputation.

Its first ascent coincided with a fast-approaching editor's deadline
for material for a new guidebook on Glencoe rock-climbing, an incentive for interested groups to want to polish off the best remaining
Buachaille routes. As a result, a cluster of rivals' scruffy tents appeared
most weekends at the foot of the mountain. Dougal Haston, Eley
Moriarty, the legendary Jimmy Marshall and his brother Ronnie also
represented the Edinburgh contingent (driven there in Graham Tiso's
old Ford Popular). 'Marshall dominated our activities,' Fraser now
reflects, 'subtly stirring up the competitive spirit amongst the young
tigers, pitting Robin against the Currie Boys, and hard men against
soft students; Edinburgh youth against Creagh Dhu classics. Rivalry
bred gamesmanship. Plans were kept secret, each nursing his own
schemes.' All along, the Creagh Dhu from Glasgow had been disdainfully regarding Slime Wall as their own domain following earlier bold
successes on the cliff.

Later that year, crutches propped against a wall in a Forrest Road
café, Fraser wrote this account of Shibboleth, thus revealing the full
facts behind the newspaper's sensational headlines:[1]

> Early in the summer Robin set his mind on forcing a Great New Route
> straight up the virgin verticality of this fearsome face, but up till June
> the weather kept him grounded. He passed his time thinking up a
> worthy name for his adversary, eventually, for reasons known only to

himself and certain of the Gileadites, to fix on Shibboleth.[2] He pondered long on the choice and was often to be seen in some small café of the town with a visionary gleam in his eye, muttering the word to himself, weighing it up, savouring its quality, testing its quantities, passing slowly from initial soft sibilant syllable to linger long on limpid labial and liquid 'l', endowing the word in a rapture of phonetic sensuality with almost oracular portent.

When at last summer arrived and the slime had drawn sulkily back into streaky patches, Robin decided to renew the attack. He lacked only a sufficiently docile second to hold the other end of his rope so, with glowing tales of a Great Natural Line, he lured me off to Glencoe. When he had tied me securely to the first belay and I had time to study the projected route, all I could make out of his Great Natural Line was a series of highly unnatural cracks and corners extending tenuously up the 500 ft of sheer rock above me, linked, or rather separated by, sections of steep smooth slab. This is one of those spots which drive home the meaning of 'vertical, if not overhanging' – a phrase which was to be much used on the ascent.

This is not the place for a detailed technical description, but a vague sketch may prove of use. The climb is 550 ft long and consists of six pitches, each of which is of Very Severe grading, then the highest standard. The first pitch is shared with a climb called Guerdon Grooves, and merely serves as a mild preparatory exercise. Pitch 2 is the hardest and never falls below VS over all its 90 ft while pitches 3 and 4 are nearly as hard. The last two pitches are more straightforward again and are even separated by a platform big enough to stand on without using the hands, though the exposure discourages this somewhat. At the hard bits a harsh croak emanates from Raven's Gully, while at the desperate bits I had a distinct impression of vultures hovering behind me, though this may have been merely imagination.

We spent two weekends on the climb. The first day we climbed the lower three pitches. Robin spent a considerable time clinging to the face below the crux, trying vainly to stem the oozing slime with a towel borrowed from an unwitting friend some months before. He abandoned this eventually in favour of simple levitation, and we made fine progress till he was turned back by approaching dusk and the severity of the resistance on pitch 4. We escaped from the face by following the magnificent flake of Revelation, which runs up beside this pitch, but further to the left.

Next day we returned by the start of Revelation to our turning point of the day before. Robin contemplated the fourth pitch anew. The sun was shining all around, accentuating the perpetual damp depressing gloom of Slime Wall. Shibboleth was exerting all her subtle insidious powers of dissuasion. No doubt malnutrition and camp life had left their mark on us too. Anyway, the more we contemplated the situation, the more obvious it became that the ideal way led up the flake pitch of Revelation to the left. From its top one could resume the original line with ease. Robin swore it would be more aesthetic to include such a unique pitch in such a fine climb, while I pointed out that it was in fact the more direct line. And so, up the flake we swarmed, revelling in its beauty and exposure, leaning out carefree on huge undercut holds over a sheer drop into Great Gully some 300 ft below. At the end of the day we emerged on to the hillside above, with the rest of our climb safely behind us.

It was then that a chill breeze of doubt first struck us, and faint echoes of mocking laughter wafted up out of Raven's Gully. Shibboleth obviously considered that by the inviolate middle pitch she retained her virtue. We could feel her exulting in her subtle triumph. Reluctantly, we climbed down by a fearful loose chimney of Cuneiform Buttress opposite to review the situation. There was no doubt about the direct line.

And so we returned next weekend, vowing to prove once and for all who was master. An alpine start from Base Camp saw us at the foot of the climb by midday. The second pitch provided some entertainment when it came to my turn to follow Robin's graceful lead. At the crux he had fixed a piton. This was the only one used in the whole climb apart from belays and was essential for security, the nearest runner being 30 ft below and the next hold being 15 ft above, up a smooth overhanging corner. Since the piton filled the vital handhold before the crux, I at least was very glad to use it quite unscrupulously. But being second, I had to remove it as I passed. The only position in which I could hold on with one hand and hammer with the other was so low as to be prohibitively exhausting. So I had to pull up to the piton and lean fully out from it with my left hand and hammer with my right while Robin took my weight on the rope from above. There was only a trace of a hold for my left foot while my right just pushed flat against the gently overhanging wall stretching massively on my right down to the last belay.

I hammered till I was exhausted; the peg wiggled freely, but was firmly pinched about its middle. At last I got permission from Robin to leave it behind. Just before continuing up I gave it a couple of

desultory blows as a final gesture – and found myself floating gracefully away out from the climb and in again to the impossible wall on
my right, clutching the recalcitrant peg in my hand. Great gusts of
drain-like laughter echoed down to me. All I could do was push off
gently again and hope to arrive back where I had come from. Somehow
I managed to wedge a fingertip in the empty piton crack and hold
myself into the cliff, but once there the situation called for urgent action.

I was exhausted. I could not rest from the piton now. I could not
climb on, deprived of the piton. I could not face the thought of being
lowered right down and starting again – without the piton. The only
solution was an inelegant but quick and effective technique specially
devised for following Robin on such occasions. It involves liberal use
of rope handholds, a jerky and positive 'tight rope' policy and unscrupulous use of such minimal rugosities as may appear on the actual rock.
Any lack of coordination tends to leave the second upside-down,
dangling helplessly at the end of the rope, but happily we had perfected
the technique on other occasions and all went well.

It is, however, a fairly energetic procedure. When I reached the belay
I was utterly shattered and had to cling weakly to the rock for several
minutes before I could find sufficient strength to weave myself into the
network of loops that constituted the belay, and let myself recover.

After this somewhat exhausting incident all went well for a while.
The virgin fourth pitch was assaulted and duly succumbed to Robin's
persuasive tactics. It proved a very worthy pitch and we emerged from
it with triumphant feelings – Shibboleth had at last fallen, nothing could
take that away from us now. There only remained two pitches. We had
agreed beforehand that I should lead the next pitch as a reward for my
patience over the many hours we had spent on the climb.

It was the easiest pitch we should encounter, or rather, the least difficult, and I had followed up it quite competently the week before. Robin
was belayed to a piton in a reasonable stance, and as I set off he was
chortling 'Shibboleth' in a happy way to himself and working out suitably laconic descriptions for the guidebook. But Shibboleth is a lady of
strong character and she could not take this defeat lightly. She had to
be avenged for her fall, and nothing short of human sacrifice could
satisfy her outraged pride!

I climbed 15 ft up and to the right, to the foot of a shallow overhanging corner. This was 15 ft high and the crux of the pitch, followed
by easier rock to the large platform and a fine stance. I remembered
that Robin's runner had fallen off as he climbed this corner so I cast

around for a better one. Classic rock spikes are not one of Slime Wall's notable features, but at last I managed to chip out a crack with the hammer so that a single strand of baby nylon would just lie in it. Hoping it was adequate, I clipped one of the ropes into the karabiner and attacked the corner. It was typical of Slime Wall. The main face sloped gently outwards over me, while the shallow right-hand wall remained obligingly vertical. There were a few sideways holds in the crack inside the right-angled corner, and one or two little edges on the walls but nothing much bigger than fingertip holds.

I was nearly at the top when I realised that my hands were feeling the strain of seven and a half hours' struggling on this cold damp steep sunless wall. My fingers began to feel soft and weak, and showed an alarming tendency to straighten out. But I just had to put my full weight on them for I was in a sort of layback position, my feet pressing in rather than down, since there wasn't enough to press down on, and my body leaning down and out on my arms, since the slope of the wall pushed it that way. My right hand had its fingers curled backhand against a vertical groove on the side wall, while my left hand was pulling sideways against the corner crack and taking most of my weight.

The next move was obvious. There was no choice. I had to lean fully out on my right hand and throw my left hand up on to a ledge above me. This ledge was quite large and flat; it sloped outwards, had a rounded edge and no trace of a grip for the fingers on the inside. I could not lean out on this hold, I could only push down on it as I overtook it. Thus my right hand would have to take my full weight as I moved my foot up to a small ledge at knee level, and gently straightened my leg – leaning right out on my hand. Then my left hand could get a push hold on the ledge while I threw my right up onto large holds and could climb out of the corner to safety.

The more I thought about it, the less likely it seemed that my fingers could hold out. Yet the longer I waited the more tired they became. I couldn't possibly rest them in this position and it was even more strenuous to retreat. To have shouted to Robin would have meant psychological defeat – my fingers would have loosened at once. I knew he was watching me in any case – he had even stopped singing his usual appalling skiffle. I just had to try that move.

I summoned up my last reserves of energy and leaned right out. I put my hand up on the ledge and moved my foot up. But I felt my hand weakening as I tried to straighten my leg and swing up gently, and then my fingers turned to putty. I seemed to be watching impersonally as

I saw them straighten out and leave the rock. I started to fall. Classically my whole life should have flashed before me but my mind remained a rather peaceful blank; it was almost a feeling of relief – I had done my best and it was out of my hands now.

The next thing I knew was a hefty jerk at my waist which doubled me up, and I found myself dangling at the end of the rope some 30 ft down, at a level with Robin, but over to the right. I contemplated cursing roundly but decided it was a little melodramatic. The runner which I had spent so long making had stayed put. The rope had not broken. Robin had held me. His piton hadn't come out. Everything seemed to have gone off classically until I became aware of a burning heat in my right leg. A quick glance down led to an instant diagnosis of broken; my foot was swinging about quite regardless of what I did with my leg. It must have hit the ledge where the runner was, for it was so steep elsewhere that I had fallen quite free of the rock and wasn't even bruised or scratched otherwise.

But the fates had kindly provided a nice ledge a couple of feet below. Robin lowered me to it. It was about a foot wide and 18 inches long, and was quite unique on the face – there was nothing comparable in sight. I managed to sit on it, dangling my legs over the edge. Robin passed over his end of the rope and I tied it to my waistline so that I was really suspended onto the ledge from the runner and couldn't fall off if I fainted. I had the rock behind me and to my right and the two ends of the rope like braces in front of me. I was as comfortable as I could hope to be, though a little cramped, and all I had to do was to prevent my foot swinging about.

We shouted for help, but our cries were swallowed up in the echoes of Great Gully. So Robin tied the end of his rope to the piton and traversed off, more or less unprotected, over some 60 ft of far-from-easy rock at a considerable exposure. From my ledge one could have spat, if one were that kind of person, straight to the bottom of Great Gully, 300 ft below.

I looked at my watch – 7.30. Then I set about examining my leg. Both bones were obviously broken clean through about halfway up the shin; I could feel the ends grinding together on the slightest provocation. As long as I kept perfectly still, it only felt hot, but any movement was distinctly painful. All the rules told me I should develop shock, but my pulse obstinately refused to rise over the 100 level. Then I wondered how I was going to be got off; there was 300 sheer feet below me and 200 ft above. As I couldn't solve that one, I tried not to think of the immediate future. How long did a leg take to heal? Six weeks, I seemed to remember. I hate to think what I should have felt if I had known it would take six months! Then my foot began to feel numb and cold, so I loosened the lace of my boot very gently.

It seemed quite soon, though it was actually two hours later, when I heard Robin's voice from the top of the cliff again. The rescue party was on its way. He climbed over to me and kept me cheerful till the experts arrived to plan the operation from the far side of Great Gully. Apparently people had never fallen off in such an interesting place before, or at least they hadn't survived to be rescued. Splints were lowered and we fixed them fairly efficiently. The stretcher was manhandled up Great Gully beneath us with much gentle cursing. The air was ringing with Glasgow and Edinburgh voices and the hillside seemed to be alive with climbers.

Ropes were lowered to us from above, knotted to reach down the 200 ft. I tied myself into a cradle arrangement, leaving my legs dangling. Then Robin tied another rope onto me – I don't think he trusted my knots – and tied himself onto a third. I tied my feet together to give me some control of my right foot. Two more ropes were brought over from the side of the cliff, where there was a largish platform on North Buttress, and we tied onto them too. Then we let the top ropes take our weight while we were pulled over and up to the platform. Robin half-climbed and was half-pulled across the face, protecting me and controlling the ropes, while I rested on his arms and fended off with my hands. It was quite a feat getting five long stretchy ropes to work in complete coordination.

Five hours after my fall, I was off the cliff and safely on the platform. I could lie down at last and stretch myself again. A unique hot drink consisting mainly of chocolate had been brewed on the hillside, thanks to Graham Tiso, who worked for Cadbury's. Then I was carefully inserted into a Thomas splint, wrapped in a sleeping bag and blankets and strapped securely into the stretcher. Familiar and unfamiliar faces floated into my sight and away again – I didn't gather who half the people were, but they seemed to be a good mixture from Scottish climbing clubs.

Now the real work started. Happily, I had chosen a fine clear midsummer's night, but even so the North Buttress is no place to take a stretcher down at midnight. So the route lay upwards. The technique was magnificent: five ropes were tied to the head of the stretcher and teams of seemingly inexhaustible climbers simply pulled me up the buttress. A Glasgow man was in the straps at the foot of the stretcher and he was pulled up too. He just had to walk up the face steadying the stretcher in a sort of inverted abseil. On the less steep bits, indefatigable relays of climbers manhandled me up the hillside, half-sliding me on the ski runners. It was a strange sensation to be relaxed and comfortable, vertically ascending the Buachaille at midnight, with the whole of the Moor of Rannoch, the Kingshouse, the campsite and Etive laid out flat at my feet in the midsummer dusk.

I was hauled up the hill for some time, then over long scree traverses under grey cliffs, the rescuers slithering and scrabbling round the mountain until we could make our way down Lagangarbh Gully and over the moor to the road. I didn't quite keep track of the whole journey, nor could I contribute much to the general flow of conversation of the party; the stretcher was so comfortable and so smoothly carried that I felt more inclined to go to sleep.

The rescue party was magnificent. A better, more experienced group of climbers it would have been hard to assemble in Scotland; most of the best-known characters in climbing were there. They had been dragged from their tents or the Kingshouse back onto the hill for an exhausting all-night expedition, many without their suppers, yet the spirit of the party was amazing. I would never have imagined that a rescue could be so cheerful; everyone seemed to regard it as the most entertaining expedition of the season. There was a lot of good-natured intercity banter and abuse; I gathered that one Glasgow fellow seemed to think that Edinburgh had been trespassing on *his* wall, and that my fall was the just and awful retribution of the gods. Another lad had the distinct impression that this was a god-sent exclusive scoop for his newspaper and promised me headlines the next day. We all joined in with suggestions that would really impress the great British public, but I have to confess the actual result was even more sensational.

We reached the roadside as dawn was breaking and everyone lay around exhausted, wondering whether to eat or to sleep first. Eventually they divided the day fairly evenly between the two; happily the weather wasn't of the sort to tempt them onto the hill again. A Bedford van took me to Fort William. When we met the ambulance after a mile or two the owner of the van just persuaded it to go home again empty and he very kindly took me all the way. And so, just twelve hours after I had fallen in the most inaccessible spot on the Buachaille, I reached the Belford Hospital and the friendly capable hands of Dr Duff and his charming staff.

'Saturday the day of the great fiasco', Robin breezily commented in a brief review of events. 'Added a fine pitch from the belay at the foot of Revelation Crack, going up and right near Nightmare Traverse to the 1st jughandle at 50 ft – no protection with the crux at the end. Then left and up an overhang corner to join the Girdle Traverse. Then Andrew peeled while leading the corner we had already climbed. Came down 30 ft on to a runner, which should have meant nothing, but was rash enough to break a leg. Fabulous rescue operations . . . Much singing all thro' the night.'[3]

Twelve months later, in June 1959, Robin went on to fashion the climb's Direct Finish up an impressive overhanging crack with John McLean of the Creagh Dhu. A few days after that, 500 miles away at Harrison's Rocks in Kent, he happened to meet the young Martin Boysen, who was to go on to become one of Britain's star climbers for almost three decades. That chance meeting added to the memorability of Shibboleth for Boysen when he came to climb the route himself in 1967.[4] The crux is unforgettable, he still believes, even though he is as aware as any that its relative difficulty has diminished as standards and equipment have moved on:

> After the brutal climbing lower down, one starts to savour on the pre-crux pitch the subtlety of friction holds, a foretaste of the delectable climbing ahead. It is precarious, steep, hard and terrifyingly exposed – there is no scope for runners. Relief follows, then admiration. Such a pitch will never, thank God, be made easy by nuts or wires. It will always remain a test of nerve.
>
> Although most climbs provide intense enjoyment at the time, the pleasure is often short-lived. For some reason, some climbs have a special significance which makes them stand out sharply, but why this should be is difficult to fathom. The climb must be good, well situated and, I suppose, hard, for the satisfaction is all the greater if one is stretched to one's limits. Ideally, too, the climb should have a certain rarity value, making devaluation in time unlikely. If, after all this, the climb lives up to, or even exceeds one's expectations, it becomes a great climb. For me, Shibboleth is such a climb.[5]

14

A NIGHTINGALE ASCENDING

On June 21st, 1958, a week to the day after the mishap on Shibboleth, Robin wrote to veteran Graham Brown, who would otherwise have had Andrew Fraser helping him sail his boat to Norway:

> It is a very great pity for Andrew, and of course for you, mucking up part of your holiday at such short notice. I hope you managed to see him on your way north. I myself am hitchhiking this evening down towards Kent, where I have fixed up a job picking peas or something – we hope to make £20 a week, then pack in on 24th July & hop over the Channel to Chamonix. For four weeks we will have nothing more than Harrison's Rocks to climb on! I certainly want to do the mountaineering routes at Chamonix – that, of course, is half the pleasure of getting out of Britain, where you spend all day on 200-ft outcrops. I would especially like to do something on the Brenva Face, and could then talk it over with you on a surer footing.

That spell of honest toil was to pass quickly for the students, however, helped by imaginings of what the Alps might hold in store. 'I leave here probably around Tuesday 22nd, cross the Channel on Thursday 24th, & reach Chamonix on Fri. for climbing on Sat., with 4 hrs en route in Paris', Robin was soon able to advise his mother, morale further uplifted by a dramatic surge in his financial wellbeing. 'I will certainly need a few days to recover – one's fingers can hardly move in the morning – and it isn't often, let alone for 4 weeks in a row, that I get up at 6.00 a.m. My date of return is unfixed.' After spending two nights at the Kensington flat of Gunn Clark, his final partner in the Alps a year previously, he reached Chamonix by train.

His first partner of the 1958 season turned out to be Trevor Jones, one who claims never to have teamed up with quite such a strange-looking individual. A large pad on the top of his head, held in place by bloodstained bandages tied under his chin, giving a rather nice Florence Nightingale look, is the Robin that Jones recalls first meeting. Robin's explanation was that he had 'missed it' running down the steep shortcuts on the Montenvers. Trees and bushes had luckily broken his fall, though at a cost, according to another English climber, Les Brown, who was on the Biolay campsite when Robin turned up 'wild-eyed, clothing torn and bloodied, his face covered in abrasions, admitting to having been a little clumsy'.

In those days the west face of the Blaitière above Chamonix was reputed to be the most technically difficult rock route in the whole of the Western Alps. Jones, a member of the Climbers' Club,[1] recalls that its ascent with Robin was not entirely without incident:

> On one very nasty layback crack, he fell off seconding me, but this was probably due to not having experience of the hundreds of gritstone cracks on which I was brought up. The best French climbers had tried to repeat the west face of the Blaitière and all had failed – the highest party failed on the crack Robin fell off. It was one of the great Alpine climbs of my life.

It was, in fact, only the second complete ascent of a route that had first been climbed by Joe Brown and Don Whillans four years earlier. A bivouac was called for halfway up at the Fausses Vires, where Jones, preparing to spend the night in a warm down jacket, asked Robin where his was. Disorganised as always, Robin was quick to reply, 'Och, it's Haston's week for it.' This tickled Jones who recalls that their twenty hours on the face was later rounded off with spectacle of a different sort:

> We came down the Spencer Couloir, me with just one crampon. He had dropped his axe. Enormous storm clouds were gathering and it was getting dark. We ran into Montenvers Station as the last train was pulling out and Robin jumped into the guard's van. I tripped and fell but he grabbed my bag and pulled me in and we laughed and laughed with relief as the rain beat down amid thunder and lightning. He had a rare dash and flashing eyes and was game for anything. What great *élan!*

In 1958, his second Alpine season, Robin, who (according to Jones) became 'the young King of Scottish climbing', went on to climb one more of the Alps' hardest routes, the west face of the Petit Dru. Starting from the Rognon du Dru with 'Morty' Smith of the famed Rock and Ice Club, they made what was reckoned to be the route's thirteenth ascent.

Joe Smith, nicknamed 'Morty' to avoid confusion with the illustrious Joe Brown, had just climbed the west face of the Petites Jorasses with Brown and Don Whillans. Naturally they didn't want to repeat it. On the other hand, Morty was keen to tackle a climb he had first attempted two years previously, at the age of seventeen, with John Sumner as his partner, when . . .

John fell 180 ft on the most exposed part of the climb which we abandoned after all his protection had broken – old slings from 1953, which he shouldn't have been using. In 1957, I again attempted the route with Paul Ross, but a storm came when we were halfway up, so that attempt had to be abandoned as well. Consequently, I was looking for a partner.

I had heard from Dennis Gray about a wild-eyed Scotsman who had a reputation as a good climber and was, Dennis said, walking around with a large bandage on his head having fallen off an Alpine path. Was his reputation true, I thought? When I first met him, he was exactly as Dennis described, but he seemed friendly. The weather was good so we decided to go to the foot of the Dru that evening. On the way we bought some bread, packet soup, cheese, condensed milk and coffee but it rained at the bivvy and the bread got soaked. This meant we had very little food – nevertheless, we decided to climb.

After setting off at 5.00 a.m. and deciding to lead through, we climbed quite fast by the standards of the 1950s and arrived at a 20 ft overhang below the 90-metre dièdre at 4 p.m. It was my turn to lead that strenuous pitch but, just as I was pulling over the overhang, the peg I was hanging on came out, due to its rotten wooden wedges, and I fell back down to Robin. I told him that I was too tired to lead again and suggested that he should have a go. He managed it without trouble and, by 5.00 p.m., we were sitting in the sunshine on a large ledge enjoying the outlook. We felt that it was too late in the day to climb the dièdre before dark so we bivouacked there. Robin told me a good way of keeping warm – put your legs in the sleeves of your jersey and wear your duvet on the top of your body. It worked and I kept a lot warmer than normal!

We arrived on the north face at 4.00 p.m. the following day in conditions of bright sunshine and soft snow. Robin was leading, his axe in the snow as a belay, when he suddenly shouted to watch out as a 10-ft-square slab fell. It slid over the rope. I thought how lucky we both were. If the slab had caught the rope we would have fallen 3000 ft.

At 5.00 p.m. we reached the top and started our descent but had to spend a second night out somewhere under the Flammes de Pierre above the Charpoua Glacier after missing the correct route down. I'll never forget how on that descent we saw the Walker Spur on the Grandes Jorasses in perfect condition. Robin said, 'Let's go and do the first British ascent', something I would have loved to have done, but couldn't, as I was due back at work in three days' time. Holidays in the 1950s were only two weeks for industrial apprentices, so the windows of opportunity for achieving good routes were rather narrow for us. I often regret not having taken that chance. Robin, of course, now had it earmarked.

Throughout the climb Robin would neither eat nor drink, not that much food was left after its soaking. The climbing was thirsty work and I enjoyed drinks of coffee in the morning and evening as well as some melted snow. Robin must have been feeling the thirst but had said he wanted to test himself to see how he felt without eating or drinking. Then, on arriving back into Chamonix, we passed a small shed where an old man sold all sorts of things. Robin said he wanted a melon. So he nipped round the back of the shed, pinched six empty wine bottles and handed them over to the old man, who gave him three francs, with which he bought the melon. I was amazed at his cheek.[2]

15

NEAR-CANTERBURY TALES

As students during their annual summer migration to the Alps, Robin,
Dougal Haston, Andrew Wightman and other Edinburgh climbers
stopped off amongst the oast-houses and orchards of Kent to work at
fruit- and vegetable-processing factories. It was there that Foster
Clark's were offering well-paid seasonal work at their vinery at
Aylsford and factory in nearby Maidstone. The harvesting of the
various Kent crops fitted in neatly with the start of their vacation and
lasted until the end of July. From 1958 to 1961, the Aylsford vinery,
25 miles to the west of Canterbury, came to be Robin's pre-Alpine base
from where he wrote a series of letters home:

> I reached Maidstone on Monday, checked in at the factory where the
> peas are canned, and was sent out the 3 miles to Aylesford – a fine Kent
> Olde English village – & the Vinery another mile out. Here we sleep
> in a large tin shed with beds & sacks for mattresses. At hand is the
> common room, like a Y. Hostel, with a couple of electric cooking plates
> and oven, & a worthy ancient known as 'Ma' who gives us lunches at
> 1/9d [9p in today's terms] & yesterday had a birthday for which she
> received from the students 2 lbs. of chocolates.
>
> The boss, 'Sid', is very decent and as there was really nothing much
> to do for the first 3 or 4 days let us loaf around fairly much at ease. We
> thus had time to inspect the local country – very pleasant, trees & ups
> & downs & a fine setting for a novel. Just behind us a path leads through
> bushes to a small lake. Around are rushes, then a sort of clay swamp,
> with small sweet strawberries & stunted bushes and beyond them, on
> higher ground, is a great tangled forest of trees. The whole is wonder-
> fully prehistoric, straight out of the Lost World, but the master stroke
> is that out of the heart of the jungle comes a fearsome roaring of lions
> and tigers.
>
> Peas began to come in on Friday – huge loads all piled high on the
> back of lorries, straight from the farms and still in the pods and on the
> vines. Two men climb on top of the load and fork the vines down to the
> ground, & 4 more fork them onto conveyor belts leading into the threshing

machines. Somehow this removes the pods & vines & washes the peas, the waste is carried off and the peas are thrown out at the other end into baskets; these are stacked on lorries which whip them off to Maidstone and in about an hour from the start of it all they are canned and ready to serve. Through this past week we haven't cleared much money, but on Monday the peas should come pouring in as the Evil Weather has suddenly changed to good, and with them comes the overtime.

We have been swimming in the lake, eating strawberries, and one evening inspected the phenomenon of the roaring – no less than the local zoo. We surreptitiously crept about, inspecting polar bears & llamas & monkeys & porcupines & the lot – even an elephant – miserably imprisoned.

Andrew Wightman:

Robin provided my introduction to Sid, the foreman, and I started immediately. Within an hour my hands were rubbed raw. In the few, painful days it took them to toughen up Robin tutored me and made sure we worked in the same gang. Pitchforking pea vines into threshing machines, we worked for eighteen hours a day.

Though the work was hard it was mostly in the open air and wonderful preparation for the Alps, even if you did waken with fingers curled, as if still round the shaft of a pitchfork, until you straightened them out, one by one, in a basin of hot water – if you could get there before the others. A metal-covered drain ran down the centre of the hut but sometimes this got blocked and you would have to wade to your bunk through ankle-deep waste. Robin took this all in his stride. One such night, amongst all the shouting and cursing, I found him lying in bed reading Kant by torchlight.

Robin:

The weather here has been fine for a week – hot and tanning, if some-times fearfully sweltering for forking peas. The vines roll in all piled high on lorries, swarming with insects of all sorts which scuttle over us as we work in our shorts. In two of the loads we have come across slow-worms, fine little harmless snakes, but very evil-looking with forking tongues, the first I have seen.

Life is very thick down here, working eating sleeping, with a steadily sinking level of living. I can't say I would be suffocated by luxury. Working among the peas induces a lethargy towards any mental efforts demanding discipline, that is, outwith daydreams. I have succeeded in going through most of Russell's 'My Philosophical Development' which I like very much. You might appreciate it. Some of it is moderately comprehensible, if sceptical.

On Saturday nights or Sundays, if they were not required to work, the Scots lads sometimes went on eating and drinking binges with their fellow Irish student workers. Here, Wightman saw Robin in a new light, 'leading the singing on the top deck of the last bus home, cajoling or threatening the other poor innocent passengers to join in!'

'Robin was a prodigious and conscientious worker,' Wightman adds, 'and, while never being ingratiating, was a great favourite of Sid's. Sid would go home at 11 p.m. and leave Robin in charge while we cleaned up, telling us to clock off at a certain time. We all liked and respected Sid so that, if the work took longer, we would clock off at the agreed time then still go back to finish the job.' Robin light-heartedly explained to his mother that his selection for the nightshift was 'the fruit of long service & diligence', going on to detail the responsibilities and benefits:

Official hours 'on the clock' for an average day would be: 8 a.m.–10 a.m., 12 noon–2 p.m., 4 p.m.–6 p.m. (these brief spells serving to relieve the various teams of the dayshift for breakfast, lunch & tea breaks) and then the night shift proper, 6 p.m. till 6 a.m. i.e. 18 hours per day – in order to clean the Viners, Winnowers, Washers, Belts, Sieves, Screens, Aprons, Conveyors, Basins, the Mobile & finally, in a combined sweeping-all-before-us, the 120 ft by 70 ft of floor; the which, in sum, constitute the Vinery. This operation however can be completed in about 4 hours of concentrated work, as our very understanding boss well knows. But as you will have gathered, there is a lot of hocus-pocus behind the face of the clock. On a good (for us) day, the dayshift would have finished vinning the last lorry-load of peas by about 6 p.m., leaving us 12 hours clear to clean up, and we would be completely finished and into the local for a pint before 10 p.m., i.e. with 8 hrs pay still to come for doing nothing – all 'on the clock' and earning 5/6d per hour at 'time and a half'. But on a heavy day, loads would be coming in till after mid-night, we would not be finished cleaning till after 4 in the morning and would retire to the Hut cursing our harsh employers.

Today I have had no work – a pity, as on Sundays we earn double time – 6/8d per hour! Lately and critically the weather has turned

Robin (left) with the other three boarders at Bee MacNeill's, c.1948.
Courtesy of Bee MacNeill.

Robin (2nd left) with his parents and brother Charlie, c.1953.
Courtesy of the Smith family.

Robin and Jimmy Cruickshank in First Year class photo, May 1951.

Fifteen-year-old Robin in cycling shorts assesses Nevis cliffs. Easter 1954.
Photo by Jimmy Cruickshank, reprinted with thanks to the Smith family.

Robin (left) and Jimmy Cruickshank heading to Bidean nan Bian, Easter 1955. Courtesy of the Smith family.

Desperate exposure on hard traverse crux of 'Deathshead's Overhang', Glencoe, Easter 1955. (A Robin fantasy.) Photo by Jimmy Cruickshank.

Robin chaired by supporters prior to the school's mock election, May 1955. Courtesy of the *Watsonian Magazine*.

School prefects. Robin (centre) with Jimmy Cruickshank (left) and Sandy Bannerman, May 1956.

Young Robin, possibly in the Lake District, c. 1956.
Courtesy of the Smith family.

Robin in the Small Quarry on Salisbury Crags, Edinburgh, 1955 or 1956.
Courtesy of the Smith family.

Robin (right) with his 'old' mentor Archie Hendry, a teacher at
George Watson's, 1958. Photo by Jimmy Marshall.

Rannoch Wall on the Buachaille. Climber is on January Jigsaw, near the skyline
of Crowberry Ridge, which Robin used to descend prior to further climbing.
Photo by Tom Weir, reprinted with thanks.

At a north-west bothy. (L–R): Phil Hill, Dougal Haston, Andy Wightman, Robin Smith, c. 1960. Photo by Jimmy Marshall.

Jimmy Marshall leads Eley Moriarty on the second ascent of Robin's classic new route 'Yo-Yo'. 1959. Photo by Tom Weir, reprinted with thanks.

On a trip to Skye, c.1960. (L-R): Jimmy Stenhouse, Dougal Haston,
Graham Tiso, Robin Smith. Photo by Jimmy Marshall.

The Jimmy Marshall Robin knew. Photo courtesy of Jimmy Marshall.

against the long chain of dependents on peas and the peas are rotting in the rain in the fields. Unless there is a drastic change in the willing of gods there will be much money lost not only to farmers & Foster's but also to students.

The cake was a fine short treat when most of the time I live off bread, porridge, cornflakes & cheap things easy-to-cook. I am glad to hear Marion got her job. With any luck I will clear a total of £60 for the 4 weeks.

The long shifts largely precluded climbing activities during those stays in Kent. Not that there is much rock in the southeast. But there is some. Harrison's Rocks, once described by Robin as 'a miserable outcrop for London picnickers', lie 15 miles from Aylesford in pleasant wooded countryside outside Tunbridge Wells, itself about 30 miles south of London. They extend for a quarter of a mile or so, their maximum height is no more than 30 ft, although some test pieces are as short as ten. Generally, the rock is sound, whilst great roots of ancient beech trees cascade down in places to provide reliable, but well-polished, holds on some of the easier routes.

It was at Harrison's Rocks in late June 1959 that Robin met the seventeen-year-old Martin Boysen and was welcomed into the wider fellowship of the Kent climbing community. Although totally unknown in wider circles, Boysen there on his own patch could climb problems which defeated all others, a fact later commented upon by Robin himself. Boysen, a local, was a protégé of Nea Morin, who died in 1986, aged eighty-one.

One of the rocks' original discoverers and pioneers, Nea had had an illustrious climbing career both at home and abroad and had passed her enthusiasm for climbing to her daughter Denise, who was married to Charles Evans, doctor on the successful 1953 Everest expedition. Her agnostic family – her father was originally a parson who lost his faith trying to convert his wife back to the doctrines of religion – was not well regarded by the respectable of Tunbridge Wells, where she was brought up. But that did not bother Nea or her brothers one bit: 'We were outlaws and rebels and gloried in it.' Robin would certainly have enjoyed hearing such stories. He might also have heard that his own septuagenarian guru, Graham Brown, a controversial character in some circles, was well liked within her family. Boysen remembers

Nea as a graceful and skilled climber with an infectious enthusiasm delighting in encouraging young hopefuls like himself and in introducing visitors, as he puts it, to the 'somewhat esoteric pleasures' of Harrison's:

> Robin was one of Nea's entourage along with several day visitors from London, including Gunn Clark, whom he already knew, and it was in their company that I was introduced to the man who was doing great things – Robin had climbed Cenotaph Corner, a climb at that time of almost mystical status and with but a handful of ascents. I was seventeen and still new to the climbing scene, so much so that I had only been to Wales once, but my summer holidays were due and Cenotaph Corner was a secret ambition. Robin was obviously a climber of stature and I was keen to observe him closely and measure myself against him.
>
> He was dressed in a red shirt and shorts which displayed his enormously strong legs and stocky powerful body. He maintained a taciturn smile and climbed with a slow deliberate style, unlike the usual quick ascents by sandstone *habitués*. A top rope was set up over Edwards' Effort; a hard problem originally climbed by Menlove Edwards, involving a peculiar and technical finger lock in a tiny runnel. A climber known to me only as 'Henry' performed his party piece by zipping up it. When Robin came to try it, he stood for a full five minutes on the crux, playing with the move, before he finally committed himself. Later on in the day, overcoming my shyness, I asked him how hard Cenotaph Corner really was. He smiled quizzically and replied: 'Hard, but not as hard as Edwards' Effort.'
>
> After a strenuous day on the rocks in which many of the famous problems such as Niblick, Birchden Wall and Unclimbed Wall[1] were dispatched, we were all invited to Nea's lovely Georgian terrace house in Tunbridge Wells at 17 Church Road where we were entertained to an elegant tea of toast and climbing gossip. Nea had an enormous range of knowledge. She had just returned from the Himalayas and the conversation was all about them and the Alps.

Around the table that tea-time in leafy Kent they were not to know quite how much their chat had promoted the germination of seeds of a notion which would lead to Robin's name forever being linked with deeds of derring-do on Alpine heights . . .

16

WALKERING IN THE ALPS

Never before climbed by a British party, the Walker Spur on the north face of the Grandes Jorasses represented one of the great Alpine challenges to climbers from these islands in the 1950s. There is no doubt that the Walker Spur, not far from Chamonix itself, was the specific objective at the start of that 1959 Alpine season. Robin had studied it the previous summer and Nea Morin had recently tipped him and Gunn Clark off about it after flying over the Mont Blanc massif as she returned from a Himalayan expedition via India:

> I was able to see very clearly the east face of the Grepon, the north face of the Geant, and in particular the north face of the Grandes Jorasses, which was strikingly black and free from snow. I told Gunn and Robin that I thought the Grandes Jorasses must be in exceptionally good condition, though, of course, they had it on their list . . .

After Robin's stint of work came to an end at the Kent vinery, he went to stay for a few nights at Clark's Kensington flat. He and Clark then set off by train from London to Paris, before travelling overnight to Chamonix. The irritations of the journey vanished when the train turned up the Chamonix valley and the Aiguilles swung into view, not a patch of snow to be seen. The sun had been shining for ten days, they were to discover at Snell's sports shop, and the great faces were said to be in perfect condition. Nea had been spot on![1] Then on hearing the rumour that potential British competitors, Don Whillans and Hamish MacInnes, might already be up at the Leschaux Hut en route for their objective, the pair decided to make straight for the hut themselves. Gunn Clark recounts the rest of the story:[2]

> At the Montenvers I caught my breath in awe. The Jorasses hung there above us, higher and steeper than I had remembered. It seemed quite fantastic that, by the same time the following day, we might be halfway up that magnificent face. Then two hours later our hopes were washed away by a violent thunderstorm. Crouching under a boulder on the

glacier below the Couvercle we debated whether to carry on or go back to Chamonix. In the end, we decided to press on, if only for the sake of spending a night in the legendary Leschaux Hut.

When we arrived there we found five assorted Continental parties [but no sign of Whillans and MacInnes]. As the evening wore on, the clouds cleared and we realised that the storm had been only local. Our hopes rose again and we took stock of the situation. It was clear from the mass of rope, pitons, karabiners littering the hut, that each party was intending to do a big route, probably the same one as ourselves. Since everyone was being rather secretive, I innocently asked if anyone was going to the west face of the Petites Jorasses, a modern rock climb. Haughty headshakes confirmed our suspicions and we retired to bed, leaving the impression that *les Anglais* would not be competing. We set our alarm for midnight and dozed off, confident that we at least would have a spot to bivouac on the following night.

We left the hut at 12.30 a.m. and started the long slog up the glacier to the foot of the face. After an hour, the great black wall loomed so high above us that it hid the stars completely. Bobbing lights started to follow us. While we were strapping on our crampons beneath the rimaye, a Polish pair caught us up. In good French they introduced themselves and told us modestly that they had just done a six-day traverse in the Caucasus. What had we done so far? Rather than admit to a couple of Sundays at Harrison's Rocks, we mumbled something about the undiscovered ranges of Scotland. Suitably impressed, they passed us, moving easily on their heavy twelve-point crampons, while we limped after them sharing an old pair of ten-point Grivels.

To avoid step-cutting on the initial ice slope, we chose the alternative start, which follows a steep loose couloir just to the left of the base of the buttress. In the dark, this couloir and the snow slope above it were very tiring. I felt sick and hopelessly weak. This may have been due to the altitude or to lack of training, but I suspect it was, rather, the result of the imagination trying vainly to cope with the unknown problems of the 4000-ft wall which soared above us in the darkness. Certainly, when dawn came and I started to concentrate on the individual pitches, this lethargy passed and I began to enjoy the climbing.

The first real problem was the Thirty-Metre Crack. From directly below, the angle appeared to be reasonable, and Robin set off carrying his sack. Bridging wide, he seemed to float up the first 40 ft. Higher, the more familiar staccato movements of hard British rock-climbing began, until with a final great heave, he disappeared against the blue sky. Meanwhile the Poles, who had been off route, arrived below us. They were obviously impressed by the pitch and so, before starting, I offered to take up one of their ropes. They gratefully accepted and, a few minutes later, I rejoined Robin, having found the upper half of the crack reminiscent of Kipling Groove.

We helped the Poles to haul up their vast rucksacks before setting off across the famous Bands of Ice, the traverse of which proved less difficult than expected. After several mixed pitches we rounded a corner overlooking the central couloir and rather unexpectedly found the Seventy-Five-Metre Dièdre. The angle was easier than that of the Thirty-Metre Crack, but the Poles insisted that we took their top rope on the first pitch. For the rest of the dièdre we climbed with them and saved each other a lot of time and energy. We arrived on easier ground, already catching the afternoon sunlight, and looked around. The weather was still settled and almost imperceptibly the Aiguilles were sinking below us.

Above, a chimney led to an exposed traverse ending on the edge of the buttress. Two fixed pitons enabled us to abseil to a tiny platform from which we crossed an awkward slab to an icy bulge. Higher up, the angle eased and we found some ledges to relax on, while the Poles continued.

The Tour Grise rose above us and we examined the Dalles Noires with interest. Although reputedly the crux of the climb, in the afternoon sun the angle did not seem particularly steep and we set off again optimistically. But the holds turned out to be small and the route far from easy to find. The resultant sense of frustration and tension was increased when a great block started to gather momentum on the slabs above. I was tied to a belay at the bottom of a slanting groove and watched fascinated as the block engaged itself in the top of the groove and approached like a homing missile. It landed on the neat coils between my feet and bounded on. When we had sorted out the bits we found that the effective length of our double rope had been reduced from 150 ft to less than 100!

Darkness was coming on and still there was no sign of the top of the tower. Robin led out two more long steep pitches with great verve and at last an exultant shout announced that he had found the bivouac site. The Poles were already installed and, rather than crowd them, we climbed down to a small ledge right on the nose of the buttress. Two pitons rang home and we snuggled into our duvets, feet dangling over the Leschaux Glacier. Having satisfied our immediate hunger with cold meat and chocolate, we filled our brewcan with chipped ice, coffee and sugar, and lit the stove. With a great sense of wellbeing we dozed off beside it as the meths flame flickered in the darkness. I dreamt undramatically, continually meeting people and shaking them by the left hand. This hand-shaking became more and more insistent until I woke to find that for increased warmth I had unconsciously leant over to the left against the meths burner: a large hole had been burnt through my anorak and the arm of the duvet jacket underneath was alight. I eventually managed to put it out, spreading burning down everywhere in the darkness. By some miracle the brewcan had remained upright during the excitement, but the precious coffee had become laced with charred feathers. Our mirth at the incongruity of nearly being roasted on a freezing north face quickly disappeared as we began to suck the vile but vital liquid through cracked lips.

At 5 a.m. our alarmclock jolted us awake to find another fine day already dawning. Memories of the previous day's stonefalls prompted us to get in front, and we passed the Poles just as they were putting on their rope. Two hundred ft of steep rock separated us from the crest of the ridge. At one point a karabiner found abandoned on a peg finally convinced us that Whillans and MacInnes had not passed that way. Once on the crest, we were in the sun. We felt considerably fitter and less tired than on the day before and the 1000 ft of ridge leading up to the base of the final Red Tower was a joy to climb.

In our enthusiasm we continued past the traverse to the right, leading to the chimney which splits the side of the tower and, by the time we had retraced our steps the Poles were some way up this repulsive-looking rift. Robin set off during a lull in Polish activity and, by a powerful piece of climbing on very loose verglased rock, arrived safely at a small stance to the right of the chimney. I started at much the same time as one of the Poles 100 ft directly above, and so was bombarded by almost everything he pulled off. For speed I resorted to climbing one strand of our double rope while Robin heaved on the other. While doing this, a large stone hit me on the back of the head, drawing some blood and all the French abuse I could muster. Once united on the ledge, we decided to let the Poles finish the chimney before going on ourselves. We remained perched awkwardly in deep shadow on the side of the tower for an hour and a half before it was safe to continue.

Above the chimney a sensational traverse 50 ft below the proper route took us to the start of the final 500 ft of the spur. It was 4 p.m.; white clouds suddenly boiled up around us, making the summit ridge seem thousands of feet away. We were getting tired and our double rope was beginning to irritate us more and more; we took it off and climbed up together, relying on the incredible position to safeguard us against carelessness. The last 50 ft were very loose, so we roped up again and broke through the cornice a few feet from the summit. My first feeling was of relief at being able to stretch out in the soft snow and relax. For a few moments a longcherished dream hovered as a reality before taking its place among other memories.[3]

Even as long as twenty-one years after it was first climbed, an ascent of the Walker Spur created quite a stir locally, and, following their arrival in the Italian town of Courmayeur, Robin and Gunn Clark 'found an ex-climbing English lady owning a chalet & willing to entertain enterprising climbers to lunch & beer & whatnot'. And why not! They had just done the first British ascent of the Spur and Robin – Nea Morin went on to add – 'didn't even find it hard'.[4] Although he had established himself as an Alpine figure the previous summer, it was this ascent that first etched Robin's name in the annals of British Alpine history.

That highlight of their 1959 season was a remarkable achievement in that they had left London on July 19th and completed it by the 22nd, just three days later. Robin later commented that the quality of climbing and the situations had been marvellous from the Thirty-Metre Crack onwards. Of particular interest was his remark that few pitons were either encountered or necessary.

Had they not made their move with such single-mindedness, however, the delights of success would have been converted into the disappointment experienced by another British party pipped at the post by just one day. Don Whillans, Les Brown, John Streetly and Hamish MacInnes were hot on their heels, as Brown recalls: 'On the Walker, we were surprised to find jammed knot runners – a British technique – and an empty packet of Smarties. But we still could not imagine another British party ahead of us, hence our chagrin in Courmayeur.'

Nonetheless, they joined forces for an appropriate celebration and, aided by Don Whillans' epic remark to Brown, 'If I'd known, I wouldn't have blewdy bothered', those few days are now part of folklore.

17

DOLOMITIC DOSSES

Immediately following the buzz attached to those first British ascents of the Walker Spur, the Alpine weather started to disappoint, confining Robin and Gunn Clark to the Italian town of Courmayeur to which they had descended on July 23rd, 1959 as the first of the two teams up and over from France. Robin explained to his mother that the bad spell caused them to wait three days before setting off for the Gamba Hut round the back of Mt. Blanc. Even so . . .

> Storms sent us back the same day & we took the Télépherique up 5000 ft to the Col de Géant, on the Italian-French border. We came on to Chamonix next day, high landscape changed from black to white, & have pretty well been festering since.[1] We had some excitement when one of the English hard-climbing youths fell off the Voie Britannique on the Aiguille de Blaitière, one of the routes we did last year. He was with Joe Smith, who climbed the Dru with me. The Guides heard about it first and went up en masse, but made a shambles of trying to locate their shouts, & 4 of us went up to help bring the boy down strapped on the back of one or other of the huge policemen who have to do rescue work as part of normal duty. The guides extort vast fees. He proved to be no more than shaken, bruised and all these things & has since flown home.

Graeme Nicol, climber-doctor on the Pamirs expedition with Robin in 1962, also participated in that rescue on the Blaitière. The injured climber, 'Matey' Metcalfe of the Rock and Ice Club, had been held by his second, Joe 'Morty' Smith, who managed to get down to raise the alarm. The last cable car to the Plan de l'Aiguille was held back for Nicol, Don Whillans, Gunn Clark and Robin, who then started up the Blaitière on the Nantillons side. They failed to reach Metcalfe that night, instead being forced to bivouac on a ledge in pouring rain and wet snow. Whillans had a cagoule and rucksack but the other three had to share his nylon bivouac sack.

In the morning they continued up over the verglased rocks and

126

got to Matey who, to their relief, had no major fractures, reaching him only a little ahead of the French rescue team which included the well-known guide Pierre Leroux. Graeme Nicol:

> Shortly after leaving the bivouac site, Don Whillans was bringing me up (fortunately roped) when I pulled a huge rock on top of myself and fell against a ledge with it on top of me. I still have the scar, and my precious duvet jacket was torn; blood and feathers everywhere. After this episode my stamina was pretty sapped but I remember Robin playing a significant role in the 'Sauvetage', taking turns to carry the stretcher, and yodelling from time to time, much to the consternation and annoyance of the guides (by this stage we were in a full-scale storm with lots of avalanche-prone wet snow). They kept saying, 'Ca peut provoquer des avalanches.'

Robin added to his letter, written in Chamonix on August 3rd, that he was 'pushing off today to Grindelwald, en route for the Dolomites, after a vast snowstorm that has plastered the Aiguilles. The 2 Marshalls & the "Curry boys", the rough youths whom you have sometimes met, have arrived full of success from the Dolomites. I am going to Grindelwald with one of them, Dugald [sic] Haston. You could write to the Grindelwald P.O. – whatever they call it in Switzerland.' He duly reached his objective even though 'hitching was only moderately good and took me very close to Lausanne. I have found a hole to sleep in among the floorboards of a house going up – some half-dozen Algerian workmen arouse me pleasantly at 7 a.m. Still waiting for my comrade'. That was still the case two days later on August 6th, so, with plenty of time on his hands, Robin found a fair bit to write home about:

> Very poor. I forgot your birthday. A very rash sort of thing to do when I have a twenty-first coming up. Many happy belated returns.
>
> I am sitting on a big wide sensible bench in the shade of a station shed. I don't know if you have been to Grindelwald – very different scene from Chamonix. Something like going from the Cuillins to Torridon. Here the hills are big steep lumps, more massive and independent. Looking southish, the Wetterhorn is the left outpost, very elegantly buttressed. I think I sent a postcard thereof. The Eiger on the right is magnificent. We look straight onto the NE face, and at an angle across the big black bowl of the Eigerwand, the north face proper, which sucks up such of the clouds as there are. Between the two, away behind,

there are other famous Horns, which every English climber ought to know by name. The Mönch & Jungfrau are hidden by the Eiger. The snow along the top of the Eiger is like a sheet of metal in the sun.

I am becoming frustrated. The weather has been fine since Monday & I got here on Tuesday night, but to date there is no sign of Dugald Haston. So I just loaf about all day, scowling at the sun & the people. With the help of the tourists and Bertrand Russell, I am full of disgust for the mass of humanity. Everything is pretty on the outside, cakes, hotels & bauble shops and clothes. Grindelwald hasn't even an atmosphere of climbing, which is the saving grace of Chamonix. The one or two climbers here seem out of place. The grass & the flowers are fine and tall, only you can't sit on them because they are full of ants. Just as we found in Norway, I don't think the great grand Alps are a patch on Scotland for looks. Apart from the snow & rock-manufactured things, almost everything is one or other shade of green. No doubt it will colour up a bit once Dugald arrives, which should be any minute.

We are here, of course, to climb the Eigerwand, which everyone will tell you is dangerous or unjustifiable or suicidal. It is grouped with the Walker Spur of the Grandes Jorasses to make up the two great north faces of the Alps, and it will have to be a lot more dangerous to be something to cry over. If we get it in good condition, it will probably be less exposed to stonefall than many of the voies normales crowded with careless novices & rushing guides. The system is to go so far up in the evening & bivouac below difficulties, ready to go right up & down next day without further bivouac or retreat without difficulty in event of an overnight storm. Right now it should be just right, but unless Dugald gets here soon we will probably miss our chance. There are always, however, the classic snow ridges, where recent storms & conditions are less crucial than for the rock routes of Chamonix.

I had some little excitement getting here myself. I suppose I am managing to look after myself, but slipped a little with my passport. I left it with Gunn Clark in Chamonix when I left to hitch-hike here &, by the time I got to the Swiss border, Dugald was somewhere ahead & I was on my own. I tried to bluff my way through with a fable or two, but they pushed me back into France, without taking my name or anything, as quickly as they could, doubtless wishing neither to help me nor to shoulder responsibility for any villainy I might be up to. This was at around 8.00 p.m. so, with Marion's tale of Hungarians in my pocket, I threaded my way through the forest on one side of the very steep and narrow pass, a vast rucksack on my back, less than 200 yds from the road, full of soldiers & police & guns & barriers. It wasn't nearly dark enough to save me from being seen, & twice I had to hare across open bits of grass, and finally had to crawl over a dry riverbed, dodging through stones to reach the shrubs beside the road on the other side. Luckily I got a lift soon, & not from one of the policemen going home for tea or something. So now I am in Switzerland without a passport, on my very best behaviour to avoid awkward contact with the police. I have sent a letter to Gunn asking him to forward it inconspicuously. I have to keep quiet in bed at night, since I doubt the authority of the workmen to let me use it and the roof of the house they are building is formed by the main road. Things have improved – I am now on the floorboards, well shielded from neighbours by walls of cement bags. I believe the workmen are mostly Italian.

Some time later. I have been to see the Italian film *Verdi*. I suppose it was better than most films, but the big thing was to hear a bit of music. That is one of the deadlier sides of long spells of climbing – you don't even hear rock 'n' roll, let alone anything 'good'. It must be a bit grim when you go to the Himalayas or the like. It didn't even matter being stuck in the 2nd front row of a very small cinema, so that all the bodies were round & squint, & the operatic ladies looked as fat as ever they were in the old films. I must now go cook myself a meal on my small & very simple meths burner, for bivouacs.

Haston, in fact, never did turn up at Grindelwald, having gone straight home instead.[2] Ultimately, Robin decided not to hang around any longer and, bitterly disappointed and angry, left for Austria, where his sister was on holiday. He then moved on to 'conduct one gentle tour of Dolomite tops', when he found himself in the heart of the Civetta Massif at the Rifugio Vassoler meeting up with Giorgio Redaelli, a crack Italian climber. 'He was so disgusted with my boots,' Robin purred, 'that he promised if possible to send me a pair to Edinburgo. He is sufficiently famous to be presented with as many pairs of different make as he wants, by way of advertisement for the makers.' Redaelli looks back on those days at the Vassoler with great pleasure. He met Robin on August 20th while waiting for Ignazio Piussi for an attempt on the most direct route up the south face of the Torre Trieste. As his climbing partner would not be arriving until the 22nd, he had a free day:

> There was nobody at the refuge except the guardian, Armando da Roit, and I asked him who the mountaineer in the shed at the back was. He

replied that he had been around for a few days and was a Scotsman. Robin didn't sleep in the shed but under the verandah of the Rifugio which was unusual, but it sometimes happened with foreign climbers far from home and without money. Perhaps he camped some nights.

I went to find him and somehow we managed to exchange a few words, to understand each other and at once became friends. In the evening we ate together in the shelter. Robin had no food, no money. He had lost everything but I don't know what happened: he didn't tell me. Over the meal we agreed to climb the Via Ratti, on the Torre Venezia, the next day. At 6 a.m. we met outside the Rifugio, ready to leave, and my gaze dropped to his boots. They looked like wartime leftovers that had been through the mill, but what made more of an impression was that the rivets/studs for anchoring and tying the laces were almost completely missing from both boots. He said: 'I have lost everything and these boots and this stuff are the only things I have left.'

In these conditions, we succeeded in climbing the Via Ratti in record time taking turns at leading. Robin was great – even the greatest. I will tell you that when we climbed from the top, roped together, I was a bit worried; I was afraid (and more than once!) of seeing his feet coming out of his boots, but his strength and his technique were great. It was a truly great satisfaction to have climbed with him and the memory is still alive in me. We wrote many times, mainly postcards, and his last was in 1962 when he climbed the Garmo. On that August 21st, 1959, a great friendship was born.

Some Scottish hospitality may be due to Giorgio Redaelli for treating Robin to not just one meal, but two, as he also forked out after their climb. Redaelli's pioneering attempt up the south face of the Torre Trieste was successfully achieved in five days.

The Dolomites might well inspire wonder in all who see them, but Steve Read believes that the first visit there for any young climber, as it was both for himself and Robin that season, is particularly sweet:

It was an exciting time for me as the yellow and golden towers of the Dollys first hove into view from the tops of the passes we crossed on our way from Austria. Dennis Gray, Beardy and I went up to the Rifugio Vassoler, at the south end of the Civetta, a three-mile long wall, reaching up to approximately 4000 ft in the centre. Of course, being English layabouts on a long holiday, we could not afford to stay in the hut, but found a very pleasant campsite among the nearby juniper bushes. We carried huge rucksacks of grub up from the valley and supplemented our diet with the odd soup and occasional beer at the hut.

The Civetta is one of the most spectacular walls in the Eastern Alps, three miles of continuous towers and faces set above beautiful Alpine meadows with the occasional small lake and stream. Stunted pine and juniper drop off this Alpine fairyland steeply into a heavily wooded valley. Various footpaths wind below the wall between the huts and from these can be heard the whine and whistle of stones falling from the face to clatter on the scree below. At sunrise and sunset, the towers gleam yellow and golden and expose the cracks and fissures which make a climber's heart beat faster. That might sound romantic, but that's how I always felt about the Dolomites – it was a magic experience I have never forgotten.[3]

A spell of bad weather prompted Read and his two companions to move to the Marmolada, where Read, who had inherited Metcalfe's Kletterschühe after the Blaitière rescue, teamed up with Don Whillans, albeit in boots that were a bit floppy, with a toe of the right foot protruding. After a desperate but ultimately successful venture on the Dolomites' ice-bound highest, Read returned to the Vassoler hut, where he found Robin camped on the spot used by his group earlier:

Robin was looking for a climbing partner so I joined him. My first impression was one of strength. He wore shorts most of the time. He was heavily built with strong brawny arms and powerful thighs. His arms appeared long and, from behind, his rolling stride reminded me of an ape. His hair was close-cropped in the style of the day and his face quite oval. But it was his eyes that really drew attention to him – quite large and staring. He was proud of the fact that he didn't even have a spare pair of underpants with him and used to strut about the campsite in the dirtiest pair I had ever seen, with a twinkle in his eye.

As a climber, he was bold. He suggested to me that we climb the NW Dièdre of the Torre Val Grande one day, the Cime Su Alto the next. In the event, we only managed the Su Alto, a 3000-ft buttress towards the south end of the Civetta. It has a very pronounced dièdre running up most of the top 2000 ft which is very steep; vertical and overhanging in places. The lower 1000 ft takes you out onto a belt of steep slabs, broken by fissures. It had the reputation as one of the hard climbs of the day – Grade 6 with a lot of aid pitches (pitches done mainly by swinging from one peg to the next). It's the kind of impressive rock scenery that is most exciting and attractive to an aspiring climber.

We travelled light without a sack to try and get up and down in the day. We tied anoraks round our waists and slung the rope and pegs and hammers over our shoulders. It was a three hour hike from the Vassoler hut to the foot of the face, which we did in the dark by leaving about one in the morning. The night was clear and starry. We began soloing up the lower slabs in the gloom of the pre-dawn light whilst 3000 ft higher, a golden glow made the top of the buttress look like a beacon. Robin stopped off for a shit near the foot of the slabs so I reached the top of them first and basked in the warmth of the sun as he emerged from the gloom below. It was here we roped up and Robin made a tricky traverse to the right, across the back of a shallow rotten cave which was dripping with slime. We had our last drink here. This led to the foot of the groove where the steep climbing began.

A few words about equipment. We were using 300 ft of 9-mm hawser-laid nylon rope, doubled and tied round the waist with a bowline: no harnesses in those days. This gave us 150 ft between us but also meant we could do 150-ft abseils on a double rope. Pegs were an assortment of heavy ex-British-Army pegs and Italian Cassin pegs. Likewise, Karabiners were all heavy steel: no alloy then. Slings were 12-mm hawser-laid nylon, 9-mm or 5-mm nylon. I had a double-headed cobbler's hammer for the pegs. As we expected much aid climbing we each had a pair of *étriers* – ladders about 3 ft long, made from 5-mm nylon line with three alloy foot rungs, and suspended from a karabiner so that they can be clipped into pegs and removed easily. There are various techniques involved in the use of them, depending how steep the rock is and how quickly you wish to move from one peg to the next. I found that I had more experience of aid climbing than Robin and was able to show him a few things here as I had been trained on Derbyshire limestone for several years.

I can remember few details of the climb. We led alternate pitches all day but, at one point, I got off-route and ended up at the top of a steep slab to the right. Robin led through following a line of pegs on the correct route, then, with him holding a tight rope, I had to pendulum sideways to reach the correct line. With 2000 ft of space below, this made for an airy manoeuvre as you put your weight on the rope and, with Robin taking the strain, ran sideways trying to keep your feet on the rock and to avoid falling and sliding across it on bare skin.

The heat reflected from the rock after midday made it like climbing in an oven and we both became dehydrated. However, the climb went well and we reached the summit an hour before dark. Down below the valley was dark, but we basked in the glow of success and a golden sunlight. We could see the descent gully off to the south on the eastern slope along the summit ridge on which the rock was very shattered. I suggested we get off the ridge and look for a bivouac site for the night. Robin said quite firmly: 'I'm not staying up here,' and off we set. We reached the descent gully to be met with 1000 ft of hard snow and this is where Robin's experience in Scotland showed. He scouted around, picked up two long spikes of rock and handed one to me: 'Use this as an ice dagger and follow me,' and off he shot down the slope. This was the best time of day to be on that hard snow as the sun had melted the surface sufficiently to provide a soft layer adequate for glissading. But only just – it was steep and hairy. Robin shot off like a gazelle and I followed more cautiously to get down that 1000 ft in one long glissade.

Then followed a two-hour flight down scree and boulders, then trees and scrub in the pitch dark, back to camp where I arrived ten minutes after Robin. We made it in eighteen hours, hut to hut. I slept all next day and I don't remember Robin trying to find anyone to do the Torre Val Grande either. That rock ice-dagger is something I have used on other occasions, and I always think of him when I pick one up.

Robin then returned to the Torre Venezia, this time with a new companion, Ricardo Blach. Unfortunately Blach fell ill at the start and had to turn back leaving Robin to go on to solo the Via Tizzi, a route referred to by Don Whillans in his book as a 'serious undertaking'. 'This was typical of the bold way he did everything,' suggests Steve Read, who had also climbed with Robin two years previously, 'and was probably the first time a Britisher had soloed anything of Grade 6 standard in the Alps'. Read, who had made its first British ascent in nine hours only that month with Dennis Gray, goes on to describe how Robin would have soloed *Via Tissi*, a climb that struck him as fairly straightforward, but exposed, particularly at a crux traverse, and sustained:

A view is sometimes expressed that climbing solo is foolhardy. I have never believed this. I say so because those who do dangerous sports solo are people who are very aware of themselves and their limitations and also very aware of the dangers of the situations they put themselves in. In my experience, soloing heightens the awareness of all the senses. I become extra-careful and my concentration is absolute. I remember Eric

Jones describing one of his many solo feats, where he said he '. . . flowed up the mountain'.

Soloing brings its rewards. There is an economy of movement as progress is not interrupted by regular belaying. Progress is generally more rapid, which brings satisfaction and sometimes safety as the mind can concentrate fully on the immediate problem, as it only has to communicate with itself.

The technique Robin used on Torre Venezia was to carry a rope, but only use it for protection at two difficult places. One was the crux pitch which is a rising traverse to the right across a steep wall – and very exposed. He tied off one end of the rope to a peg at the start of this pitch then passed it through karabiners at available protection points, each time tying the rope to his waist again with a length of slack; enough to reach the next point of protection. Once the difficulties were passed, he would tie off the rope above and reverse the pitch to retrieve the equipment, now using the rope as a safety line from above. He also needed a rope for various abseils on the descent from the top of the tower.

Looking back to those days at the Vassoler hut, Read recalls that Robin did actually stay in a tent, '. . . in other words somebody else's!' It was a matter of pride as well as necessity to avoid paying for a single night's sleep during Alpine trips, he explains: 'So bivouacs and dosses in the most unlikely places became the order of the day, and part of the challenge of a long holiday – half-built houses, bus shelters, garage fronts, private verandahs etc. In the mountains payment to stay in a hut meant failure. Bivouacs under large boulders were usual.' Two members of Read's own club once slept in a large, roadside grit container with a swing lid that opened up next morning when a bucket of ashes was dumped on them. 'Robin,' he now appreciates, 'was obviously a master craftsman at finding a free doss.'

Robin from Padua, Italy, August 1959: 'Am peacefully meandering over the Continent, mainly, if miraculously, by train. I have now some 30 minutes in Padua then 2 hours in Milan & if I choose 2 hours in Basle & as long as I like in Paris. I may go tour the Louvre & Sorbonne & read original Cartesian manuscripts.'

18

THE BAT AND THE WICKED

Of all of Robin's classic new climbs, the Bat alone was spiced with a scarcely palatable brand of Currie seasoning. Pioneered on Nevis with Dougal Haston in September 1959, when the relationship between the pair was not at its best following Haston's recent failure to turn up at Grindelwald for an attempt on the Eiger, its evolution nonetheless merited recording, Robin decided:

> You got to go with the times. I went by the Halfway Lochan over the shoulder of Ben Nevis and I got to the Hut about two in the morning. Dick [Holt][1] was there before me; we had to talk in whispers because old men were sleeping in the other beds. Next day we went up Sassenach and Centurion to spy on the little secrets hidden between them. We came down in the dark and so next day it was so late before we were back on the hill that the big heat of our wicked scheme was fizzling away.
>
> Càrn Dearg Buttress sits like a black haystack split up the front by two great lines. Centurion rises straight up the middle, 500 ft in a vast corner running out into slabs and over the traverse of Route II and 200 ft threading the roofs above. Sassenach is close to the clean-cut right edge of the cliff, 200 ft through a barrier of overhangs, 200 ft in an overhanging chimney and 500 ft in a wide broken slowly easing corner. At the bottom a great dripping overhang leans out over the 100 ft of intervening ground. Above this, tiers of overlapping shelves like armour plating sweep out of the corner of Centurion diagonally up to the right to peter out against the monstrous bulge of the wall on the left of the Sassenach chimney. And hung in the middle of this bulging wall is the Corner, cutting through 100 ft of the bulge. Dick and I lay and swithered on a flat stone. We wanted to find a way out of Centurion over the shelves and over the bulge into the Corner and up the Corner and straight on by a line of grooves running all the way over the top of the Buttress, only now it was after two in the afternoon.
>
> But we thought we ought to just have a look, so we climbed the first pitch of Centurion, 50 ft to a ledge on the left. The first twisted shelf on the right was not at all for us, so we followed the corner a little

farther and broke out rightwards over a slab on a wandering line of holds, and as the slab heeled over into the overlap below, a break in the overlap above led to the start of a higher shelf and we followed this till it tapered away to a jammed block poking into the monstrous bulge above. For a little while Dick had a theory that he felt unlike leading, but I put on all the running belays just before the hard bits so that he was in for the bigger swing away down over the bottom dripping over-hang. We were so frightened that we shattered ourselves fiddling pebbles and jamming knots for runners. We swung down backwards in to an overlap and down to the right to a lower shelf and followed it over a fiendish step to crouch on a tiny triangular slab tucked under the bulge, and here we could just unfold enough to reach into a V-groove cutting through the bottom of the bulge and letting us out on a slab on the right just left of the Sassenach chimney.

And so we had found a way over the shelves, but only to go into orbit round the bulging wall with still about 40 ft of bulge between us and the bottom of the Corner now up on the left. The way to go was very plain to see, a crooked little lichenous overhanging groove looking as happy as a hoodie crow. But it looked as though it was getting late and all the belays we could see were very lousy and we might get up the groove and then have to abseil and underneath were 200 ft of over-hangs and anyway we would be back in the morning. We could just see the top of the Corner leering down at us over the bulge as we slunk round the edge on the right to the foot of the Sassenach chimney. A great old-fashioned battle with fearful constrictions and rattling chock-stones brought us out of the chimney into night, and from there we groped our way on our memory of the day before, leading through in 150-ft run-outs and looking for belays and failing to find them and tying on to lumps of grass and little stones lying on the ledges. When we came over the top we made away to the left and down the bed of Number Five Gully to find the door of the Hut in the wee small hours.

We woke in the afternoon to the whine of the Death Wind fleeing down the Allt a' Mhuillin. Fingery mists were creeping in at the five windows. Great grey spirals of rain were boring into the Buttress. We stuck our hands in our pockets and our heads between our shoulders and stomped off down the path under our rucksacks into the bright lights of the big city.

Well the summer went away and we all went to the Alps. (Dick had gone and failed his exams and was living in a hole until the re-sits, he was scrubbed.) The rest of the boys were extradited earlier than I was, sweeping north from the Channel with a pause in Wales in the Llanberis Pass at a daily rate of four apiece of climbs that Englishmen call XS (X is a variable, from exceptionally or extremely through very or hardily to merely or mildly severe). From there they never stopped until they came to Fort William, but the big black Ben was sitting in the clouds in the huff and bucketing rain and the rocks never dried until their holidays ended and I came home and only students and wasters were left on the hill.

Well I was the only climber Dougal could find and the only climber I could find was Dougal, so we swallowed a very mutual aversion to gain the greater end of a sort of start over the rest of the field. Even so we had little time for the Ben. We could no more go for a week-end than anyone else, for as from the time that a fellow Cunningham showed us the rules we were drawn like iron filings to Jacksonville in the shadow of the Buachaille for the big-time inter-city pontoon school of a Saturday night. And then we had no transport and Dougal was living on the dole and so to my disgust he would leave me on a Wednesday to hitchhike back to Edinburgh in time to pick up his moneys on a Thursday. The first time we went away we had a bad Saturday night, we were late getting out on the Buachaille on Sunday and came down in the dark in a bit of rain. But the rain came to nothing, so we made our way to the Fort on Monday thinking of climbing to the Hut for the night; only there was something great showing at the pictures and then we went for chip suppers and then there were the birds and the juke-box and the slot machines and we ended up in a back-garden shed. But on Tuesday we got up in the morning, and since Dougal was going home next day we took nothing for the Hut, just our climbing gear like a bundle of stings and made a beeline for Càrn Dearg Buttress.

This time we went over the shelves no bother at all, until we stood looking into the little green hoodie groove. It ran into a roof and from under the roof we would have to get out on the left on to what looked as though it might be a slab crossing to the bottom of the Corner. I was scheming to myself, now the groove will be terrible but nothing to the Corner and I will surely have to lead the crux, but Dougal shamed me with indifference and sent me round the edge on the right to find a decent belay under the Sassenach chimney. There it was very peaceful, I could see none of the tigering, only the red stripes down the side of Càrn Mòr Dearg running into the Allt a' Mhuillin that was putting me to sleep if there hadn't been odd faint snarls and scrabblings and little bits of rope once in a while tugging around the small of my back. But once Dougal was up he took in so much slack that I had to go and follow it myself. Half-way up he told me, you lean away out and loop a sling over the tip of a spike and do a can-can move to get a foot in the sling and reach for the sling with both hands as you lurch out of the groove and when you stop swinging climb up the sling until you can step back into the groove; and his sling had rolled off the spike as he left it, so I would have to put it on again. I came out at the top of the groove in a row of convulsions, which multiplied like Asdic as I took in the new perspective.

Dougal was belayed to pitons on the slab under the Corner. The slab and the left retaining wall went tapering down for 20 ft till they merged and all heeled over into the general bulge. Above, the Corner balanced over Dougal like a blank open book with a rubber under the binding. The only big break in the bareness of the walls was a cleancut black roof barring the width of the right wall. The crack went into the right wall, about six inches wide but tightly packed with bits of filling; and thus it rose in two leaps, 35 ft to the black roof, then out four horizontal ft and straight up 35 ft again; and then it widened for the last 30 ft as the right wall came swelling out in a bulge to meet the top of the great arc of the sky-line edge of the left wall. And if we could only get there then all the climb would surely be in the bag.

Well I had stolen the lead, only some time before I had been to a place called Harrison's Rocks and some or other fellow out of London had made off with my PAs. Now PAs are the Achilles' Heel of all the new men, they buckle your feet into claws and turn you into a tiger, but here I had only a flabby pair of Kletterschühe with nails sticking out on both sides of the soles, and so I worked on Dougal to change footwear at which he was not pleased because we stood on a steep slab with one little ledge for feet and a vision before us of retreating in our socks. We had two fullweight ropes. Dougal had one rope that was old before its time, it had once been 120 ft long but it lost 5 ft during an experiment on the Currie Railway Walls. (This last word to sound like 'Woz'.) A Glaswegian who was a friend had one day loaned us the other, and so it was even older, and he mentioned that it had been stretched a little, indeed it was 130 ft long, and so Dougal at the bottom had quickly tied on to an end of each rope which left me with 15 ft on the one to get rid of round and round my middle to make the two ropes even. This was confusing, since I had a good dozen slings and karabiners round my neck and two bunches of pitons like bananas at my waist and a wooden wedge and a piton hammer swinging about and three or four spare karabiners and a big sling knotted into steps.

The Bat and the Wicked

But I could still get my hands to the rocks, and I made slow progress as far as the black roof. I left about six feeble running belays on the way, mainly so that I would be able to breathe. And as there seemed little chance of runners above and little value in those below and nowhere to stand just under the roof and next to no chance of moving up for a while, I took a fat channel peg and drove it to the hilt into the corner crack as high under the roof as I could and fixed it as a runner and hung the knotted sling from it and stood with my right foot in the sling. Thus with my hands in the crack where it came out horizontally under the roof, I could plant my left foot fictitiously away out on the left wall and peer round over the roof into the Corner above. Deep dismay. The crack looked very useless and the walls utterly bare and I shrunk under the roof into the sling. Shortly I leaned away out again to ponder a certain move and a little twist and then something else to get me 10 ft up, but what would I do then, and then the prepondering angle sent me scuttling back like a crab into shelter. In a while I got a grip and left the sling and heaved up half-way round the roof and sent a hand up the Corner exploring for a hold, but I thought, no no there is nothing at all, and I came down scarting with a foot under the roof feverishly fishing for the sling. And there I hung like a brooding ape, maybe there's a runner 10 ft up, or a secret keyhole for the fingers, but how are you ever to know for sitting primevally here, so for shame now where's your boldness, see how good your piton is, and what's in a peel, think of the Club, think of the glory, be a devil. I found a notch under the roof in which to jam the knot of a sling which made another runner, and I tried going up a few more times like a ball stopping bouncing until I realised I was going nowhere and trying nothing at all. So I jacked it in and left all the runners for Dougal and Dougal let out slack and I dribbled down to join him on the slab.

Here I sat a while and blew, then I took my coat of mail and put it on Dougal and Dougal wanted his PAs back and we untied to swop our end of rope so that Dougal could use my runners and I tied myself on to the stance while Dougal rotated into the tail end of the longer rope and the time went by. But Dougal caught it up a little by rushing up to the black roof while I pulleyed in the slack. And here we had a plan. Just above the lip of the roof, the crack opened into a pocket about an inch and a quarter wide. There should have been a chockstone in it, only there was not, and we could find none the right size to insert. If there had been trees on the Ben the way there are in Wales there would have been a tree growing out of the pocket, or at least down at the stance or close to hand so that we could have lopped off a branch and stuck it in the pocket. But here we had a wooden wedge tapering just to the right size and surely it once grew in a tree and so maybe it would not be very artificial to see if it could be made to stick in the pocket. Blows of the hammer did this thing, and Dougal clipped in a karabiner and threaded a sling and the two ropes and pulled up to stand in the sling so that he could reach well over the roof and look about at ease. And sure enough he could see a winking ledge, about 25 ft up on the right wall.

Now Dougal is a bit thick and very bold, he never stopped to think, he put bits of left arm and leg in the crack and the rest of him over the right wall and beat the rock ferociously and moved in staccato shuffles out of the sling and up the Corner. I shifted uneasily upon my slab which tapered into the overhangs, making eyes at my two little piton belays. As Dougal neared his ledge he was slowing down but flailing all the more, left fingers clawing at grass in the crack and right leg scything moss on the wall. I pulled down the sleeves of my jersey over my hands and took a great grip of the ropes. Then there came a sort of squawk as Dougal found that his ledge was not. He got a hand on it but it all sloped. Rattling sounds came from his throat or nails or something. In his last throes to bridge he threw his right foot at a straw away out on the right wall. Then his fingers went to butter. It began under control as the bit of news 'I'm off', but it must have been caught in the wind, for it grew like a wailing siren to a bloodcurdling scream as a black and batlike shape came hurtling over the roof with legs splayed like webbed wings and hands hooked like a vampire. I flattened my ears and curled up rigid into a bristling ball, then I was lifted off my slab and rose 5 ft in the air until we met head to foot and buffered to a stop hanging from the runners at the roof. I could have sworn that his teeth were fangs and his eyes were big red orbs. We lowered ourselves to the slab, and there we sat in a swound while the shadows grew.

But indeed it was getting very late, and so I being a little less shattered heaved up on the ropes to retrieve the gear, leaving the wedge and the piton at the roof. We fixed a sling to one of the belay pitons and abseiled down the groove below with tails between our legs and a swing at the bottom to take us round to the foot of the Sassenach chimney. By now it was dusk and we thought it would be chaos in the chimney and just below it was very overhanging, but I knew a traversing line above the great roof of Sassenach leading to the clean-cut right edge of the cliff. My kletterschuhe kept slipping about and I was climbing like a stiff and I put in two or three tips of pitons for psychological runners before I made the 50 ft of progress to peer around the edge. But it looked a good 200 ft to the shadowy screes at the bottom, and I scuffled back in half a panic out of the frying pan into the chimney. Then two English voices that were living in a tent came up the hill to ask if we were worried. We said we were laughing but what was the time, and they said it would soon be the middle of the night, and when we thought about the 700 ft of Sassenach above and all the shambles round the side to get to our big boots sitting at the bottom of the cliff, we thought we would just slide to the end of the rope.

So I went back to the edge and round the right angle and down a bit of the wall on the far side to a ledge and a fat crack for a piton. By the time Dougal joined me we could only see a few dismal stars and sky-lines and a light in the English tent. Dougal vanished down a single rope while I belayed him on the other, and just as the belaying rope ran out I heard a long squelch and murky oaths. He seemed to be down and so I followed. Suddenly my feet shot away and I swung in under the great roof and spiralled down till I landed up to my knees in a black bog. We found our boots under Centurion and made off down the hill past the English tent to tell them we were living. When we hit the streets we followed our noses straight to our sleeping-bags in the shed, leaving the city night life alone.

The next Sunday we left a lot of enemies in Jacksonville and took a lift with the Mountain Rescue round to Fort William. They were saying they might be back to take us away as well. We had thick wads of notes but nothing to eat, and so we had to wait in the city to buy stores on Monday, and we got to the Hut so late that we thought we would house our energies to give us the chance of an early start in the morning. Even so we might have slept right through Tuesday but for the din of a mighty file of pilgrims winding up the Allt a' Mhuillin making for Ben Nevis. We stumbled out rubbing our eyes and stood looking evil in the doorway, so that nobody called in, and then we ate and went out late in the day to the big black Buttress.

This time we went over the shelves and up the hoodie groove no bother at all. It was my turn to go into the Corner. By now I had a pair of PAs. I climbed to the black roof and made three runners with a jammed knot, the piton and the wooden wedge and stood in a sling clipped to the wedge. Dougal's ledge was fluttering above but it fooled nobody now. At full stretch I could reach two pebbles sitting in a thin bit of the crack and pinched them together to jam. Then I felt a lurch in my stomach like flying through an air pocket. When I looked at the wedge I could have sworn it had moved. I seized a baby nylon sling and desperately threaded it round the pebbles. And then I was gracefully plucked from the rock to stop 20 ft under the roof hanging from the piton and the jammed knot with the traitor wedge hanging from me and a sling round the pebbles sticking out of the Corner far above. I rushed back to the roof in a rage and made a strange manoeuvre to get round the roof and reach the sling and clip in a karabiner and various ropes, then trying not to think I hauled up to sit in slings which seemed like a table of kings all to come down from the same two pebbles. I moved on hastily, but I felt neither strong nor bold, and so I took a piton and hammered it into the Corner about 20 ft above the roof. Happily I pulled up, and it leaped out with a squeal of delight and gave me no time to squeal at all before I found myself swinging about under the miserable roof again. The pebbles had held firm, but that meant I hung straight down from the lip of the roof and out from the Corner below so that Dougal had to lower me right to the bottom.

By now the night was creeping in. Peels were no longer upsetting, but Dougal was fed up with sitting on a slab and wanted to go down for a brew. But that was all very well, he was going home in the morning, and then coming back for a whole week with a host of terrible tigers when I would have to be sitting exams. So I was very sly and said we had to get the gear and climbed past the roof to the sling at the pebbles leaving all the gear in place. There I was so exhausted that I put in a piton, only it was very low, and I thought, so am I, *peccavi, peccabo,* and I put in another and rose indiscriminately until to my surprise I was past Dougal's ledge and still on the rock in a place to rest beside a solid chockstone. Sweat was poring out of me, frosting at my waist in the frozen mutterings flowing up the rope from Dougal. Overhead the right wall was swelling out like a bullfrog, but the cracks grew to a tight shallow chimney in which it was even blacker than the rest of the night. I squeezed in and pulled on a real hold, and a vast block slid down and sat on my head. Dougal tried to hide on his slab, I wobbled my head and the block rolled down my back, and then there was a deathly hush until it thundered on to the screes and made for the Hut like a fireball. I wriggled my last slings round chockstones and myself round the last of the bulges and I came out of the Corner fighting into the light of half a moon rising over the Northeast Buttress. All around there were ledges and great good holds and bewildering easy angles, and I lashed myself to about six belays.

Dougal followed in the moon-shade, in too great a hurry and too blinded and miserable to pass the time taking out the pitons, and so they are still there turning to rust, creeping up the cliff like poison ivy. Heated up by the time he passed me, Dougal went into a long groove out of the moon but not steep and brought me up to the left end of a terrace above the chimney of Sassenach. We could see the grooves we should have climbed in a long line above us, but only as thick black shadows against the shiny bulges, and so we went right and grovelled up in the final corner of Sassenach where I knew the way to go. The wall on the left kept sticking out and stealing all the moonlight, but we took our belays right out on the clean-cut right edge of the cliff so that we could squat in the moon and peer at the fabulous sights. When we came over the top we hobbled down the screes on the left to get out of our PAs into our boots and back to the Hut from as late a night as any, so late you could hardly call it a bed-night.

Some time next day Dougal beetled off and I slowly followed to face the examiners. The tigers all came for their week. On the first day Dougal and the elder Marshall climbed Sassenach until they were one pitch up from the Terrace above the chimney, and then they thought of going left and finished by the new line of grooves. Overnight the big black clouds rolled over and drummed out the summer and it rained all week and hardly stopped until it started to snow and we put away our PAs and went for hill-walks waiting for the winter. They say the grooves were very nice and not very hard. All that was needed to make a whole new climb was one pitch from the terrace above the chimney, until we decided that the way we had been leaving the terrace as from the time that Dick found it when we first climbed Sassenach was not really part of Sassenach at all. By this means we put an end to this unscrupulous first ascent. The next team will climb it all no bother at all, except that they will complain that they couldn't get their fingers into the holds filled up with pitons.

The above was originally published as an article in the 1960 *Journal of the Scottish Mountaineering Club*.[2] Geoff Dutton, creator of the 'Doctor' stories, had just taken over as editor when Robin submitted his work. Robin's mother kept a number of his letters to Robin, exhorting, cajoling, jesting, deprecating a too-barbed excess now and then, whilst a common addiction to punnery seemingly helped bond the pair. Dutton now writes:

143

I do not want it to appear that I feel competent to pontificate on Smith the Man off my own *bat*. It reads rather egotistically; but you did ask for *my* impressions of Smith – ie the impression he made on *me*. So it's excusable. And it's strictly on his writing, for that's where we clicked; & I had not long enough to know the rest of him – as so many regret. You will have collected Each Man's Smith; hopefully the many facets will come together, and apparent contradictions will season the mix into something approaching Life.

I first encountered Robin Smith as a bundle of closely-inked MSs sent to me when I took over from Dr JHB Bell as editor of the *Scottish Mountaineering Club Journal*. I had a sort of brief to bring the *Journal*, always a sensitive social indicator since its inception in 1890, up to date. It was the beginning of the 1960s and a great wind was shaking the walls of established institutions like the SMC, flushing out both climbing and societal norms. Bell himself had opened windows when he began over twenty years before, and understood. He told me that Smith, one of these wild young men, had promised me something for the *Journal*. It was up to me to get it.

'Make it,' I wrote to Smith – in the process of getting it – 'as graphic and dynamic as you like.'

He did. 'The Bat and the Wicked' arrived two months later.

The apparently puerile titular pun served to cock an urchin snook. I groaned (as I was meant to). But what followed was an intensely serious and disciplined composition. Further snooks were cocked but always with a purpose. I was entranced. The right thing at the right time.

From this very beginning, Smith's style suggested to me an inner strength, delighting to break through the disguise of an apparent disorganisation – whether of narrative, teetering icefall, or casual public behaviour. He seemed much more than a wild young man. Shortly afterwards, I met him in the flesh at an Edinburgh bar, with the inevitable chipper to follow, and then the usual seedy flat. From what I remember, he stoked the conversation, playing no overbearing part in it, but whipping the hoop along, a ribald but essentially detached observer. Several times afterwards we came together, though never on the hill. His ancient jacket bulged with books bent back and thumbed by his powerful 'banana fingers', as Marshall called them. I found him in the Union one day stuffing down soup, Eliot's essays open beside him at 'Tradition and the Individual Talent'. Appropriate enough.

He deeply respected Tradition. He was fascinated by old climbs, old climbers, old climbing journals, old clubs. Tradition reinforced, as Eliot observed, the sense of his contemporaneity. And – a further point from that essay – it ensured a continuous extinction of his own personality: his climbs and articles were quite free of self-advertisement, any brandishing of *me*. His writing remained objective, refreshingly free of mateyness and pleasantries, formalised, yet mock-pedantically adorned with wordplay and puns (which he explained to me patiently or impatiently in numerous letters), and flagged with hilarious extravaganza – like the whoops which punctuated his climbs. This basic restraint of the artist contrasts with the effusions allegedly 'inspired' by him in others. Tiresomely unnecessary expletives and school-bus bawdy are absent; he calmly achieves his most cathartically black effects without a single oath. But these effects were built up by brains, imagination, wide reading and sheer hard work; he would sometimes write me several versions of a sentence, before its rhythm satisfied him. I had to wait the last deadline of Press Day. Just as he would surmount a slippery pitch, testing and towelling it while his companions froze.

As contributor, he was the antithesis of other brilliant climbing writers, like say, Tom Patey, who sent in chaotic and barely legible script, sometimes contradicting itself – hilarious and uncomplicated prose, but requiring much putting in order, often indeed carrying a plea such as 'do what you can with this!' Smith forwarded meticulously crafted contributions and jealously and rightly guarded them from editorial meddling; occasionally we sparred over minor clarifications I considered necessary for the readership – a literary tournament we relished, for the two of us shared the same zest for new forms and grips of language. Though kind and considerate himself, his simplest and most innocent-looking sentences were carefully shafted barbs and stings, obvious only to textual obsessives like ourselves.

It is because we both enjoyed – or suffered – this passion for literary experiment that I have presumed to write here on Smith at all. I never had time to find out much about him personally. And of the great sweeping climbs he created or followed so effortlessly, I appreciated only their gusto, and that from afar; I was physically incapable of grasping their subtleties, their first difficulty threw me off. But in his writing, we moved together; and never more so, I think, than when I published (or republished, they being mostly written for our old *alma filia*, the *Edinburgh University Mountaineering Club Journal*) those of his stories which first appeared to a wider public *post mortem*. His dark grin was ever present then.

Would he have developed further as a writer? Of course he would, with such talent, consciously exploiting tradition. His last letter to me, from some tent in the Pamirs, sketched, with a fine understanding, the characters of his companions. He was reaching out. The closing sentence stays in my memory. Indeed, I can only quote it from memory: by an astonishing accident, I threw out with the rubbish, when I retired as editor, all his letters – which I had kept in a separate envelope even more carefully than those of Bell, Patey and suchlike giants. No doubt the shade of Smith, powerful as ever, arranged this mischance: for he hated well-intentioned scavenging around the untransmittable centre – from which he fashioned his climbs and his writing. As far, then, as I recollect, his conclusion ran: 'I must stop now, it's getting dark, the paper's finished, and my pencil is only half an inch long.'

Robin's efforts on paper and rock enthused others too. In 1979, twenty years after the first ascent of 'The Bat', by which time Dougal Haston had also been killed, a film (also called *The Bat*) by climbing cameraman Jim Curran. It has been shown regularly to moun-taineering groups around Britain since and became generally available in modern format in 1997.

Curran, who had approached Robin's mother for her blessing for the project, kept in touch with her about the progress. 'During the days spent camped under Càrn Dearg Buttress,' he wrote of the film's shooting, 'we all felt very close to the spirit of the article and hope that the film will do justice to the men, the climb, and the magnificent writing ["The Bat and the Wicked"] that inspired us in the first place.'

19

OLD MAN JAMES AND I

The winter arrived and in February 1960 Smith teamed up with Jimmy Marshall for a week on Ben Nevis. What followed was to be the most written about and analysed goldrush ever in Scottish winter climbing. Conditions were superb, whilst both Smith and Marshall were at their physical and psychological peaks, and well aware that they were creating history. Both wrote articles on the climbs and these too have become part of the legend. A welter of routes, The Great Chimney, Minus Three Gully, the superb Smith's Route on Gardyloo Buttress, and Observatory Buttress, all new and all hard, were climbed on consecutive days. There followed the second ascent of Point Five Gully, a seven-hour romp achieved in far better style than the original, multi-bolted, five-day siege conducted by Ian Clough the previous winter. A well-earned rest day was next for Smith and Marshall, featuring a marathon 20-mile hill walk, pub crawl, arrest and return to the hut by midnight. The final two days saw a return to exploration with Pigott's Route on the Comb, and the gem of the week, Orion Direct, one of the finest winter lines in Scotland. This climb more than any other by Smith and Marshall captured the spirit of the week, and the imagination of Scottish climbers for decades. Orion Direct ventures through similar terrain to Smith and Holt's Orion Face,[1] and may be no harder, but, more than any other winter route of the time it was Alpine in both scale and conception.

(John Inglis writing in 1993 about the most momentous week in the history of Scottish mountaineering.)

Lines like Orion Direct and Smith's Route were far ahead of their time, their level of difficulty such that there were to be virtually no attempts at repeat ascents for over a decade. Even today, in fact, the advent of vastly improved gear has in no way prevented them from being amongst the most sought-after climbs in the whole of Scotland.

News of their success spread fast that February and Robin soon found himself in receipt of a note from WH (Bill) Murray, a senior figure in Scottish mountaineering circles, whose role as a pioneer of new routes had been constricted by the exigencies of war, much of it spent in a Japanese prisoner-of-war camp:

> My congratulations on Point 5. To my mind, that is the first ascent. Nothing in Scottish climbing has stirred me so much since 1937.
> PS – I have dropped a similar note to JRM.

Murray was in effect telling Robin and Jimmy Marshall that he discounted the relevance of the ascent of Point 5 the previous year when 900 ft of rope was used for a climb that took no less than five days. Uncertain of which 1937 event Murray had in mind, however, I contacted him for clarification. Murray confessed that he did not know either! I reminded him that his own ascent that year of Garrick's Shelf on the Buachaille's Crowberry Ridge was subsequently referred to as a prototype of modern ice climbing. 'But I'd not have made a reference to it in writing to Robin,' he said, adding that a wayward pen might have put 1937 instead of 1957, when Patey, MacInnes and Nicol made a memorable first ascent of Zero Gully in five hours. 'I must have meant Zero in '57, but it's anyone's guess. The slip of the pen might have occurred from a mental cast-back to Garrick's? . . . One of life's mysteries,' he chortled.

The much respected Murray wrote in 1964 that history is made by individual men, small in number, who have ideas and the vigour to put them into effect.[2] Those who had done most to shape the recent history of Scottish climbing were, in his opinion, Tom Patey, Jimmy Marshall and Robin Smith. This they had achieved not only through their climbs, but also through their great influence on others, he believed:

> All of us who have done long new routes know how greatly the times can be reduced on a second ascent. Psychological barriers are down. Hesitation's gone. We know what is wanted and do it faster. The same thing applies from one generation to another – as we have seen it happen in Scottish winter climbing. It will happen again. A sobering thought.

Murray, who died in March 1996, met Robin only once, for just a few minutes as they were walking in opposite directions between Altnafeadh and Lagangarbh, when they exchanged a few civilities before passing on their ways:

My immediate impressions were: (1) that I liked him, (2) that he had a strong personality, and (3) that like nearly all young climbers he beheld his elders with a certain irreverence. I too at his age felt that men over thirty had one foot in the grave. A view that time evaporates! But I could tell that he was already destined for the world stage.

When Robin's account of the week's climbing, 'The Old Man and the Mountain(s)', came to be published, David Hughes as editor of the *EUMC Journal* misprinted the title by including the 's'. 'Looking back,' he says, 'I must have been rather unimaginative not to have detected Robin's play on the title of Ernest Hemingway's popular book— just one Sea sufficed his Old Man. Things then took a turn for the worse. The whole article was republished in *Mountaineering* magazine complete with mistakes, much to Robin's displeasure.' Which he did not conceal as he swung into action with a letter to the magazine's editor:

> How is it you have been so discourteous as to publish an article written by me without ever asking my permission? If I had been asked for, and had given, permission, then at the least I could have corrected misprints. In your reprinting, I have counted thirteen misprints. Not all of these appeared in the *EUMC Journal*.
>
> You claim to be 'indebted to the EUMC for permission to reprint this article'. I presume therefore that one D. Hughes said it wouldn't matter. Last May I explicitly told you that I strongly objected to the reprinting of my article in any such magazine as *Mountaineering*. I know of at least one BMC officer who knew of this objection. I cannot believe that you had no knowledge of this objection. Apart from Hughes, no member of last year's EUMC committee was approached for permission. That committee demitted office last June. As from then, Hughes has not been a member of the club, let alone a committee member, let alone journal editor. As from then, the position of journal editor has been held by myself. No member of this year's committee was approached for permission.
>
> Thus it appears that no person holding authority in the club, let alone in the journal, was approached for permission. Further, I believe that as author of the article, I hold the copyright rather than either the club or the journal editor.
>
> I believe that your magazine sells at 2/- per copy. My fee for submitting articles to such magazines is 5 guineas, and I will be pleased to

hear from you as soon as possible. I will not object if you deduce 2/- to cover my complimentary copy of *Mountaineering*.

The outcome of Robin's letter is unknown. The erroneous title, however, was set on a course of self-perpetuation in reprints . . . until now:

The Old Man and the Mountain

Old Man James and I on a Friday night in February went to the Hut halfway up the mountain. Stackalee and Typhoo came as well because Typhoo has a car and needed someone to climb with. All nine days long the moon grew big and round and all the big black Ben was shining white. On Saturday we had breakfast for lunch and went and climbed the Great Chimney on Tower Ridge. We shambled up soft snow slabs, then I went up a pitch of Chimney with my eyes on the crux, only the rope just sort of stuck when I was just below it, so I made a belay and the Old Man went and fought it out sitting in a sling under an over-hanging chockstone and pressed on to the crest of the Ridge below the Little Tower. I dropped my ice axe, so when I reached the top I fixed a sling and abseiled back down the Chimney into the gathering night. I was right at the end of the rope and had to let go with my bottom hand and the ends were just sliding over my shoulder when I came upon my axe. The Old Man, who is very bold, went solo down the crest of the ridge and came upon terrible difficulties in the moonlight, but in the end we got to the hut for a big brew.

On Sunday we made an early start in the wee sma' hours of the after-noon, only I forgot my axe and had to go back for it and we were quite late starting up Minus Three Gully. I was scheming for the crux, so I took a belay and James went up in nice ice grooves into a great ice cave. I climbed halfway up the back of the cave and through a hole in the curtain of ice and out on to the face of a terrible icicle, but here there were great jugs ready to be cut and places to bridge and you went up no bother at all and the next pitch was longer and harder and I had to sit and gnash my teeth while the Old Man led through. We came out on to the Northeast Buttress ridge and wandered up to the Plateau and down by diverse routes screeching at the moon.

By then our transport had left for the big city but chosen men of the Mountain Rescue came up to the Hut to train for a week with lots of food. The next day we were really late because I was hunting my ice axe

while the Old Man squatted at the foot of Tower Gully hurling oaths at
the Hut. In the end I thought, we won't climb two at a time if it gets
steep, and I went up the hill without it. We went to Gardyloo Buttress.
The top half is split by a couloir which was pouring vast waves of ice
down the middle of the steep bottom half. James went up an ice groove
on the right and made a peculiar piton belay, and settled down for a real
deep freeze. I hacked away up and left over the icefield for 90 ft till I
came upon a bit of rock probably on the line of Kellett's summer route.
By then it was going dark and I couldn't think whether to go straight
up or go to the right or look for a runner or look for a belay. I tried all
four and picked on the last and put in two pitons so that they didn't fall
straight out and threaded a sling round a bit of snow in a crack and said
I had a belay. But the Old Man is very wise and analysed my tone of
noise and decided I was shattered and using a manky belay to pass the
buck so he sat tight. Then I dropped the axe. It stuck in the ice on top
of an overhang 5 ft below and I crept down to pick it up in a sweating
terror of kicking a bit of snow on it. At least you might say I had a runner
now, and so I decided to go up and right across a great barrel of snowice
strangely shaped and leading nowhere evident. The top six inches were
crusted snow and no use to anyone. I had to use our monster ice piton,
knocking it in as high as I could and using it for balance while I cut steps
and pressing on until it was down about my knees and pulling it out and
putting it in again. Then I dropped it at the biggest bulge and it disappeared into the night. That meant I couldn't go back, unless (as it were)
out of control. Then I lost my grip of the axe and it started somersaulting
in the air with both my arms windmilling trying to grab it and my feet
scarting about in crumbly holds. Somehow all was well and I came to
an ice arête below where it still cut away into vast overhangs but above
the angle fell back one or two degrees and I went up till the rope ran
out just as I came into moonlight on the snow at the foot of the couloir.
The Old Man was moaning in throes of misery, but he came up on his
knees groping for steps in the moonshade and led through easily to the
plateau while I took a piton hammer belay. We shambled down Number
Four Gully and I found my axe.

I was still exhausted the next afternoon so we went up a wiggly line
of snow and ice grooves on Observatory Buttress for about 600 ft until
it gets very easy where Good Friday Climb comes in from Tower Gully.
Nothing very exciting happened except that Old James got the crux.
We slid round into Tower Gully up to our stomachs in powder snow
and we got back to the Hut almost in daylight.

On Wednesday we were monstrously early; we were up by halfpast eight, but the weather was manky and thawing at the Hut with bits of rain and sleet. But around ten it faired up, so we struggled out of the Hut with stacks of gear and this time wearing Duvets and went to Point Five Gully and here conditions were great. The first pitch was a doddle on snow-ice; what took time was finding cracks for piton belays. James led pitch Two, an ice wall very steep for 20 ft. Then I went up a groove to a great boss of ice, but here you could stick your hands under the boss and away up behind it and clear the gap running round it on the right and semi-layback on the snow above. I pressed on up a chimney full of evil crusted snow and took an axe belay at the side of the gully. Then the spindrift started drooling down, and just as the Old Man spread himself halfway over the boss of ice it grew to a hissing torrent and piled up on his great stomach and pushed him out from the ice while he clawed away for the holds and through the tips of his gloves. It seemed half an hour before it ran dry. The next pitch was beautiful, a long funnel of ice, mostly vertical but just curved enough to let you bridge. Then the gully opened out and we charged on whooping through swirling clouds and pools of moonlight to the plateau.

In the morning there was mist and a big wind. Around midday we attacked the slopes of Càrn Mòr Dearg, with lots of pounds in our pockets and no map, whistle or compass. We went into the fangs of the wind over Aonach Beag and all the Grey Corries to Stob Choire Claurigh and round to the Spean Bridge Hotel. Shortly we took a bus to Fort William for fish suppers, only Hell's Kitchen was shut, so we had to turn to drink. They threw us out at nine o'clock and we walked a bit and thumbed a wee car and here it stopped and two great policemen leaped out and arrested us. They took us away to the Station and put us under a bright light for interrogation by a grim circle of sergeants, but it was all a mistake, something about dominoes, and they let us out for the last bus past the Distillery. We beetled up the path and entered the Hut on the stroke of midnight.

The next day it was foul and cold and we were feeling ill, but in so far as it was the Ben it was good weather and about two o'clock in a state of disgust we felt obliged to heave our way up the mountain. We went up Pigott's route on the Comb, from bottom left away up right to the end of a tapering shelf of snow, then up a short fierce chimney and long ice grooves, and along the crenellated crest to the Plateau. We tossed a coin for the chimney; Old James won.

Overnight the wind died and Saturday was so fabulous that one o'clock found us under the Orion Face. Between Slav Route and Beta Route a great tumble of ice fell out of the Basin to the foot of Zero Gully. Even the Old Man recognised he had had his share of cruxes, so he offered me the choice and I chose the first because the third looked terrible, but here the second turned quite hard and the third was a wee doddle. It was all fabulous climbing, 500 ft of ice to the Basin, then over the snowfield and out on the right by iced slabs, and next thing I found myself belayed below the Second Slab Rib of the Long Climb and the Old Man was turning it by a great pitch on the right. Then I went by iced slabs and he went by iced slabs and I went over a snow-field and we found ourselves into the night with the moon hidden in clouds, below the final towers at the crest of Northeast Buttress with 1400 ft of climbing behind us and the perishing Old Man in the lead again. Above it looked drastic; I just saw murky white overhangy shapes and a shadow sidling very slowly through them. He couldn't really see more than 10 ft, and he hadn't a clue what way to go or even if there was a way. First he wandered leftish, but 100 ft without any runners he came back right and sent all his rubbish thundering down on my head while I froze from cold and terror and thought about the twenty-four points of his crampons. When he got up I had to follow through a maze of grooves and bulges and icicles groping for holds that had all filled up again and taking double-handed pulls on the rope. We battered up snows to the Plateau and back to the Hut for a final feed.[3]

Late in the Sunday afternoon I ran my pack over the CMD arête and the lowest pass in the Mamores for a lift on the JMCS bus from Glencoe to Edinburgh. James went down the Allt a' Mhuillin and round by the road on his thumb, but then he's getting old.

References to the pair's encounter with members of the Fort William constabulary will not have passed unnoticed. Rumours have been bandied about over the years about this incident – with a notable lack of fair-mindedness, it always struck me. Rather worryingly, however, I came across this letter to Robin from the Fort William Burgh Prosecutor:

You are charged at the instance of the Complainer that about 9.00 p.m. on 11 February, 1960, from the Argyll Public Bar, High Street, Fort William, you did while acting together, steal one set of Dominoes.

Had that Jimmy Marshall character led him astray, or something? What now? It was then that I uncovered Robin's reply dated February 27th:

James R. Marshall and myself have received a complaint at your instance. The facts are as follows. In the Argyll Bar where we had both been drinking, I by way of a weak joke stuck the dominoes into Marshall's rucksack and thereafter found it impracticable to remove them without becoming in such difficulties as have in fact arisen.

I had not thought about it very hard at the time, but I am fairly certain that the dominoes would have been returned before we left Fort William since they were of no particular value to us. We are sorry to put the Polis and the Court to trouble, but as you will see we did not have any criminal intention and there was no pre-meditation or conspiracy. I do not know whether this amounts to a plea of Guilty or of N.G. to the charge as it stands, but we can assure the Court that such an incident will not occur again.

To which the Prosecutor replied:

When the case against you and JR Marshall on a charge of theft was called at today's sitting of the Court, it was agreed to adjourn same until 14th April 1960 at 11.00 a.m. when your letter pleading guilty will be considered. Marshall failed to appear and a warrant has been granted for his apprehension.

I asked around. A number of people were pretty shaken. Marshall could, for all people know, still be on the run . . . [4]

20

JIMMY MARSHALL LOOKS BACK

An architect, born ten years before Robin, and held in high esteem by his climbing peers, who have long called him 'The Maister', Jimmy Marshall remembers Robin well:

I first met Robin Smith as Archie Hendry's protégé on a meet to the Etive Slabs at which he kept a very low profile and even seemed surprised that our geriatric group could derive entertainment at all, let alone by exploding beached Brasso cans on the large driftwood fire. In retrospect, I know it was an early indication of his independent nature and innate good sense in avoiding the undue influence of the more dominant climbers of the time. He couldn't have been very impressed, for we wasted the whole day climbing grassy rubbish to the left of the main slabs, totally missing the fine exposure of the great routes which make climbing there such a unique experience.

Robin was an avid collector of information right from the very start, initially quizzing Hendry, then climbers chanced upon during trips, for any available new route data. His development over those early years was rapid and intense, not specialised insularly as a crag-rat but nurtured by a potpourri of naïve outings over mountain terrain in all types of weather, summer or winter, climbing whatever, wherever, with whomsoever chanced to fall under his spell, often inevitably on his own. In this he was fortunate, unhindered by preconceptions, and blessed with the intellectual capacity to analyse the character of his companions and the fears and reactions provoked by primitive struggle. His self-reliance enabled him to embrace the specialised demands of new ascents with a maturity beyond his years. Robin's independent initiation did, however, produce strange results, in that he would take excessive time and trouble on some climbs reputed to be 'hard' – almost as if trying to make it difficult – then he would put up a more difficult new route of his own without trouble.

His natural ability to climb rock was quickly apparent. His style was not that of a 'cruiser' but, rather, he displayed a limpet-like ability to persist at a problem for great lengths of time: a major feature of his first ascents. When I came to repeat his routes, I was often amazed at what he had held on to for so long. On Aonach Dubh for example, my brother Ronnie and I did the girdle from Ossian's to the 'barrier' in fast time but, when I saw the pitch close at hand, I abandoned the climb. Well, next day, Ronnie, laid-back, 'almost horizontal', they used to say, sat on the ramp for nigh on five hours managing the ropes whilst Smith grappled with rock and conscience (about levels of aid) before making the spectacular 40-ft ascent. This tenacity is typical of today's climbers who, whilst they climb at much higher standards, do so with considerably reduced risks, which probably evens out the relative standards of achievement.

As he matured, Robin quickly gained confidence and changed from the quiet, inordinately shy boy I first knew. As with climbing, he was a fast learner but, having known him since he was a boy, I could always detect in him a shyness, a vulnerability, an innocence. No matter how tough he might have appeared to some who knew him solely as a climber, and not well, a gentle and sensitive nature was at the back of his unbounded enthusiasm. This brought out the protective streak in some of us, perhaps not quite how those who got his back up found themselves reacting, for he could be a real terrier towards anyone he considered pompous or officious. In some ways I knew little about Robin, as he rarely talked about his background or childhood and I have since wondered if those brought up away from their parents tend to keep things close to their chests.

Robin was fortunate to arrive on the scene when he did. He knew this – he was very conscious of the history of mountaineering and aware of recent developments from which he was to benefit directly as an heir. During the five years prior to his arrival, Lancastrians Joe Brown and Don Whillans had set new standards on rock, standards we Scots were in danger of failing to match. The Creagh Dhu, with climbers such as Bill Smith, Cunningham, Noon and Walsh, made regular trips to the Lakes and Wales to sample these Whillans–Brown routes. In turn they applied those higher standards on their own new lines at Arrochar and Glencoe. This Creagh Dhu roll produced a host of fine climbs, which Robin used for 'finishing school'.

He was then able to set his targets higher, eventually taking over and spearheading the way forward. This was an exciting time when the strong nucleus of talented climbers who frequented the Glen most weekends were quite prepared to team up outside normal associations on grounds of mutual convenience. This was the gateway to Robin for, as in most things, he was an original thinker. It wasn't long before the extra dimension he introduced inspired a fresh wave of activity and, with it, a further host of young climbers. Without doubt, he raised himself into the highest echelons of climbing to become as good as any climber in Britain.

Robin's natural ability on rock did not transfer to the medium of snow and ice with the same ease, understandable in that step-cutting methods in those days required a fairly long or intensive apprentice-ship to acquire the skills to read the subtle variations of ice and angle, so essential before one could 'motor on' in winter conditions. However this didn't stop him trying and, just as on rock, he had the eye for the quality line. This knack led him to try the gully on Meaghaidh I named after him when he failed, an emotive reaction on my part in response to his 'impertinence' in attempting such a route with so little winter background. The jibe, however, did act as a considerable spur to his burgeoning ambition thereafter. Of course he returned this favour by naming one of his rock routes Marshall's Wall after I had failed to brass the crucial moves. In retrospect, it's quite a good ploy to impress one's name in relative perpetuity in the annals of our sport.

Even whilst coming to terms with the esoteric demands of winter ascents, Robin nonetheless made impressive progress and, within as little as two winters since the Meaghaidh incident, made his fine ascents of Comb and Orion faces. As with rock climbing, of course, he had before him the example of the older generation of protagonists. The Aberdeen and Glencoe factions in particular had been pursuing new thresholds at considerable pace, and Robin appreciated how they recog-nised winter ascents as one of the most satisfying expressions of extreme mountaineering.

Coinciding with Robin's coming of age in the climbing sense was the emergence of the Currie Boys – Dougal Haston, Eley Moriarty and Jimmy Stenhouse, guided by my brother Ronnie. Even though the Currie contingent had climbed no more than a few Munros – and even fewer named climbs – they had developed quite an advanced ability on their local railway walls and bridges. They were a breath of fresh air on the Edinburgh scene. Their drive, raw keenness and talent made an impression on me, so I took them to local crags for encouragement and even saw them as potential partners for myself. Soon I was plying them with suggested routes, some of them unclimbed. This helped advance their abilities rapidly and it was not long before they were performing, on rock at least, to a high standard. Suddenly I had an abundance of suitable partners.

Dougal and Robin became excellent friends, if not so close as Dougal and Eley Moriarty who, near neighbours as children, had been great buddies even before starting climbing. Certain credence has been given to animosity or friction between Smith and Haston, which is entirely misleading. They were always close friends who enjoyed a good deal of climbing and, even more, socialising together. The misunderstanding possibly arose from a degree of reluctance to climb together, in that the role each played within the partnership might in due course be misrepresented by others, much as had already happened with the Whillans–Brown partnership down south. They did of course have a bust-up after Dougal failed to turn up in Grindelwald for an assault on the Eiger in August 1959, the month before they climbed the Bat together, and it may be that the soured relationship alluded to by Robin in 'The Bat and the Wicked' – with tongue in cheek, it has to be said – created an erroneous impression of animosity in the minds of many who did not know them. I can't understand why Dougal did not set the record straight in his book, *In High Places*. Robin and Eley also climbed a lot together, and got on very well.

The climbing styles of Robin and Dougal were very different. On rock, Robin tended to be canny and not fast, with a great ability to stick with a problem until, in his mind and perhaps hours later, it was resolved. By comparison Dougal, also talented, threw himself into things with remarkable abandon and came off now and then. Apart from a couple of peels when he climbed the Bat with Dougal, the mature Robin didn't come off, even on his new routes, as far as I know. Without harness or helmet, peeling was no cushy thing. Certainly I was never keen on it myself, but it didn't bother Dougal a bit.

In my mind there is no doubt that Robin had a considerable edge. This was obvious on rock all along, but it was not until later, and Robin's 'ice bogey' overcome, that it became the case under winter conditions. 'The Winter Week' with me was perhaps all Robin needed to give him the confidence to move onto a higher plane.

While the Currie Boys regularly sought guidance and advice from me, Robin was strongly independent. When it came to planning new routes, not only did he scavenge information from all and sundry, but he used his own eyes and instinct to detect lines no one had thought of. Shibboleth is a first-rate example of this. Nobody had 'seen' that line, perhaps his finest and still an absolute classic. When one considers the number of top climbers theorising over and debating the chances and means of forcing a route up a particular face in that era, it is remarkable for the concept of any hard new line to be envisaged and accomplished by one and the same person.

But not all of Robin's new routes could be classified as his own original ideas – the Needle, for example. Often the candid 'theorising and debating' about possible new rock routes made for exciting times as to who would be the first to get there. Robin, of course, had more than his share of success in this as well. Not only did he climb as often as almost anyone else, but he could rely on a blend of innovation *and* ability beyond that of talented contemporaries.

The ideals and brotherhood of climbing filled both Robin's sporting and social life. In this, of course, he was not alone. It applied to everyone in our so-called 'team', to myself until my proclivities were diluted by my willing and rewarding ascent of the altar steps, indeed to everyone who was part of our climbing network: my brother Ronnie, the Currie Boys, the Creagh Dhu lads, with whom we exchanged social visits during the autumn, after summer had passed but before the mountains had a chance to come into winter condition – in fact, almost every climber who was in the higher echelons of the sport. We had some wonderful times together, both on and off the hills.

However, it wasn't all decadence when the autumn monsoons hit the Highlands. Most weekends in those pre-climbing-wall days were spent climbing gloriously illicitly on Salisbury Crags. Impaired by hangovers from the Saturday parties, performances were not that brilliant till the brewer's haze wore off, but the chat was good and ideas were conceived of rock and ice climbs on northern cliffs when they came into condition. Parkies then had no Land Rovers or walkie-talkies and only patrolled the lower roads – on scooters. Otherwise it was Shanks' pony for them throughout the park, which left us time between their visits to enjoy the rocks and develop skills on little test-piece eliminates or greatly overhanging traverses a few feet above ground from where, should a parkie make an unexpected appearance, one could step off and pretend to be a geologist. Confrontations occasionally occurred and names were demanded. The name of Bill Murray was the most frequently offered, though not always accepted.

The use of Hunter's Bog as a firing range by the Territorial Army was another source of irritation in the park at the time, as one of our favourite crags was in the firing line. I well remember one officer with a somewhat Sandhurst voice ordering us to remove ourselves from the area but the lads, naturally reluctant to comply with such an unreasonable and arrogantly put request, pranced about on the crag, mimicking baboons, telling him across the 150 yards or so, to go f . . . himself, whereupon he unleashed a patrol, rifles and all, up the hill to roust us out. We whisked off in all directions to appear on sundry knolls, yodelling and taunting the aspirant soldiers as they floundered amid the unforgiving gorse below whilst we, their tormentors, wafted like smoke over the hill to the ice-cream parlour in Newington for yet another binge of Coupe Jacques (at something like 1/6d a throw), then the inevitable debate whether to continue on to the Pentlands and the 'bona fide' havens winking on their far horizons.[1]

Around February each year I usually spent a winter week in the Highlands but in 1960 I was engaged to get married in the March and it occurred to me that the comforts of the marital state might dull my appetite for mountain asceticism. Therefore I'd better do some of the routes I had in mind, lest I fall by the wayside, so to speak. I canvassed around for a kindred spirit, to be met by little enthusiasm. Then, out of the blue, Wheech [Smith] volunteered. I was taken aback for, though we were good friends, he had over the years more or less shied clear of me as a rope-mate. But the thought intrigued and, despite a little concern about his pace, I agreed. It turned out to be a great week: stable weather conditions with a couple of mini-thaws to set up good conditions, generous snow- and ice-cover, and we were fighting fit. We were both using ten-point crampons and short axes.

Robin was his usual disorganised self, dropping or forgetting things, so I spent the first two days swearing at him but, knowing I was given to this habit, he simply grinned like the Cheshire cat and climbed on. He went on and on about Gardyloo Buttress, which I confess to have thought of then as trivial, and acquiesced only to get it out of the way. The icicle was always his intention but, though intact, its formation didn't look good for step-cutting attempts. At least that's what I argued and bullied him out of it – I didn't fancy holding him and a ton of ice on a manky belay. As it was, his superb lead over the upper edge proved at least as problematical and unsafe, but it did demonstrate that a new level of face-climbing was possible, and we were lucky enough to have perfect conditions and the time to exploit the situation to the full.

From then on we unified as a *real rope*, almost telepathic in understanding, rarely needing to converse on ensuing climbs on how or where to go. Everything fell into place naturally. The remarkable enduring friendships which evolve from partnership of a rope are a constant source of amazement and one of the great rewards of memorable struggles on the mountain walls of our youth.

Not that we were silent, far from it, for the Ben was at its most magnificent and as each exciting new vantage was gained, yet another dramatic vista would unfold, moving us to wild babbling eulogies to the Ben and tuneless songs into the void. The tempo changed on gaining the plateau, usually in filtered moonlight, whence we drifted down by diverse ways, awed by the light and shadows of the corries, enshrouded in the silence and tranquillity of the night, musing on the insignificance of our endeavour in the face of such profound beauty, till passing through the hut door into the world as we make it.

That week was another crucible for Robin. It was the perfect opportunity for him to consolidate, then hone, his snow and ice techniques sufficiently to let him move faster in difficult situations, with no reduction of confidence or increase of risk. In our short exploratory endeavours he had developed sure-footed, fast movement over steep snow and ice commensurate with the demands of such routes. Further, he realised that the limits of winter climbing on the open faces could be extended. This all augured well for the future of Scottish winter mountaineering.

Stimulated by the experience, we agreed to write it up to encourage the host of new climbers, inspired by recent advances made on rock, to take up the torch. Somehow, this never really happened on the hills and more than a decade was to pass before other climbers moved out on to the winter walls. Other than on Salisbury Crags, however, we never again had the opportunity to climb together. But Robin was in full flight, climbing here and in the Alps with various members of a very active élite.

When the Russians visited Scotland in the summer of 1960, Robin and Eley Moriarty struck up a very good rapport with their 'avant garde' and Robin, at his usual inquisitive best, was hooked by descriptions of the huge unclimbed 'Eigerwands' of their mountain ranges. When a return invite was issued, we in Edinburgh assumed that Smith and Haston, as the most proficient members, would be invited to represent the SMC. Of course, this was not the case, so I and, no doubt Archie, encouraged Robin to press for inclusion within the club element of the expedition. This he duly did, sadly with the success that accompanied most of his endeavours.

The loss was cruelly timed. He had achieved the fullness of skills on the mountain and was soon to launch on a philosophy career, all to be dashed on some mundane mountain in the Pamirs. I mourned his passing but, in ways, mourn the loss of his potential more, for he was poised to take Scottish climbing much further in quality and standard and to extend the same concept, through small-scale expeditions, to the greater mountain ranges of the world.

Smith led a full and vital existence, with achievement enough for any man. Nearly forty years on, I recall him as if it were yesterday and warm to the remembrance of his uninhibited joy in the freedom of the wilder side of Scotland's Bens.

21

THE MOSTEST FANTABULOUS

Sheets of flame reveal partner Wheech doing a dervish dance round the hut's mangled old stove; his fat-fingered fumble provides an amusing ten minutes of cosy reflection before the soothing hiss and familiar gloom swallow the hut. But thoughts of prolonging the horizontal are rudely thrust aside as his hacked and filthy visage, that could frighten lesser men, peers over the bunk to pronounce the day 'the mostest fantabulous' of the week . . .

As he gathers his senses in the CIC Hut on the morning of February 13th, 1960, Jimmy Marshall is already speculating on what fate might hold in store for himself and Robin that day on Nevis. Now that the weather has turned out to their liking, he knows they are set for a venture that could gild an already amazing week with an extraordinary climax:

An hour later, bellies filled with rich greasy omelettes and all goodies that happened within reach, we are toiling towards the tall white face of Orion, intent on making a superb Direttissima by the great ice fall which pours from the 'Basin' to the foot of Zero Gully.

By the time we have staggered to the base of the wall, the route is dissected into his and mine sections; so Wheech leads off, up a pleasantly fat ice slope, whilst I sort out the many slings, hammers and karabiners from the bag.

At 50 ft Wheech's tour had misled him onto a thinly-iced slab, where it was obvious he would either waken up or roll back down to the hut; his bow-legged bumbling at the foot of this great ice wall seemed as out of place as a can-can in the Swan Lake; however, by performing an exciting traverse of crampon scarts to reach thick ice, the rapid progress is resumed and a large ledge reached 150 ft higher; joining Wheech after being truly stung by his *mauvais pas*, we searched for a peggable crack with delayed success. The situation was magnificent: above us a great groove, rich with ice, swirled into obscurity; rightwards, Zero Gully took on the air of an escape route, whilst the great iced slabs to the left promised future 'joyous days upon the mountainside'.

Fully whooped up and anxious to reach the key passage to the wall which we both felt was somewhere about 100 ft above, I climbed over Wheech into the groove and hacked and whooped the way up over grand bulges, howking immense jug-handles in the ice; an ice column runner gave joy at 90 ft, then a little higher the angle eased, and a small hole under a rock roof 40 ft above promised security. Gaining this hole, I hacked away a curtain of icicles and squeezed in like a frightened ostrich, to manufacture a belay on an inverted channel piton in the rock roof; this didn't instil a sense of security so with an incredibly awkward manoeuvre the axe was driven into the floor and a cowardly sprauchle backwards performed to stand secured by slings above the void. Feeling brave once more I took in the rope as Wheech came on, babbling back and forth about character, quality and senility.

We were now at the question point of the route; to the right, the difficulties were obvious and in sight, whilst above nothing could be seen but a steep icy rib and a skyline begging the question; naturally the unknown appealed, so the bold climbing machine hacked away up and round the rib out of sight, but unhappily not of sound. A few minutes after he moved from sight, a horrible flow of oaths seared down the sterile slopes; I thought he was in a cul de sac, but no, he had climbed into easy ground, with the way to the Basin clear, and the share of labour too small for a step-hacker of Wheechy's calibre. With an added sense of satisfaction, I watched the rope snake out at an increasing pace and soon the ostrich act was repeated, as I removed our comforting anchorage. The climbing above was delightful and somewhat reminiscent of the slabs of the Crowberry Gully junction, but continuing for greater lengths.

A short wall above Wheech led onto a long snow rake, where a quick cramponing crawl brought us to the snowfield of the Basin. From a rock belay on the right edge of the depression, Wheech cut up an ice slope for 100 ft, then made an icy 50-ft traverse rightwards to belay at the foot of the Second Slab Rib of the Long Climb. Standing at the belay in the Basin I couldn't help recalling the last visit, when Patey and I had made the girdle traverse of Ben Nevis; there had still been traces of the Smith–Holt rope leading out by the 'V' traverse to the Northeast Buttress, from their ascent of the Long Climb one month earlier, which, unfortunately, owing to a lack of time, stopped short at the Basin. It was this sense of the unfinished that was partly responsible for our very presence on the face at the moment. However, Wheech was finished with the work above and I hastened to join him, where I was rather disappointed to find the rib above too thinly iced for comfort. An exploratory traverse 10 ft round the corner disclosed a well-iced wall, shining green in the evening light and perched over the now impressive drop of the wall beneath: 130 ft higher, the hunt for peg cracks failed in the gathering gloom of night and a belay in powder snow brought sharp edges of frost and fear into the struggle: Wheech came and went, swapping wet gloves for dry, trending left and up by shallow grooves, over treacherously difficult breaking snow and verglased rocks; night was fully launched when the rope ran out, but the moon stayed sly behind a blanket of cloud. Following up was like walking on eggs, the dark pit beneath our heels sufficient warning to take care; a short step of ice above Wheech led onto the high snow slopes which form beneath the terminal towers of the Orion Face. Here the expected respite failed to materialise; knee-deep and floury, they whispered evil thoughts, threatening to slide us into the black void and extinguish the winking lights of the CIC hut. Floundering up this snow, doubts plagued the mind; our original intention to spiral up rightwards round the towers lost its appeal in the face of such threat; perhaps a move left would bring us onto the crest of Northeast Buttress? But again the snow. Great shadowy forms confused the issue, so we persisted with the straight-up as being mentally the least trying.

A yell from above lit the night; Wheech had found a rock belay. A jumble of talk awakened vague morning memories of the face, then, by right of sequence, I deprived partner Wheech of his dry gloves, leaving him to fight the cold war whilst I tackled the obscurity above. A scrabble up a cone of snow above the belay led to a well-iced groove; it was necessary to feel the angle ahead with the hands, as up here everything was whitened by fog crystals and in the misty gloom distance was incalculable. Up above, there appeared to be an immense cornice; the thoughts of an enforced bivouac beneath the icy beak passed absently through the mind as I chopped away at the ice. About 40 ft up, the groove steepened to a bulge; finding the holds with the cramponed feet was extremely awkward at times, and often moves were made hanging from the handholds whilst the crampons scarted about in search of the 'buckets' cut below. Above, the bulge loomed more ominous, so a trouser-filling traverse was made onto the right wall, along a short ledge; then a frightening move, leaning out on an undercut ice hold, to cut holds round a rib onto the slab wall of a parallel groove. The ice here was only about an inch thick and moving into the groove was very difficult; the cat-crawl up the thin ice remains imprinted in the memory, for at this 'moment of truth' strains of an awful dirge came up from the Blackfoot 90 ft below, 'Ah kin hear the hammer ringin' on somebody's coffin . . .' Other ditties may have followed, but that particular one registered and stimulated progress across the slab to a comforting snow-filled groove, where the calf muscles could recover.

At last things were beginning to take shape; a large cornice at my level closed the top of the first groove, and above me was a steep wall, thick with ice. This looked the way and, having no desire to freeze, a short traverse was made up the thinly iced slab to an accommodating ledge; then the great hacking resumed. Strain on the back of the legs was becoming very trying, and I had to cut a deep step occasionally to stand on to relieve the calf muscles. I began to worry about the length of rope, feeling much more than 140 ft had passed; the thought of having to continue without a belay gave further chill to the night; then suddenly there was no more ice to cut, and in front a gentle slope catching the cold filtered moonlight shone in a heartwarming scene. Whoops of delight went down to thaw out Wheech, then up a couple of feet to discover the rope was out, a retreating belay from the edge as Wheech came up the snow cone enabled me to take an axe belay 10 ft back. It was grand to be able to sit down and relax. A whooping session began as Wheech came up in a series of frozen jumps, purring about quality and character. 'What a climb!' was our chorus, then his amorphous shape appeared over the edge, covered in snow, ironmongery clanking, like some armoured beast from the underworld. Gathering up the rope, we rushed up to the plateau, to arrive at the point where the Northeast Buttress branches from the summit plateau. Then stowing heaps of rope, slings and snow into the frozen sack, we pushed off across the misty plateau making for the hut, heat and the big sweet brew, occasionally stopping to howl into the night what a 'mostest fantabulous' climb we'd had.[1]

22

NIGHTSHIFT IN ZERO

The celebrated WH Murray thought that Zero Gully would never fall. The big, green ice overhangs looked too savage to the man who had probed its defences in pioneering forays before the Second World War put paid to all that. His way of thinking seemed justified when good English parties fell out of it in the early 1950s. Those and other failed attempts by Britain's leading climbers of the day, at a cost of no less than three lives, helped create an impression of impregnability.

When it did finally go, in 1957, it was to a party led by Aberdonian doctor Tom Patey in nailed boots. No crampons! It was the first of Nevis's major gullies to be climbed and was seen as an exciting breakthrough in winter climbing. Murray described the ascent by Patey, Hamish MacInnes and Graeme Nicol in only five hours as a truly great achievement in the history of ice climbing. However, their efforts did little to dissipate the feeling of awe its nihilistic name tended to inspire. In more pragmatic terms, it may have been the unrelenting high-angled ice of the first four pitches, a stretch with minimal protection regularly swept by avalanches of spindrift, that continued to deter repeat attempts – for a further three years, that is. Then, in 1960, the new kids on the block thought they would give it a go.

On March 21st that year, Dougal Haston was at the SMC clubrooms in Edinburgh sleeping off the effects of a night out on the town when another city kid came rolling in. Raring to get off to the hills, Andrew Wightman feverishly shook him out of a dazed slumber. Without further ado the pair were on the road, heading north to Fort William, lecture time a forgotten inconvenience of student life. That night they walked up to the CIC hut below the cliffs of Nevis.

The morning dawned icy, bright, crisp and full of promise for an attempt at Zero Gully's much awaited second ascent, when suddenly . . . panic and desperation. In their muddled rush to get away from town, they had forgotten the rope! Dougal Haston explains how the problem was solved:

The Hut was full of steadfast English muttering earnestly, up Three down Four, up Two down Five, and other Nevis Gully permutations, so we waited until they had departed and went scavenging for rope. Sure enough, there was a nice shiny one hanging on a hook. After swallowing a foul breakfast, we grabbed it and staggered up the hill feeling like junkies on a cure.

There was enough blue ice gleaming in the Gully to satisfy the aesthetic eye, but it was demoralising for arms whose only exercise for a month had been a table-to-mouth motion – of little use in the cutting of steps. Andy got stuck in a corner moaning the blues while I pecked miserably at the first pitch. I had done 10 ft in half an hour when he told me to get a grip and move, so I threatened to drop on him, putting twenty-four holes in his head in the process. That shut him up, whilst the slanging had warmed me up, and I charged up 70 ft within the hour. Arm exhaustion then reflected my inactivity in the city, so I decided to go down, have a rest and a sleep, and come back on the morrow.

The evening was full of hateful mutterings about black rope-stealing and bed-thieving Scots in a hut that was fully booked. We had just got to bed when a grubby Smith arrived. He made a brew and we talked of scoops, birds, parties, punch-ups, draught E, draught C, honks, ulcers and all the happenings of a city week, before Wheech admitted that he too had no rope. To be with-it in the Scottish winter you don't want to think about climbing till noon. So we slept on and waited to see what the afternoon would bring. When we did get up the nail-booted early risers of the long axe were long gone, leaving, as all good university clubs do, a selection of ropes for use in emergency. 'Emergency' was, after deliberation, equated to 'Scotsmen without rope', so a nice red-and-white one disappeared into the rucksack. About one o'clock we made a big effort and shambled up to the foot of Zero, past English parties returning from a good day's climbing elsewhere.

Fit from a holiday with Old James, Smith thought he should lead the first pitch, so we quibbled, tossed up, and he won. Andy belayed and I stomped around to keep warm as Wheech's middle name is not Speed. Two hours of Zero Gully on our heads later, he was 30 ft higher than the end of my steps of the previous day when a manky belay was announced. As we didn't want to leave him there I followed in a blue reverse, but was so shattered and icicle-like that I left him to lead the next pitch.

This was an evil winking little bulge which turned out to be a pseudo. Even Wheech, using my axe because it was better than his, managed to outwit it in less than half an hour. In fact, he got so chuffed that he battered my axe into the ice with such enthusiasm that the pick came flying past me and just missed the coat of ice which was the frozen Wightman in a great huff 'cause he had thought we were fast.

I shouted on him to come up. He shouted on me to come down and said he was going to untie, but by then his hands were so cold he couldn't undo the knot. When I pulled in the rope, I did it so fast that he had to run up the pitch, which wasn't bad for a wee boy on his second winter climb. Andy should be called Willie the Weeper for all the moaning he does. Sure enough, the manky belay set him off again, and I left him mumbling and grumbling to himself while I went up the bulge to curse at Wheech for breaking my axe.

We had a ten-minute session. Then I got the urge to lead and started up the next pitch. This got me gripped and eventually I stopped under an ice bulge leaving a line of buckets to salute an evening sun that was charging down with so much haste that it had forgotten to tell the moon to come up. Andy was brought up to Wheech and Wheech to me before he led through to the bulge. This was mountaineering at its wonderful best. The still, lonely silence of glorious nature in all its twilit splendour was broken only by the sweet schoolboyish voice of Wightman uttering foul vicious oaths and tirades against the certainty of the origins of his partners on the rope.

Wheech was up above, carving great steps round the bulge and rejoicing in the safety of my traditional ice-axe belay which kept popping in and out of its widening hole in the powder snow as if looking for the other half of its mutilated head somewhere down in the depths. Darkness fell completely just as he reached the top of the bulge, and Andy and I quickly followed up the line of potholes which would have done credit to any *Manual on Snow, The Climbing Of.*

On the first ascent the party had only taken an hour to climb from here to the top as all the difficult pitches are in the first 400 ft. We now reckoned on half an hour as they were all old men.

We sat eating Mars Bars and were all friendly again, or we were at least until only one torch was found in the rucksack, when we relapsed into the usual mutterings. Proceeding upwards through a waterlogged snow bulge made us all wet and more bad-tempered. For the next few hours we meandered around in the dark, keeping seeing great winking bulges and black evil rocks which forced us to traverse back and forth with no appreciable gain in height.

We then decided to go rightwards hoping to find Observatory Ridge. While scrambling round a crummy snow arête with belays at a premium, the torch beam suddenly caught a line of steps about 60 ft vertically downwards and to the right. This set us chortling again to the tune of great spark-producing leaps on the end of a pendulary rappel, eventually landing us one by one on large English-smelling steps. The rest was now a wee doddle and we stomped up fast to the windswept plateau.

It was all hell let loose up there. So we quickly beetled off down Four Gully in the dim light of approaching dawn to face court-martial for rope-thieving by the English dayshift.[1]

23

A MAN AMONGST MEN

With a great thump and thrashing of arms, the man threw himself onto the police officer, who appeared to lose all interest in Bruce and Keith and the open fire hydrants and turned his attention towards a more serious threat to good order. In due course, another constable arrived, and the fighting stranger – whose only offence was that he didn't like policemen – was dragged away to another place, Bruce and Keith being left, apparently forgotten, to fulfil their responsibilities to the guests from Scotland.

The time was now March 1960, the place the Oxford Ballroom in Newcastle, and members and friends of King's College Mountaineering Club, John Cheesmond reminisces, were busy showing Robin a good time. For some years it had been the club's practice to invite famous climbers to give talks: Peter Harding had spoken of great doings on gritstone and on the West Buttress of Clogwyn Du'r Arddu, Hamish MacInnes of climbs in the Alps, Himalayas and New Zealand, and John Cunningham of fierce things in Scotland and Wales. However, all was not quite right as Cheesmond, a King's College, Newcastle student at the time, goes on to explain:

> While all these evenings were exciting and memorable, the visitors obviously belonged to an earlier generation – in their thirties or possibly even older. But, as term started at the end of the Great Summer of 1959, it was apparent that there was a new star in the north, who took photos, could talk and – even better – was the same age as us.
>
> I had first heard of Robin Smith a year or so earlier, when a friend had returned from an Easter trip to Llanberis with many tales of an Edinburgh student who had been making fairly short work of a selection of Joe Brown's climbs. It must be almost impossible for climbers whose careers began in the 1970s or later to imagine the aura which surrounded the routes of Brown and Whillans, at least until the Great Summer. In addition, information about these routes, and about those who were daring to make subsequent ascents, was passed around in covert ways, akin to the workings of a secret society. To those who were

only on the fringes of this society – like most of us in the northeast of England – the thought that someone could visit Wales for the first time and climb the most notable problem, pulling over the top with a 'So much for the fucking great Cenotaph', inspired nothing less than awe.

Robin's reputation was reinforced for us a month or so later, when Geoff Oliver reported seeing him lead two new climbs in a day on the East Buttress of Scafell. Again, apparently, this was his first visit. Further tales of his first ascents in Scotland, and of the Walker Spur in 1959, plus a few chance meetings, resulted in an invitation to him to speak to the club.

He arrived from the train late on the Friday afternoon, in company with John, another Edinburgh student, who provided musical accompaniment throughout the weekend in the form of 'The Fair Maid o' Fyvie O!' Initially, both intended to return north later in the evening. However, after the talk – inspiring and humorous at the same time – and a few pints in the Union bar, plans were modified. They would stay at Keith Bancroft's flat, in borrowed sleeping bags, and on Sunday would go on a club meet to Crag Lough, then seen by us as the finest outcrop in the north of England outside of the Lake District. No worries about the outdoor gear. All would be provided from Keith's stocks.

In the meantime, the Oxford was the best place to complement our high spirits and round off a really good night out. During our meandering departure from the Union, Robin's attention was caught by a very attractive girl, whom he then approached. Unfortunately, she was attended by a boyfriend, understandably a little peeved, even belligerent – particularly when Robin offered him a five-pound note (his lecturing fee) as a possible exchange for his beautiful companion. We kept wary eyes on all this, while chatting and listening to yet another rendition of 'The Bonnie Lass o' Fyvie O!' But Robin was more than a match for the occasion and a credit to his course at Edinburgh. Before the debate was brought to a conclusion, a near observer detected what he thought were tears in the boyfriend's eyes as he sank to his dialectical knees. However, the conquest remained in the philosophical, if not moral, domain and, in due course, away we lurched, to new meetings and thrills at the dance-hall.

On Saturday, there was less drinking and singing, more eating and talking, as we discussed how the day at Crag Lough might proceed. By the time we arrived at the foot of the crag on Sunday morning, Robin had been provided with an old canvas anorak and a pair of Arvon's Lightweights – leather uppers and hard rubber Marwa Kletterschühe, and excellent up to Very Difficult on rough rock. John was having to

172

make do with the clothing in which he had arrived from Edinburgh, but was keeping his spirits up by humming a now-familiar tune.

Crag Lough forms the natural, grim and greasy rampart to the north side of Hadrian's Wall, much of it remaining untouched by the sun most years between July and the following May. With only a passing nod to the season and borrowed equipment, but with thoughts of Robin's reputation, the High Girdle of Central Buttress was chosen – Keith, although agreeing to lead through, expressing a good deal of concern. This was understandable as the route is 250 ft long and, at Hard Very Severe, was seen as a considerable challenge at the time even for local climbers.

We didn't know then that the form and texture of the rock of Edinburgh's Arthur's Seat was similar to that of the Whin Sill in Northumberland but, for whatever reasons, Robin was very impressive. He made rapid, if awkward, progress up the first crack, Sciatica, and from then on, the more open and athletic style of climbing enabled him to demonstrate his dynamic confidence – both to Keith and to watchers on the ground. This was most surprising, as we recognised that since the previous autumn, Robin's efforts on the hills had been devoted to lengthy plods and frozen epics with axe and crampons. In addition, we were aware that other well-known climbers had found the friction-free strenuosities of the crag rather daunting. On the other hand, we knew that they hadn't benefited from Keith's nervous, but encouraging, patter at the other end of the rope, nor been able to borrow and modify his comb into a hook in order to thread a tricky line-runner – significant bonuses enjoyed by Robin and, no doubt, contributing to his unfailing cheerfulness during the day.

The length and complexity of the climb and shortness of daylight meant that, by the time they completed the last pitch, it was time to go. But the journey back in the club bus was also notable for me as I spent most of it chatting to Robin, hearing amongst other things of Dougal Haston and the Currie Boys, and of his recent magnificent winter spell on Ben Nevis – the difficulties played down in the characteristic style of climbers, but with humorous insights and an enormous regard for the experience of Jimmy Marshall shining through. I can recall him saying that he learned 'a great deal' on that outing.

They didn't leave for home until the following morning. However, for most of us the partings – with the accompanying flatness of spirits – took place that evening. Naturally we didn't realise it then, but the recollections of Robin and the whole weekend were to last us a lifetime and, even now, any bar of 'The Bonnie Lass' serves to prick the memory. There were other meetings during the next year or so – in the Dolomites, the Lakes and Glencoe – and by the summer of 1962, I had been able to recognise some of the fullness of his exceptional abilities, not only on the mountains, but also in his writings and the quality of fun which imbued his dealings with others.

I heard of his death in the bar of the Kingshouse. It was front-page news in the *Scottish Daily Express* but, strangely for the Scottish press, my recollection is that the lion's share of the coverage was given to Wilfrid Noyce, no doubt reflecting his membership of the successful Everest expedition and his status as a well-established author. But sadness for Robin – combined with youthful anger and callousness – found this odd and unfair. Surely, in his forties, Noyce's day was past. Why didn't the journalists recognise what I felt was the greater loss? It may seem odd but, more than thirty years later, my feelings on this haven't much changed.

Geoff Oliver of the Fell and Rock Club was also in Newcastle that weekend and can still remember how Robin's eyes bulged with delight when he received his fee . . .

. . . as if money were something of a novelty in his world.[1] He was quite taken too with Newcastle Brown Ale and my impression that this was 'a Man amongst Men' was formed when he awoke on Saturday morning, picked up a flat, dead pint – a left-over from the previous night's revelries – and downed it in one. But he was equally impressive, and passed with honours, at the usual testing of visiting VIPs at Crag Lough. He said that he preferred to hear someone say 'Try this' with a demonstration, rather than 'Try that' and step back.

One February our Newcastle team spent a week based at the CIC hut in splendid conditions. 'Too good for novices,' Robin joked with us and later strolled off in his very worn ten-point crampons (no front points), one axe and minimal clothing, to solo Comb Gully, at a time when for most people it was a major expedition. The Ben was his home patch, a scene in which he was positively majestic.

I noticed too that the lads had renamed him 'Wheech', probably because it was more fitting to his character and role as a 'hard man'. But I was impressed most of all by the squalor in which they lived. Cooking was kept simple by using the same pot, which was topped up regularly but never cleaned. Three spoons seemed to complete their equipment.

On another occasion, on Scafell, two of my friends fell some 600 ft down Deep Ghyll in beautiful ice conditions. As we were evacuating the wounded, we heard two Scottish voices (raised in derision) from high up. I discovered later that it was Robin and Dougal, who said they had come to Cumbria to escape the crowds in Glencoe. They had climbed Moss Ghyll but – as it was 'only England' – they were sharing one pair of crampons and finished in the dark!

What an appetite for adventure! Robin even seemed to encourage epics by his approach. For instance, his first British ascent of the Walker Spur was made immediately after jumping from the train, with no attempt at acclimatisation, while, at home, he would 'give the mountain a chance' by his outrageously late starts.

Not everyone, however, looks back on Robin's extravagances with Oliver's uninhibited delight. There have been those who have critically interpreted some of his ventures as the deliberate engineering of 'epics' through foolhardy flirtation with the outrageous. 'So what,' retort his supporters, angered at the very idea of such negative thoughts about one so talented.

Clearly, Robin's penchant was deep-rooted and goes back to his days as a schoolboy when he had me climbing up and down this or that and tramping here and there in the dark. I just put it down to his not being good at getting going in the morning. But there may be more to it, as Dougal Haston suggested when he wrote: 'This was his challenge. He had to increase the challenge by climbing at night, in the wet or sometimes solo, often in bad conditions and always with the worst of equipment. This was the way he played the game.'[2]

24

AN ODIUM MEETER HIKES TO KINTAIL

Words bordering on the romantic in the university club's journal may have popularised Kintail with students of Robin's generation. For whatever reason, many including Robin held Kintail in gentle regard despite the lack of serious climbing there:

> Not for the tourist is this most beautiful country. It has all the advantages of isolation and if you find charm in the Scottish Highlands at all, then you will find it in full measure beneath the Five Sisters. Munros stretch almost from the door as far into the distance as any eye can travel and there is hill-walking in any direction, limited only by human energy.[1]

It was in this area to the north of Glen Shiel and Loch Duich, and no more than 20 miles from Skye that the club held regular Hogmanay meets. Whilst the students based themselves at their bothy five miles into the hills in Glen Licht, the Glasgow branch of the Scottish Mountaineering Club brought in the New Year at the local hotel run by climber Norman Tennent and his wife Mona. An experienced mountaineer in her own right and former university club member, Mona ensured that students were welcome to use the stables and barns throughout the year. When the Hogmanay holiday period began to draw to an end, students tended to gravitate towards the hotel before returning south. In this way Robin got to know the Tennents.

Robin and Norman corresponded regularly, and as they engaged in a game of postal chess, they exchanged mountain talk, particularly of the Karakorum in north Pakistan where an expedition was planned for 1963, with Tennent as leader and Bill Smith, Haston, Moriarty and Stenhouse the other likely participants. In the end permission could not be obtained. Norman's letters survive, and one of them reminds Mona only too vividly of her anger over arrangements: 'The Karakorum expedition was planned without my knowledge or agreement to take on sole responsibility for the hotel. Robin, of course, would not know this when he arrived, nor that Norman had been seriously ill and that I was trying to nurse him back to recovery.' When Robin turned up at the hotel Mona showed him to where her husband lay convalescing from hepatitis after two weeks in hospital. Within half an hour of his arrival, Tennent was out of his bed and the pair were heading for Glencoe! Tennent's letter discloses that Robin sensed Mona's displeasure, but discharges him of responsibility. On the other hand, Mona recalls that she had made the seriousness of her husband's illness clear to Robin, and it is not surprising that she considers him one of the guilty, although she did try to conceal these sentiments from him at the time. Mona can understand why Norman liked and admired Robin: 'Both put climbing before any other interest or obligation.'

She had met all sorts of climbers, some of whom believed that, while it was quite in order for a woman to do the cooking and generally to serve, they should not be expected to participate in conversation at the table. In Mona's eyes, however, Robin held a positive attitude towards women and was most personable and courteous. Her friend, Jean Thomson, then newly qualified as an architect, describes him as 'gentle' and 'charming'. Nevertheless, she also detected that he was well capable of being self-centred, turning up at meets with neither food nor sleeping bag and taking it for granted that others would feed and shelter him. Tipped off by friends about this practice and advised not to succumb to any pleas of hunger, she was amused by his 'rather sheepish waif-like act' when he did duly make an approach.

Keen to get away to the hills more often, Jean also attended the club's pre-weekend get-togethers in Deacon Brodie's pub. It was there that she began to hear of Robin's achievements:

> It was rather hard to relate this rather shambling, not apparently very bright character (my mistake!) with his growing reputation as a very hard climber indeed. Physically he looked quite unusual – short, stocky and amazingly loose-jointed; bandy legs; very long arms, with huge hands like bunches of bananas; a large head; and a lot of charm, which he knew how to use when necessary, combined with a shy, even sly, smile which at times verged on a 'foolish' grin.
>
> To say that I *climbed* with Robin would be far from true, although one Easter a group of us went to Skye in a parental mini-bus. Arriving

at Glenbrittle early afternoon it was generally considered a kind idea to 'take the girls climbing' before getting down to the serious stuff the next day. I can't recollect what we climbed, certainly nothing difficult, but Robin was happy to go along with it, took me up and let me lead through in his usual cheerful, good-natured, laid-back way. Next day we girls went off and enjoyed ourselves on something simple. However, the man who partnered Robin came back extremely shaken, saying he would never climb with him again as he was 'quite crazy'!

Later that year I saw Robin in action on some low-level crags in the Lake District, where he soloed a route so hard that even though we had a 'ringside seat' on an adjacent crag, we couldn't even see the holds he was using. Nothing special nowadays, but gripping stuff thirty years ago.

Did I use the word 'self-centred' of him? It's not really the right term, though it could have seemed that way to someone who was not involved in his world of total dedication to climbing. An enigma, certainly, and another word which keeps coming to mind is the Scots term 'fey' – not the 'doomed' bit (though maybe something of that too) but the 'eccentric, slightly mad, elfin' bit.

At Hogmanay 1959 David Hughes, who had partnered Robin on Yo-Yo, was one of the party staying at the Kintail Hut with others including Jean herself and Andrew Fraser of Shibboleth renown. Almost on the stroke of midnight Robin and a couple of others burst through the door with healthy appetites following a 'gentle stroll from Glenfinnan', 40 miles or so to the south, across some of the wildest terrain in the country. Immediately they were welcomed into the festivities. However, the revellers were not to know that the rucksacks of the newcomers contained little for the celebrations, and it wasn't long before people were looking around for missing items of grub.

Returning to the hut several years afterwards, Hughes found himself flipping nostalgically through the logbook in the hope of reviving memories of those halcyon days. Lo and behold, Robin had not only signed the book but, taking advantage of reflective solitude after the rest had left, had actually confided there his own account of that unforgettable gathering under the heading 'Memoirs of an Odium Meeter':

Thirsty-First: Snaked and lathered up from the Deep South. Wet outside. Sneaked Fraser's chicken from under his nose. He knows. Fraser's chicken. Fraser's foul but fowl is fair. We are the three whiches.

Food goes missing and all know it's one of which (but not which one of) three. Who'd go missing here? May as well get lost. Bloody boots. Iron in their soles, rough on the heels. Giggled at Elizabeth: 'We must drink to Pris.' Seen at not-ours end of pantry. Scene. Found lot of odium (Ours is Bare). Gave Hughes (singing songs) water bucket; went to his head, foul. Went to bed. Fights. (Put out songs; Hughes put out).

Thirst: Now sated. Many sored but few rises. Wet inside. Fraser the Teetotal wholemeal rich-tea twice-cooked two-bit deep-fry basket rose, phrasing, smelling of soap and tea rose totally vertical but thorny as a green horned toad so desiccatedly croaking that he would have been twice as much by the horizontal ones if they could have ris and would have got his chips and croaked and kicked the bucket that was going in his sleeping bag beside him. Also was he one of a prickly pear, two-biters-in-the-night. (His complement bit at we three whiches for abusing her Primus, but Fraser had her first. More odium.) The other leg of the Jeans was eating a ginger nut. There were too two cling peaches like an order to commandoes: 'Move in together in the dark and lie lo on landing and keep a grip and spread out in the morning.' I spread down stairs after noon and sat and got a cold looking at the sun on Ben Attishow.

Second: – wind. Back on our feets (of harms) Harma Virulenceque Canis. In the grip of odium. 3 Addicts we, foil to double, treble, trouble, multiply (sic), 8 times 4 are 32. Hate times for our thirty-two. We dog them. Are now each feeling still-a-bit-Grey-but-like-a-Dash-Hound. And so to the races. We fan our sickened wind of whispering fiction, spirit of competition, stir the pygmies and Amazons onto the Clownic Ridge. Go dog go. The whiches leap into BRM sticks and brm along the Ridge. The rest just sticks, we knew they would, it's no ill wind that bodes no glue; honking behind, like geese, with salt (25 Odium) on their tails. We go by saddle horse-shoe and all. The rest go bare-back, each fails even to end the Ride, id est. Blow home on the dying wind – oh, panefully. Even the ill hills have their phil. Go doggo, collapse into pits for feats on our backs for days and daze.

Third: Stirred.

Fourth, Fifth, Sixth, Seventh, Eighth . . . ? Some or other day is ris. I wonder where the bodies is. Gone with the wind. Caught even Strork slipping out of the corner of an eye. Migrated. Maybe I grated, they got cheesed off. Welched. Rabbited. Thus I have but now am won, am self undone, am left so lo, odium winds up, runs down, nothing to hate, nothing to rob, nothing bewares, no wind in my sales, have got windead, panting for odium, allodium exhausted, mine run dry, must get out or I will die.

<u>Nine . . . Teen</u> Squared Sun Sets To Wait.

Well, now we're all in the picture!

25

I KNOW A WEE LINE SOMEWHERE

Several Glasgow climbers shared in the development of Robin's new routes. Two former members of the Glasgow University Mountaineering Club once more find themselves immersed in Robin's schemes and dreams . . .

Summer 1959: At the end of a great week of hazy summer days, warm rock and superb routes two climbers gradually make their way up a long steeply vegetated ramp. Little clouds of midges lazily gnaw at their calves. Above them, at the far end of the cliff, lies an unexplored line at the edge of Pleasant Terrace. Its massive corner, blocked by a large overhang, beckons as they slowly get nearer. Robin Shaw has fallen for Robin Smith's chat about a new route on the north face of Glencoe's Aonach Dubh:

> Robin is ahead as we amble up the ramp under his magnificent Yo-Yo. The ramp steepens to a scramble, easy but exposed. Ahead of me Robin stops, looking upwards. I wait, light a fag, and look up at the possible route in the big corner. He moves up a bit, then down, then a few moves up and back to his ledge. 'Let's get the rope out,' he says. 'Pass me the end and get a belay.'

Nervously stubbing out his cigarette and uncoiling the rope, Shaw thinks: 'This has to be hard.' To his astonishment, however, Robin waltzes upwards without a pause. When Shaw joins him at the top of what turns out to be a steep but simple scramble, Robin laughs, shaking his head. 'Some chance we have with the real thing!' he blurts. (Not many have been in Shaw's position of witnessing Robin roping up for a Moderate.) Two hours later, and with Robin now functioning normally, they still haven't managed to solve the problem of getting into the corner – 'a bit like Hangman's on the Buachaille, only with the moves to the crack steeper and the 40-ft wall a formidable barrier,' warns Shaw. A rotten rib has to be passed and neither of them can summon up the bottle. With shadows purpling on the Aonach Eagach ridge across the glen, they give up, continue along Pleasant Terrace, and solo the top pitches of Shadbolt's Chimney in the gloaming, disappointed but determined to be back.

A couple of weeks later Shaw returned with a friend, managed to get over the rotten rib into the corner, and, with increasing confidence and excitement, led out a long pitch up the steep corner. Then at the belay, to his horror, he found an abseil sling. Someone had been there before but had obviously retreated. Thinking that the next pitch must be even harder, Shaw looked up in dismay:

> But hard though it was, it was much easier than the preceding pitch. What had happened? Could the next pitch leading to a large ledge be the problem, but it seemed straightforward? It was, and on the ledge I found another sling. It began to dawn on me as I looked up. A grass curtain reared about 100 ft, dripping and unpleasant. The climb was over and the best way off was by abseil.

On getting back home, Shaw received a letter from Robin explaining that he had done the climb the previous weekend with Haston. Shaw had not been available and Robin was apologising for having left him out. Rather than climb the grassy choss above the corner, they had abseiled off as Shaw had suspected. The letter continued in consoling tone: 'The climb had been enjoyable . . . We could give it another go together. And there's another good line I've sussed out.' Thus it was that Shaw learnt that he had made no more than the second ascent of a climb called Stook.[1]

On another occasion, on Nevis, Shaw and a friend were trudging up to the flanks of Tower Ridge in great conditions in winter. Only one other party was on the hill, sighs Shaw: 'So you can tell immediately it was in those halcyon days before you could drive from London for a weekend's ice climbing.' He had done a new route to the left of the Italian climb the previous day when he lost his axe at the end of a long, unprotected, steep run-out, attempting to lasso a spike of rock – fear and trembling getting the upper hand! They were looking for the axe when they heard climbers on Càrn Dearg opposite and, abandoning the fruitless search, went across for a look:

> It was Dougal Haston and Robin. When we reached the top of the ramp leading onto the middle of the buttress, Robin was sitting on a

platform with his characteristic grin. The rope inched back and forth as, up above, Dougal was trying to make progress on the corner of Route 2. He returned puffing and we sat around swapping stories. I was never as comfortable with Dougal as I was with Robin; sometimes in his company, Robin seemed to put on a mantle of toughness that was absent when he was alone. Today however, Dougal was uncharacteristically generous and suggested I have a go. Probably he had assessed that I wouldn't succeed and after about half an hour I came back, thankful to be off the steep verglased rock. Then Robin tried with no success either.

Haston set off again and this time, to their astonishment, having found a safe runner just below the breakout onto the slab, he took off his boots. Sure enough, his socks would hold better on the glazed rocks, but they all thought this a bit over the top. Naturally they didn't say so, recalls Shaw, adding that they just exchanged glances and continued chatting about other possible routes on Tower Ridge:

> Then shouts and curses told us all was not well: 'I've dropped a bloody boot,' screamed Dougal and minutes later was hirpling around beside us on our ledge. We stifled grins, but on the way down Robin mimicked Dougal's lopsided gait and kept breaking into cackling laughter in which Dougal joined once we'd found the boot.

Shaw also has vivid memories of a trip to Ardgour – of pouring rain as Robin and he lay in a tent below the cliffs of Garbh Bheinn. With water everywhere and the ground like a water bed, they talked philosophy while managing to keep philosophical in spite of a fairly major snag with plans. 'You bring the tent and the stove and I'll get the food,' Robin had said. 'We can divvy up after.' The problem lay in his having forgotten the food.

'It would have brought tears even to the eyes of a Stoic,' reflects Shaw. 'And I had trusted him, not even, to my regret, asking what delicacies he had in his pack before we left the road. So here we were with about five teabags, a few Knorr Swiss cubes and a packet of biscuits that had been festering in my sack for ages. But somehow I could never bring myself to be angry at Robin. It was just the way he was.'

By morning the rain had slowed to a mean drizzle, and they squelched their 'stiff damp underfed bodies' to the foot of the Leac Mhor which was living up to Robin's name for it – the Great Leak.

Recalling that they obviously had no guidebook and no idea of where the route went, Shaw asks:

> Would Mozart carry a guide to the composition of symphonies in his pocket? Up we went, and God knows where, over slimy unprotected slabs and vicious little overhangs. Irrepressible Smith held it together. With anyone else I would have said 'No!', and insisted on getting the hell down to the nearest warm pub. The only bit I remember in detail was when we were brought to a stop below a shiny bulge with a hold-less slab to its left. Robin managed to fix a sling on a rare spike and swing about 20 ft across the dripping slab to lodge in a crack. I think I just surfed over on a tightrope.
>
> Despite the prospect of no more than a couple of biscuits each for dinner and another day of wet desperation, Robin wanted to stay. But it was my tent and I wasn't playing, so we ended up at the pub at Corran Ferry, a pub suddenly tolerable in view of our deprivations.
>
> To his credit, after a pint or three, Robin didn't hold it against me for aborting the great Garbh Bheinn expedition. Some of my friends found Robin a difficult character. If some of their stories are accurate, he could be insensitive and boorish. For my part, I found him kind, thoughtful, unpompous and modest and I consider it a privilege to have shared some great times together.

Jimmy Gardiner, another Glasgow student at the time and now a head teacher in Dunblane, also has vivid recollections of Robin, no more so than of when they met towards the end of August 1961 at the Creagh Dhu hut, Jacksonville, in Glencoe. The weather was looking as if it might be on the point of taking a turn for the good. Robin was newly back from the Alps where the season had been bad, and was seeking an Eiger-substitute. Gardiner, himself with nothing better to do, was prepared to stay on at Jacksonville whilst everyone else returned to the city.

On the Monday it rained heavily in the morning and was only slightly drier later. According to Robin it was ideal weather for an attempt on the Buachaille's Carnivore, a route as hard as any in the glen in those days. Nevertheless, they headed in that direction about 2.30 p.m. Eventually they reached the top of pitch 2 in the early, wet and very gloomy evening and decided to abandon it. Given the weather, Gardiner was amazed that they managed any climbing at all:

In fact it rained every day except Wednesday, which was a good day, and that morning, with the immortal words – 'I know a wee line somewhere' – we headed down the glen to the west face of Aonach Dubh. I gathered that Robin had attempted it before since he offered me the early lead. However, I was unable to get round the nose on the second pitch which, I think, had been the limit of his own previous attempt. Robin led thereafter. I remember being very impressed, not so much by the difficulty of the climbing as by the exposure, particularly on the belay at the start of the last pitch. Robin again offered me the lead but I was sufficiently impressed to decline. The Big Top was soon in the bag.

Robin was a regular at 'the ville'. He might have known how to climb but he was a terrible card player. That said, he then managed to hustle me out of 50p in old money by beating me at chess after pretending to know little of the game. Since I later played chess regularly on a competitive basis, that was no mean achievement, I've since thought.

On the way to the pub that evening Robin was all for a midnight traverse of the Aonach Eagach. I've never been sure if he was being serious, but I remember being impressed by the boldness of the suggestion.

To Gardiner, and to many others too, it was already apparent that Robin was a climber with monumental talent, one who thought big and whose determination was truly irrepressible.

26

REBEL WITHOUT A CAUSE?

The 1950s was an exciting time for Robin and his contemporaries to be approaching maturity. With respect for the Establishment and its conventions already in decline and Youth discovering a voice of its own, it was an era that saw the coming of the rebel, with or without a cause: James Dean, Teddy Boys, Elvis Presley, Rock 'n' Roll. All along, however, some groups of young men had been able to flout behavioural conventions with impunity and get away with wildness that would have been condemned in others. Some young climbers jumped on the bandwagon.

Many of their actions were little more than mischievous or amusing. Gatecrashing the Chamonix Guides' Ball and Robin's purchase of a melon with refund money from a few stolen empty wine bottles can perhaps be regarded as examples of this. But more serious incidents did occur. One lad snaffled a chicken from a spit without realising how hot it was, to be seen running along the street juggling it from hand to hand. Another young climber snatched a pair of gloves on display outside a shop, only to discover that several were stitched together as a security precaution, and sped off with them trailing behind. Doing a runner (leaving a restaurant without paying) was commonplace. Once, a large tin of cooked chicken filched in Cortina was taken from the original perpetrators' bivouac before they could savour it themselves! On one occasion, Dougal Haston reputedly feigned a fit in a climbing shop with the help of some toothpaste while Robin exited with a rope.

So, over and above mischief, some of the younger element could be both antisocial and criminal, generally under the guise of larkabout. Most climbers, however, would not condone, let alone participate in, such ventures. The legendary figure of British mountaineering, Joe Brown, says that the only 'down' he had on Robin was his shoplifting in Chamonix with Haston. It further irked Brown and friends of his age group that the duo claimed to be poor students and 'philosophised' accordingly in justification. These older climbers called Robin and Haston 'a pair of little crooks'. Andrew Wightman:

> A coterie of the British climbers cultivated something of a grunge look, epitomised by Robin. The French, who clearly did not sleep in their clothes, who had sweaters with hole-free sleeves and duvet jackets without food or candlewax stains were the antithesis of this group and generally the subject of terrible vilification by our lads. From that standpoint it was no major leap to start taking from the well-stocked shops, the line of thought being that the businesses were clearly owned by mercenary Gallic plutocrats ripping off poor climbers. It was also a risky game that could be seen as reinforcing the hard-man, outsider image.

At home, abuse of climbing huts and a surly or sneering attitude towards older climbers was more distressing to some. An SMC veteran reflects that Robin was part of a bad lot who behaved like none before and none since. They left the huts 'in a right midden' and did not take kindly to suggestions that they show consideration for others. Two young climbers painted the Lagangarbh hut in outrageous colours, while money removed from the hut's electricity meters – by techniques allegedly taught by members of a Glasgow climbing club – was used either to provide free electricity or to enhance gambling kitties. Letting down others' tents was a Smith–Haston joke though they quickly became bored if their goading was ignored or if they were not considered objectionable. As time passed, however, such enfant-terrible ways moderated. Sheila Samuelson, for example, can recall no inclinations towards wayward behaviour during their 1961 Alpine season when she was in their company throughout.

Here is what Andrew Wightman has to say of the era during which Robin grew up as a young climber. Wightman, now a long-standing SMC member, probably knew Robin better than most:

> In the late 1950s in spite of heroic efforts by a few, the SMC (the main mountaineering body in Scotland) remained almost moribund and failed to grasp the opportunity to exert leadership with the goal of matching developments in climbing elsewhere. The young climbers instantly felt the frustration. Consciously or otherwise, they realised that, to achieve change, you needed to go to extremes. Depending on your position, they were either natural hooligans or iconoclasts. With hindsight, the truth is that they were both. Huts not booked and found

locked on arrival were entered, bunks were commandeered and their rightful owners either left on the floor or forced into some outhouse, and behaviour during a hut stay could be boorish.

Robin's background made him much more schizophrenic and often reluctant as a participant, but he was as committed as anyone once started on a particular escapade. Some of the loose-knit group Robin moved with simply had no qualms about stealing. Others rationalised their behaviour as protests against disparities within society or as rejection of conventional mores, though it has to be said that most of the group took no part in its more antisocial excesses. While there was much he disliked about the 'Currie' behaviour, it was marginally more acceptable than the then general attitude within the SMC. What was and still is surprising is that a strong character like Robin's was so influenced. The only justification he ever gave, which I am sure he never really believed, was that the stealing was from undeserving rich bastards and hooliganism was against an establishment that resisted any change.

Robin and I spent a lot of time together in the city, the mountains and vining peas in Kent. There were occasional alcohol-inspired boisterous acts in Kent, but no stealing. I also don't think that Robin ever stole when he was alone. You have to keep any thieving and antisocial behavioural excesses in context and I am an unreserved apologist. It was the exception, not the norm, and what little occurred did so over a relatively short period when Smith was not just pushing back climbing barriers but testing his own limits.

Why would such a strong personality as Robin's be part of, or follow, the crowd in a manner more usually associated with someone dominated by others or easily led? Gordon Greig:

It is commonplace that those who have shared hardship, danger, even riveting experiences, tend to form sodalities, to see themselves as a group even when those comprising that group are pretty rugged individualists. Thus the more extreme the hardship, the more shared the thrill addiction, the stronger the bond. Such a band of brothers may become a mini-mob, with all the paradoxes that entails, doing what few members would singly contemplate, whether in anticipatory excitement or in pent-up release. Individualists, as opposed to nature's loners, may have standard gregarious instincts and be disproportionately reassured to find that there are others somewhat like themselves, and come to place a high premium in being of their company. The more exclusive and elite the group and the more the teamwork is essential, the greater the bonds that bind, making non-conforming seem kin to petty treason. As with any mob, hot-heads dictate the flow and a misbegotten, finally specious, 'loyalty' prompts the rest to follow.[1]

Realisation that he was influenced by that trait, his individuality compromised, no doubt contributed to the schizophrenia identified in Robin at the start of escapades. Of course, he was different things to different people and, to David Hughes' mother, he was a very quiet polite and well-mannered young man, a view not untypical of how older women regarded him. Hughes himself, however, saw both sides of the coin:

> He did sometimes give an appearance of being other than that, as we all know, especially when he hung about with the Currie Boys. They were what we now call 'street-wise' and Robin was in this respect, as were many of us at that time, naive. He was experimenting with life, like all of us, Dougal Haston and the Currie Boys as well for that matter.

Haston publicised himself as working-class and portrayed Robin as privileged. Certainly, Robin's was a high income family until his father died when he was seventeen. It was a family steeped in the tradition of university education. His mother had an Honours degree in English. Robin did have advantages, and Haston had a point. How one regards being raised at a distance of several thousand miles from one's parents is another matter. Haston, son of a baker, was born and brought up in a Currie housing scheme. The area is, however, the opposite of deprived. It is neat, clean, tidy, respectable and close to open fields, even though it is very different from the tree-lined neighbourhood of bungalows where Robin lived.

When they first met in the summer of 1957, Haston was already part of a wild crowd bent on cocking a snook at recognised Establishment bodies. After getting to know Robin, his impression was 'that he often found it hard to shake the traditions of his good upbringing. He vandalised with the vandals, also part of the game, but I don't think his heart was really in it. He tried to steer a path on both sides.'

Seeing both sides of the track was undoubtedly a new experience for Robin after he left the sheltered environment of his school boarding house. This was a source of embarrassment to him, well illustrated when he and ex-army officer Graeme Nicol met at Lagangarbh not long after they had participated in the dramatic rescue on the west face of the Blaitière. Nicol was with army friends, Robin with Creagh Dhu climbers. 'After our previous meeting,' Nicol remarks, 'you might imagine we would be bosom buddies but in fact it was a very awkward strained atmosphere with Robin definitely preferring his Creagh Dhu companions.'

To an extent, Haston lived in the shadow of Robin. Academic progress apart, Robin's climbing abilities were rated higher in both summer and, in particular, winter, conditions. Then, after Robin's death, when memories of his powerful personality and intellect had become part of the equation, Haston's accomplishments were qualified as some instead wondered what Robin might have achieved had he lived. However, there was no such stumbling block abroad, where Haston went on to be recognised with willing acclaim.

Reactions towards Robin and Dougal Haston differ. While Robin usually tends to evoke feelings of gentle warmth, Haston is rather seen as the dour 'hardman'. Of course, Haston had a bit more time for his personality to develop (he died at the age of thirty-six), while Robin was still a very young man when he died, and only just out of university. In fact, the Haston Robin knew was both voluble and outgoing, though he became taciturn and intense as he matured. One person who knew them both put it that Robin's 'mature and *serious* approach to living' should be underlined, adding that 'he was not just a healthy animal like some, or anxious to *prove* something like Haston: he was an *explorer*, of rock, ice, and people and their culture.' As soon as comparisons are made, admiration in some quarters for Robin's talents draws to the surface a pejorative attitude towards Haston. That has led to Haston's intellect being unfairly dismissed. Moreover, some would prefer to believe that Robin would neither steal nor vandalise whilst Haston's deeds do not surprise them.[2]

While Robin's letters home, not written for public consumption of course, ratify that he was invariably considerate, responsible or deep-thinking, he too was deeply affected by a need to *prove* something, as his own diary about early climbing confirms. His experiences as a child may have induced reticence about his past too. Andrew Wightman and

Jimmy Marshall, two who came to know Robin as well as any, knew little of his background, and Wightman has no doubts that this was deliberate on Robin's part. He cites Robin's revelation that he had worn leg braces as a child at night to try to straighten his bandy legs: 'I often thought he regretted having told me that. He was a very private person.'

Despite his well-recognised rebel image, Robin was welcomed into the folds of Establishment bodies with remarkable consistency: prefect at school, SMC committee man (at twenty-one, the youngest ever), and member of Sir John Hunt's Pamirs expedition. During that expedition, very much an Establishment set-up in Robin's eyes, he nonetheless came to blend in with a group of men several of whom, in his estimation, did not merit selection. This is evidenced in a letter from John Hunt to Robin's mother: 'Your Robin was beginning to see that we older ones actually could climb, had done some noteworthy things and – the only important point – were people he could like and respect.'

As an SMC committee man, Robin represented Edinburgh's group of hard climbers and their supporters in a quest to wrest back influence, as they saw it, from a Glasgow clique of moderate climbing ability. Robin, by his own admission capable of being impetuous, was encouraged to get stuck in and, driven by a dislike of pretentiousness, was occasionally unfair in his efforts to knock people from their self-made pedestals. One veteran is still a little hurt that he was classified in that light.

In view of the warmth in which Robin is held generally, however, those he upset are hesitant to write of grievances. Another elder, still annoyed with what he calls behavioural difficulties in Robin, also refuses to put pen to paper. His beliefs run along lines that young men have leanings towards obnoxious or antisocial traits which almost all sooner or later lose. Robin, he feels, did not reach that stage. A woman climber, who wishes her remarks to remain unattributed, judged Robin this way: 'All I can say is that to me he was two people – the single-minded climber who probably at times was not a very nice person, and the young man who was so different in a non-climbing setting.'

Generally, however, Robin responded well to elders who extended the hand of *partnership*. Philosopher Willie Stewart and Brenva veteran Graham Brown are examples of those who offered non-condescending consideration. He respected them. The words of mountaineering father-figure WH Murray, written thirty-three years after Robin's death, are pertinent here: 'I *can* say of Robin that omens seemed to be good, that all men I respected thought so too . . .' Though he may have frustrated other older people, in reality he seems to have distressed few. More evident is the contrasting aspect of his character demonstrated in a letter to his Granduncle George in Australia in 1958:

I really am sorry that I have not written you sooner, but I persuaded myself that a recent crux in my work prevented me. Thank you very much for sending me that very valuable book, the *SMC Guide to the Western Highlands*. It is always a risk to send me a book on climbing, but it so happens that although I already have two of the volumes in this series I had very little knowledge of the one you sent and am taking pleasure in getting to know it.

The *Geographical Magazine* is also exceedingly interesting – I have never known the story of the Alpine Club, and one article on Persia describes a mountain range which I had already tucked away among ambitions.

I have read the varied snippets and articles you sent, and of course I have often heard elsewhere of your very well-known friend Dr Robertson.

I had never realised that you had been a climber yourself. The methods of climbing have very greatly changed since your time – nowadays we favour an 'Alpenstock' probably half the length of the one you used, and you may have heard vague mutterings about the pitons and étriers and complicated rope techniques which we use on the harder climbs. But the motives remain much the same, and I find a very deep and healthy force in the mountains.

We at home are keeping very well. Charlie comes through from Glasgow for most weekends, although of course he is working very hard for his finals. Marion too is busy – I hear her downstairs now, practising at the piano. I myself have recently started to play the clarinet. Our mother is at last beginning to bring the housework under control, and she is beginning to find rather more free time. She sends you her love, and says she will write when she can. With love from me as well, Robin.

Certainly, Granduncle George must have been unaware of any rebelliousness in his Edinburgh great-nephew. Robin's sister Marion, however, was as aware as any of her brother's foibles, although she too found that there was more than one side to him. Describing life in their Comiston Springs Avenue home where she, Mrs Smith and Robin lived from 1956, she remembers affectionately how Robin kept in touch so regularly by postcard or letter when he was away and how, after late-night study sessions, he often used to join their mother for long chats if she had not managed to get to sleep. When he was studying Robin tended to sleep during the day and stay up much of the night, and his mother and sister would sometimes waken in the morning to find strange constructions he had built in the small hours – books, pens and pencils, various orna-ments and all sorts of bits and pieces carefully balanced in elaborate and fantastic sculptures in the sitting room. When he was off to the hills Marion used to listen for his safe return, usually at some late hour as she lay in bed on a Sunday night, this despite him having been amused when she broke her scapula in a fall on Nevis! Robin was very keen on jazz and was teaching himself to play the clarinet, as Marion recalls: 'His chief aid to learning was to put on a record, and then play along with it – often excruciatingly! But he enjoyed classical music too. In particular I remember his liking Bartok's *Concerto for Orchestra.*'

She adds that Robin was a stimulating if unpredictable person to live with, tempting one to wonder how 'stimulating' the treasurer of Edinburgh JMCS might have found an exchange of correspondence with Robin. Here, an understanding of Robin's attitude towards authority and pretentiousness may give meaning not only to what has been said above but to a file of papers handed down from baffled club secretaries to their bemused successors since 1961. The point in ques-tion was whether or not members of the Junior Mountaineering Club should pay for the use of its parent club's rooms of which Robin was the appointed custodian:

> GJ Ritchie, Hon. Treasurer, SMC, members of SMC Eastern District Committee and myself are somewhat upset to hear from your Hon. Sec. of vacillation on the part of your Section Committee in regard to payment of stipulated fees for hire on several occasions of SMC clubrooms, projector, screen, bulbs, gas fires, gas cookers, electric fire, electric lights, library, floorboards, doors, bog, etc., and I would be greatly obliged if you could advise me of the true and veracious situation in this matter.
>
> Yours humbly,
> (Sgd.) Robin C. Smith
> Custodian, SMC Clubrooms
> Member, SMC General Committee
> Convenor, SMC Eastern District Committee

The angry recipient referred the matter to a likely sympathiser in the SMC who in turn protested to another member, applying sneer quotation marks to his comment that it had come from a so-called *responsible* official. Robin was sent a copy of the letter, which spoke of a disgraceful idea, of it being contemptible to charge a club with limited funds, of the scheme being beyond local powers, of the screen they had been asked to pay for being one the junior club had loaned, gratis, to the SMC, of a misguided attempt to poison relations between the two clubs, of the discourtesy of not first informing the SMC committee members who may also be on the junior club committee, etc, etc . . . Then came the threat of matters being passed over his head to the secretary or president, which drew the following response:

You can't spew the cud and have it. Your days of vegetable rumination are done.

Here are some home truths for your reception qua spittoon. These I submit to your unofficial capacity solely to void my rheum.

(On policies of Trade her Majesty's Government does not consult the paddle steamers that ply about the Channel.)

On your own precedent we now charge a guinea a day for use of the clubrooms. The clubrooms are self-supporting and a guinea is not contemptible. In proportion as acceptance of X is contemptible, refusal of Y is curmudgeonous. By way of concession we ask of the JMCS 3 guineas for one year of unlimited use of the clubrooms. (For fear of sophistries I will not list the amenities. Let us fixate on electricity. Does not the whole of your argument rest on a screen? This is a smoke screen.) I am sure the JMCS have done many things congenial to the SMC. For instance, they invite a representative to their dinner. So do the EUMC. So what?

Some weeks ago, Tiso wrote Douglas, communicating the decision of the competent body. He has had no answer. I met Douglas in the clubrooms, and inquired how matters stood. Information was withheld, beyond this, that discussion was under way at a higher level. Searching high and low for this level, I found nobody knowing anything of it. Therefore I wrote Clarkson and asked how matters stood. I have had no answer. (Let us therefore hope that the JMCS course of meetings has terminated for the season. For until they address themselves to me or to some proper authority, they also will void my rooms. Any SMC member introducing them will be required to lay down a guinea flat.

Squads of police are standing by. For they are aware that the person to be contacted regarding these premises is Mr Robin C. Smith.)

I am considering calling a meeting of the General Committee with a view to instigation of disciplinary action with regard to your egregious subversive super-rogatory and inexcusable conduct.

Yours gerontocidally,

Smith.

PS: You could always RESIGN.

Such a retort typified Robin's bolshie attitude towards those who flaunt titles (his own having been spelt out in mockery in his first letter) and at the power and authority they expect to wield. Consequently, the recipient is unlikely to have perceived him in the same sympathetic light as one of Robin's friends who remembers a chance meeting near the Royal Edinburgh, a psychiatric hospital where Robin worked for a short while after leaving university:

> What Robin told me really summed up his attitude to people in general. He found it very easy to communicate with the mentally deranged and adult patients who had remained infantile. Another climbing friend once said that Robin was the finest bloke he had ever met. I think that was true for us all. More than three decades on, it's still true for me.

Maybe that disgruntled treasurer could have better subscribed to Marion's lasting memory of her brother's nature – or at least to part of it: 'He was very lovable but could be infuriating.'

27

TALES OF THE FIESCHERWAND

Another June/July in Kent, another season in the Alps, and another British 'first'? Robin was no doubt scheming to establish that as an annual pattern after his feats on the Walker Spur and in the Dolomites the previous summer. His 1960 spell of work at Aylesford and Maidstone nearly complete and his finances again empowered, he informed his mother of developments:

> We have been working in the factory at Maidstone as soon as the peas stopped rolling in, for the cherry harvest is simultaneously at its height. There is a great hissing & steaming & pounding of machines all day long and often through the night, and a great milling of students & casual & regular labour, mostly looking for soft options. Dozens of hawk-eyed overseers, men in white coats & women in green, all with grim faces, set frenzied examples of industry & are eager to be furious. By contrast, at the Vinery, there is a constant body of some 35 students all sleeping in the one Nissen Hut & eating in the one canteen, & always the same local women working on the washers, the same fitters & odd job men, and over us as the only man in a position to command, the one boss whom we know as 'Sid' and who bears all responsibility. Everyone knows everyone & has a unique part, not so much like that of a nut in a machine. There is a much greater unity & purposefulness in the work, a great deal of co-operation from the students & much more efficiency than at the factory.
>
> Everything for the Alps appears to date to be under control, though problems can crop up in seconds. Either eight or nine of us will be crossing the Channel from Dover on the afternoon of Wed. 20th and making for Paris that night in the large Volkswagen 'Caravanette' Dormobile owned by Andrew Fraser's parents. Five of the party are already assembled and employed by Foster Clark's. Will be leaving here afternoon of 19th – but must presently go to bed since it is approx. 2 a.m.

Despite Robin's passport having gone astray the group managed to leave Kent as scheduled, first heading for Paris where they dropped in to Pierre Allain's shop on Rue St Sulpice. After sleeping the night on a pavement on the Versailles side of the city until woken by office workers at the start of the morning rush hour, they headed south for Grindelwald in the Bernese Alps.

Robin had designs on the Eiger, but it was the vast icy north wall of the Oberland's Fiescherhorn (13,280 ft) that first attracted his attention as a realistic option in view of conditions. Measuring almost two miles in width and, at its highest point, more than 4000 ft high, it is one of the very biggest Alpine faces. Riven by constant rockfalls and avalanches, that wall is seen by some as a dark, foreboding and oppressive place – an impression underlined by its situation at the head of a remote glacier and by the frail wooden cross on the approach erected in memory of those killed attempting the face.

The Fiescherwand was first climbed as long ago as 1926 and, although not often repeated until recent times, now carries a number of other serious routes. In 1960 none had received a British ascent. The route that was to be the subject of an article by Robin[1] takes the obvious spur – the Nordpfeiler – on the right (western) edge of the main face. It is out of the line of rockfall and avalanches and is, without doubt, one of the great Alpine classics. The difficulties can vary dramatically from season to season but, over recent years, it has been robbed of much of its icy shell. However, in the summer of 1960 the route was still in heavy winter garb, severe even by standards of the day. Robin and his colourful long-suffering climbing partner were to discover that 'step-cutting for 3000 ft and unpremeditated bivouacs before, during and after' were among the surprises that lay in store, as Robin wrote:

Goofy is a grubby fellow who lives in a sleep. Here is how he climbed the Alps in his sleep.

We drovedovertotheoberland under little Phraser. We were many and odd and odd, and therefore, smartly, doubleyoked and teamed in twos in furrows into the snows. The sleepy two-timed residue, Goofy plus two, sloped away last and so not least. Phraser and I, that olden team, had boldly struck out white wands well in hand. For ruminant idling little profits, we wander-lustily theorised. But alas describing the circles of the schools we carried each other away and passed a number of days circling base. But at last we opened our eyes and rose through the forests and snows to a desolate hut in a golden silence under the gleaming walls. But herd again from ober the land, here were all the many and odd, Goofy disgruntled with negative plus-two and nobody very positive and each aspiralling sortie come to nothing. Wherewith the well-laid teams of men closed in a scramble and set with the sun.

Out of this confusion Goofy and I turned up our collars and loped into the big night wild with stars. We nosed through moraines and crevasses and looming cliffs of rock and ice away up and round, and sat on the snow as the light came slowly, fumbling into bitter crampons under the long 'schrund of the Fiescherwand.

The North Wall of the Fiescherhorn is snow and ice and bits of rock, miles long by 3000 ft of climbing. The spur in the middle looked to be the best (but not the fiercest) line, for all the wall was quite plastered but less so out on the spur, with the angle a little less and the line more defined and less threat of loose stones or avalanches down your neck. Fiercely therefore leaping the 'schrund, we flung ourselves upon the spur. (Only first try, Goofy fell in the 'schrund, for he was half asleep, and so he stayed throughout this insomaniacal sortie.)

From here till the end of the day we were lost in the wrinkled humps of spur, shambling ribs and grooves and shelves, great bulges bald or bristling, sly sidlings round the sides, crusty snow and rubber ice and piles of crumbling rock, axes picking or hacking at almost every step, always threading, thrutching, balancing, bumbling, cunning, where to go, how to save, will it hold, will it go, with always the next bit of hump hiding the spur that lurked above, and awesome gauge of height-not-gained in views to left or right over the sweep of the vast ice walls of the Fiescherwand. And most of all, those slopes of ice too hard and steep to climb without holds, but dotted all over with inset stones from bigger than yourself to the size of your thumb; and saving hours of cutting steps, you plot a course from stone to stone, from tip-toe on one to leap for another, from scarty slab to thumbnail mantel, cutting maybe once or twice to clear the top of a stone, creepy-crawling heart in mouth and trying to push not pull. The ground went down, the day ground on. Huge slow hissing mists coiled around us. Unfit, ill-fed, necks half-wrung, we fluttered up with axe-arms flapping, until at last the spur hardened and reared into one last fearful hump. Sheer rock walls fell away to the right and a grisly couloir swept the left, leaving no ways round, and above the bulges piled out of sight and threatened a full stop; but a questioning scoop curled up and rightwards, and blindly we slow-wormed through its folds, champing and pawing at bits of ice as always the bulges thrust us right, and little white mice of panic whispered round the walls of the brain that the light was beginning to go and the scoop was going nowhere. Then we came out at 300 ft at an overhung ledge on the teetering edge of the spur, with no way up, and no way right, and was there, was there, yes there was, a spidery ledge swung back leftwards through the gloom over the bulges under an overhang onto the crest of the spur. By now the sun was buried and the last light going. With seized-up arms and rumbling bellies, we fumbled leftwards under the overhang past the one and only piton we found on all the climb to 30 ft of do or die on knees and elbows up the great hold of an over-hanging flake and round the lip of the overhang into a short steep icy groove which twisted up and right to a neck at the top of the last hump of the spur. And there above us a prow of snow soared the last 300 ft into the vast luminous cornice booming out of the night.

But here, as we broke the back of the spur, in us, too, something snapped. We hadn't brought any bivouac gear, because we had planned to be down in a day; and now that we were stuck for the night, we could have thrashed on to the cornice and burrowed for ever into the deep snow; but we hadn't eated any goodies all day long, so now all light-headed we just nodded around the neck, Goofy like a totem pole swaying in a dozent trance while I went round about in a mumbling delirium. The neck was a right-angled rock step, 6 ft horizontally and then 4 ft vertically, cutting into the profile of the narrow crest of the spur, but filled in with a triangular ridge of crusted powder snow, the shape of one of those crummy one-man tents. Abysmal steepness fell to the right, and the icy groove up which we had climbed twisted back down to the left into the bulges below us. A chill wind blew no good from the right, so starting from the top of the groove we hollowed out the ridge of snow till only the crust was left. There wasn't room for us side by side, so thoughtfully I stood aside for Goofy to sidle in and li lo. Then, classically bridged across the groove, seat on one bump of ice, feet on another, and nothing under my knees, and thinking of Goofy's toes turning black in the night, I took off my crampons and my drooling boots and socks and wrapped my feet in a spare jersey and put them all into my rucksack and knotted the sack into a great club. By now Goofy was asleep, but not for long, for seizing hold of him, heaving and shoving, I struggled by every mounting method to get myself into the one-man tent. But I couldn't get over his great knobbly knees, and all I came near to was demolishing the tent and rolling us over in a stotting clinch back down 3000 ft of steps. And so I reverted to the classic bridge, muttering unmentionable spells to hypnotise my knocking knees to lock in animated suspension between my back which slowly gelled to one spine-chilling wall of the groove and my great club-foot planted on the other with crampons, boots, socks, feet and jersey milling about inside. However, I was firmly belayed, to 300 ft of rope, lying in fankles under Goofy, sleeping again, grinning like life-in-death, and lashed to an axe thrust to the hilt through the crust of the far wall of the tent. And so the night rolled on, with Goofy like a pupoid grub while I wriggled in the open like an early worm, and all the while vulturous mists wheeled slowly around us, and sometimes, through them, lights, incredible as stars, winked from the lost world of valleys and resorts, and so till the ghoulish shrouded daylight rose again from the grave.

Then for half an hour, while Goofy rubbed his eyes, I chewed four tasty socks and two boots and crampon straps. When they could bend I battered them on, then we rose all weak and creaking, kicked our happy home to bits, and dragged up 300 frostbitten feet of steepening prow of deepening snow to inside the open beak of the biggest bit of the beady-eyed double cornice. We thrashed through the lower cornice, up to our waists in powder snow, folded under the upper cornice curling 30 ft outwards over our heads. But now that it was light of day, we didn't want to burrow for ever, and away to the right a break in the cornice looked like saving time. And so for 100 ft of rock-gymnastic nightmare, we bridged, straddled, chimneyed, lay-backed, mantelshelfed and stomach-crawled through convolutions of floating snow friezed by demoniac winds, along the tunnel between the cornices, through the break in the upper cornice, out of the climb and on to the summit ridge.

To the left, the summit of the Fiescherhorn called from swirling clouds on high. So turning right, we widdled off homewards. It was just a walk, but miles around, and mostly in the mist, with fleeting pools of sunshine, into which we belly-flopped for sleeps. Half way down we found another hut, and people, who fed us; and then we stopped for forty winks and hours later staggered on, and then a labyrinthine ice-fall trammelled us for hours and hours, and just one hour from home, night fell, all mist and dripping; and so for hours and hours we huddled in a sodden cave, with that inhuman fellow Goofy sleeping again. But daylight came, and we petered on, and there was the hut, and all the teams, and bits of bread, and down below there were cafes, with chandeliers and tailored waiters and menus as long as your arm, and bars; and as for Goofy, ever since, all he does, he drinks as well as sleeps.

FIESCHERWAND: THE TRUTH

With the thought that Goofy should be given a chance to give his version of events on the Fiescherhorn, I set about tracking him down in France where I heard he now lived. Here Goofy tells the story in his own words:

Dear Mr Cruickshank,

I'm partial to a bottle of Château Morgon '92 with my Sunday lunch and this normally puts me in the mood for a pleasant afternoon nap whilst musing over the past. Since moving over here to France life has been blissfully calm and all those stories about the Fiescherwand have been put behind me - until you happened to phone.

Let me remind you that no one is going to get away with reprinting that wheechy account of the Fiescherwand - not without me having an opportunity to give folks one or two facts. No way am I going to let some smart-arsed biographer publish all those fabrications and downright lies again without me telling the truth - the truth that people like you have kept quiet about over all these years. This, Mastermind, this is what you are now going to publish:[1]

* * *

Let me begin by going back to those heady days when a trip to Edinburgh conjured up the thrill of not only climbing on some old railway walls, but also the excitement of a city with licensing hours newly extended to ten, hand-jiving in dark-lit howffs, Bungey's dishy-dolly waitresses, late-late coffee bars (open till eleven!), High Street Wee Hairies, Leith Street bar patrons kickin-sassenachs'-heids-in (an ancient Pictish custom), multi-hatted welly-booted tramps, reekie stairway entrances, thrown-up haggis suppers, the Hall Bar . . . In a word, Edinburgh was where it was all at.

The city's off-beat climbing circles of that time, in which Robin moved, appreciated the good things in life. These, it was generally agreed, came out of three taps marked Light, Heavy and Export in an establishment in Teviot Place. Occupying the ground floor of an otherwise boarded-up tenement block, the premises had long been designated for demolition. The planners, however, had not reckoned on its landlord and 'vibrant' father-figure Willie McDonald. This impressively corpulent ingurgitator of Fountainbridge ales was obstinately soldiering on – his tremulous hands defiantly continuing to serve an endless flow of rattling pints for his small but appreciative clientèle of hoods, free-loaders, wasters, drop-outs and dossers.

True the place was perhaps a little primitive – dour, even. But Willie was not one to allow the tone to be lowered. It was here, on Thursday evenings, that the Spartan decor acquired an unusual degree of animation – Jack the barman busily to-ing and fro-ing a constant stream of glasses which our globular friend behind the taps was pouring for a meditative group huddled around a beer-soaked table in the room at the back. Who would have guessed that, amongst this heteromorphous group of way-out weirdies, here sat the cream of Auld Reekie's climbers?

And yet wasn't that shifty-eyed character with the twitch the man behind the theft of the Glen Etive cake? Wasn't it in his Currie abode that the suspected hordes of borrowed gear were almost certainly to be found?[2] And that well-groomed city type with the attaché case and clean livin' look – his every utterance and gesture greeted with the reverential deference worthy of an oracle? The awesome silence surrounding him was such that you could easily have been forgiven for thinking he was the Social Security Inspector checking up on skivers – except, that is, for the tell-tale scar on the forehead. No mistaking that incongruous septuagenarian sage in the middle, however: Thomas Graham Brown of Brenva, the bespectacled, porkpie-hatted, pipe-puffing professor – geriatric hard man.

Going on now to those with their backs to us, sinisterly hunched over the gargantuan piles of glasses littering the table. From left to right: the Baron, an extraterrestrial druidical hermit from the far side of the zoo out Clermiston way. Next to him, a cherub-faced mastodon with big fists, greedily scoffing his umpteenth pint of the evening and rumoured to have been involved in the disappearance of the Ben Nevis lead. And, finally, the group's weekend chauffeur: Typhoo-Piggy, more prosaically known to those who considered his climbing shop privi-leged to have their trade, but never in receipt of the discount commen-surate with this honour, as . . . 'The Pig'.

Oh yes, I almost forgot that rosy-cheeked youth sat in the corner, sweet angelic smile over his face, grubby hands clutching a half-empty glass, and wearing beer-stained stovepipe trousers plus tatty suedies long since worn through to new-look peek-a-boo style by city climbing. Wasn't he that drunken fellow seen sneaking past the cash register of that High Street restaurant, bulging inside jacket pocket dripping with greasy sausage, bacon and eggs, squashed in between a conveniently folded menu? Wasn't he that puking individual squatting on the kerb-side by St Giles, sheepishly feigning to ignore the horrified stares of well-bred uncle and aunt who had, unfortunately, chosen that very moment of intimacy to pass by? No, it couldn't be. But yes. Yes, it was. It was the man himself: pal Robin!

[. . .] During such evenings weekend transport was fixed, climbing partners arranged, projects discussed. Which all goes to explain how I came to be accompanying Robin on the sun-soaked slabs one Easter weekend in Glen Etive. It was there, for the first time, I saw Don Whillans in action. His simple unpretentious low-key style was the complete antithesis of today's glitzy climbing mutants. The *Whillans Bumper Book of One-Liners* hasn't yet been published, but when it is, maybe it will recount how he finally met his equal one sunny spring day below the Slabs. Robin was enjoying goading an increasingly fidgety Whillans about the bigger routes north of the border when:

Whillans, eyes narrowing:	'*Aye lad, booteet went yewlotte oo-pootooppe Sassenach ann Cent-urion*' (Leans back with barely concealed satisfaction at putting a cork in this Pictish heathen's blethering)
Batman Robin, in English:	'*Ah, but we then came along and did all the hard bits you left out in between*' (Cheeky grin)
Whillans:	'*!!¿? ! †P†? †Q††† †††††† †††* . . .

[. . .] A similarly arranged outing saw Robin at the CIC hut on a final visit to the Ben before leaving for the Pamirs. I had managed to tag along behind, although plans to rock-climb were soon foiled by an unseasonal freeze-up and fall of snow. The wintry spell left us wishing we'd left the rock boots and midge cream at home instead of our crampons and ice-axes. Never one to be put off, though, Robin began rooting through the odds and ends left behind in the hut for repair work. Hardly an hour later, we were proudly heading up towards the icy grip of Tower Cleft, brandishing a rusty old coal shovel and – what was undoubtedly the precursor to the dropped pick – a peculiarly bent door handle.

Such escapades into back-to-basics wizardry lay behind many of Robin's Pythonesque goings-on. One which particularly springs to mind is the rescue he carried out of a panic-stricken girl in a party caught out on Tower Ridge. In those days Robin was one of the few to know about the 'back-door' exit down onto the snow slopes of Tower Gully, and a growing storm was emphasising the urgency of getting them all off the ridge via this route. However, the prospect of learning to abseil in the dark and in rapidly worsening conditions had dramatically compounded this particular beginner's fear. The struggle that followed as he finally succeeded in getting the, by then, completely berserk damsel in distress off on the end of the rope into the swirling night void below was a scream. At least that's what he said, and I had to agree it must have been hysterical.

[. . .] Not that all weekends were spent on the hills however. Those were the days when the highlight of the climbing calendar was the annual exchange visit with a Glaswegian nihililst brotherhood parading under the name of the Creagh Dhu Mountaineering Club. During such weekends the SMC clubrooms – to which Robin, as custodian, had the key – were transformed into a convenient unofficial doss for his Creagh Dhu friends from the west. This had the advantage of having entertainment laid on down the stair at The Howff, folk-singing hot-club of the north. That is, if one was admitted, for this somewhat Presbyterian hall of music was the haven of the temperate, where nothing less than best behaviour was tolerated and the slightest smell of alcohol meant certain refusal at the door. Difficult conditions indeed. However, those who had managed the feat came back with enticing tales of the comely lonesome virgins frequenting this Calvinist club of the abstinent . . .

* * *

[. . .] *This now brings me to the bit where you, Mr Wiseguy, you said I could get my own back: The Fiescherwand!*

* * *

I've got a mate over here who, unlike me, is keen on long-distance running. He's been doing it for years. However, he keeps on saying 'Faut pas brûler les étapes' – which, roughly translated, means 'gently, gently or you'll bugger yourself up' [. . .]

Well, as we stood there like Lilliputian midgets below the soaring ice slopes leading up to that menacing headwall on the Fiescherhorn's north face my thoughts were not very different from those of this mate of mine. After all wasn't this my first ever Alpine season? Hadn't we just stepped off the Dover–Calais ferry only a few days previously? Weren't the climbing journals littered with tales of first-timers over-whelmed by the cataclysmic ferocity of the storms, the annihilating roar of the avalanches, the chilling whine of the stonefall, the sheer intimi-dating scale of it all? It was obvious we risked embarking on some-thing where 'Il ne faut pas brûler les étapes'.

A seductive line thrutched sensually up through that threatening headwall and the thought of tackling it was beginning to worry. However, Robin's gaze was already latched onto it, his eyes following each frost-shattered crack, each icicle-fringed overhang, each snow-banked ledge, each ice-choked chimney. [. . .] Preferring a less provoca-tive spur on the right, I argued for caution, given the wintry conditions, this being my very first Alpine route, us not being acclimatised, that the Teutonic Swiss barmaids were perhaps not so Teutonic as all that after all, that Willie McDonald might miss our trade, etc, etc. Such closely reasoned logic was the staff of life to someone like Robin, student of philosophy as he was. Neither Kant nor Descartes could have done better. *Der Nordpfeiler der Fiescherwand* was about to receive its first British ascent.

I can't really remember at what point the niggling voice began to gnaw away about the wisdom of having abandoned the Hall Bar for the Alps. Anyhow, by then we were being forced off to the left of the spur's flank, getting closer and closer to those terrifyingly exposed ice slopes. Thinking 'Christ, Robin's not going to take us out there after all!', that niggling voice was beginning to take on a decidedly persua-sive tone. Continuing leftwards would have been fine for the certifi-able, rabid nutters. Even regaining the crest, however, meant a bold and poorly protected run-out back up the spur's now-vertical icy flank. We were still hardly a third of the way up and it was impossible to see what lay above. Moreover, time was already beginning to tick by. Back home Willie would, by now, already be busy preparing for the first customers of the day. [. . .] Robin, in the meantime, had moved out

205

under the spur's flank, latching onto its gleaming carapace by his front points like an over-starved Highland sheep tick. Outside the Hall Bar, a small queue – seemingly entombed in funereal silence – would be gathering on the pavement. [. . .] Back on the spur where I was, in the cold comfort of my stance, it was obvious that it was getting really serious. And yet, only hours earlier, from down below, the spur had looked such an easy option: a north-face route with a tender soft touch, an almost friendly air to it. What had happened? Where had we gone wrong? Surely, if the Fiescherwand had had so few ascents, wasn't it more to do with it lying hidden behind its Eigerwand rival, stood full frontal to the Kleine Scheidegg voyeurs, than with any inherent difficulty? Had we simply strayed off route? Yes, that was it! Obvious really! Above we would find easier ground. Bound to be more hospitable there. Less ice, less steep. Plain as a pikestaff, when you think about it. Better get back to the crest quick. Just a slight hiccup this. Bit of a laugh really. After all, wasn't Robin planning this as yet another of his well-known text-book ascents: the sort I had heard were models of their kind, and that all who came back from climbing with him talked about with such knowing looks? Yes, without a doubt, our ascent would be quoted for years to come as 'a model of its kind'. Comforted by such reassuring thoughts, I settled back on my belay to admire Robin labouring away, arms and legs hammering away at the now-vertical ice below the crest, as if in the final throes of a convulsive fit. My mind, at least, was free to concentrate on other, less demanding, things . . . Hundreds of miles to the north, in bustling Teviot Place, the sound of stodgy fat fingers fumbling with the bolts on the other side of the door would be signalling an end to that doleful waiting. Watches would be checked, readjusted, wound up, put to the ear, shaken, tapped, banged, or simply smashed against the wall. [. . .] The door to Nirvana was about to open. It must have been about then that Robin, higher up on my left, finally managed to arrange some protection and things suddenly began to look better again. Back at the Hall Bar they would already be beginning to silently shuffle in one by one, in single file. You would have been forgiven if you had got the feeling that this was no ordinary group of devotees – a secret sect perhaps, or maybe even a bunch of Masonic tic-tac men? [. . .] A sudden tug on the rope announced that Robin had made it, safely belayed on the broad crest of the spur above. The thought of getting back to easier and safer ground was motive enough for me to throw everything at it, and, eventually, I managed to claw my way up. Breathing a sigh of relief, I joined Robin at the stance, the difficulties now over. It was, at last, possible to see what lay ahead. 'Cccchhhrist!!! Christ all bloody mighty! The whole f . . . . . . route's covered in ice! It's yards thick!!!' Angrily grabbing me by the collar, Robin wasted no time in tying me down with such a knot that would have got even Houdini wondering if he was going to get out of this one alive. Before I could shout *'Hilfe!'*, Robin disappeared up the following pitch as if it were the way to paradise. Dragging me up to the belay, Robin had obviously not grasped that, given the distance still left to go, it might just as well have been Paradise Lost and that, anyway, if I wanted to look for Paradise right now, I'd prefer, if you don't mind, to join Willie's clients in their quest for it. Nevertheless, the half-two closing time came and went, with Robin still out in front and going strong. Occasional sightings of a celestial cornice, still light years above, were, however, starting to drive home the disturbing reality of the Fiescherwand's seemingly cosmic dimensions. By the time the Hall Bar reopened at five, the spur was beginning to narrow slightly. Could it be that we were at last nearing the top and, hopefully, easier ground? Time was not on our side. Like Hall Bar patrons approaching 'Last Orders' we too had an eye firmly fixed on the clock. Light began to fade just before closing time. [. . .] By then, the spur was rearing up in a final jumbled mass of dark overhanging walls and chimneys, a bivouac now looking inevitable: a sobering thought as, of the two of us, only Robin had served an apprenticeship in the Scouts where they taught you to Be Prepared. How was I to know he hadn't even been awarded a single medal, let alone promoted to Patrol Leader? If he had, perhaps he would have made sure we were carrying whistle, compass, spare underpants and the various other bizarre accoutrements unfamiliar to such a fundamentalist mountaineer as himself. Not that a whistle or a compass would have been much use in the circumstances. [. . .] Defiantly refusing the obvious and struggling to keep a stiff upper lip, Robin said to be brave and not to go wobbly. Solemnly adopting a grave voice he asked me to continue on with him, up into the dark unknown above, adding that it would be 'do or die', 'women and children first', 'coûte que coûte', or something heroic like that. So he said. You could almost hear the stirring strains of 'Scotland the Brave' as we threw caution, dignity and honour to the wind and charged intrepidly on up into the night air, hands and knees, hit and miss, smash and grab, hand over fist to Valhalla. 'Such courage, such valour,' I can hear you saying. 'The very stuff of *Boys' Own*, *Dan Dare* and *Dick Barton* all in one! Real adventure indeed!' Well, that's what we thought too until we suddenly ground to a halt, empty-bellied, on a knife-edge of crumbly snow above the final rocky bit. There we were, just one long single run-out below the exit cornice, and fighting over who should get a seat for the night and who would have to stand. Tough that Robin got a bad deal though. The following morning, tunnelling through the final cornice (nothing quite like it on the Ben!) to emerge onto the sunny side of the Fiescherhorn like beady-eyed weevils in a cataleptic torpor, the sweet taste of success was dampened by a feeling more usually associated with the after-effects of a night on the bevvy. At least for one of us . . . Which all brings me back to this mate of mine I was talking about. He's got a point: il ne faut pas brûler les étapes! N'est-ce pas?

29

MOST FOUL AND ABUSED SEASON OF SEASONS

Conditions played down by Robin as 'moderately foul' at the start of the 1960 Alpine season doubtless contributed to the deaths of two Dutchmen on the same mountain as Robin and Goofy, whose overdue return from that epic first British ascent of the north spur of the Fiescherwand came as a relief to their university club comrades. They turned up just as a rescue mission was starting to look inevitable, both showing signs of suffering, due largely to the effects of the unplanned bivouac at 13,000 ft without appropriate gear – 'endeavouring to be not miserable and unfrostbitten', as Robin put it. The regrouped party then moved to Chamonix from where he wrote home on July 29th:

> I have your letter sent to Grindelwald, & am not displeased that you wrote not sooner, & will assume if you like that I left the land with your uncommunicated wishes for good weather, in so far as they could have made no difference.
>
> We left Grindelwald invisible, but here & now it is scorching & cloudless & shows no signs of changing. May well stay aloft until Tues. & then go down to Italy where food & climbing gear are cheaper, maybe at long last to return via Mont Blanc. Being bloated with city feeding & nights of sleep etc., we are eager to rise again & single minded & ready to struggle about, but although they take some time to come the little homesick twinges sure return after two/three days of cracked lips & snow to drink & scrubby eating & snowblind eyes & middling exhaustion, there seems nothing more desirable than feet up, listening to radiogram, & excellently eating. This of course works both ways like grass across the fence.
>
> Toes still tingle reminiscently, but insufficiently to prevent myself & another leaving today for a jolly climb in the eastern flank of La Chaîne de Mt Blanc.

However, the weather did not match up to expectations and Robin had to potter around Chamonix for several days before setting off for the northeast face of the Droites with Andrew Wightman. When they stopped off at the Argentière hut they found that, as Wightman says, 'the other occupants were well-equipped Frenchmen who looked rather askance at the two young scruffs with short ice-axes, who were planning this difficult climb. Then Robin's record began to leak out and finally someone recognised him. The atmosphere changed immediately, but not the weather, and we never did make progress on the face.'

Meanwhile, the rest of Robin's Dormobile van contingent were camped on the Biolay campsite where they were about to be joined by Dougal Haston and Eley Moriarty, fresh from the Dolomites. Once Robin and Wightman were back from their abortive sortie, a vanload of them left France for Courmayeur in Italy from where several planned to tackle the west face of the Aiguille Noire de Peuterey. Having managed just one climb, and keen to do another, Goofy was nonetheless wary about attempting it. Rarely repeated, the route was held in a degree of awe by those who had read the accounts of Buhl and Gervassuti. It still awaited a British ascent. Robin, Haston, Moriarty and Wightman were the aspirants, along with Goofy himself:

> We set off for the hut in the evening, got hopelessly lost in the pitch-black pinewoods and spent the night in a deserted cowshed crawling in rats. Arriving at the hut next day, beads of sweat (panic?) were beginning to appear as the huge face came into view. It was my first season. There had been a fall of snow – not much, but enough to make the route impracticable. I guess you'll understand my relief when it was decided to head back down the valley after the hut *gardien* told us that the weather and conditions were not good for an attempt. Apart from that particular moment of ecstasy, I also remember Dougal tripping on the steep descent: we watched him rolling away towards a ginormous vertical drop, thinking 'Will he, won't he?'

Haston was spared, although tragedy had already struck the party when Jim Rorke was killed in an abseiling accident. Only a few days earlier Robin had done much of the organising to get the body of his friend down, and dealt with the formalities in Chamonix. Rorke had only recently been a member of the Saturday-night-bus 'choir' after nights out in Kent.

When the time came for Team Dormobile to return to Britain, the tentless Smith and Haston were last seen settling in for the night under the awning of unsuspecting French campers. 'The weather continues to be reediculous,' Robin went on to complain back in Chamonix on

August 14th, his postcard showing a picture of the Dru. 'Every break in the rain is to be the start of a fortnight's sun but maybe one of them (this one?) will be. We are now only 2, others having gone home or elsewhere, & we are purchasing great supplies & ascending to approximately Point X on foot of photo to set up Base Camp maximally watertight for assault on middle of face above. No stone falls, avalanches, etc. If our strength of purpose remains, you will not hear for some time.'

Chamonix, August 16th:

Hoping to reach you before you leave for the jolly Alps, & hoping that the weather will be better for you and incidentally me, I am bound to report continuing foul weather and not a single climb since the one at the beginning.

We camped as I indicated in a 3-ft-high cave out of the snow which fell about us to a depth of about 4 inches in one night & left the W. Face of the Drus, whose little nooks we had eagerly watched shedding their last patches of snow, one great plastered pyramid of white once more.

We have met up with a large bundle of English friends so as to provide between us such diversion while confined to these foul plains sunk in soporific hollows between the ranges.

But: the old story repeats itself, here we are once more at the close of the 2nd day of beating sunshine, the night is cold & clear, gleaming jagged silhouettes of needles all around, and this might very well indeed as before be the start of that fortnight which will make it the season of seasons. In 2 days the big routes would be ready to be climbed, & tomorrow we will leave for high camps again, given weather, probably to the Drus again. Will probably be home for early September.

Send briefly Marion's & your forthcoming addresses, to Cham. Also your dates.

Grindelwald, August 21st:

You shouldn't be spring-cleaning but sun-bathing in the summer, & anyway your results will vanish in Autumnal degeneration with me alone in the house. I will cut the grass & eat raspberries & may study & intersperse & little bit of climbing.

We are still quite routeless, after another tentative on the unclimbed S. face of the Fou, when we joined forces with one Joe Brown & his second man from Manchester but penetrated wet clouds no further than the foot of the snowed-up soggy & seemingly eager-to-avalanche couloir barring the way to the wall.

Joe Brown referred to that tentative in his book *The Hard Years*, putting it that Robin's pace made the rest of them look like old ladies. He added that, as conditions started getting trickier Robin turned to him: 'He said: "You give the word and we'll follow you wherever you go." I said "Right", and turned to go down.' And so they did.

Dennis Gray was Joe Brown's second man that day, Haston making up the party of four. The way up to the Envers des Aiguilles hut, covered as it was with snow and ice, was dangerous and they kept losing the way. Once on easier ground after soloing up smooth snow-covered slabs, however, it became a race between the Scots and the English. There was nothing in it as they approached the final incline in their heavy packs but, on this stretch, Gray concedes, Robin even managed to burst into song (as best he could), as his southern rivals dropped behind:

Thus he won a famous victory for the honour of Bonny Scotland! When I first met Robin, I was not too impressed. But later, after being in his company, I learned to appreciate his dry humour, his incredible fitness and stamina, and his sense of adventure.

I well remember the time Dougal, Ron Cummaford (a member of The Rock & Ice), Robin and I gatecrashed the Guides' Ball in Chamonix that same month. We must have stuck out like a sore thumb dressed as we were in jeans and sweaters, whilst all the guides and their ladies were in evening dress. Every time a group got up to dance, we would swoop onto the table as soon as they had departed, knock back all the drinks (mainly champagne) and disappear back into the anonymity to be found at the back of the hall as quick as we could. It says a lot for French tolerance that we were not beaten up or kicked out on our arses! But how we killed ourselves laughing as we staggered back up to our tents on the Biolay campsite, inebriated but happy as only Scots and a Yorkshireman could have been at getting drunk at someone else's expense!

As they waited in Grindelwald for 'ridiculous-for-summer quantities of snow to disappear', Robin and Haston had opportunities aplenty, had they wished, to muse on those adventures with Gray and Brown. However, they could not hang around indefinitely, fortunately so since the Eiger's north face never came into condition that season. Back in

Edinburgh whilst his mother was on holiday in Austria, Robin wrote to her of matters that would torture the soul of any red-blooded man of the mountains:

> Home again, still too disgusted to think of studying after this most foul and unanimously abused season of seasons. We sat 10 days under the Dreaded Eiger, plenty of sun but far too much snow, & bathed & sun-bathed & ate & slept to the drone of insects (stinging) & avalanches. Thence miserably thumbed home in many slow stuffy cars like Jonah in a whale but have no fear for tribulation is the parent of maturity and All may be for The Good On The Whole and Wisely Ordained. All seems to be well in the house. The Cat is Fat. Resignedly, Yr. Son.
> PS: Many thanks for Magnificent Birthday Card.

Mark you, he was to grump even more the following summer:

> Now we are sick of the Dolomites. Also we are fairly fed up with the Alps. This is little wonder. I haven't seen Scotland in July or August for about 5 years, nor any but the dregs of an Edinburgh Festival. To hell with another month of perambulating the Alps with an odd route when the weather permits.

At least Maggie the cat was happy!

30

MATTERHORN MUTTERINGS

In the summer of 1961 Robin was again working in Kent. Meanwhile, his mother was off on a cycling holiday back in Scotland as he prepared for his fifth Alpine season. 'I will be surprised if you have reached S.Uist without any breakdowns. Send me some note of your travels. Don't park your saddle-bag of tools near any hoodlums or for long spells in towns,' he chaffed her with a variant of her own advice to him, making play of the fact that her route down the islands of the Hebrides would take her through such trouble-free and sparsely populated countryside. 'I was hunting for the Arden Shakespeare Edition of *Hamlet* for you but have finally found that it has not even yet been issued, so I have thought of nothing else by way of substitute except for things which you might not choose yourself. I could always send you 5 guineas. I hope the weather is something near as hot & cloudless as here. We are all sunburned brown (some red). It is now 3 a.m., we have just swept the last of the stray peas down the drains, and by 8.00 a.m. the 5 of us will be swinging pitchforks with our numbed blistered & illegible hands. Consequently I am presently going to bed.' Edinburgh sage, Professor T. Graham Brown, was also kept in the picture:

> The hours drag but the weeks fly and in about 2 weeks Dougal & I plan to go to the Alps. Dougal has failed all his exams but is not greatly worried. Andrew failed his Chemistry and says he is staying at home.
>
> Big Eley is going home shortly to finish his apprenticeship, and then, on the 19th July – believe this if you can – to get married. It is meant to be a secret, even from us, so spread it as far as you can. It is a terrible thing to happen to a 7-ft 14-stone hill of a man in the prime of life and good at climbing too. His very sweet cuddly little sharp-fanged girl has got him well and truly by the tail. We are disgusted.

A later note home mentions hearing of…

> … nothing but thunderstorms & snowfalls in the Alps, but this is all to the good, it gives them a chance to get it out of their system, & who

knows but that an anticyclone may blanket out the thunderbolts for months on end, & then we will have a tale or two to tell . . . Peas have very nearly run their course, beans don't start for another fortnight, and so there is very little work at the Vinery. Most of the Irish students have left already. During the first four weeks I had little time to leave the Vinery & so there is no news other than that of work & sleep which devolves into a dull routine of no great interest. Being fed up with forking peas, I expect to leave today & cross the Channel tonight. I don't expect I will fork another pea in my life, not with a pitchfork anyway. Dougal Haston, whose job pays less, can't afford to leave till Friday. I will probably hitchhike at leisure & meet him & our transport some- where abroad.

Sheila Samuelson and fellow student, Rosemary Brindle, had agreed to provide that transport, which is how Robin, free of weighty clobber, came to step off the Dover–Calais ferry at 4.30 on the morning of July 20th. A lift straight to Paris got him there before the train:

I spent the day variously in Paris, took an evening *train de banlieue*, and then a lift took me to Sens where I passed a roadside night under poplars all lit up in the moon. In the morning I joined up with a Parisian student of Russian, a philosopher to boot, *nihiliste, pas croyant*, voluble, very good for my French, & we proceeded together all the way to Geneva in a remarkable series of long lifts – a mere 5 or 6 altogether. We slept on a bench in the heart of the City under glittering hotels & fountains & parted in the morning, I for Visp, where our multiple rendez-vous was (surprisingly) realised.

We are four sitting in a tent – rain & all last night on arrival, but this morning only steamy rolling clouds around the base of the big mountains & steaming away to nothing in the rising sun. The Matterhorn has just come quite clear, black & white against blue sky, we (2 of us, the climbers) will enquire & prospect as to the conditions & if they seem good enough will take a trip up the North Face. Of course it could all go horrible again but there's nothing like optimism. We will shortly be leaving for a night in the Hornli Hütte, 5000 ft above Zermatt . . .

I'm sorry I won't be reaching you on the 4th, but if I had written earlier I would have been too early, as we just came down yesterday from 3 days on the hill. I wish you a happy birthday all the same.

At Zermatt we had great weather but lousy snow conditions. We set out at 3 of a morning for a big tentative on the Matterhorn north face, surmounted the bergschrund & lower ice slope, and reached about 1/3 of the way up the Face before deciding that we weren't enjoying ourselves. Here the route should follow rotten & slabby rocks, with several patches of snow & ice, of no great difficulty, but all the slabs were coated in wet melting snow which made progress slow, miserable & dangerous. Also we were within 300 ft of the ordinary route, the Hornli Ridge, as erst surmounted by Aunty D. & Uncle A., and willingly enough therefore we escaped & shambled down to get back to the Hut around 4 in the afternoon. The Matterhorn is a monument to the gap between getting worked up over looks & getting to grips with reality. You would hardly believe what a heap of slag that proud uprearing etc is.

And yet, while looking up at the Matterhorn on a recent family skiing holiday to Zermatt, Sheila Samuelson could not help but reflect on those golden days of youth when joy was unconfined . . . well, most of the time:

Really, Robin was a right pest. If it hadn't been for him Rosemary and I would have stood on top of that in 1961.

At the Zermatt campsite we all four stayed together in a two-man tent, one of those old Black's Good Companions with an 'A' frame and the opening on one of the long sides. We slept in a row with our heads to the rear and our feet sticking out at the front – I can't remember ever waking up with wet feet. Nor can I remember there being any friction, possibly because both Rosemary and Dougal possessed extraordinarily calm temperaments and Robin had a knack of getting his own way so had nothing to grouch about.

In the morning we all humped our gear and tramped severally up to the Hornli Hütte. Robin's and Dougal's plans were to slip up the north face of the Matterhorn before moving on to more exacting stuff! They were already widely considered the two most talented climbers in Scotland (and therefore, Scottish climbers would no doubt have maintained, in the British Isles), but I don't believe they had climbed together very much before this season. After circling around each other for a while they had finally got together for a series of major assaults.

Their climb would take two days, with a bivouac halfway up. Meanwhile Rosemary and I had arranged for a guide to take us up the Hornli Ridge on the second day, giving us a day to scramble about and acclimatise. We all slept on the Matrazen Lager, that interesting experiment in international relations, and Robin and Dougal departed before the night became morning to tackle the north face. Rosemary and I spent the day reconnoitring the lower slopes of the Matterhorn which close up is more like a huge pile of rubble than the noble pillar it appears from a distance. In the late afternoon a disgruntled Robin and Dougal stomped into the hut uttering imprecations against the mountain. The weather had not been cold enough to glue the north face together and they had been forced off by unstable conditions. They were all for leaving instantly. 'We can't,' we told them. 'We've ordered a guide for tomorrow.'

'Cancel him,' said Robin magnanimously. 'We'll take you up ourselves.' Rosemary and I ran down the track towards Zermatt to intercept our guide. We were to wish we had left things as they were.

At 3 a.m. we got up and woke Dougal and Robin. Or at least we woke Dougal. Robin refused to budge. Dougal submitted to the porridge we made for him and we waited for Robin to bestir himself. Other parties departed to climb the mountain. Rosemary and I watched them in frustration while Dougal conferred with the recumbent Robin. 'He's not feeling too good,' Dougal told us. 'We'd better give him a while longer.' Dougal, who had a soft voice, always addressed Robin by his pet name of 'Wheech'. They obviously had a great respect for each other, even an affection.

At 11 a.m. with the Matterhorn melting in the hot sun like a great inverted ice-cream cone and Robin still stubbornly cocooned in his sleeping bag, Dougal, Rosemary and I set off to climb the Hornli Ridge together. Not only were we six hours late setting off, it was also extremely slow caterpillaring along with three on a rope. Dougal was amazingly patient. He would have preferred to dispense with the rope and swarm freely up the side of this majestic slagheap unencumbered. We were not keen. There is no technical difficulty on the tourist route up the Matterhorn but it is a hell of a long way to the bottom and we were nervously aware that there would not be much left of all we saw and knew if we let go. Nor is the Hornli Ridge quite the straightforward tramp it looks from afar. It is a great jumble of tottering pinnacles and shattered slabs and the route is not always easy to discern. We wandered gormlessly off across the east face before finally locating the Solway Hut. By now it was 3 p.m. and those climbers who had set off at the appropriate time were already descending. We continued some way further, then, not wanting to spend the night on the mountain, decided to call it a day. When we got back down to the Solway Hut we found Robin squatting, gnome-like, cross-legged, on a rock ledge above it. He had apparently recovered from his malaise and decided to take an afternoon stroll.

We roped up on two ropes for the descent, dispensing with belays. 'Just run down the mountain,' Robin instructed us, 'in a kind of controlled fall.' Eyed disapprovingly by the descending guides shepherding their clients this is what we did. Robin was a great inspirer of reckless confidence in the normally cautious. Pity he couldn't get out of bed a bit earlier, though.

SNAKES AND LADDERS ON THE CIMA OVEST
DE LAVAREDO

After those unedifying skirmishes with the Matterhorn Robin couldn't wait to shake the grit of Zermatt off his boots. Sheila Samuelson recalls the morning of August 2nd, 1961 as Robin, Rosemary Brindle, Dougal Haston and she set about packing the car:

> Having failed wholesale to reach the summit of the Matterhorn we slammed the boot shut on our gear and, leaving with more of a bang than a Whymper, we sped off to the Dolomites: the promised land of cohesive verticality where Robin had his eye on the north face of the Cima Ovest, not so much a rock face as a geological blunder. Nothing so overhanging was ever designed to be climbed, but Robin was determined to bag the first British ascent of the Direttissima. He became increasingly cheerful as the distance between himself and the Matterhorn widened. Meanwhile he entertained us hugely with his linguistic expertise. He was extremely competent in French but knew no Italian. 'It's easy to speak Italian,' Robin informed us airily. 'You just use a mixture of English and French and throw in a lot of Italianate endings.' When we stopped at the street market to provision up Robin jumped out of the car and produced a gush of quasi-Italian accompanied by a lot of dramatic arm-waving. It certainly got results.

Robin:[1]

> We hairpinned up to Lavaredo, 3 in 1 and 2 by 2, S. and R. for the wheel and meals and Haston and me for the Cima West. The cold at dawn would have blackened the toes of a brass monkey. So around 10, Haston and me, we ambled round to under the North Wall (having made a cunning plan with S. and R.) with 300 ft of rope, doubled, 1 sack, 1 camera, 2 hammers, 6 slings, 8 étriers, 40 karabiners, and (cunningly) 300 ft of line to save us taking bivvy gear.
> Cassin climbed it years ago, two men and three days and just a few pitons, 800 ft up the far right edge, then 500 ft of hairy traverse, above

the biggest overhang you ever saw, in to the middle of the wall, then, 1000 ft up couloir and over the top in a thundering storm, babbling. But nowadays they go for Direttissimas, straight up the biggest overhangs with a great beating of pegs and drums. A first ascent can last for years, with time off for rest cures, with an average of more than a piton a yard, and just a few expansion bolts where the rock won't take pitons, and just a few free-climbing moves, rudely disrupting the rhythm of swinging free. The powers of the pioneers to pitoneer and persevere are far beyond the grasp of Stone-age Britons, but all the pitons are left in place so that later ascents are comparatively easy. In 1959, inevitably, they finished a direct start to the Via Cassin; and here is how we cunningly climbed it.

We tied on to the double rope, and divided the gear, and one man took the sack, with the line and the camera, and the other took the krabs and stepped up off the path. For 20 ft you climb the rock, because it's only vertical.

The wall has the look of an elephant's hide, flat and smooth from a distance, but riddled all over with pocks and warts, piton-cracks, sharp little finger holds, crumbling jugs, loose flakes, shallow grooves, sharp little roofs, and ledges to stand on once in a blue moon.

The route is a wandering line of pitons, 400 ft hither and thither up a shallow, gently overhanging bay, to under the monstrous arch of a roof jutting out about 80 ft, and then 200 ft along a magnificent zigzag piton crack, twisting up and out and leftwards all at once, and round the lip of the roof, and then by another 400 ft of gently overhanging wall easing off to the plumb vertical just as it joins the Via Cassin at the end of the hairy traverse under the couloir.

But we had had but a nibbling foretaste of unelementary pitoneering. So up we bumbled, up two down one, clawing krabs and thrashing air, hurling holds at audiences, otherwise avoiding the rock like a hot tin roof, but nonetheless trapping fingers, baring knuckles, dripping gore on krabs and ropes and beating knees to black and blue balloons. To play it cool, you harmonise your ropes. 'Tight on white, and slack a bit of red.' Only ours were both a dirty white, synchronically turning speckled red, obtusely clipped at acutest angles, writhing into tumorous kinks, and hideously twisted like a pair of loving snakes, with the man who was climbing too throttled to speak and the man at the reins too sleepy to listen and the two of us linked by nothing but hate and discord. One man would follow the pitons till he ran out of rope or krabs or couldn't drag the rope any further, then he would sit and swing in his ladders while the other man followed, collecting all the krabs, and clambered over the first man and up the next pitch. Easy; but night fell at the end of four pitches, which is to say, right away out on the lip of the monster roof.

This was not cunning, but we had a cunning move in hand, and scanned the gloomy screes below and bawled to left and right. But no S. and R., so we passed a worried hour spinning our webs for the night. Haston was laughing, he was at a belay, a rugosity for his seat and one foothold. He faced out, lopsidedly crucified across a ring of pitons, head jammed under a bit of roof, and held in at the belly by criss-cross bits of hoary abandoned rope. I was 20 ft down and right, hanging free from a holdless scoop, but with pitons all around. So facing in, I wove a net of krabs and ladders and bits of sling, slung around me under my armpits, under my seat and under my knees, with toes against the rock an inch above the biggest bit of roof, seated, as it were, on a bottom-less closet, and feeling that way too.

I had the sack, so while Haston yelled the odds I took out the line and unravelled it 300 ft down into the night. This was the first, but we feared it was the last of the steps of our cunning plan.

Sheila:

I can't remember whose stupid idea it was to haul the dinner up that monstrous overhang on the end of a rope. The theory was that Robin and Dougal would be provided with nourishment and sleeping bags at their first bivouac without having to haul provisions or have the onerous task of brewing while swinging in étriers. Well, the idea was fine but . . .

Provisions were low and Rosemary and I descended to the valley to stock up. It was quite a trek on a Hitchcockian nightmare of a road and the afternoon was well advanced when we returned to camp. We brewed a delicious savoury stew, wrapped the pot in a sleeping bag and put the whole parcel in a rucksack with a few other nourishing morsels and Robin's duvet jacket. We trotted off with this up over the ridge and along under the black shadow of the north faces, where loosened stones whined down constantly from above, like enemy fire. This was our mistake. We should have kept 100 ft or so out from the base of the cliff and then we would have been underneath where Robin and Dougal were dangling and spotted them more easily (if we hadn't been caught in the gunfire). Eventually a distant cavernous bellowing attracted our attention and at last we had the sense to move out from the rock face – and out, and out – until, rubbernecking upwards, we could see them trussed up like victims of medieval torture hung out on the castle walls for the ravens to pick at. It was becoming seriously dusk.

Robin:

But then the plaintive voice of S. rose from the screes. We answered warmly. They had driven down to town to buy us fruit and goodies and bread and jam and butter and chocolate full of brandy, and cooked a thermos of coffee and a dixie of stew and potatoes, and wrapped them in duvets and sleeping-bags with knife and fork and spoon, and tied them all into a great rucksack. By now it was so dark that I couldn't see more than a blur of Haston, but we both untied from the double rope, and undoubled it, with some confusion, into a single length of 300 ft. Then Haston tied onto one end, and I tied the other end to the top end of the dangling line and carried on lowering so that the bottom end of the line would reach all the 500 ft to the screes. But meanwhile, hanging loops of rope had embrangled themselves around the dangling line, and as I lowered the rope the line came back up in a loop-the-loop, and I found myself lowering it all over again. A fankle ensued. So I went to work like a fizzling computer, speaking coaxing words to all the little knots, with Haston somewhere up above turning cold and repetitive. Meanwhile S., with the sack and R., had been back for quite some time; we could see them waving torches at the bottom. In two hours all but the kernels of fankle were solved, so I lowered as much as I could, and sure enough they caught it in the beam of a torch, snaking down to the screes 100 ft out from the base of the wall.

Sheila:

We attached the rucksack to the poor cobbled-together ophidian and Robin began to haul it up. This proved an exhaustingly strenuous task. The rucksack spun giddily, maliciously turning upside-down. Robin's arms grew longer. Oaths curdled the chill Alpine air. It became too dark to discern the upward progress of the rucksack and we slunk off, hoping for the best.

Robin:

From where he was, Haston was useless, he just froze and swore and moaned, while the rope came up in tiny jerks and down in the depths the invisible sack was monstrously spinning and leaping through the night.

The pulley was all wrong, and once in a while there were bits of

222

fankle to get past the krabs, and the more I pulled in the worse the fankles grew, till even my arms were all seized up in knots and not until the first faint glimmer of dawn did the sack swirl into sight. I gaffed it to a piton and slumped in my slings, but then I was roused by Haston's groans, so I put on a duvet and sleeping-bag, and gobbled coffee and handfuls of goodies and stew, and Haston pulled up his share, with goodies and stew unhappily all mixed up, and then we slept.

Sheila:

The following morning, though far from early, we returned to the dark side of the mountain to pick up the rucksack. We thought it would be waiting for us on the scree. It was not and, peering upwards, we saw that Dougal and Robin still hung inert and askew in their cocoons. We hailed them and they began to make feeble movements like moth chrysalides reluctantly metamorphosing.

Robin:

So loth as sloths we unbedded ourselves and packed the rucksack, keeping duvets and goodies. Then I lowered it, that was easy, but the ropes were so fankled it stuck half-way, so I had to pully tup (pull it up) and start all over again. Next time it stuck about 60 ft from the screes, but I wasn't going to pull it up, so Haston untied from his end of the rope, which gave me another 20 ft, and I added a chain of tatty slings, and not for a dismal number of hours did we start to climb.

Sheila:

A hissing altercation between Robin and Dougal far above brought to an end Robin's solo vocal accompaniment. Then the malignant rucksack bounced almost to within reach. I scrambled onto a boulder and made cat-like swipes at it and finally got a finger hold, unhooked the thing and hauled it down. Shortly afterwards an end of the ill-omened line came wriggling through the air and slapped onto the scree at our feet where it lay like a dead snake, all malice spent.

Robin and Dougal had laboriously begun to unravel the knitting which held them to the face. It seemed a long process. Exhausted by their exertions we moved out of the black shadow and sprawled on rocks in the sun, where we watched their painfully slow dangling progress. It was about as excruciating as watching two flies trying to extricate themselves from a spider's web.

Robin:

Haston recovered an end of rope and we tried to redouble it for climbing, but the strain had left it twisted and kinked in psychopathic convulsions.

The climbing was just the bleeding same, with nothing but the beginnings of cunning to balance the loss of blood and vigour. We reached the hairy traverse of the Via Cassin just in time for an hour of beating sun-set, and here was the very first ledge of the climb with plenty of room for two. So we settled for a reasonably typical hunched-up twitching, chittering, wriggling, burbling, hellishly freezing bivouac. Then half an hour of tepid sun-rise hustled us onwards. The Direttissima really finishes up a lot more pitons just left of the Via Cassin couloir. But it looked daft and we were sickened, so stuffing our ladders away, we finished up the crumbling tumbling couloir. At noon we came out in the frizzling sun and hobbled down the other side all sweat and blood and stiff and sore, with fists rolled up like hedge-hogs, and they never opened till S. and R. had fed us full of food and wine and wheeled us home to the land of rolling Munros.

Sheila:

They arrived back at the tent looking as if they had aged ten years and having hated every minute of the climb. Well they didn't have to do it. Did they?

Robin:

Such is the modernest climbing, a savourless progress up a blind alley. It moves right away from the natural thrill & flow which are the best things in hard climbing. It is like a lot of modern jazz.

Sheila:

I vowed never to return to the Dolomites. However I must have been the world's greatest sucker because I was persuaded to return the following year. Fortunately, though, I spent an enjoyable time doing a number of classic routes with less driven members of the club rather than running a soup kitchen for the gods.

32

THREADING THE NEEDLE

On June 7th, 1962, Robin made his way westwards to Clydebank in his quest for a new route in the Cairngorms, apparently 90 degrees off course. His target was Shelter Stone Crag or, more precisely, its central area, which had recently been publicised by the Aberdonians as being all 'very problematical and intimidating'. Their conclusion that a route there was 'manifestly impossible' acted as a tantalising piece of bait to rivals, no more so than to climbers from Edinburgh and the Glasgow-based Creagh Dhu.[1]

Tentative efforts first started to be targeted at the centre of the crag in 1961, and Robin would have heard of these failures. Two cards home, as it happens, indicate that he was in the area himself towards the end of that summer. Their dates coincide with his first ascents with Graham Tiso of Clean Sweep and Hellfire Corner Direct on nearby Hell's Lum Crag:

> On our way to the Shelter Stone, passing Loch Morlich in grey but dry & promising weather watching out for Deer Stalkers Tourists Grey Men & other dangers of this region. We will probably be going north tomorrow but may stay here – you never know. Yachts on the Loch. Maybe we will stay to instruct for free board at Glenmore Lodge . . .
>
> For the 3rd time in a row, the rains fell upon us just as we fell upon the Shelter Stone. Eagles saving eggs from the foxes. We climbed a little & scuttled north to Garve for the night. Revictualled, we are going West along Loch shown [Loch Luichart], then North, to Loch Fannich & the Fannich Hills – unknown but rumoured precipitous – in search of its secrets. At the moment, it is not raining & even looks like turning fine. You never know. Midges hanging on.

It is safe to say that Robin assessed the line of a possible new route up Shelter Stone Crag during that trip, prior to heading north. He would also have examined photographs of the crag during the winter. Perhaps unknown to him, however – for far from all information was pooled – two other Edinburgh climbers had detected that same potential route, as Jimmy Marshall reveals:

In late May 1962 my brother and I climbed all the lower slabs by the initial pitches of Steeple but turned left which, to our disgust, took us to a long grassy slope where Ronnie's interest in it as a credible new route ended. From there we abseiled off with a view to returning soon, for we knew what had to be done.

Robin clearly sensed that the route was on the verge of falling. The weather during the first week of June was brilliant. He must have known the line would be in perfect condition. Time was running out for him, as he was going to the Pamirs at the end of the month and, after nine weeks there, followed by a stint in the Alps, summer would be over.

It was no doubt with such a projection of events in mind that Robin arrived unannounced on Clydeside to recruit the help of one of the Creagh Dhu lads. Wrestler Davie Agnew, serving his apprentice there as a 'keelie' in a shipyard, was about to find himself on a climb that with the passing of time has become one of these islands' great classics – the Needle:[2]

Early Thursday evening, June 1962. I was cleaning up in the kitchen having just completed another day in the yards when I heard my younger brothers and sister yelling. 'Davie, Davie, there's a man oot here tae see ye.' Drying my face, I headed for the door thinking proviman, polisman, tickman. It was with great relief and surprise that I opened the door to find Robin 'Walker' Wheechman!

He said 'Do you want to go climbing? I've got this great line in the Gorms. If we leave right now, we can get it done this weekend. It'll really upset the Aberdonians.' I consented immediately, feeling pleased that Robin had dared to venture into the nether regions of Clydebank to find me.

I quickly packed my gear: six slings, six 'biners, my PAs, a few manky pegs, and my trusty home-made peg hammer, which was Clyde-built and no two are alike. Leaving a note for my mother to pick up my pittance at the yard gate the next day, we left Clydebank on a Corporation bus. It dropped us off at Buchanan Street Bus Station just in time to catch the 7.00 p.m. Perth bus.

We arrived in Perth just before 9.00 p.m., Robin having talked almost the whole journey about the route. It was time to eat. We got a fish supper each, to keep us company, while we walked from the bus station to the Inverness road. I'll always remember when we were at the edge of the road, on the outskirts of Perth, hitching up to Aviemore. It was getting dark and across the road from where we stood was a band of gypsies, camped in a field beside a wee burn. Watching them kept us from boredom while waiting for a ride. Meanwhile, we were both thinking on how similar the gypsies' and our own lifestyles were, except for the hedgehog stew part.

At last a car stopped, a salesman on his way to Inverness with loads of goodies for our Highland brethren. He gave us a lift to Aviemore, letting us off at Loch Morlich junction. We thanked him profusely, telling him that 'Highlanders preferred lollies to Cadbury's any day', a reference to what ex-Cadbury rep Graham Tiso had told us. (The canny economical Highlanders of his sales area liked longer-lasting lollies more than the chocolate he happened to supply.) Anyway, as it was late, and with no chance of a lift to Loch Morlich, we hotfooted it a mile or so up the road and crashed in the woods over the dyke, very happy with our progress since 7.00 p.m.

The next day dawned dry and clear. We had a quick brew while we stuffed our bags. We were on the road by 7.00 a.m., ready for the early morning Cairngorm chairlift traffic. Within a few minutes a car did stop! It was driven by Tommy Paul, one of my Creagh Dhu pals. Our luck could not have been better. Tommy was going to work, up at the chairlift. Great, and when we got to the middle station on Cairngorm, Tommy fed us tea and doughnuts. Then fired us up the White Lady Chairlift. Robin and I couldn't believe it. We would be over the head of Coire Cas and down to the Shelter Stone by 10.00 a.m., and it was still clear and dry.

We reached the Shelter Stone and looked up at the Crag: 1200 ft of gleaming granite, with an awesome head wall. It occurred to me then that this was going to be a wee bit more than a dawdle. I suddenly understood why the Aberdonians had stayed away from it. We had a brew, while I tried to calm Robin down. He was very excited! 'Look at that corner! Look at those roofs!' he yelled.

'Have a Penguin and slow down,' I said. 'Now, show me the line.' He did, and I must say he got my undivided attention. Well, down to business. We sorted our combined hardware: about a dozen slings, twelve 'biners, one rope, two hammers and ten assorted pegs. Robin had already figured out the pitches he wanted to lead and, as it was his line and they would probably be the most difficult, I had no objection. Without further ado, we set off. I was odds, he was evens. The first two or three pitches were fairly straightforward . . . slabs! Nae bother!

The fourth pitch was much steeper and, I guessed, harder as Robin's singing became more raucous and jumbled for a few minutes as he figured out the moves.

'On belay. Come on up! You'll really like it,' yelled Robin. I did enjoy it, especially when I was on the blunt end of the rope. The next pitch was my lead. A quick transfer of gear, and I was on my way. It wasn't too hard. There was plenty of sun and good rock. A great pitch, ending in a big belay ledge.

'Come on up. Belay's a bomber!' Up came Robin, chortling with delight, until he saw the next pitch. *The dreaded crack for thin fingers.* We didn't know that yet, but we were soon to be acquaint.

'Davie, dae ye want to switch leads?'

'Naw, Robin, a deal's a deal.'

So, away the bauchle went, mumbling and grumbling, thrutching and pedalling. 'Tight rope. Slack rope.' Assorted cursing and then loud chortling and screaming, 'I'm up. A piece of cake. You'll love it!'

I did not exactly love it at the time. I thought it was the hardest pitch I'd ever done. Robin only used three runners on the whole pitch, a tribute to his talent. The remainder of the climb was anticlimactic. Still superb climbing, but not as desperate.

The last pitch, threading the Needle, was definitely Robin's. It capped a fantastic day and really hadn't taken that long for a new route: about nine hours. We were very chuffed with ourselves.

The run down the scree to the Shelter Stone was 'Très Grande Vitesse'. Back under the Stone, we brewed up gallons of tea and ate every morsel we could find in our packs. We talked about the climb and life till the wee hours, wrote up the route in the doss book and eventually fell asleep.

Little did I realise it would be our last evening together.

A few weeks later, I heard on the BBC that two British climbers had been killed in the Pamirs: their names were Wilfrid Noyce and Robin Smith. Later the same day, I received a postcard from Robin. It said,

The Hills are mighty big here.
Keep climbing.
Robin.

Yes, my friend, sometimes the hills are mighty big, but I do try to keep climbing.

PART THREE

THE PAMIRS: 1960–62

33

WILFRID NOYCE

Wilf was wearing the same blue anorak he had worn on Everest as he lay, nine years later, closely bound to Robin Smith in the tight coils of their rope, on a little shelf some 2000 ft up the West face of Pik Garmo. For those of us who found them there, it was a moment of indescribable pathos. Yet it seemed to symbolise a new-found friendship between these two men. They were, in age, a generation apart. Each had attained high academic distinction; both were brilliant mountaineers. There they lay, in death united.

John Hunt recalling July 26th, 1962[1]

A book about Robin Smith would be incomplete without some appreciation of the man with whom he was to die. Like Robin, Wilfrid Noyce was born in India, his father, Sir Frank Noyce, a member of the Viceroy's Council. He was forty-four, twenty-one years older than Robin, and married with two young sons, when he fell to his death.

Noyce was educated at Charterhouse, where he was head boy, before going on to study at Cambridge where he gained firsts in both Classics and Modern Languages. The Second World War interrupted his studies, which he completed in 1946. Noyce then became a Modern Languages teacher, at Malvern and later at Charterhouse, prior to taking up writing as a full-time career in 1961. He also lectured and was competent enough to give presentations in French, German and Italian about the successful 1953 Everest expedition of which he was a member. His *Times* obituary ascribed to him a 'poet's approach' towards mountaineering. About ten books by Noyce, one of them poetry, were published. The most successful, 'South Col', is credited with having conveyed not just what happened, but how it felt, on Everest.

Noyce was introduced to rock-climbing as a boy by his cousin, Colin Kirkus, and climbed intensively as a young man with Menlove Edwards. Climbs by Edwards and Kirkus in the late 1920s and 1930s are legendary. Noyce in turn became a leading climber just before and following the Second World War. He was lucky to survive several big falls, the most serious a pre-war 200-ft sheer drop from the East Buttress of Mickledoor Grooves on Scafell on a rope held by JM Edwards (with whom he compiled guidebooks to Tryfan and Llewed). 'Edwards's strength and skill saved him,' *The Times* said of this incident, 'but he was terribly injured, especially in the face. His boyish good looks were gone, but plastic surgery did marvels, and his rare personality proceeded to stamp itself on his new-made features.'

Apart from Everest, Noyce had been on two other big expeditions, to Machapuchare, western Nepal, in 1957 and to Trivor in the Karakorum in 1960. Bad weather forced him to turn back 150 ft from the summit of Machapuchare after pioneering the entire route himself. Previous to this he had made two expeditions to the Garwhal in 1943–44 while on service in India. His aptitude for big mountains was reinforced in 1945 at the age of twenty-eight by an ascent of the 23,385-ft Panhunri, where he disregarded acclimatisation because he was on strictly limited army leave.

John Hunt wrote two articles about Noyce. The first appeared in the December 1962 issue of the *Geographical Journal*, the second, written jointly with David Cox thirty years later, in the 1992 *Alpine Club Journal*.[2] Their combined essence is as follows:

> Wilfrid Noyce was a close friend of mine for over twenty years. Particulars from his life have been adequately told elsewhere and it is as a friend, not as a biographer, that I prefer to write of him.
>
> I already knew of him by repute from his great climbs and from two remarkable accidents before the last war, through mutual climbing friends. But our first meeting was in quite a different setting: a hutted camp in Norfolk, when he joined 1st Battalion, the Rangers (10th King's Royal Rifle Corps, KRRC) in early February 1942: he as a newly fledged second Lieutenant, I as Second in Command of the unit. The bond of climbing drew us together in that bleak environment – this and the fact that we had both survived serious accidents in the previous two years.
>
> Despite his neat new uniform, it was obvious that Wilfrid was not a warlike person; moreover, he was the reverse of ostentatious authority. I do not think he enjoyed commanding a platoon in the motorised battalion of an armoured brigade. But I soon appreciated his tolerance of, and adaptability to new situations, even those as unfamiliar and uncongenial to him as this one; he could see the need for it and was willing to play his part despite a distaste for the precision and discipline

of military life – even despite an almost complete lack of 'know-how' about matters mechanical. While there were times when he appeared almost absent-minded, preoccupied with his own thoughts, he could also be practical and efficient when these qualities were needed.

But he was soon to find an outlet for his tastes and talents and apply them to the exigencies of training for war. How we enjoyed ourselves when, a few weeks later, I obtained the Brigade Commander's approval to run a course in North Wales for a group of all ranks from trooper to major – and mis-named it a 'Toughening Course'! To our surprise, everyone else enjoyed it too and this was due, in no small degree, to the informality of Wilfrid and the other climber-instructors. In this role the diffident, seemingly dreamy young officer, who was wont quietly to drift off on his own after a long day's training, in search of some new line up a cliff, was seen in a different light: a man content to commune with himself and with nature, whose approach to mountains revealed a new meaning to the title of our course.

Our ways parted during the rest of the war, though we kept in touch. Wilfrid, already an accomplished linguist, studied Japanese and was sent to Delhi in an Intelligence post. From there he was later to find an outlet to the mountains once more, as an instructor successively in Kashmir and in Sikkim at RAF Aircrew Rehabilitation Centres. From mutual friends who shared this work with him and from Wilfrid himself, I learned how much he enjoyed giving a taste of his preferred form of adventure to men in need of change from a very different kind of risk. His gift for teaching, whether to soldiers or schoolboys, was always best in this medium; he was a person whose message was imparted rather by sight and sense than through the spoken word.

Of his skill as a mountaineer, his magnificent record is adequate tribute. But I count myself fortunate to have seen so much of it at first hand; often on difficult climbs together. His sense of balance, sureness of foot and rhythm of movement on steep ground were a wonder to behold. He seemed quite unaware of exposure and would stand with his hands in his pockets on narrow, sloping ledges where other people would have been eagerly looking for a handhold, or wanting to drive in a peg for a bit of security. A natural climber loves movement and Wilf was an outstanding instance of this; also it was probably for this reason that the more laborious techniques of artificial climbing made no appeal to him: 'they would have removed the wings from his heels' [Geoff Sutton, 1963 *Climbers' Club Journal*]. This is perhaps another way of saying that Wilf, however talented he was as a rock climber and mountaineer, was above all a lover of the hills and of movement among them.

Memories come flooding in: of a day on Pillar Rock, when we met again soon after the war, over Easter in 1946 – he was just back from climbing Panhunri and I from the crags of Olympus. He led Harry Tilley and myself up the 'Very Severe' Savage Gully, down over the famous Nose and the North Climb, then again up the exhilarating north–west route; all in quick succession with effortless ease and apparently, with a wide margin of safety. Yet, only two days later, he was lucky to survive when he was blown from his holds and fell, breaking a leg, while climbing the Shark's Fin on Tophet Bastion, Great Gable, in a gale. So, from an earlier fall in Wales, when I had held him on the rope, and later in the Alps, I sometimes wondered whether this margin was not a narrower one for him than he, with his superb technique, believed it to be.

Wilfrid's part on Everest has never been adequately told. When all combined so splendidly to produce the final triumph, it has always seemed to me invidious to single out individuals. Yet it is right now to recall my view of him, a tiny speck of blue anorak, breasting the ridge above the South Col at over 26,000 ft, followed by the sturdy Annullu. For us all at Advanced Base in the West Cwm, this was the break-through to the final citadel of the mountain, which we had begun to question our power to reach. For me, who knew him so well, it was no surprise; I had chosen him to give this lead.

A few days later, knowing his phenomenal stamina and resources of will, I asked him to climb a second time up the Lhotse face, so as to be in support of the second assault. We met at Camp VII, I on my way down with Evans, Bourdillon and Ang Temba, he on his way up with Wanh. I do not know how we, in our extreme exhaustion, would have fared that night but for Noyce's ministrations.

Two days later he went onto the Col with one Sherpa, shouldering part of the burdens of two others who turned back after starting out from Camp VII.

Without doubt he could have reached the summit and I know, from a quiet uncomplaining word to me at Base Camp on 8th May, after I had explained the plan for the assault, that he felt this too. It was some comfort to us both that we were to have made a third attempt together, if such had been needed.

In three successive Alpine seasons, 1954–56, with Michael Ward and David Cox, we made a number of fine climbs. Of these I remember with most pleasure our failures and successes on Mont Blanc. The failures due to bad weather on the Innominata, Peuterey and Frontier ridges are no less good memories now than the four glorious days in August 1955 of a double traverse of the mountain; from Les Contamines to Courmayeur over the Aiguille de Bionassey, Aiguille du Gouter, Mont Blanc and Mont Maudit; then back from Italy to France up the Brenva Face, diverted by the weather from the Route Major but not deterred. I recall his lead up the seemingly endless steep and exposed face which leads from the Sentinelle ridge to the summit of Mont Blanc, kicking small toeholds for the rest of us, hour after hour. On completing that great route and descending via the Grands Mulets to the Plan de l'Aiguille, his companions were only too glad to complete the descent to Chamonix in the *téléférique*: not so Wilf. Apparently as fresh as when we had left our bivouac some fourteen hours earlier, he hastened down on the path.

His later climbs on bigger mountains, such as Machapuchare and Trivor and, no less remarkable, on the harder Welsh routes with Don Whillans and other leading cragsmen, bear witness to his continuing stamina and skill as he passed the forty mark. In the Alps, the fourth ascent of the Furggen ridge on the Matterhorn in 1959, in which he took part with Colin Mortlock, was an outstanding feat.

But testimony to Wilfrid Noyce simply as a great mountaineer would present a quite incomplete impression of the man. His scholastic attainments and literary gifts are recorded elsewhere and add to this picture. But as with others, his true worth was in himself, as a person. His deeds helped to form his personality as he fulfilled them and he stands out from this background of achievement: a quiet man, yet someone of whom no-one could fail to be aware: a man ever seeking the truth, yet accepting the mystery of the infinite: a man at peace with other men and with the world around him, who made others in his company feel at their ease. He was such a splendid companion, an ideal man with whom to share a tent. If one wanted to talk, he was an excellent (and very widely read) conversationalist; if one wanted just to lie in one's sleeping bag and doze, he was equally happy. I never heard him say an unkind word about anyone, though he always spoke honestly. It is hard to imagine him quarreling with anybody, or ever losing his temper. This quality of kindness and his constant thoughtfulness for others made him greatly loved, without his seeking affection or popularity.

In the last few weeks of his life he was winning new friends in our strangely different company. This is, when all is said and done, why we went to climb in the Pamirs and it provides a sufficient reason for all that men and women strive to do.

34

RUSSIANS ON OUR HILLS

As the 1950s became the 1960s, international relations between East and West became more and more fraught. Some British climbers felt strongly that personal contact with Soviets might, in a small way, help international relations, a sentiment echoed by some Soviets. Robin's level of concern about international relations is not recorded, but those of his vintage were aware of the real possibility of nuclear war.

In early summer 1960 a party of Soviet climbers visited London, Wales and the Lake District before coming to Scotland with a few English climbers as guests of the SMC. The visit was reported in the *Scotsman* on June 20th by Tom Weir, who first met the Russians at Lagangarbh Hut below Buachaille Etive Mor. Dressed in light blue tracksuits, they had the look of athletes. They confirmed this impression with a display of handsprings and somersaults before getting into their climbing breeches – something of a contrast to British mountaineers' more relaxed approach towards their sport. Whilst the Russians undoubtedly climbed for pleasure, competition was encouraged back home by Soviet officialdom, to the extent that medals were awarded annually for the best climbs and biggest mountain traverses. Weir's overall impression was emphasised in the *Scotsman*'s introduction: 'Incidents during the recent visit of a party of Soviet climbing enthusiasts have signally contributed to better relations between the nations.' One wonders.

At any rate, a little bit of history had been made. Recognising that nobody was better placed to write of it than Robin Smith, *SMC Journal* editor Geoff Dutton set about eliciting an article and published the resultant work with these caveats:

> The Russians were, inevitably, shown Glencoe and Skye. But there was no bear-leading: they were happy to explore by themselves, enthusing over the mountains and the sea, but not over the weather or the slime. Feasts and lectures followed in Edinburgh, where the projected film suffered a technical hitch. Though one wonders how much of Scotland

as a country, not as a countryside, they did see, the Russians appeared to have enjoyed their stay; their hosts certainly did. The usual distortions were made by the gutter press; but if what our propaganda tells us about what their propaganda tells them is true, they would expect that.

However, we do not print the following as a mirror of truth; it rejoices in its own distortion, a picture of the proceedings seen by one of the thrawnest participants [Robin Smith]. Allowances must be made here, too!

Sunny Lagangarbh crackled under the brooding Buachaille.

Then 'Hear that clutch?' said Ritchie. And higgledy-piggledy here they were, Dr Slesser and Kenneth in the van, weaseling down the dirt track, AC evergreens down from the Red Snows, overlapping meets of ladies, six climbers from Russia, and in the rear Tommy Weir, Scotland's greatest chronicler, here to put another page to Annals of the Mountain World.

'Take these chaps to something tough,' said spirited young Wraith Jones.

Ritchie fled with Big Brother. Big Eley, James and I took Eugene, Misha, Tolly and Tommy to Great Gully, Glencoe's grimmest grotto.

Notes on Climbing in Great Gully 1894–1961:

This fine yet frightful line fell direct to NC solo (1894), 137th equal in shades of ferocity on this mountain, this line never flags, and yet essays on this line have not been repetitious, while novel lines have broken out on all sides. 1930: AJ and JHBB scaled ponderous Cuneiform. Great balance required. 1937: JC de-BN (and party) plucked Raven's Gully. 1946–1956: CDMC opened ways of some importance over walls on right and also pleasant ways of passing merit over walls on farthest left too. (Black Dan, Snotter Blob and new exciting trends will be cleaned up in a later tissue).

With then a sense of history, we crept up and down cracks on the far right and up the far left edge of Slimey Wall. Poised on the very Gully bed, Tommy composed and cool as a cooker snapped his jaws. 'Dynamically posed,' said Tommy. The rest of us went to the summit, and lay in the sun, exchanging harmonious pidgin notes on capitalism, dinners and England. Thence we rushed to Lagangarbh, very late for schedule for journey for dinner for Russians for furthering paths to peaces. Ritchie, Eley, James and I went up the Lost Valley, we made a great new route.

Scavaig stravaiged around the beetling Cuillin.

They hove to. Still with this crew, we lent a hearty hand to heave-ho chests and firkins to the Hut. Skye! Mecca to these chaps, all in a froth for Gabbro.

Of an evening we four put an end to the Crack of Dawn to lend that route some matter and form. The Russians tight-roped the razor Ridge, they cut their feet to ribbons. 'At home we haff not such feats,' they said, dismayed. Jones led out the fiery Inglish, fishing.

'Now,' said Big Brother, 'there will be Discussion.' With ears for hours on end we witnessed bottling of priceless notes on inseminative education of Scholars of Sport and spotty Outward Bounders.

And so we left this happy Isle, wedding of thrusting rock and sucking sea.

Last Anglo–Russo Goal was Edin Berg. Of natives, Eley and I alone hazarded this expedition. Plotting multiple courses, homaging mighty lamas, swallowing monsoons, led on by gaping snaking gorges, at the last we faced the final dinner.

Eley and I, in the lead, not in tails, swung into the George, and open arms of Dr Slesser, sheathed in smiles, Kenneth and Tommy, rows of pillars of the Club, and Sir John Hunt who was the conqueror of Everest. Dinners downed, all rose as one, and bubbled up the Mound to the Clubrooms. Crowds had gathered. The excitement was terrific. And here – peak of the week – Red Snows flashed past 200 goggled eyes, never have we seen such Cinema. 'Here was a Summit made,' declared the great ovation and another brick was laid for salvation of the nations.[1]

Anatoli Ovchinnikov, one of the Russians on our hills that week with Robin, reflects that meaningful summit talks could sometimes be difficult even for climbers:

I was roped to Robin for the ascent of Pik Garmo and for the first part of the descent, so, of the Soviet mountaineers, my contact with him was greatest. However, although I was trained to translate technical English, I didn't speak the language, and couldn't understand him sufficiently to give a detailed description of his character. For several years after 1962, I and Anatoli Sevastianov, also on Garmo with us, exchanged letters and New Year greetings with Robin's mother. In particular, I remember that she once wrote: 'If you or any Soviet mountaineers are in Scotland, then you will always find a bed for one or two of you in my house, even though I live modestly and my house is small.'

Memories of joint ascents between British and Soviet mountaineers in the Caucasus in 1958, in Wales, Scotland and on the Isle of Skye in 1960 and in the Pamirs in 1962, come to mind. We gained great satisfaction from our contact with British mountaineers, who, in spite of our accepted opinion of them as reserved and cold, were in fact sociable and pleasant people. We shared with them the joy of successful ascents and the bitterness of loss.

Sir John Hunt first visited our country in 1954. He won over the hearts of Soviet mountaineers with his stories, in particular of the 1953 Everest expedition with Sir Edmund Hillary and Tenzing Norgay, and the film of its ascent. It is possible that Sir John's stories led to the desire of the Soviets to organise our own Everest expedition. In 1956, Soviet and Chinese mountaineers climbed Mustagh Ata and Kongur in the Karakorum and, in 1958, as preparation for a joint ascent of Everest, Pik Lenin in the Pamirs. However, following disagreement between Soviet and Chinese political leaders, the expedition planned for 1959–60 was cancelled. For our dream to come true, we still had a long path to travel and it was not until twenty years after the 1962 British–Soviet expedition to the Pamirs that the ascent of Everest became a reality for us.

Soviet mountaineers responded to Sir John Hunt's initiative to develop joint climbing contacts and mutual understanding. And so, in London on May 21st, 1960, Sir John, British mountaineers and a representative of the Soviet Embassy met our small party. I shall write about the whole of our visit to Britain. I always talk about Britain and not England because during our stay it became clear that England is only part of the British Islands, that the inhabitants of Wales do not consider themselves English and as for the Scots . . . well, no more need be said.

We considered the British strong on rock and knew that Westerners were apt to climb solo, whereas Western mountaineers seemed to think Russians were hardy but couldn't really climb. We always had to prove ourselves. So our team members had taken leave from work to go rock-climbing for three weeks in the Crimea, where, not wishing to disgrace ourselves or our countrymen when we got to Britain, we climbed 5b routes without top protection to ensure we were mentally prepared for any situation.

We were given a very warm welcome and were accommodated in the Park Court Hotel, opposite Hyde Park. We particularly wanted to see Piccadilly Circus which we had heard about in the wartime song.

In general we liked London which was for us a very different environment. During those two days we visited the Alpine Club and a mountaineering equipment shop (which even now do not exist in Moscow). We were also at Buckingham Palace and Downing Street, heard debates in the House of Commons, walked along the Thames embankment, and visited Oxford. We also showed our mountaineering films, which were well received. Naturally, despite our late return to the hotel, we still did an hour's exercising in Hyde Park each morning.

On May 24th we set off for North Wales via Stratford-upon-Avon. Overnight a tented village had grown up around our hut and we were surrounded by newspaper correspondents. This for us was amazing. Cameras clicked and people were looking at us as if we were Martians or people from another world. At that time, of course, you very rarely met Soviet people in the streets of the capitals of Western Europe, never mind in the provinces. There were many stories about us: some true, some total fantasy. We were looked upon as unusual, strange, perhaps even semi-wild. A Frenchman was once disappointed with our appearance, I remember. 'Ah, they're just normal,' he was heard to say after we were pointed out. I was delighted – we were normal people! But many former Soviets come to the West now, not just tourists or scientists but also as representatives of various Mafia organisations, if you believe what the newspapers say.

Next day John Hunt said that, as in the Soviet Union, he would set a control time for our climbs – we were to be back by 3.00 p.m. In our mountains, where non-obervance is exceptional, a search would be organised immediately a party is late. However, Sir John did not return until after 4.30 p.m. and, as we were not accustomed to criticising our leaders, we pretended not to have noticed!

We arrived in Scotland, in Glencoe, on June 3rd and met climbers from Edinburgh among whom were the ever-cheerful and restless Robin Smith and his friend Jim [or James 'Eley' Moriarty]. The weather in Glencoe was overcast. The rocks were soaking, covered in moss and our feet, especially in our type of boots, often slipped. I climbed with Misha Khergiani and Robin climbed with Jim. Robin was a good rock-climber. He knew the routes and he and Jim moved quite quickly while we had to go flat-out in order not to fall behind. That day we each covered two routes and I got to know Robin a bit. The following day Misha and I went to the Isle of Skye with them.

Sunday, June 5th: The weather was cloudy. For the first time in my life I saw the tide coming in. I gathered mussels. After lunch John Neill

239

took us to a viewpoint to show us the peaks, but visibility was poor. It was only at about noon that it cleared up a little and we did a traverse of most of the peaks of the island's main ridge. Towards evening it cleared up totally and visibility was exceptional. It was clear that we were on an island and, in the distance on the mainland, also an island, were the mountains of Scotland including the peak of Ben Nevis. Scotland, being in the north, has light nights just as in Leningrad or Karelia, where there are also many lakes.

June 7th: Misha Khergiani and I were to go to Nevis, where Robin was to take us to some difficult routes. It rained all night and by morning it hadn't stopped. Only at 3 p.m. did the ferry arrive and in half an hour we got off at Mallaig. We missed the train. Jim and Robin put Misha and myself in the tent outside the town and they themselves went to spend the night at the station. In the morning Misha and I got up at 5.30 a.m., packed our rucksacks and went to the railway station where we found Robin and Jim asleep, but by 6.30 a.m. we were on our way to Fort William, a journey of about 60 km. It was raining. In Fort William, we left part of our gear with a friend of Robin's, took a short bus journey, and walked up to the mountain hut up the damp, muddy path. In general the terrain was similar to the Caucasus. Unfortunately it was still raining, the mountains were covered in cloud, visibility was nil, and we wouldn't be able to do the climb Robin had in mind.

After lunch at the Captain Charles Inglis Clark [CIC] hut we climbed Nevis by the easiest ridge route – up Observatory Ridge, then down Tower Ridge – and returned to Fort William in the evening. On the way there, Robin and Jim practised climbing on an arch across the road. Their climbing was masterful and they suggested that we should try it too, but we didn't accept their offer as we thought it not right to climb on public buildings in a foreign country.

The following day we arrived in Edinburgh, where we again met Robin at a function in a hotel. En route we had been invited to lunch at the house of a Scottish lord.[2] Unfortunately I don't know his name as we didn't exchange visiting cards – I didn't have any and he perhaps didn't consider it necessary. Robin and Jim were also there. Not only did we taste Scottish dishes but found out about certain original features of Scottish culture, that is the kilt and the bagpipes.

There were also amusing incidents when we were in Britain. In one of the morning papers I saw the familiar word 'vodka' and read the article carefully. A journalist had come into our hut in Wales, had seen the vodka and caviar we had brought for social occasions, and decided that the

Russians had got up in the morning, drunk the vodka, eaten the caviar and gone climbing. We all had a good laugh. Only Eugene Gippenreiter, the official representative of the Soviet State Committee for Sport, was worried about possible consequences when we returned to Moscow.

I was especially amused to discover that I was suspected of being a member of the KGB. On a piece of paper found under the table at one of our receptions were descriptions next to each of our names, with many question marks against mine. Our leader, Michael Borushko, and I were both senior lecturers at Technical Institutes, though I, for some reason, was listed as a student. We had our work in common and, during discussions on our programme, he often asked, 'What do you think?' The British thought that each USSR delegation had to have a KGB agent as secret leader to sanction the actions of the formal leader.

Our delegation to Britain received a lot of publicity. Even in the London newspapers, there were reports about our stay almost every day. We were advised then by Soviet authorities not to take newspapers home, but I have given those I kept to Misha Khergiani's museum in Miestia. Of course I understood that the attention was not the result of our personal qualities but rather an interest in the Soviet Union and respect for our country. On the one hand, this was due to the Soviet army's contribution to the successful conclusion of the Second World War in Europe, an indisputable fact, and also to the first space flight by Yuri Gagarin just one year before our visit. Western nations were amazed that our country, with its destroyed economy, could achieve such an outstanding success. On the other hand, it was due to the authority of Sir John Hunt who led the Himalayan expedition in 1953 when Everest was conquered for the first time: the world's third pole. Not only had we met him during his lecture visit to Moscow in 1954, but we did so again in 1958, when he was returning home from his expedition to the Caucasus.

An important result of our trip was the idea of organising a joint British–Soviet expedition with the aim of climbing the Soviet Union's highest peak which at that time was simply called 'Pik 7495 Metres'. Sir John took on the responsibility of organising this and we promised the full support of Soviet mountaineers.

241

35

INVITATIONS[1]

Influenced by the hospitality extended to their climbers in 1960, and in recognition of British support for the USSR's application to join the International Mountaineering Federation, the Soviets made it known that applications by British mountaineering clubs for permission to climb in the USSR were likely to be considered favourably. As it turned out, British support was not enough for the application's success, the nub of the problem being the goal of communist expansionism set forth in the Soviet Federation's constitution.

Two men, John Hunt and Malcom Slesser, already knew of each other's ambitions to climb in the Pamirs, having discussed this when the Russians were in Britain. Each sent off an application, the Glasgow-based Slesser writing under the banner of the SMC, while John Hunt was acting as joint spokesman for two London-based clubs, the Alpine Club and the Climbers' Club. On May 23rd, 1961 the SMC and John Hunt received identical telegrams from Moscow:

AGREE TO VISITS OF UNITED GROUPS OF ALPINE CLUB AND SCOTTISH MOUNTAINEERING CLUB TOTAL TWELVE PERSONS JULY–AUGUST 1961 CENTRAL CAUCASUS FOR 30 DAYS STOP 1962 PAMIR PIK STALINA REGION FOR 65 DAYS LETTER FOLLOWS REGARDS
USSR MOUNTAINEERING FEDERATION

In his book, *Life is Meeting*, published in 1978, John Hunt reflected wryly on his reactions to the invitations: 'The issue of nationalities within the United Kingdom was neatly solved by the Soviet authorities. I have since wondered whether their underlying purpose might have been to divide, rather than strengthen, the Act of Union 1707.' The Caucasus offer was of no interest to him or to Slesser. Indeed, John Hunt was unaware that an application to climb there had been made by the SMC.

The Pamirs, the former USSR's highest mountains which form

242

the northwestern extremity of the Himalayan chain and rise to more than 24,000 ft, are located in central Asia in Tajikistan – close to Afghanistan, China, Pakistan-controlled northern Kashmir (under dispute with India) and Pakistan itself. In the eastern Pamirs, the average height of peaks exceeds 20,000 ft, but summits are no more than 3000 to 6000 ft above high surrounding base levels. In the western Pamirs, target area for the expedition, mountains are both higher and sharply disjointed, low ranges alternating with high snow-capped ridges that overlook glaciers. Fast rivers flow in deep narrow ravines and debris has filled the valleys leaving few places suitable for human settlement. Other mountain ranges lie within sight from Pamir summits: the Karakorum to the southeast, on the Himalayan range, the Hindu Kush to the southwest and the Tien Shan to the northeast.

Marco Polo described the Pamirs as 'the roof of the world' when he ventured through them in about 1273. The north–south alignment of part of the range was a barrier blocking the old silk roads from China. Caravans from the east were forced to veer north via Samarkand, or south and west across northern Afghanistan, before reuniting near the frontier of Iran and continuing for a further 2000 miles to the Mediterranean. Historic Samarkand lies 400 miles north-west of the expedition's destination.

Three Empires – Russian, Chinese and British – once met at the remote Pamirs. In the 1880s and 1890s, some border frontiers still had to be fixed in the region and Russia and Britain manoeuvred against one another for military and political ascendancy. During those decades the Pamirs were explored and mapped by soldier-explorers of both empires and their efforts reflected in treaties concluded in 1895. New boundaries, formed naturally by mountains and valleys as dividers, were agreed. Most significantly, Afghanistan was reshaped to include the Hindu Kush and the Wakhan valley, the tongue of land extending east to China; the Karakorum, now part of Pakistan, became the northern limit of India–Kashmir; the Pamirs and land to their north and west, which had once belonged to Persia, were annexed to the Russian Empire. By 1895 the distance between the Russian and British Empires, about 2000 miles at the beginning of that century, had shrunk to no more than twenty. Some British statesmen saw that as a threat. However, earlier sporadic Cossack incursions beyond those demarcations towards India, the British Empire's 'jewel', had come to nothing. The boundaries still exist 100 years later, and were respected until the Soviet invasion of Afghanistan in 1979.

After the 1917 Bolshevik revolution the area became almost inaccessible to foreigners. One such, the celebrated German traveller and mountaineer WW Rickmer-Rickmers, who had first visited the Garmo glacier in 1913, seems to have been the only one to have reached the heart of the mountains, in an expedition to the Western Pamirs in 1928. By then, Soviets had begun extensive exploration, of a military nature initially, then geographic, and in 1931 discovered the summit which became known as Pik Stalina. Pik Stalina was first climbed in 1933 by Vitali Abalakov, whom Robin by coincidence came to meet. By 1962 all Pamir mountains in excess of 6000 metres (20,000 ft) had been ascended, some by more than one route. The highest was renamed following Stalin's fall from favour. Pending the choice of Pik Kommunisma in 1962, it was temporarily called Pik 7495 Metres. Rickmer-Rickmers' findings became invaluable during the expedition's planning stages, and his notes and a unique map were collected from his Munich home in spring 1962.

Upon receipt of the Soviets' invitation, John Hunt immediately wrote to Malcolm Slesser, on May 25th, 1961:

I have in front of me the welcome news, intended both for the Alpine Club and the Scottish Mountaineering Club, that visits are approved for this year to the Caucasus, and for next year to the Pamirs.

I have passed this on to Emlyn Jones, Honorary Secretary of the Alpine Club, so that he may be in touch with the SMC about it forthwith; officially, it is none of my affair although I have had a hand in bringing it about.

As far as I know, the SMC has not made a bid to go to the Caucasus this year and this was exclusively the enterprise of the AC [Alpine Club], in arranging a meet in the Caucasus. Unless we hear to the contrary, therefore, I imagine the AC will wish to avail of all twelve vacancies, if they can fill them.

As regards next year, I would hope that an amicable arrangement can be made between the two clubs, by which a combined group of twelve climbers go to the Pamirs, on a ratio to be agreed mutually. Of course, the matter goes further than that as someone will have to be in charge and that, 'someone' will have to be happy about the choice of members of the combined group! I say this with some feeling as it might conceivably be myself.

Slesser replied from Glasgow:

> The Russian decision was one of the three possibles I expected, and poses problems for yourself and myself. I have yet to get the letter promised in their telegram, and that might marginally modify any impressions gained, but in essence it asks that the SMC and AC parties combine.
>
> I have talked this over with all of our party, save George Lowe and Iain Smart; and with the SMC secretary. We are all agreed that the joint party is perfectly workable, provided you are the leader. I am most sincere in this, and want you to know that nothing would please all of us here better than that you were, are, the leader.
>
> I realise that the Russian suggestion must pose difficulties to that CC/AC [Climbers' Club/Alpine Club] group who originally approached you to be their leader and spokesman, but I feel I mustn't enter into that problem. Save for Alan Blackshaw, whom I like very much, I know none of them personally at all.
>
> On the face of it, that should be a party composed of 50 per cent SMC and 50 per cent AC. I can see that many will think that since the AC has done more sponsoring, they should have a bigger say, and I am inclined to agree. On the other hand we have been pretty active in working on the Russians, through the Foreign Office, the USSR Federation of Mountaineers and others. However, when you look at my party, you will see that three are members of the AC and two of these are not members of the SMC (McNaught-Davis and George Lowe [both also CC members]). Of my party, you know everyone well enough, I think, to satisfy your excellent criterion of knowing each man personally, except for Don Bennet. Of him, I can only say that he is a good man, quite well-known up here, active climber, and knocked off several 20–21,000 footers in the Ladhak Himalayas with the RAF expedition some years ago, and close friend of Dan Stewart.
>
> I put forward a definite plan to the Russians, concerned with making a base on the Garmo glacier, and trying a new route up Pik Stalina. This they seem to have accepted. George Lowe may have told you of this idea.
>
> Please regard this letter as quite off the cuff, unofficial, and merely to assure you of our genuine feelings that you are the man we feel is best to lead the joint party, that we don't mind the joint party, but that we do feel that SMC group should have a good say in the party and its composition.

Here is our party, as it was: Self, leader; Mac [Iain McNaught-Davis], deputy leader; Ken Bryan, climber; Iain Smart, doctor; George Lowe, climber and cine-photographer; Donald Bennet, climber. Our plans had also encompassed two to four Russian members.

John Hunt's role as leader and Malcolm Slesser's as deputy leader of a mixed club party were effectively formalised.

The two non-SMC invitees, Lowe and McNaught-Davis, had joined Slesser in an expedition to Greenland the previous year. Slesser accorded them recognition as high-altitude men.

A few days later, identically worded letters, dated May 29th, duly reached both John Hunt and Malcolm Slesser from the USSR Mountaineering Federation:

> Further to our cable of May 23rd, we advise you some details connected with the visits of British climbers to the mountain regions of the Soviet Union in 1961 and 1962.
>
> Since the Scottish Mountaineering Club has applied to the Mountaineering Federation of the USSR with the analogous requests, both of the contemplated visits can be realised on condition of organising joint groups of not more than twelve members, ie six climbers from each of the clubs. This will facilitate considerably the preparation and organisation of the said undertakings, especially with the expedition in 1962, since it will be operative in the remote and difficult region of Pamir. I can inform you in a preliminary way that a tentative region for the operations of the expedition will be Garmo glacier with Pik Stalina, its southwest side in particular, as the object for ascents as well as other neighbouring summits. Duration of the expedition will be up to sixty-five days in July–August 1962.

The Soviets also stated that expenses for the British part of the joint expedition would be expected to be borne by the Alpine Club and Scottish Mountaineering Club and indicated that they would like to meet a representative of the British party in Moscow later in the year.

Robin Smith, c.1960, on Steeplejack Staircase, Salisbury Crags, an extreme route first climbed by Derek Haworth. Photo by Jimmy Marshall.

Dougal Haston on the second ascent of Robin Smith's Glueless Grooves route on the Cobbler, 1957. Photo by Jimmy Marshall, who shared in its second ascent.

At Courmayeur shortly after the ascents of the Walker Spur. (L–R): Don Whillans, Les Brown, Robin Smith, Gunn Clarke, John Streetly. 1959. Photo by Hamish MacInnes.

Ben Nevis, northeast face. The Orion Face is in sunshine on the far left.
Jimmy Marshall and Robin did some epic climbing here in 1960.
Photo by Tom Weir and reprinted with thanks.

Gordon Greig (left) and William Stewart, Robin's University tutors, 1960.
Courtesy of Gordon Greig.

Robin keeping up his ridge-walking skills . . .
Courtesy of the Smith family.

In August 1960 Robin and Goofy climbed the 3000-ft North Spur of the
Fiescherwand in near-winter conditions. The spur is to the right of the summit.
Photo by Jimmy Cruickshank (taken end of June 2001).

Setting off for the Pamirs, June 30th, 1962. From back (L–R): Ted Wrangham, Graeme Nicol; George Lowe, Ralph Jones; Joe Brown, Derek Bull; Wilfrid Noyce, Robin Smith; John Hunt, Ian McNaught-Davis. Photo © *Mirrorpix*.

Robin (right) and Eley Moriarty while with the Soviet climbers visiting Scotland, 1960. Photo by Eugene Gippenreiter, provided courtesy of Anatoli Ovchinnikov.

Robin and Wilfrid Noyce on Pik Garmo, approximately one hour before they died, 24 July 1962. Photo by Anatoli Sevastianov.

Pik Garmo (6595 m), showing the line of the Robin/Wilfrid Noyce fall on 24 July 1962, and the location of the bivvie site. Photo by Anatoli Sevastianov, reprinted with thanks to Anatoli Ovchinnikov.

Robin's note to Davie Agnew (see Chapter 32), which he received after Robin fell to his death. Reprinted with thanks to Davie Agnew.

The memorial built for Robin and Wilfrid Noyce by a group of Soviet mountaineers. July 1962. Photo by Malcolm Slesser.

Moscow 1993. (L–R): Eugene Gippenreiter, Alasdair Forrest, Anatoli Ovchinnikov, Olga Thulojay and Anatoli Sevastianov. Courtesy of Alasdair Forrest.

36

PARTY POLITICS

Slesser visited John Hunt in London at the end of June 1961 and
followed up this visit on July 11th with a letter about the delicate issue
of the role of the Climbers' Club, whose members had helped initiate
the expedition. He failed to see how the CC could be associated with
the venture on any official basis. 'The Russians have given permission
to the AC and SMC, and that is the way I should prefer to see the
joint expedition labelled,' Slesser stated. 'Naturally, there is no objection to anyone from the CC coming on the expedition and some of
the proposed party are members of the CC. I feel most strongly that
the planning of this affair should remain an AC/SMC matter.'
Recognising that his load was now much lighter, as he no longer had
an expedition to organise – whereas it was the reverse for John Hunt
– Slesser offered to help in any way he could.

On July 19th John Hunt wrote to AB Hargreaves, President of the
Climbers' Club (CC) about 'the most helpful part' his club had played:

> First, you will remember that, when we met to discuss the project last
> autumn, it was decided to make the application on behalf of the Alpine
> Club only, despite the interest of the CC, owing to the known attitude
> of the Russians towards requests from climbing groups to visit the Soviet
> Union. In the outcome, as you know, the USSR Federation has given
> permission for a combined AC/SMC party; a request from the SMC
> having been made independently of that from the Alpine Club. In these
> circumstances I do not feel that it would be politic to have the expedi-
> tion officially associated with the CC, much as I personally would like
> to do so. I very much hope that the CC committee will be understanding
> of this viewpoint.

He went on to suggest to Hargreaves that the more important issue
was the actual representation of CC members within the party.
Climbers already invited from south of the border were Iain
McNaught-Davis, George Lowe, George Band, Alan Blackshaw,
Ted Wrangham, Ralph Jones, Derek Bull, of whom Lowe and

McNaught-Davis, both Climbers' Club members, had been proposed by the SMC. 'This may seem curious to you (as it does to me!),' John Hunt reflected. 'But it is a happy chance that they both belong to the CC. The remaining four are Scots and members of the SMC. I do not propose to justify my choice of the party, but you may care to know that I have tried to achieve a combination of high-altitude experience, general mountaineering competence and, not least important, good public relations potential!'

John Hunt then received a letter from Bennet stating that, provided he did not prolong his stay in Vancouver to work for a higher degree, 'I might be able to return to Britain and join you in early July.' Feeling that Bennet must now be regarded as a reserve, John Hunt wrote to Slesser on September 12th:

> We must discuss this at our meeting on September 21st, but I would like you to know my feeling, which is that we should replace him with a very strong climber. Although there is a nominal 50:50 basis as between the SMC and the AC, I think you will agree that on the present membership we should not necessarily be too strict in adhering to this, bearing in mind the whole expedition as I have tentatively outlined it . . .
>
> On the above premise, I would like to invite Wilfrid Noyce to join the expedition. He is, in general terms, the most outstanding mountaineer in Britain today . . .

Slesser discussed with President Ian Charleson the implications of a proposition that would cut SMC participation to three members. They decided it was unacceptable, and Slesser wrote to John Hunt on September 14th to advise him of this:

> We are agreed that the combined party should continue to be 50:50 SMC/AC. Even as it stands, the bias is considerably in the AC favour through the fact that Mac and George happened to be in my party. We should not wish to see the SMC representation fall lower, and indeed, would rather see it move the other way.
>
> I am all for regarding the expedition as a single entity, and have no wish to see any division into this or that grouping, but the fact remains that the Russians have given permission to the AC and to the SMC, and have ordained that the two shall amalgamate and I cannot see that, whatever the attractive choices in personnel that you could make south of the Border, this can be got round.

It follows that, however much I highly regard the possibility of Wilfrid Noyce joining, it is clearly impossible, unless some vacancy falls in the AC ranks.

John, I can see your difficulty. You are faced with a joint party, and yet have insufficient personal knowledge of the potential SMC candidates. This is unfortunate but surely out of a club of almost 400 members, there are two or three who can fit into the scheme of things. In addition to a number of strong and well-known climbers like Smith, Patey or Ritchie, there are umpteen younger blokes, both likeable and deserving of a chance to go on a trip like this one.

All of this could be rough ground, which I think should be right behind us before 11 a.m. on the 21st [the date of the first committee meeting in London].

On September 15th Iain Smart, doctor and SMC man, wrote to John Hunt to apologise for not being able to attend this meeting. He continued:

I realise how important this initial meeting is and I regret my defection. I am particularly concerned as it will weaken the SMC representation and I understand that there are moves from the AC to weaken this still further. I would like to stress that I have complete confidence in you as leader of a united party and I shall undertake all the tasks given to me in connection with the organisation of the expedition and shall strive for its unity. At the same time, Malcolm has my complete support in the matter of parity. In an international expedition such as this, involving three countries, it is a point which must be settled at the outset and I have confidence that you are above any local London parochial influences.

John Hunt to Slesser on September 19th:

From your letter, I gathered that the SMC intends to insist on the terms of the invitation from the Russians which do not incidentally mention the exact numbers to be provided from each club; nor, in any case, do I feel that we should have this kind of dictation from across the Iron Curtain. The essence of the matter is the need to have a homogenous party which will play its small part in furthering British–Soviet relations. I thought I would write you this letter to give you further food for thought before we meet, as I detect in a letter from Iain Smart that he at any rate is thinking in terms of three countries being involved in this visit. Personally, I find room for only two countries, Britain and the Soviet Union.

The first expedition committee meeting was held at the Ski Club, London on September 21st, 1961, attended by Sir John Hunt, Malcolm Slesser, Alan Blackshaw, Ken Bryan, Derek Bull, Ralph Jones and Ted Wrangham. Apologies for absence were noted from George Lowe, Iain McNaught-Davis, Iain Smart and two noted as being abroad: George Band and Don Bennet. The Secretary was Sue Bradshaw, and her minutes recorded that . . .

Sir John opened the meeting by defining the aims of the expedition. It was unique in that it was a joint party with the Russians and, for that reason, it was most important to make it a very friendly party, not only before but during and after the expedition. As the aim was to get together with the Russians, little would be achieved if it was not a happy united party, and in fact a good deal of harm might be done. Sir John wanted to make sure it would be a worthwhile trip.

Applications to the Mountaineering Federation of the USSR had been made through the Alpine Club and the Scottish Mountaineering Club only because the Russians would not entertain the idea of private individuals going. Both clubs had accepted the role of sponsor. This did not mean however that it was a representative AC/SMC party. The spirit of a club or a nation was inimicable to the unity of the expedition. The leader must take people who were acceptable to him. Therefore the choice lay with Sir John to make up a homogenous party of friends. They were chosen through the agency of the AC and the SMC, but Sir John wanted to feel they were a composite group.

In the discussion which followed, it was pointed out that an opportunity of this kind had not come to the SMC before, and for that reason they would like to see it as a representative party. However it was also pointed out that the Climbers' Club who had initiated the application to the Russians, had subsequently stood down in the interest of the party as a whole.

It was also thought important that the Russians should realise that in Britain the emphasis was on the individual, rather than the group, to which Sir John replied that it must be, first and foremost, a party, not three separate countries – Russia, England and Scotland – that were involved. The most important thing was that the party should not be split when it got there.

The twelve, both those at the meeting and those absent, were classed as having been proposed either by John Hunt or by the clubs concerned and as having accepted. The level of SMC participation was a crucial point of debate and it had been agreed that, in the event of resignations from the SMC contingent (non-SMC members Lowe and McNaught-Davis included) they would be replaced with SMC members. The minutes went on to state that 'it is agreed to be most important that the party should be a single team, and not two groups owing separate allegiances to the sponsoring clubs'.

Amongst other points, the Soviet Mountaineering Federation would be approached with a view to increasing the party to fourteen members, 'in order to enable a larger number to profit from this unique opportunity and to get more done in the short time available'.

A major planning exercise was about to start. John Hunt had already prepared a 'Planning Calendar' showing dates for completion of major tasks, dates of future meetings, including a 'Weekend Party Meet' on Nevis the following March. A 'Planning Responsibilities' sheet listed those who had agreed to take on responsibilities under the following headings: Policy, Diplomatic Contacts, Finance, Travel, Rations, Photography, Research and Maps, Equipment, Transport, Publicity. Purchase of equipment (mountaineering, tents and bedding, cooking, medical) and responsibility for its transport with that of the rations was allocated to the Scots under Slesser's delegation.

As matters stood on September 21st 1961, the party of twelve was complete. On the 22nd, however, George Band withdrew. Over the course of the next two months, an AC replacement would also have to be found for Alan Blackshaw. From SMC ranks replacements would be needed for Iain Smart, in the specialist role of doctor, and Donald Bennet.

The party's composition soon became common knowledge. That it lacked strength in depth attracted attention and comment from those in the top echelons of the sport. South of the border, the young Chris Bonington, president of the hard-climbing Alpine Climbing Group (ACG) which Robin would shortly join, put his views on October 28th, 1961 in reply to a letter from John Hunt. It discloses the feelings of the more accomplished climbers on both sides of the border, and highlights party strength as a major consideration underlying much of the activity and correspondence around that time:

I felt it my duty to make heard the feelings of a large body of leading modern Alpinists. I fully appreciate that prejudice never dictated your choice of party. However, I feel the very fact that you had to give your expedition official status immediately imposed obligations on you. The Russians are allowing the expedition in on the understanding that it is representative.

Even with McNaught-Davis, Brown, Patey and Noyce though [if included], this gives it a strong basis, it is certainly not representative. Don Whillans, undoubtedly our best mountaineer (Brown has done nothing major in climbing for six years), has been ignored. None of the climbers who are doing outstanding routes in the Alps have been asked.

Quite a few of your party, though very pleasant people, are not particularly good climbers, and I doubt if they have much endurance. It is important that they were among the founders of the party. However, once you had to go under official guise, I feel you took up many extra obligations. There is no doubt about it, that once the membership of the party becomes public, it will be examined critically, and I think justifiably so.

In conclusion, I would strongly urge that, if any vacancies should occur, they should go to people like Don Whillans, Dennis Davies or even one of the younger generation like Ian Clough. I greatly appreciate the trouble you took to write.

Well before the conclusion of correspondence with Bonington, John Hunt was conscious that an effort was needed to strengthen the party. On October 10th he had again made reference to this to Malcolm Slesser in a letter which dealt in the main with the proposed visit to Moscow, a task to be undertaken by Slesser, as Hunt was too pressed by other commitments:

> . . . As regards the party, I have invited Wilfrid Noyce [a replacement for George Band], following my last letter to yourself; I await his reply. I have also written to Donald Bennet in the sense of my last letter. It therefore remains to fill Donald's place from someone up your way. In view of the difficulties of first selection by myself, I suggest that you make the initial choice, leaving it to me to confirm it when I meet the person in question. I would hope this might be done on 23rd November [the date of the next meeting in Glasgow]. In making your selection, I know you will bear in mind the various desiderata, competence and good public relations potential . . .

Iain Smart to John Hunt:

Thank you for your letter accepting my apologies for absence at the recent Pamirs meeting. I would like to congratulate you for the way you have sat on English nationalism and have insisted that both of the United Kingdoms be equitably represented. Under such circumstances, it logically follows that we shall be a loyal party of friends.

By a cruel stroke of irony I am scheduled to be in London on the 23rd and 24th November to read a paper to one of the learned societies there. As it happens to concern a field in which London is about twenty-five years behind the rest of the world, I feel it is my bounden duty to attend in order to shine a light in the darkness. I am trying to arrange for my papers to be read on the 24th which would enable me to be in Glasgow on the day of the 23rd, travelling to London overnight. I shall do all in my power to be present at this meeting as I am sure you must want to re-establish personal relations with all members of the party as soon as possible.

Meanwhile I shall proceed with planning the medical side. I am very much looking forward to meeting you again and supporting you in your onerous task of organising and leading this difficult expedition.

John Hunt sent Smart's letter to Slesser for advice. Slesser replied:

I, and anyone else who has come in contact with Iain, has always found him to possess a finely-drawn subtle sense of humour. I am used to Iain's letters. You are not. Had the letter been addressed to me, I should have been tickled, but then I know what he was trying to say; that is, I know in advance.

But it isn't the letter I should have thought he should have sent you, for very understandably, it is capable of misunderstanding; and much depends on how it's read.

It's no part of my business to explain away Iain's faux pas or his ways. But I should help you by interpreting his letter, for he is being quite earnest (in his first paragraph, for instance) and at the same time giving you a playful poke in the ribs. He is alluding to the fact that the English as a race seem to the Scots to be much more Anglocentric, than British-minded, relative to the Scot. Whole libraries have been devoted to the subject, and I have always enjoyed a book by Moray McLaren and James Bridie called *A Small Stir, or Letters on the English*, in which they compare the two nationalities, largely to the advantage of the English.

Anyway, the point has been made that we're a party of friends, and British, and I for one hope that that's that.

Yes. I'll deal with substitute for Donald Bennet, and write again . . .

On October 16th John Hunt continued his deliberations about the strength of the party in a letter to Slesser:

Thanks so much for your letter, returning Iain's; I see that I shall have to cultivate a Scottish sense of humour as well as a working knowledge of the Russian language! However, do not worry; I had not taken it unduly seriously.

On a much more serious note, however, rumours have reached me that there is a certain amount of concern in the mountaineering world at the absence, in our ranks, of any of the younger climbers at present in the forefront of achievement. Without intending to alter the general requirements for membership as I have discussed them with you from the beginning, I share your own concern that we should, if possible, strengthen the party from the point of view of mountaineering skill.

One opportunity to do so is now open to you, following the decision about Donald; from a talk I had with Charleson on the phone, I gather that the SMC is helping you with advice on this point. By inviting Noyce I have (I believe) made another move in the same direction.

There remain two other possible ways of strengthening the party from the technical point of view:

(a) That we increase the size of the party, as agreed at our last meeting, rather than leave it until your visit to Moscow. I have cabled today for permission from the Russians.
(b) To accept any resignations. Naturally I would not withdraw any invitation already made and accepted; moreover I would be sorry to see any withdrawals. On the other hand, Derek Bull offered me his resignation as he is so deeply impressed by the point of view expressed in certain quarters among top climbers. I am considering accepting his offer and would, in this event, like to invite Chris Bonington.

John Hunt concluded that, one way or another, the party would be both 'adequately strong and reasonably analogous in other respects'. However, the Russians, by return cable, refused permission for the party to be increased to fourteen. Slesser replied to John Hunt on October 17th, unaware of the Russians' decision:

Thanks for your letter of yesterday's date. This is us running into the trouble of having had official SMC and AC backing. I still feel that you, as leader, have the ultimate choice, and that the fact that a young climber is in the forefront of achievement doesn't necessarily give him a right to come on the expedition. This isn't Everest, and nor do the mountains of the Pamir represent the hardest mountains of the high sort, so that other factors come very much into selection.

I would very much deplore Derek Bull resigning. This expedition has deeper roots than that. Furthermore, is Alpine technical skill all that is needed? Anyway if Derek Bull was to resign in order to give his place to stronger men (and younger men) I should certainly accompany him, for he has as good a right as myself to be on the party, and I have as little claim to hard mountaineering, or less probably, than him. But I don't intend to resign.

I think the matter will sort itself out. I feel sure that even of the present party some event or other will take more of the original party off the list. Re Bonington, I got the impression at our meeting on the 21/9/61 that he was felt to be too much of a prima donna, though as an individual I've heard nothing but good about him.

I don't know how you've found it, but with myself I've always found that when it comes to thinking of a party for a big trip, some of the best climbers turn out to be intolerable! My view is that you should not increase the size of the party unless to accommodate certain people who you feel very strongly would be an advantage to the party. Otherwise, have them as reserves.

I have now heard from Tom Patey, to whom I wrote in guarded terms. He is free to come and, from his letter, would obviously like to. I've enclosed his letter, because it might let you see him directly, not through any impressions I may pass your way. I would strongly urge you to ask him, for these reasons:

1. He was and is one of the best climbers ever to come out of Scotland.
2. He is a doctor, and while no good to the expedition as the *only* doctor, would be an excellent additional man, and he is likely to be effective at high levels, for he is just so fit and able.
3. He is mature, past his prima-donna stage.
4. He has a certain international acclaim.
5. He is a proven high-altitude man.
6. He plays the accordion wonderfully. Such a musician could

bring us tremendous advantage in dealing with the larger groups
of Russians.

Charleson has written me about others; of these Patey is one. Robin
Smith and Dougal Haston are others. The rest are too young or too
inexperienced, I think, to want to take. Smith I have written, but had
no reply. If you were thinking of a party of fourteen, I would suggest
it be Bonington and Smith. Smith, with no Himalayan experience, is
quite brilliant as a climber, certainly the hardest man north of the border.
He has been deplorably cliquey, so that even those of us in the west of
Scotland hardly know him. This expedition could be the making of
him. He has just graduated in Honours Philosophy.

But supposing it stays at twelve, *then with Patey*, we would have the
following men of proven high-altitude experience: Yourself, Noyce,
Mac, Patey, Wrangham, Lowe – not a bad bunch! – and Ken Bryan
alone represents 'young' Britain.

So much for my musings. All is fixed for Russia but the Russians. I
need a letter or telegram from Moscow supporting my visit in order to
obtain a visa, and hope to get this from you as soon as it comes in. I
can hold my plane bookings till ten days before departure.

37

WILF'S HESITATION

Reviewing the era for a moment, the Cold War between ideologically opposed East and West was at its zenith during the 1960s. The Berlin Wall was under construction. With the 1962 Cuban Crisis, a few months after the expedition, the world teetered on the brink of a nuclear abyss. At an individual level, there was little contact between people from opposite sides of the Iron Curtain. Few Soviets then had opportunities and permission for foreign travel, and Westerners were generally not welcome in the USSR nor trusted once there. Derek Bull, for example, came to be arrested in Dushanbe for taking photographs and was put in jail for a few hours until his link with the expedition could be established. Strict travel restrictions were imposed on the few Westerners who did go. In border areas, sometimes depopulated, and where radar and other military installations were concentrated, Soviet authorities were wary of visitors to an even greater degree. Consternation in the West about Soviet spying also ran high. There was great distrust on both sides.

That backcloth was to affect the final composition of the party. Wilf Noyce had great reservations about going and was unlikely to have gone but for strong feelings that international relations could perhaps be favourably influenced by interaction at personal level. John Hunt came to reflect: 'Initially he decided not to go. From some notes found in his effects at Base Camp, it was clear that Wilf had hesitated about joining the expedition. Should I have persuaded him to join me, this once more? Well, it was too late now.' Noyce's ideals can be gleaned from the piece John Hunt found:

A LARK SANG. I opened an eye. There were the Downs, soft, with villages nestling beneath them. Spears of corn pricked up from fields rich for all their rubble of flint and chalk. Great stupid sheep stared, unaware how ridiculous they looked after shearing. This earth held me as in a cup to the wide sky, lord of this landscape of quilted fields, little churches and cottages.

And I thought: men from this soft land have taken their dreams to farther and vaster ranges, and have come back and have seen here the chapels of their faith, as the Himalaya were the cathedrals. And other men go from wider country which they love no less, from the frostgirt plateau of Moscow or from the Georgian slopes; not to find cathedrals, for they do not believe in them, but for other ideals which they believe as high. And when these two races meet, perhaps they find they are not so far apart as at first they thought.

When I was sitting on the summit of Trivor in the Karakorum, I noted the line of fairy summits away to the northwest. Mechanically I realised that the Pamirs of Russia were before me. But I felt no emotion, no zeal for a Promised Land. Even when I knew that an expedition was being organised, it did not occur to me that I could or should go with it. And when the chance came my way, I was filled with doubt.

What moves a man who sits brooding over an invitation? For some no brooding is needed: this is the chance of a lifetime. For most, work or home supply the age-old dilemma. To me, brooding, it seemed that mountaineering had hitherto been a private adventure, a self-seeking. Days in the mountains had given me personally something, whether I was alone or with companions. I could understand much, despite the bar of imperfectly understood speech. To be with those who thought and spoke quite differently, yet on common ground and with common aims – this might be a bridge, not only of my understanding of other men's motives in the sport of mountaineering, but perhaps even, in a small way, of the gap separating East and West over all other fields of thought.[1]

Noyce's line of thought was remarked upon by his widow, Rosemary, in a letter written when I was compiling this biography decades later:

I appreciate that a few notes about Wilfrid would be appropriate, but am not sure that I can add much to what you already know or even whether I am prepared to delve too deeply into painful memories. Also there are large blank areas and I could possibly be misinterpreting the facts.

I think it may be correct to say that, basically, this was an ill-fated venture for Wilf from the start. He had just given up his job as a schoolteacher in order to concentrate on writing and lecturing and he had several projects on the go. Luckily two books were far enough advanced to be published after his death. He was forty-four and at this point in his career he did not need a diversion, so at first was reluctant to break off and join the Russian expedition. But he was finally persuaded that his climbing experience and linguistic skills would be useful in this attempt to break down barriers. International communication was always close to his heart. So, with hindsight, you could probably say he went against his better judgement and whether he had premonitions that all would not be well I do not know. He certainly took out much more life insurance than before, a fact I only became aware of later. And, as the time drew near to leave for Russia, he became very depressed and run-down and suffered a series of minor ailments. The last straw was he developed a foot infection and was hobbling about with slippers and a stick during the last days at home! I do not know if Wilf continued to be in a poor state of health during the expedition.

For myself, I married a mountaineer, so mountaineering was something I was prepared to live with, though not necessarily be happy with. Like Wilf, in 1962 I felt that three major expeditions in our twelve years together was about enough and we needed to get on with our lives together as a family. But it was not to be.

Graeme Nicol, who ultimately went as expedition doctor after Iain Smart withdrew, states that Noyce was not unwell in the Pamirs and, albeit by the unimpressive standards of the party generally, not unfit. According to *Welsh Rock*, written in 1986 by C. Trevor Jones and Geoff Milburn, however, Noyce lacked his usual equanimity and was sufficiently out of sorts before the expedition for the former to record it. And the *Daily Herald*, for whom Noyce was expedition correspondent, thought that words used by him in his last communication merited repetition: '... if, of course, nothing happens'. It also reprinted an extract from an article written by Noyce before leaving Britain, this time with the last three words printed in italics: 'I have a hankering after places that have not been trodden by anybody, and both the shapely Mount Moscow and Mount Garmo seem to have *secrets in store.*'

Noyce to John Hunt, August 14th:

I feel a general worm not having written since the Easter weekend. Particularly on the question of the Pamirs.

As said then I was, and still am, interested apart from the financial aspect, and one or two others & it is these which have kept me in a state of indetermination, which seems to be becoming chronic.

You have probably given me up (I expect you were expecting me to write first) and from what David [Cox] said this weekend your plans are forming at any rate so far as the party goes. That would be very understandable & resolve the difficulty in its own way, particularly as I haven't yet mentioned the Pamirs to Rosemary. She did, however, say, reflectively looking at the paper, 'I see John's going to Russia. I suppose you'd be able to go now you're not teaching.'

Anyway, if you had time to drop a note it would be very interesting to hear how things are going along.

Noyce rationalised reservations about inclusion and, on October 16th, 1961, sent a letter of acceptance to John Hunt:

The great answer is yes, with one very important 'if', and that concerns the return date.

You must be to some extent in the same boat over this. Rosemary and I had planned a bit of camping with the boys. We haven't had a family summer holiday since 1959. If the return was in September, too late to do anything before school, then it would make the whole thing very difficult if not impossible. Ideally, I could come out as early as you liked if only one could get back before say the end of August. You will doubtless feel the same way with Prue and Jenny. It seems a small point, but important.

I have just come down from the Welsh dinner and had a word with Ralph Jones and Alan [Blackshaw], and gather other people may have time difficulties. I suppose an earlier return party, perhaps going out earlier, would be completely out? You may not know dates exactly at all yet I imagine. The money seems very reasonable indeed.

Thank you very much once more for this invitation. It will be grand to climb together again and in those surroundings. Certainly I'd be very ready to do a chore. Last year I looked after clothing and travel, and steered far from food and finance. This doesn't express properly my appreciation of the invitation & your consideration. Thank you.

John Hunt to Noyce the next day:

This is excellent news and I am delighted; I am equally sure that everyone else already in the party will welcome you.

As regards the dates, these will be a matter for negotiation with the Russians when Malcolm Slesser visits Moscow towards the end of next month. For the same reasons as yourself (and possibly a few more!) I may have to press for a period which will terminate not later than 1st September; moreover, I doubt whether I personally can manage more than the total of sixty-five days prescribed.

We shall certainly want you to shoulder part of the burden, and I will let you know about this shortly. Meanwhile would you be good enough to send your share, £100, to Derek Bull as early as possible?

A few exchanged pleasantries, a joke by Noyce in a letter dated October 19th, 1961 that his wife, Rosemary, would be out with the chopper were he to get home a day later than end of August . . . and Wilf Noyce was 'in'. He had replaced George Band.

38

LAST MEN IN

As mid October approached, debate about Robin's participation had scarcely begun, though Slesser had twice mentioned his name in letters to John Hunt. The proposed composition of the party was a hotly discussed issue amongst the Edinburgh SMC contingent in view of the rapport Robin and Eley Moriarty had struck up with the Russians the previous year. When a return invitation was issued, they in Edinburgh assumed that Robin and Dougal Haston, as the most proficient SMC members, would be invited. When that failed to happen both Jimmy Marshall and Archie Hendry, SMC vice-president at the time, encouraged Robin to press for inclusion within the club element of the expedition.

The thrust of popular feeling had been filtering through to Malcolm Slesser who, looking for a replacement for Bennet, was meanwhile awaiting Robin's reply to this undated letter:

> Behold this impressive notepaper. And you will observe that the SMC is one of the sponsors. As a member of the committee, and listener-in to rumours, and talk of rumours you will know all about that; but it is in a way quite a triumph to have got the SMC in a strong position vis-à-vis the AC. The only trouble lies in the fact that Sir John will not invite anyone on the expedition whom he neither likes nor feels he would [not] get on with nor whom he distrusts. A most reasonable proviso. Unfortunately, it cuts across Scottish cadres like the old Iron Curtain itself, for he just doesn't know them well enough. The situation at the moment is that there is in all probability going to be a vacancy on the SMC side of the party, which Hunt will want to fill with an SMC man. Who and what sort of person will depend on the general balance of the rest of the party. But Ken and I are keen that you should have a chance of coming on this trip. Permission has been got to climb from the Garmo glacier (a shorter approach march – four days ex-Moscow) on new untried flanks of Russia's highest Cime and hill-walking on neighbouring Munros. Personally, I think there can probably be better mountains to climb, but none so interesting taking the situation geographical and political into consideration.

The time will be seventy days, starting about July 1st 1962. Cost initially £100 each, but money back with bonus almost certain. If you're interested, and can tolerate* the rest of the company (Bryan, Smart, Hunt, Blackshaw, Noyce, McNaught-Davis, Lowe, Bull, Wrangham, Jones, etc) I should like to arrange a chance for you to meet John Hunt informally. We are having a Pamir Committee meeting here in Glasgow on 23rd November, and hope to have a few drinks after it. How about joining the party that evening?

Had a great first week in the Alps, then it snowed.

*Who may not be able to tolerate you!

As it happened, a meeting of East of Scotland members of the SMC committee had been arranged for Saturday, October 14th, 1961. Robin had been on the committee for almost two years. Slesser, a former committee man, was considered by the Edinburgh contingent as part of the 'Glaswegian clique' whose influence on general SMC matters they had wanted to see reduced. The Glaswegian group regarded Robin as part of an 'Edinburgh clique'. It is well known that Robin and Malcolm Slesser did not get on with one another. At this meeting Robin was up in arms about a couple of points. On one of them, that non-SMC members were taking two of the SMC's six places, he pressed a resolution that both Lowe and McNaught-Davis be asked to stand down. That was voted down. A national SMC committee meeting took place in Glasgow the following Saturday, October 21st, with the same outcome according to the minutes:

> There was a very full discussion on the composition of the 1962 Pamirs expedition. The initial approach by the club had been made at the request of a private group of members for a party which included two non-members of the club. The Russian reply had invited a party of twelve, six from the AC and six from the SMC. A motion that the two non-members be asked to stand down was defeated by a majority. It was agreed (RC Smith dissenting) that a circular to members might give them the opportunity to contribute financially.

Robin, however, was not prepared to let matters rest there and on October 22nd he wrote to John Hunt:

> I am writing to you as leader of the British–Soviet Pamirs Expedition 1962. Slesser has written me to say that 'there is in all probability going

263

to be a vacancy on the SMC side of the party, which Hunt will want to fill with an SMC man', and he suggested that I might be offered that vacancy. I would certainly appreciate the offer, but as matters stand just now, it would be dishonest to accept, and I would be obliged to turn it down. I am sorry to labour you with local grievances, but I feel that I should try to tell you why.

The invitation from Russia came through, I believe, around June of 1961. I do not wish to delve into the murky history of Scotland's part in securing this invitation, but I would like to pinpoint one factor which seems to have been overlooked: the SMC *as a national body* were hosts to Russian climbers both in the hills and in Edinburgh in May 1960. As to the invitation to climb in the Caucasus this past summer, the Russians gave only about five weeks' notice. By then, so far as I know, most of those members of the SMC who might have been interested had made other plans, and, in the time remaining, the club could not have organised anything on a national basis. It is obvious that an expedition to the Pamirs would be more attractive and important. As to this part of the invitation, the wording states loud and clear that the Russians expect six members of the SMC to make up one half of the joint SMC/AC expedition. Further, I think it is clearly implied that the Russians expect not just a group of friends, but a group thoroughly representative of the club as a whole and representative of the club's best climbing ability.

The representatives of the SMC as advertised in the national press are Slesser, Bryan, Smart, Bennet, Lowe and McNaught-Davis. But neither Lowe nor McNaught-Davis are members of the SMC, (I believe they are both members of the AC) and to include them within the Scottish contingent dishonours the black and white letter of Russia's invitation. Further, Slesser, Bryan, Smart and Bennet are a group of friends from Glasgow, in no way representative of the club as a whole, and not representative of its best climbing ability.

On these two scores, and especially on the former, it seems to me that Slesser's team would be exploiting the name of the club under false pretences. Now that Bennet is unlikely to be going, Slesser has approached myself from Edinburgh and also I believe Patey from Aberdeen. But this leaves the former score untouched, and on the latter it looks like an unsatisfactory compromise, a sort of sop to Cerberus. Until very recently, very few members of the SMC have known about this expedition. I raised the above objections at a meeting of the General Committee last Saturday, when they took no action. However, the feeling is now running high in

growing sections of the club, and I expect that the issue will be raised
again either at or before our AGM on 2nd December.

Please let me be quite clear that I am not in any way trying to blame
yourself for this unfortunate situation. Indeed, I do not believe it has
been entirely calculated by anyone. But although there are, of course,
some arguments in Slesser's defence, I believe that they are outweighed
by the above objections. This view concerns the name of the club as a
whole, it is *not* just the view of a body of rivals. You may feel that it is
unfair, or that it overlooks important factors; if so, and if you could
spare the time, I would be very grateful indeed to hear from you.

In the meantime Slesser had heard of the committee debates and
replied on October 23rd to a (now untraceable) letter from Robin:

Thank you for your letter saying that you would like to come to the
Pamirs with the party led by John Hunt. However, it would be idle for
me to pretend that I haven't heard something of what went on Saturday
last. I believe you put up a vigorous case. But what a pity you didn't
come and see me sooner if you or any others wanted to go. I had desisted
in asking you in the early days of planning because I was led to believe
(by George Ritchie I think) that you were included in an East of
Scotland party: and you must admit I haven't had much in the way of
encouragement to mingle with your crowd.

But it may be too late to sort out this mess, for that is what it is. Your
need to argue on Saturday stemmed from an inadequate knowledge of
the facts of the matter. Should you wish to know them, I have all the
documents here, and you are welcome to come over and look at them.
Secondly, you presume an expedition is compounded of just so many
good climbers. Such an expedition recently went to Nuptse. Any expedition I am associated with, and this goes for John Hunt too, is
compounded of people; and people are chosen by the leader. And the
expedition should return, whether it has attained its publicised object
or not, with its members still friends.

Before I could reasonably ask John Hunt (who *is* the leader) to invite
you to join the party, which I should very much like to, I should need
to be happy in my own mind that you would accept him as leader, and
that means giving him your unstinting support.

As for asking that McNaught and Lowe stand down! Had you
considered the practical consequences of such an action had your motion
been successful? The SMC would have been the laughing stock of the
UK, which surely wasn't your wish.

I hope, Robin, that if you still want to come, and I hope you do, you will reply very soon. The jelly has almost set.

At expedition headquarters Robin's letter to John Hunt was the catalyst for two letters on the latter's part; to Slesser and to Robin, firstly to Slesser on October 25th:

Forgive a hurriedly dictated letter, but a very great deal is going on down here.

I have decided to invite Tom Patey and hope to hear from him shortly. Despite his other preoccupations, I hope very much that you will be able to give him some preparatory work to do, from among the responsibilities allocated to your end. I know you will agree that this is an important part of building up a team.

At this end, Alan Blackshaw has had to withdraw and I have invited Joe Brown.

You should know that I have had a very reasonable letter from Robin Smith, which, however, makes the point very forcibly that the Scottish element is unrepresentative both of the SMC and of Scottish achievement today. I do not suggest that you need do more than take note of this! I will send you a copy of my reply to Robin when I write to him.

John Hunt to Robin, October 26th:

Thank you so much for your letter dated 22nd October, raising the question of the membership of this expedition in relation to its tasks, as they are viewed by yourself and other leading Scottish climbers. I realise there is a good deal in what you say and I thought it might possibly help if I told you of the background to the party and the present position. I am also most grateful to you for giving the opinions an airing.

Briefly, the two applications, which were made quite separately in the names of the AC and the SMC, were conceived as private parties and were composed before permission was received. The two Clubs were invoked as sponsors only because we knew – from the Russians themselves – that they would not entertain approaches on the part of private individuals. So, you see that Slesser's group and mine were in an awkward position when the invitation reached me, to combine forces in the name of the AC and the SMC and join in a British–Soviet expedition. We could, of course, have disbanded and handed over to the two clubs the onus of selecting a more representative party, whether within or outside the membership of these clubs, with such aims as the clubs saw fit to achieve through this combination. We felt that this would be most unfair to those who had taken the initiative and were expecting to take part, and we preferred to stand as we were; the two clubs agreed to abide by their nominal sponsorship.

Having said this, I maintain that the combined group is a reasonably strong one from the viewpoint of experience and technical competence for the type of climbing I anticipate; no less important, I believe it to be balanced in other respects also. The viewpoint on this will naturally vary, depending on the concept of the enterprise. It would be possible to vie with the Russians purely in the field of technical expertise but this, for reasons which I believe to be in the best interests of mountaineering, I do not wish to do. For one thing, it smacks of competition, which I find alien to the spirit of the sport.

In short, given the handicap of the background of private parties of friends as described, I have aimed at achieving an experienced balanced party, including a few whose stamina and proven capabilities at high altitude are unquestioned. These include Noyce and McNaught-Davis; also, I hope, Patey and Joe Brown.

I apologise for this rather long screed but I felt I owed it to yourself, who was good enough to raise the matter on the part of a number of others, to let you know how things stand and why.

Thank you very much, once again, for ventilating the feelings of a number of people; you may feel free to ventilate mine, which really do not derive from any prejudices whatever!

On October 31st John Hunt then kept Slesser posted of developments with Robin. Amongst other things, he referred to Iain Smart's earlier withdrawal from the expedition:

Thank you for your letter dated 24th October. The news about Iain came from you as a complete surprise to me: I have, however, now heard from him. For personal reasons I am sorry, but we must look immediately to his replacement.

If, as I hope, Tom Patey comes as a doctor as well as a mountaineer then I am inclined to think that it is not essential to look for another medical officer. If you agree with this, then the way is clear to fill the vacancy with another leading Scottish climber; he must, however, bid fair to fulfil the other requisites which we have agreed.

As regards Robin Smith, his letter to me (I enclose a copy of my reply) indicated that he would be unable to accept the invitation. If I am wrong – or if you can persuade him to change his mind – then, on the recommendation of yourself and Ian Charleson, I will be quite happy to take him along.

By now Robin had visited Glasgow to read the documents Slesser had earlier invited him 'to come over and see', following which he informed Slesser that he could now see that . . .

There are a number of dampeners to the, at first sight, great glare of this paradox and that I will do my peaceful best to get six SMC places.

Since you seem to be working heartily (though with two reservations) in the SMC interests, it is clear that the Metropolitan inner circle would have to be persuaded of the relevance of the SMC and of their more than nominal right to six places.

Robin to John Hunt:

Thanks for your courteous and very fair letter. Naturally, I don't agree with all that you say.

The tone of my previous (impetuous?) letter was somewhat anti-Slesser; but now that I have seen Slesser and read the correspondence, I require to back-pedal part of its force. It seems that Ritchie specifically applied to climb in the Caucasus in 1961, that Slesser specifically applied to climb in the Pamirs in 1962, and that both were given the nominal support of the SMC. Therefore, it is out of order to complain at this late stage that Slesser's group is not representative of the club as a whole or of the club's best climbing ability. Further, matters are improved with Patey's inclusion. I still maintain that the Russian letter implies that they expect a representative group, but this, I agree, is not explicit.

However, it remains very explicit that the Russians have invited and expect six members of the SMC. And yet, only four are scheduled to go. (I have heard it said that the CC and others find even four too many.) It emerges that Slesser has put up quite a struggle (with only the two reservations) for the interests of the SMC and I appreciate that he would not want to ask two of his original group to stand down on a technical point; rather, I believe that the SMC Committee, whose loyalties lie with the SMC and not with Slesser's original group, should have courteously pressed that point.

Thus it seems that the club has little quarrel with Slesser in person. And I appreciate that none of the present twelve are going to be asked to stand down merely to smooth a grumbling appendix to Britain's mountaineering system(!). But most of this club would agree, that it would be a pity if you could not arrange in the end of the day, for the SMC to take their six right and proper places. You may disagree, but we would be very grateful if we knew that we had your sympathy.

John Hunt's acknowledgement of Robin's letter cannot be traced, but it is evident that during the course of November cogs and wheels interacted. Robin would go. He and SMC president Ian Charleson were invited as observers to the expedition committee meeting in Glasgow on November 23rd. Robin found the scenario rather daunting, but met John Hunt, who issued an invitation that was formalised in writing the following day. Planning details were still scanty, the letter explained, and a 'substantial contribution in the order of £100' would be expected from each member of the party. Some part in the preparation and planning of the expedition would also be expected of each member. There would be occasional meetings in London or Glasgow. 'I very much hope,' John Hunt ended, 'you will be as keen as I am to take part in this expedition; may I add that I will be personally delighted if you accept.'

Robin replied on November 25th that he was 'very pleased to accept', adding this postscript:

> I had not realised that the £100 contribution would be wanted as soon as possible, and I may have a lot of difficulty in getting hold of it before the last one or two months (May or June). As for dates, I am at present completely free and easy, although I may need to be back for the start of the academic year (October).
>
> I would like to thank you very sincerely for the invitation. It will be a very new experience for me, not only as an expeditionary, but also, for the very first time, as a Gentleman-Climber; and I am sure it will be a very valuable experience. Hoping to see you at the CIC, Yours, Robin.

Robin too was now 'in', and the party almost complete. However, the selection of the last man in – Graeme Nicol – also attracts interest. He went as replacement for Tom Patey, himself approached following Iain Smart's withdrawal. Patey, a powerhouse in Scottish mountaineering who was killed in a fall from a sea stack in 1970, told John Hunt on November 12th, 1961 of his need to step down from the expedition:

I am sorry for keeping you waiting so long for a definite answer – the more so, because I'm afraid it will have to be in the *negative*. I'm sure you will understand that I would sacrifice a great deal to go on this expedition but, as things stand, I have no hope between now and next summer in saving sufficient, not only to pay my way on this expedition but also to maintain the family in my absence. I would have liked to imagine that something would turn up, & carried on with preparations regardless, but I am afraid I might let you down at a later date, & be the cause of further confusion.

If you should find it difficult to fill my place (which I doubt), I would be doubly grateful if you would get in touch with me again. I shall meanwhile continue to explore every alleyway for funds, on the off-chance, that this may be so.

I know you require an immediate estimate for the medical stores. On both my previous expeditions, the entire medical stores did not cost the expedition a penny – I had dealings with over twenty drug firms & not one of these failed to cooperate. I still have the relevant correspondence & could pass it on to your expedition doctor if he wanted it. Also I would be only too keen to help you in any other way particularly in the medical line.

I am writing today to Malcolm to tell him the sad news. I shall also mention that if the requirement still exists for a Scots doctor & SMC member, Graeme Nicol, who was originally a prospective member of this team, is now demobbed & working in the hospital here. I know in confidence that he would accept an invitation now that he is in a better position to do so, & would have no difficulty in getting leave from the hospital. I believe that he withdrew originally because of his connections with the SAS. – & that this was on the advice of the Service Authorities. He is now however a civilian, & although it is perhaps presumptuous of me to say so, would make an excellent addition to any Himalayan team – one of the best companions I've had in the mountains, and in the forefront of Scottish snow & ice climbing developments, with also three or four Alpine sessions to his credit. Above all, he is an excellent man to get on with & has a sense of humour. However, as I say, I am now unconnected with the expedition, so this information is perhaps rather irrelevant.

Once again, my sincere apologies. I sincerely hope that I may hear from you again but imagine not.

In consequence of Patey's letter, Nicol was 'in', the final party being: leader John Hunt (aged fifty-two), deputy leader Malcolm Slesser

(thirty-five), Joe Brown (thirty-one), Ken Bryan (twenty-six), Derek
Bull (thirty-four), Ralph Jones (thirty-two), George Lowe (thirty-
seven), Iain McNaught-Davis (thirty-two), team doctor Graeme Nicol
(twenty-six), Wilf Noyce (forty-four), Robin Smith (twenty-three) and
Ted Wrangham (thirty-three). Thirty years later Wrangham came to
reflect on its composition:

> It was rather an ill-assorted party. John Hunt was of course a great
> leader and the Russian members of the team staunch mountain compan-
> ions, but the English–Scottish mixture was not a success, though Robin,
> I seem to recall, somewhat distanced himself from any problems. I was
> relieved to find, when we split up into three groups to go climbing,
> that our group consisted of the two Anatolis (Ovchinnikov and
> Sevastianov), Derek Bull, Wilfrid Noyce and Robin Smith.
>
> Robin was younger than the rest of us, but neither this nor the differ-
> ence in nationalities mattered and we all got on well together. Unlike
> Robin, I had never been in the top echelons of mountaineering but he
> was most companionable. He seemed to admire Noyce for his obvious
> earlier achievements and also John Hunt, not part of our group, for his
> mind-over-matter attitude; he had seen him toil badly on the first long
> haul with provisions from Base Camp and then manage to keep up
> with the best after that.

Despite having previously described John Hunt as an 'army planner'
to his cousin, Peter Lothian, Robin nevertheless came to hold him in
high regard. Of Robin, John Hunt recorded the thoughts he felt shortly
after the accident:

> I thought of Wilf and our friendship over twenty years . . . And Robin,
> who had shown so much youthful promise and who, despite his
> academic honours, lived only for climbing. I remembered my first
> impression in the CIC hut under Ben Nevis, as he lay cosily in his
> sleeping bag watching me, with what I took to be cynical appraisal, as
> I busied myself sweeping up the mess on the littered floor. Robin, about
> whom I had written in my diary at Base Camp 'is doing his best to be
> a good member of the party'. And later, at Camp 2: 'Derek, Robin and,
> of course, Wilf are wonders of selfless labour in the common weal'.
> Robin had decided to be one of us . . .

39

PREPARATIONS

Now that an expedition had been agreed in principle, Malcolm Slesser prepared himself for the trip to Moscow for discussions with the USSR Federation of Mountaineers. Much of his recent correspondence with John Hunt had related to tactics for that visit. Meanwhile, John Hunt had been primed by JMK Vyvyan, who had climbed in the Caucasus with SMC members earlier that year. Coming home via Moscow, Vyvyan had visited two members of the USSR's Mountaineering Federation – Kaspin, the secretary, and Gippenreiter, who spoke excellent English and had responsibilities for international matters. The Federation, John Hunt was told, reported to the 'All Union Council of Sports', an influential body in the corridors of power. In the eyes of the Communist regime, any contact with Western organisations was high profile and Soviet committee members knew that a false step could adversely affect prospects, not just for their sport but for their own careers. For example, if the British team's intention of climbing the USSR's highest mountain were to come to the attention of an unsympathetic senior Soviet political leader, he might regard it as an insult against the Soviet State, in which case the invitation would almost certainly have to be withdrawn.

The series of meetings started on November 29th, 1961, chaired by Antipinok, the mountaineering representative on the 'All Union Council of Sports'. Others present were Kuzmin (vice-president), Kaspin, Ovchinnikov and Gippenreiter. Below are core details of Slesser's report to his colleagues:

> Five Soviet climbers, and a radio operator, to be assigned to the expedition; Ovchinnikov likely to be the Soviet leader, probably Gippenreiter and two others who had visited Britain in 1960 as members – good news that: Soviet safety standards to be adhered to including scheduled return times from climbs; the Garmo basin, and Gando to the north, already designated for the visit; Garmo agreed as ideal for Base Camp; ascent of their highest mountain Pik Stalina [shortly to be changed to

272

Pik Kommunisma and called 'Pik 7495 Metres' pending that] permitted as far as those present were concerned, but publicity in the UK of this intention advised against, lest this news finds its way back to Moscow; once in the Pamirs they could do what they like; the stay not to exceed sixty-five days; Intourist vouchers not needed as they would be treated as a delegation; heavy kit to be sent in April for storage by the Federation in Dushanbe; en route to the Pamirs, heat and dust, not insects, are the main problem; travel by road uncomfortable; use of helicopters (to a maximum level of 3200 metres) economical – horses bought as an alternative would have to be resold for sausage meat at 40 per cent of the buying price; a lightly laden caravan will leave Tavil Dara in advance of the British party with oats for the horses and to prepare a helicopter landing-place; some horses at Base Camp were advisable for carrying wood, mail, injured men and evacuation at the end; most gear to be abandoned unless more horses, and associated cost, taken on; the 'walk-out' at that time of year said to be very lovely, rivers low; nailed boots strongly recommended; urged to take double-skin tents as temperatures at 7000 metres can fall below -30° Centigrade; wood readily available at Base Camp for cooking; radio operator to cost nothing; telegrams sent free of charge to nearest post office; mail from UK will easily reach Dushanbe, but then a matter of luck, dependent on the plane flying from there to Tavil Dara, where there is no post office, then by horse or hired men, to the expedition; about six walkie-talkie sets to be provided; a fund-raising philatelic scheme all right, provided not launched until the new year; wearing of shorts in Dushanbe would cause offence to Moslems; horses may bring gadflies, but there would be no mosquitoes; fifty-six days' food to be taken from Dushanbe, perhaps some sheep on the hoof; Soviet climbers keep off alcohol prior to an expedition but willing to drink to excess after; as much whisky as possible to be taken for the 'celebrations'; Soviets cannot understand why SMC not represented 50 per cent but that is an internal matter; best climbing period is last three weeks of August when winter snows were consolidated; therefore part of this period being lost; arrival/departure dates not permitted to be changed; 1st July arrival in Moscow and 3rd September departure agreed; generally rock is poor and the snow seldom hardens to good neve – in the exceptionally dry air conditions, the snow sublimes rather than settles; dry air increases volume of liquid intake; the main glaciers are frightful, ablated into 15–20-ft-high ice pinnacles with ensuing route-finding difficulties; unquestionably no porters; costs in the USSR come to £3090.

Basically the timetable was: fly to Moscow (Day 1), fly south to Dushanbe (Day 2), sort out kit already there (Days 3 and 4), kit by lorry and men by plane to Tavil Dara (Days 4 and 5), by helicopter with all food and equipment to Base Camp 8 km above the snout of Garmo glacier at 3200 metres (Days 6 to 10), climbing in the area of the Garmo basin (Days 11 to 52). The remainder of the sixty-five days available would be needed for withdrawal, initially by horse caravan.

Reality was to differ on a number of points. Walkie-talkie radios were not available. Helicopters took the gear to 2000 ft lower than originally planned. Horses and sheep were not needed, possibly to Robin's chagrin, perhaps to his relief, as responsibility for the horse caravan out from the mountains to Tavil Dara was his as transport officer. The walk-out at the end was dropped from plans and helicopters substituted. For many, the walk-out from expeditions was considered a fulfilling experience. The walk-in, the traditional means of getting fit by members of big British expeditions, was not part of the plan.

Attitude to fitness was just one of the marked differences in approach between the Soviets and the British towards big expeditions. Competition in that era was the basis of all sporting activities in the USSR and climbing conformed to that pattern. Given this attitude, training was done with rigid discipline and there was almost total abstention from smoking and drinking. Objectives were stated in advance and had to be achieved. A different philosophy in mountain strategy was used. The competition in high-altitude climbing gave greatest points to teams with the largest number of people to complete the objective, whether a single summit by a new route or a long-distance high traverse. Therefore, the method used was to move the whole party from camp to camp, carrying all equipment and food with them. It is a method which worked well among peaks up to 6000 metres (20,000 ft). Some of the British wondered whether it would be as satisfactory in the higher mountains of the Himalayas, but it had two obvious disadvantages. The first is that, having planned for a given period, the party may meet prolonged bad weather at the furthest point out and, with no fixed camp to retreat to, would be short of food and fuel. Secondly, if any member of the party were to fall sick, he would have to be evacuated to the nearest camp which could be some days' journey away.

The British approach to big-mountain climbing was different. They then regarded it rather as a pleasant pastime and disapproved of any competitive approach. It was usual to employ porters and to operate from a series of fixed camps stocked with reserves of fuel and food. Their principal objective was to get a pair of climbers to the summit. That method, based on Himalayan experience, tended to be slower, but surer. They acclimatised and got fit as they advanced.

It was agreed that Soviet methods should be adopted in the Pamirs and the suffering that lay ahead for the British can be imagined: no porters, no walking-in, no training in advance. By various accounts, Robin was to be the exception. Joe Brown, for example, has written about the imposed porterage due to helicopters not being able to take supplies as high as the planned Base Camp:[1]

> We duly set off together but the Russians soon drew ahead. Halfway up, the British party was tottering. The Russians passed us on their way down, with Robin Smith in their midst. He was the only one of us who could keep up the pace. He was so obviously the youngest and liveliest of the British party that he soon became the Russians' favourite.

Meanwhile, in the early stages of the expedition's planning, Robin had been put in touch with expedition treasurer, Derek Bull, to whom he sent £20, the sympathetic Bull agreeing to accept the balance of the £100 in instalments as soon as Robin could manage it. 'Dreadful business this money, but at present it is still our only source of income,' he quipped in acknowledgement.

Robin's finances around that time were very tight. Over and above normal outgoings, he had now told Bull that he would send him payments of £20, yet the expedition was scheduled to coincide with his regular well-paid seasonal work at the Kent vinery. As a student Robin had never been flush, though he was seldom seriously short of beer money. His passport has shown that he could take tidy sums on Alpine trips after working in Kent where annual earnings, in today's values, were £2000 or more. Additionally he had the Post Office work at Christmas and, most vitally, his student grant.

Now no longer a student and his grant terminated, he had a spell working as a porter in an Edinburgh mental hospital, Archie Hendry, his old French teacher, recalls. Hendry was asked if he would like to buy Robin's Rolex Explorer watch which each Pamirs team member had been given. He asked how much Robin wanted but, thinking that Robin was chancing it and uneasy about taking it, instead offered the money as a gift which Robin refused. In fact, suppliers' 'freebies', according to an expedition member, were normal perks on that sort of trip, although Robin's entrepreneurial initiative extended this practice to its limit. In the end, it seems, Robin never got round to paying the full balance despite a degree of enterprise in selling off surplus expedition audio tapes.

Later, during the course of the expedition, Mrs Smith was far from relaxed about being unable to respond to a request for further finance: ' . . . I shall not be able to put much in 'the hat' as our family income is very low at present – none of my three offspring earning as yet, and all three requiring a lot of help with their varied adventures. My daughter is in British Guiana for a year doing Voluntary Service Overseas – but one has to assist for fares . . .' She was gently told not to worry. Most likely she did not know that a partial refund, perhaps even a profit for participants, had been forecast, and that the expedition's cash problem was temporary.

*　*　*

As 1961 drew to a close, Robin's regular correspondence with Dennis Gray started to focus on the Alpine Climbing Group which Gray, its new secretary, was attempting to persuade leading Scottish climbers to join. Founded in 1953 for those on the leading edge of mountaineering, the ACG expected members to give evidence of climbs annually, and those who failed to maintain an adequate standard had to retire from membership. After a number of years, the group became associated with the Alpine Club, largely for administrative support, but still retains its separate identity even today.

Gray's predecessor as ACG secretary, Chris Bonington, had written to tell Robin that the club was 'as dead as a dodo' and that he wanted it brought to life: 'I don't think there are more than twenty climbers scattered over the country who are interested or capable of doing the hard routes. The ACG could give useful contacts, especially when one has a long holiday and can't find anyone similarly placed . . . what would you say to joining forces?'

Gray's first contact with Robin may not have been in Bonington's mannerly style. 'A move is afoot to attempt to get all the bums and ne'er-do wells in,' he wrote. 'The insurance still holds good: £100 towards a rescue, £1000 if totally obliterated – and a bulletin worth reading once a year.' But the timing wasn't right for Robin, leaving Gray with 'a fever of indifference'. However, in November 1961, Gray threw in a further incentive: 'You certainly would not be welcome in some quarters! . . . but if the ACG is to come to anything we must get every Alpinist who is active into it now!! We need you dreaded Scotsmen. It's up to you to bury your haggises and get a grip.' Robin duly joined the Alpine Climbing Group, though not before receipt of another letter dated January 16th, 1962. After the banter was through, and after mountain talk of the Pamirs, Karakorum, Lhotse and Everest had ended, Gray went on to say: 'You were nearly invited as one of the two guests of honour to the Rock & Ice dinner in Manchester this year but it was thought to be a hell of a way for you to come. Next year it may be in the Lakes so possibly you could make it?'[2]

Earlier that same week Robin had written to the Pamirs expedition secretary, thanking her – 'but abysmally belatedly' – for her card. 'It was delivered through a blizzard to a camp at 2500 ft (in which I was selling my amateur status to the army) – this may be a record', he told her, though what he did to earn his money is not known other than that he was somewhere in Wales. He gave Chamonix as his next point of contact. Consequently he expected not to be in Britain for the next Pamirs committee meeting, but was confident that he would make the Nevis meet of the Pamirs party in March.

On January 24th Robin duly left Britain by train, with Dougal Haston as his climbing partner. He updated his mother of progress two days later from Chamonix: 'Snow all over the place, but undiscouraged, we are hiring skis & climbing painfully to a certain log cabin some 3000 ft higher than Chamonix & close to the climbs. Weather quite settled-looking. I sent you a book from Paris, you should have it before this. Don't expect more for maybe a week or so.'

Winter Alpine expeditions were not then the norm for British parties and those undertaking them can now be looked back on as pioneers. Robin and Haston, however, did not lack confidence. There was even talk of their going for the first winter ascent of the Walker

Spur. Certainly their ventures might have made ideal training for the Pamirs, but they spent two days reaching the Montenvers after ineffective use of skis and a consequent bivouac below the treeline. 'This was obviously all part of the learning process, judging by Dougal's later exploits,' surmises Geoff Oliver who had lent them a special bivvy sack/tent designed by Don Whillans. Robin's undated letter arrived home from Refuge des Amis de la Montagne, Chamonix:

Living as it were in a low quarter hotel, in a room with bunks & a basin under the eaves & over the living rooms of the proprietor, we peer out (on the 3rd day) from under the eaves & our scowling brows to the snow-bound tips of the Aiguilles, showing above the first forested slopes. However, the forests are turning in a thaw from speckled white & black to black (or green) with a faint speckling of grey, & even the peaks (we imagine) are shedding tiers of snow. On the first day we set off under 70-lb packs towards Montenvers, at the top of the trees, along the electric-railway line but, the railway being non-operative, the snow lay all over it & grew steadily deeper till we ground to a halt at a railway hut some 600 ft (of the 3000) from the top. Yesterday we skied, abortively but not without learning a little, & today we return to the assault of the railway. From the Montenvers we plan an assault of indefinite duration, we plan to carry food for 6 nights but, being the traverse of a series of rock ridges, the route would not be exposed to the omnivorous avalanches which must presently be sweeping the walls & faces. Furthermore, increasing depths of soft snow on the approach from Montenvers to the col at the start of the ridge are quite likely (apart from all question of weather) to put us quite off. In which event, I will return to the exacting pursuit of Doctor Faustus, full of Bach & Beethoven but with little of the Devil so far.

We had thought never to be allowed to darken these doors again (of the refuge, that is), in that for the past few years we have amused ourselves by staying here without ever paying & escaping by ever more complex means from the proprietor (a stunted & evilly-grinning Parisian Apache) & his huge & Amazonic wife. But he is really a good fellow, & we heard that he has une *Amitié pour le Scotch* (Whisky), & therefore brought an ingratiating bottle from the boat. We are now *bienvenus*.

The music was very cheap. If by any chance it was the wrong volume, let me know here. *Also if you want any more music* or any other French things it will do no harm to let me know in case I call in at Paris. (Which is quite likely).   Cheers.
Robin.

In a further note home on February 3rd, he told of a 'fresh fall of snow last night, besides which it has been too cold to encourage bivouacs up in the hoary hills. We even got touches of frostbite on our only attempt at an approach march – swinging up & down through trees trying to traverse a hillside buried in deep soft snow. Good for my French anyway, but I may leave soon.' Any thoughts Robin might have had of gaining pre-expedition high-altitude experience in winter had been thwarted, although in Chamonix he did manage to research the prices and quality of karabiners, rock pegs and ice pegs on behalf of the Pamirs team.

On March 10th and 11th the Nevis meet for expedition members went ahead as planned, enabling participants to acquaint themselves with one another. Some had met only at committee meetings. I contacted some of them, and in the remaining chapters they give their impressions from that time. Ted Wrangham:

> Robin and I talked a bit about some rock climbs I had started and of which he had completed the first ascents, Thunder Rib on Sgurr a' Mhadaidh in Skye and a route left of the big corner on Carnmore Crag (he called it Gob). Clearly Robin was a fine rock climber, but he was really in his element on snow and ice.
>
> Most of our party got going from the CIC hut at a reasonable hour and went off to climb some of the classic ridges and gullies, but Robin pretended to ignore our preparations and was still in bed when we left. Some of us went up Observatory Ridge and, as we rose, I looked across to the Orion Face and saw that Robin had now arrived on the hill. In crampons, with an axe in one hand and a peg in the other, he strolled casually up the verglased face, stopping at intervals to chat with us, and with his companions below. As a demonstration of ice-climbing technique performed with no apparent effort, it was quite remarkable. Robin was without any doubt the finest winter climber I have ever seen.

Ralph Jones, 1995:

> When the composition of the Scottish part of the expedition was originally announced, the English and Welsh were somewhat taken aback because almost nobody with experience outside Great Britain was included – when I say 'experience', I mean of having done high-quality routes or been on big expeditions. Since Tom Patey had come and gone, it was eventually a great relief to find that Robin Smith was to join the

party. I had met him just the once, at Glencoe in 1960, when we climbed with the Russians who visited Britain that year. But I don't think many of the others had met him before the Nevis meet, which turned out to be a catastrophe in some ways and assumed fairly rapidly the sort of aura of playing an away match on Scottish hills.

I hired a car, took Joe Brown up, and we met Robin. It was quite funny to see a sort of stand-off, as it were, between two champions meeting 'in the ring' and weighing each other up. However, they seemed to have an almost immediate rapport on the basis of climbs already done. It was very noticeable to us, the English/Welsh, that the Scottish attitude towards Robin Smith was very unlike our own. They seemed to regard him as a climbing yobbo and didn't really conceal their feelings, but at the same time were obviously in awe of the routes accomplished by him in Scotland and abroad.

Robin proposed that Joe, I and he should climb Tower Ridge the next day and we thought this a good idea. He said he would show us around Ben Nevis 'in winter conditions'. This was a dig at Joe – though I don't think Robin realised that Joe had actually done a lot of winter climbing on Nevis but Joe, being Joe, had probably never said much about it. What ensued was a trial of strength up Tower Ridge which, as a disinterested but exhausted observer, I found entertaining if not a little wearing. Joe and I roped up occasionally but were mostly unroped. Robin climbed alongside us, discussing routes, cracking jokes, taking the mickey out of the English/Welsh and generally disporting himself on the crags. I must admit that I was absolutely knackered. I don't know what the record is from CIC hut to the summit of Tower Ridge but I bet we beat it by a handsome margin. It was pretty obvious that neither of them was going to give second best to the other, so all the most difficult variants were tackled at lightning speed plus, I suspect, one or two that no one had ever thought of before. During the whole ascent Robin kept up a running commentary of anecdotes and playful criticism and Joe interspersed when appropriate with the occasional cutting comment about Scottish climbing. I was too exhausted to say anything at all. When we got to the top Robin announced that that seemed a good start to the day – I thought it a good finish to the day as well.

Robin and Joe by then obviously held each other in high esteem and Robin proposed that they should go off and do something that had not been previously climbed, a gully I think, as a mark of respect, as I saw it, for the maestro on Scottish ground. I thought it all quite entertaining.

I trudged slowly up to the summit of the Ben and met them at the top of the gully adjacent to Tower Ridge. Frankly, I can't recall its name, but Robin, when we met up again, said that this was probably as good a way down as any and proceeded to run down it in large leaps and bounds, which Joe and I found quite impressive, all the more so when he caught the spike of one of his crampons in his socks and looped the loop several times.

Joe Brown:

Whereas I had been climbing much longer than Robin, I was profoundly impressed by the economy of his techniques. As an 'over thirty' I had perhaps forgotten what it was like to be young and bursting with energy. He was quick and careful on difficult ground, yet he was completely reckless on easy terrain. Coming down Number 3 Gully he started running, overbalanced and flew out of control. He broke the fall after 200 ft crawling out of the avalanche debris that buried him with a sheepish grin on his face.

Ralph Jones:

After he recovered and then went tearing down the rest of the gully, Joe turned to me and said, 'We'll have to watch this chap', which I thought was one of the understatements of the climbing year.

The following day unfortunately was pretty abysmal in terms of weather and in terms of our deputy leader's attitude. Several times arguments of a very heated nature were cooled down and it all got a bit wearing.

We offered Robin a lift back to Edinburgh. At first he turned it down, saying he could do it quicker on the train. I expressed doubts over this because at the time I was rather aware of my rallying abilities. So we took on the train and, though I can't remember the exact route, I know that for several miles we were parallel to the railway track. Gradually the train hove into view; we overtook it and left it behind. When we got to Edinburgh Robin remarked that, while he wasn't too impressed with my climbing, he thought my driving amazing.

During this period, equipment procurement for the expedition was being undertaken by the Scots under the delegation of Malcolm Slesser, who turned to Robin for little. Sue Bradshaw recalls that Robin was 'just a young student'. She knew how, in the most charming of ways, to boss him about. Wilf Noyce could happily write to Sue that he had received something from Robin 'cheerfully late'. But with Slesser, matters were different, and contemporaries know that Robin did not willingly recognise his authority.

Within a few weeks, the expedition's organisational phase was reaching its end. The main party was due to fly to Russia at the end of June. Heavy gear would be shipped from Tilbury in advance, accompanied by Slesser and Bryan who would meet up with the rest of the party in Moscow. On June 12th Robin sent a multi-questioned letter, principally on the subject of recording tapes, to Slesser: 'As usual I am at sea. When do you go to sea? I can't find the Tilbury address. Could you please send me the date for latest arrival of goods, the addresses for lists of what is going, etc, so that my muddled mind can see clearly what to do (no doubt post haste) to avoid chaos.' Seeking means whereby he might approach yet closer to his £100, he advised Slesser that he had '60 super-swift-knitting women friends who want to knit me last-minute knick knacks. Can I get a bale of free wool? Yours in poverty.'

Robin added the postscript that he had 'been doing fabulous climbs if nothing else'.[3] Only four days previously, with Davie Agnew, he had made the first ascent of the Needle, one of the hardest routes of the day in the Cairngorms, and still a classic. Then on the 19th he wrote to Sue Bradshaw:

I sent a 15 lb parcel to Lep today, by express, they say it will arrive tomorrow. I have lost the instructions (the latest ones) sent by Mac., but Malcolm gave me the address –

British–Soviet Pamirs Expedition,
Lep Wharves
Corney Rd
Chiswick
London W4

However, as I recall, we were to send two or three copies of a list of items, only I have no addresses. Could you please either do this for me or let me have the addresses? Sorry.

I list, overleaf: 1 Black's Icelandic Inner Sleeping-bag, 6 Prs Stockings, 1 Pr Hebdencord Breeches, 2 Prs Underpants, 3 Vests, 4 Shirts, 2 Jerseys, 1 Felt hat, 1 Balaclava, 3 Hankies, 1 Tie, 1 Pr Socks.

I will probably be leaving home, not to return, on Sun 24th/Mon 25th, probably going to Wales (so that an emergency address which might me would be, c/o Pen-y–Gwynedd Hotel, Llanberis). In emergency up till Sunday, my phone no. is – FAIrmilehead 1532. I got my passport & visa today, thank you, & will bring them, together with anti-smallpox certificate and a handful of roubles and not more than 44 lb of baggage to London airport (I presume there is only one, or that this is the main one) for departure in an Aeroflot at 10.30 a.m. on Saturday 30th June. Alright? Please don't trouble to answer unless to correct bloomers.

On June 22nd Robin wrote a further letter to Sue enclosing his next-of-kin form:

I hope you have found some sign of my parcel to Corney Rd. If it has managed to go by sea, good & well. If you have traced it or it appears before Saturday, could you arrange for it to go to the airport to meet me on the 30th, & I will try to keep the rest of my baggage down to 29 lb. If it is not traced till after the 30th, it would be a great inconvenience but not a catastrophe. I will expect to be hearing from you by Monday morning as to how things have gone so far.

Could I put my foot in it again? A plan has just materialised for me to go straight to the Alps after the expedition to meet up with a friend who will otherwise be on his own. It would be very much better for me to fly direct Moscow–Geneva, or possibly to take some more interesting route, part by train, since I will have all that I need for the Alps with me. Do you know if this can still be arranged? Say through Lep or else direct through Intourist, or even from Moscow? If any immediate move had to be made, before we leave London, I would be happy to settle for a flight to Geneva. (I don't suppose I would get off with London via Geneva . . .) But please don't trouble much about this, I imagine that if I kick up enough fuss in Moscow I can arrange it on my own account.

Sue replied to Robin on June 26th, advising him that the last she saw of his parcel was on the deck of the *Estonia*. 'It was brought on at the last minute by the Lep agent,' she wrote. 'It wasn't labelled or anything, so I hope it will be all right.' However, as there were also expedition crates on deck, there seemed every chance that all would be well. But Robin was due for a disappointment about hopes of returning via Geneva: 'I'm afraid the answer to your question is a *very definite no*. The tickets and places were all booked *months* ago, and cannot be changed now. Another reason is that there have to be ten people in a party to qualify for a reduction in fares.'

In 1995 Sue Bradshaw looked back to her most vivid memory of Robin, when he made one of his infrequent visits to the expedition office in Paddington Street. It was in the spring, the sun was shining, and Robin was sitting in an armchair facing her as she sat at her desk with her back to the window: 'I was most struck by his eyes – dark, intelligent and sparkling. He was one of the most alive people I have ever met and I was struck by how nice he was too, with a good sense of humour.' Wilfrid Noyce, on the other hand, was in and out the office frequently. 'Quiet and gentle,' was Sue's initial impression. 'Only later was one aware of his inner strength and experience of life. A good mentor for Robin I expect.'

With the expedition due to leave Britain at the end of the week, Robin – preparations complete – started to make his way towards London Airport. 'I did very well, got a long lift from Carlisle through all manner of very rustic by-roads to within 20 miles of Joe Brown's home, on Wednesday night, & made my way there for a lift on Thursday', he wrote to his mother.

Val Brown, Joe's wife, remembers Robin's visit. 'He was fascinated with our little daughter, Helen, who was then a two-year-old toddler,' she says. 'He played with her for ages and she really took to him. At our home climbers came and went all the time, but until then I had not been aware of them taking much notice of her. Thinking at the time that Robin had studied psychology, I did wonder if he might have been interested in her reactions for some sort of informal research or the like, but soon saw that his attention was spontaneous.'

Robin's letter of June 29th, written in a London park that Friday evening and posted in Paddington, continues:

I reached London in time for a few pints with Barry Aston, with whom I am staying. Today I have been fixing up what has been left of my various deals. Brown & I are well set for Ilford Cameras, valued around £35 each, with a lot of film, we are to pose suitably with them at London Airport, & may subsequently appear in the corners of magazines. But the higher places in the expedition have mismanaged my efforts for another 2 cameras. Further, the jerseys & stockings are costing 70 per cent of wholesale price – not so good, although they are certainly alright jerseys. Maybe I can arrange for the expedition to pay.

I trust your fire is set for you, your dishes are washed, your grass is cut. My regards to Claire if she isn't away, she can reveal Paris to me if I pass through in September. I will be flying back to London on September 3rd, & may or may not come back to Edinburgh, probably not. But don't *forward* any important-looking mail to Russia. I may phone you on the 3rd Sept. or around to give you a forwarding address.

If you want to write to Russia, it seems you write Dushanbe direct. Maybe you could put 'the British Embassy, Moscow' as a 2nd address should the first fail. There are likely to be 2 deliveries from Dushanbe to Base Camp, by mule, during the time we are there. If not I could pick it up on the way out. The Address is, in Russian words but English Letters, exactly as follows:

R. Smith,
British Pamirs Expedition,
Dushanbe (note 'n')
Pochtovoe, otdelenie 22 (which means PO 22)
Russia.
I seem so far to have forgotten nothing.

All participants had by now received a letter of good wishes from the leader, John Hunt. After explaining that he had written to thank all who had helped in whatever way, he continued:

There have been a number of problems to contend with and the successful way in which they have been overcome augurs well for the success of the expedition itself. As I said at the meeting the membership of this expedition has not been easy to compose and some of us have not been able to get to know one another well beforehand. I believe the biggest problem as well as the most rewarding prospect ahead of us, is to make a success of our relationships, with each other as well as with the Russians.

I know I can count on you to help in overcoming this problem which will have, incidentally, quite a bearing on our climbing prospects!

The party was now ready to leave Britain the following day, Saturday June 30th, 1962.

40

LOWLAND USSR

The expedition was now under way, Robin could tell his mother from
Moscow on Sunday July 1st, on a postcard featuring the Red Flag with
images of the Kremlin and a space rocket in the background:

> We arrived last night, were driven to the Hotel Armena, & spent today
> touring the city streets by bus with guide. Tonight, a Tchaikovsky opera
> in the Bolshoi Theatre. Tomorrow morning round the public parts of
> the Kremlin & flight in the afternoon to Dushanbe for a day or so of
> organising. All goes very smoothly. Moscow at first sight is not unlike
> a city of French buildings & Scottish people, although the domes &
> towers & the high-boots & great coats of police & soldiers, are very
> Russian. Busy streets, cars trams buses, high heels nylons & lipstick
> sometimes, open necks or snazzy ties. A dance band in our dining room.
> Please write me, Brit. Sovt. Pamir's Exp., c/o British Embassy, Moscow,
> NOT at Dushanbe. But don't bother writing more than once or twice.
> Lousy Weather.

He expanded the scenario slightly to his aunt and uncle in Gullane,
writing that the party would soon be in 'Dushanbe, 2000 miles SE, in
Samarkand, for a day or two before flying by helicopter to Base Camp.
We are having bad weather but a great time.'

The highlights in Moscow in John Hunt's opinion were
Tchaikovsky's *Oprichnik* and the visit the following evening to the new
Hall of Congresses for a world premiere of a ballet, *Legends of Lovers*.
He noted in his expedition diary that both were 'quite stupendous',
even though it was noticeable that the audience gave a lukewarm
reception to the latter.

Anatoli Ovchinnikov, Soviet expedition leader who climbed with
Robin in Scotland in 1960, looks back to the Soviets' part in the expedition's planning:

> It took two years of intensive work to make this idea a reality. Firstly,
> it was essential to convince the leadership of the Sport Committee of
> the expediency and necessity of such an expedition. Sasha Kaspin, the

Executive Secretary of the Mountaineering Federation of the USSR, showed tremendous energy, initiative and ability in solving the main problems of organisation and preparation.

In talks with the leadership of the Sport Committee of the USSR it was agreed that helicopters would be used to transport freight and the expedition's participants to Base Camp, and also to air-drop the freight to intermediate camps along the ascent route. A certain amount of experience had already been gained in mountain flights, as a helicopter was used to drop off freight at the weather station in the Pamirs, and was also used as a medical ambulance. But the pilots did not have experience of *landing* at heights of 3000 metres and above.

Before the start of the expedition I flew into the town of Frunze, now called Bishkyek, to solve practical problems about selection of helicopter routes, landing strips, places for the air-drop of freight etc. Here I met the helicopter captain, B Miroshchim, and the navigator, V Krivoshchapov. A landing strip was chosen beside the Garmo glacier, not far from Base Camp. Possible routes there were identified as via Tavil Dara or via Jirgital. Via Tavil Dara didn't suit because the British participants could not be accommodated there. But that was our usual route and we knew it well – after Tavil Dara, up the valley of the river Obihin-Gou as far as Pashimgar, then along the Garmo ravine. The second possibility would use local airline planes as far as Jirgital where there was helicopter fuel and more suitable conditions for the British participants. To the Garmo ravine from Jirgital, the journey was then by helicopter across several mountain ranges.

In Dushanbe, Krivoshchapov and I put forward these possibilities for consideration by a Commission made up of border guards and KGB officials. The route via Tavil Dara was cheaper since the helicopter could carry twice as much freight when flying along the ravine. The Commission recognised the expediency of taking the British participants through Jirgital, and the Soviet participants and all freight through Tavil Dara. Krivoshchapov and I were made responsible for flight safety.

Nikolai Shalaev, who was the head cook, was responsible for the domestic side of the expedition. He was careful and totally reliable.

Wilf Noyce acted as the day-to-day expedition correspondent for the *Daily Herald* and he now takes up the story. With fees contributed to expedition coffers, the *Herald* ran a series of weekly articles by Noyce, some written in advance of the expedition, others in the USSR:

Five days in Russia. A jumble of impressions. The welcoming smile of Eugene Gippenreiter at Moscow Airport, and the confused sightseer's glimpses of Moscow. The towers of the Kremlin against a midnight sky not quite dark; the rich music of Tchaikovsky in the Bolshoi Theatre; the chocolate-box bizarre cathedral of St Basil and the endless weary length of the avenues at the Exhibition of Soviet Achievements; above all the streets and squares, some of them, as one of the party had it, 'a mix-up of Glasgow and Manchester with the lettering the wrong way round'. And the frustrations.

Travel in the Soviet Union is not yet free of pitfalls. Our 2000 mile flight to Dushanbe, capital of Tajikistan, was delayed by a day for a complicated series of reasons. On the 3rd day, however, we were speeding smoothly southeast for five and a half hours, from Europe into the heart of Asia. That same sultry night we were being greeted at Dushanbe Airport by Anatoli Ovchinnikov – small, smiling, alert, with finger-breaking handgrip – and the other Russian members of the party.

Anatoli Ovchinnikov:

At last all the preparations for the arrival of the British mountaineers, including the programme for their stay in Dushanbe, were complete. And then, completely out of the blue, we received a telegram saying that the British mountaineers would be flying out to Dushanbe on 3rd July. It was late in the evening, it was warm, it was a dark southern night, and above the aerodrome the lights of the huge Tupilov 104 appeared in the sky. The plane landed, then the tedious moments waiting for the gangway. The Britons appeared smiling. We introduced ourselves. Among them was Robin Smith. At first he didn't recognise me but then he gave me a friendly pat on the shoulder and spoke about climbing Pik Kommunisma by the southern face. I nodded my head as a sign of agreement. We got on the bus, travelled to the hotel and then the whole expedition team had dinner in a restaurant. You could say the expedition had begun.

The Britons got to know Dushanbe and its surrounding area in the next few days accompanied by Eugene Gippenreiter. Meanwhile Nikolai Shalaev and I were agreeing hire of transport with local organisations, finalising dates of departure and checking that they would be observed.

Wilf Noyce:

We have begun to get to know the Russians in the last days. The 4th was spent in sweltering heat, unpacking and sorting our mountain of gear. The Russians helped us, showing great interest in our boots and butane stoves. We have not yet seen their equipment. Then we bathed in the local lido; and we bathed again later in a glacier torrent that descends from the snow peaks which one can see beyond this wide, fertile basin.

Meanwhile, however, we had suffered a shock. We arrived, confidently expecting to fly on to the airfield at Tavil Dara in a day or two's time, there to trans-ship to the helicopter. On the night of our arrival John Hunt learned that for security reasons we would not be allowed to visit Tavil Dara at all. Our kit would go that way with the Russian members. But we, on the 7th, would be flown to the airfield of Jirgital to the northeast, and thence straight to the glacier by helicopter. Moreover, this helicopter, a hard-worked creature, will have been operating with an expedition to the Tien Shan range and must be fetched.

Would we contribute one third of the cost of flying it over – about £480? The lines on the party treasurer's brow have furrowed deep. We, and what we stand up in, will fly in on the 7th, but apart from the cost of helicoptering in, there will now be the cost of helicoptering out at the end. It may be possible for us to walk five days out, stopping short at the forbidden area, but all the heavy baggage must be flown out. The pleasure of walking out at the end is the keenest of pleasures. Apart from which 'there is much profit in the observation of human customs', and we shall have seen no one but another Russian group of climbers among the glaciers.

John Hunt:

It was on this basis that our contracts and our budgeting had been drawn up. Malcolm Slesser was incensed by this change in plan and he demanded that I should call what he believed to be the Russians' bluff. He even suggested that we should pack our bags, depart for the Afghan frontier, and climb in the Hindu Kush instead. I disagreed. We had no permission for that area, we had no maps or essential contacts. It was very doubtful if we could carry out such a threat without cutting off our noses to spite our faces; it would merely be a counter-bluff. However much we might dislike the decision, the Russian authorities doubtless had reasons which were important to themselves; I did not think they would back down. In any case, as guests in a foreign land, we were in no position to throw our limited weight around. Above all, I was anxious to maintain a happy relationship with our Soviet climbing companions who were not, themselves, responsible for political decisions. A confrontation at this point would have ruined the prospects of unity in the mountains on which the success of our climbs would largely depend and which was, as far as I was concerned, the main purpose of the whole exercise.

The incident passed and we flew to our destinations as the Russians wished. Fortunately there was a solid core of good sense and moderation in our company which helped to smooth over the raw edges. But the incident demonstrated a weakness within the British party of individuals who had taken separate initiatives towards realising this privileged journey, and whose thinking on the issues and objectives had not fully blended. It left a scar which was never entirely healed. What were the Russians' reasons? As we flew up the Obihin-Gou valley we looked down upon the shells of homesteads in a landscape apparently deserted by human beings. 'Avalanches' was the explanation given to us. I remembered the ruins of the old Bezingi village in the Caucasus, from which Stalin had evicted the Balkari tribesmen. 'Avalanche' was the reason given for that too. Both explanations seemed very implausible to me.

Whatever the reasons and despite this setback, there was one important matter on which we were all agreed. From now onwards the whole party, Britishers and Russians, should work as a team; there should be one leader. It was flattering, if a trifle daunting, to be invited by the Russians to fill that role.[1]

Anatoli Ovchinnikov:

We agreed on tactics for our climbs in an original way. I would meet Sir John; he would ask me, 'Anatoli, how do you suggest we organise the climb?' I would express my point of view. He would answer, 'We'll do as you advise.' Then half an hour or an hour later we would meet again. Sir John would say, 'You, of course, are perfectly right but, taking into account our experience, we have decided to do things a little differently.' He would explain his suggestion. I would agree because I had been told to do so by the upper leadership, who said, 'In the mountains do everything as the British want but you must ensure safety.' I was also aware that, during the stay of British mountaineers in the Caucasus in 1958, they expressed displeasure when they thought we were being excessively careful or if we didn't allow them to do something.

Wilf Noyce:

Individuals' whims such as ours may be less catered for because, to the Russians, the individual, at least officially, is less important than the system. However much they may want to help us as individuals, our Russian friends here recognise the immutability of the system and respect it.

It is instructive to see the way it works in their training, for instance. They go to bed early: 'Abalakov would be very angry if he knew that so-and-so had stayed up.' Gippenreiter announces that he has not drunk alcohol since January, and was genuinely horrified, I think, when the cigarette-hungry members of the party broke into the cigarette chest with an ice-axe (in Moscow). At Dushanbe he was concerned to find that Ralph Jones had given a boy a cigarette: 'That will teach him bad habits, we think it is very bad.'

Some will smile at the apparent naïvety. The other side of the picture is to be seen in Dushanbe itself. In three villages at this site, the Emir of Bukhara in 1920 tried to reorganise his forces after being overthrown by the Bolsheviks. The modern town of 224,000 inhabitants dates from 1929, and was, till recently, named Stalinabad. It is a prosperous industrial centre.

Thus it has the advantage of being a new town, with remnants of the old villages interspersed. In no other Eastern city have I seen the same cleanliness, absence of flies and beggars and mange-ridden dogs. One cannot but admire the way in which the Soviet Union has ordered these things. Spacious public buildings, not unpleasing to look at, overlook straight streets bordered with plane, willow and white acacia to keep off the fierce summer sun. Along these walk the Tadzhik, colourful and handsome, of whose ways we hope to see something these two days. Those of the plains are square-faced or round, but there are also the mountaineers, long-faced and often striking to look at, the girls wearing brightly striped dresses to below the knees, and trousers. The bazaar is clean, orderly and surprisingly free of flies – and beggars. Even service is not followed by a demand for 'baksheesh'. A young boy guided us from our swim to the restaurant. We asked what we should give him. 'He will not want a tip. You thank him, and he is glad to have served you.' No tips are given as a rule.

July 5: Our kit went off by lorry on its twelve-hour journey to Tavil Dara. When unpacked it was found that the medicinal oxygen cylinders contained no oxygen. By a masterly piece of fitting, a Soviet firm contrived to make a connection and transfer oxygen. Thus we are now poised ready for the flight into the Pamirs.

July 6, Dushanbe: Only one or two of the Russians have been with us enough to leave an impression. Eugene Gippenreiter – slim, dark, moustached, a smiling face – has been our guide since the beginning. His English is excellent but with his companions we sometimes resort to dictionaries, sign language, fragments of English. Anatoli Ovchinnikov, their leader, is a small man, with sunken eyes and a very strong springy body. He and John Hunt get together over a Russian/English lesson each day. Vladimir Malakhov is broader, fresh-looking, with an open face and charming smile, and some English. As someone said, Joe Brown, also small and powerfully built, could well pass for one of the Russians. Joe surveys the world serenely, takes things as they come, takes a lot of photographs and listens politely to a language of which he claims not to understand a word.

A certain ebullience, in speech and action, seems to please. This is supplied in the wisecracks of Iain McNaught-Davis (which Eugene is never quite sure whether to take seriously) and of Ralph Jones. Ted Wrangham's Etonian wit they may find harder to understand. Robin Smith, the wild man of Scotland, goes down very well. And, of course, John Hunt, very popular in Russia, mixes dignity and friendliness in a right royal manner. John pursues his Russian studies indefatigably.

We visited yesterday one of the two comprehensive boarding schools of Tajikistan. It takes all ages from two, boys and girls, holds 840 children, and has room for over 1200. Everything possible is done for them, and the equipment, presided over by portraits of Lenin from early childhood, is first-class. John found out everything that was to be known about the school and system of education. But the great success was scored by Malcolm Slesser. After a little concert given by the seven-year-olds, he played back their songs and music on the tape, to their great delight.

Today we have been by bus up a gorge of the Gissar Range, and walked up to a tiny village of the pattern one sees as widely apart as Morocco and Pakistan: flat-roofed mud houses, walnut trees, a woman washing maize, girls reaping the thin wheat crop. In the torrent we bathed (the temperature had been 109° in the shade) and bathed again: long delicious bathes which we shall remember in the next weeks. Then back, to pack up and be invited out to tea by the hospitable Association of Tajik Mountaineers.

John Hunt:

It was a wholly delightful, if gastronomically exacting occasion. After consuming great quantities of *shashlik* curries and flat bread, we repaired to recover in an upper chamber normally reserved for the elders, for quiet conversation over cups of green tea. The tradition was as civilised as in any Oxford college, notwithstanding the fact that we sat shoeless and cross-legged on the floor. One of the waitresses, a motherly character, took a fancy to me; to my embarrassment, but to the amusement of everyone else, she addressed me with unmistakable meaning in her voice. 'What do you want to have to do with all these immature young men?' she enquired. 'Why not let them go off to the mountains and have their fun, and you and I will enjoy each other's company here in Dushanbe?' Not sure whether to be flattered or dismayed by this revelation of her feelings and my age, I compromised by accepting another cup of tea.

Robin to his Edinburgh climbing fraternity:

We are whooping in Dushanbe, oriental city of sun bazaars and lovely Tajik Maids. Helicopter to Base Camp tomorrow. Big Time.

I will be in the Alps, all being well, straight from London or Paris, by 3rd–7th September. Write to say what has been climbed or who will be where in September.

Malcolm Slesser:[2]

One man was in a veritable paroxysm of joy over the piles of bright new mountaineering gear, and that was our untamed tiger, Robin Smith. His great elfin face was one vast smile. Stripped to brief, ragged bathing trunks and covered in sweat and dirt, he was running pitons through his hands with all the relieved feeling of a sourdough who has discovered gold and fingering the thousands of feet of Swiss Perlon ropes with the reverence of one touching the holy hem. As an impoverished student, these things had been virtually beyond his reach . . . In abandoned ecstasy, he linked a hundred krabs together; then, winding them round himself, he was photographed in the attitude of a twentieth-century gladiator.

Later that day Robin impressed his personality more forcibly on me. While cooling off in the Lake of Communist Youth, we had a horse fight, during which he held me under so long that I started to breathe the water.

Robin to his mother:

I can write no more than a scribble. All day we lounge or bathe, in the heat, and now it is midnight local time & in 6? hours' time we fly for

Base Camp. This is 6 times better a town for the likes of us than Moscow. We haven't looked at a museum. Our tours, to a country village, a very startlingly modern school, a bazaar, all among the very colourful natives, turbaned, bearded, in flowing robes, on donkeys, etc, mostly Tajiks but very mixed. 2 or 3 times a day we swim in hot lakes or cool rushing rivers. All goes well.

I have shot off dozens of my free snapshots, they may (one or two) come out. Even within our party we are still friendly. But a lot of (predicted) officialese has disrupted our programme here & there – eg we are unlikely to be allowed to walk right out, Tavil Dara is taboo for no given reason, obviating the need for mules & my small contribution.

None the less, the Russians we see are obviously friendly & helpful, have given us a good time, & soon we may even be climbing. Behave.

41

IN THE MOUNTAINS

Anatoli Ovchinnikov:

On the day we were due to fly out to Jirgital there was an earthquake, but this didn't prevent us from arriving on time at Dushanbe airport for our flight there in an ME2. It turned out that the helicopter didn't come from Frunze because of unfavourable weather along the route and so we spent an unplanned night in Jirgital. We slept in the open air where we could. Robin Smith slept in the garden of the airport chief. The following day, July 7th, we were transferred to the tip of the Garmo glacier, at an altitude of 3000 metres. The helicopter landed and for five minutes we were shrouded in clouds of dust until the engine was switched off. Boris Miroshkin suggested that we prepare the strip for future landings and that we must water the area to prevent dust. Base camp was set up in a birch copse from where we could see the summit of Garmo. The whole population of Base Camp, under the leadership of Nikolai Shalaev, not only helped set up camp but set to, levelling the ground for the airstrip, and putting up flags to show wind direction. The following flights then started to bring in other participants and freight.

Wilf Noyce:

July 7th, Base Camp: In almost exactly a week from London Airport, we have arrived at the snout of the Garmo glacier. This has been made possible by the remarkable skill of the helicopter pilots.[1]

The day started dramatically at 5 a.m., with earthquake tremors at Dushanbe strong enough to shake the walls and send the lights swinging. By 6.15 we were on the way to the airport. Against a stormy sky we were soon flying up the U-shaped valley of the Surkh Ab River; we passed over Qala Khoit where green fields now mark the site of a village obliterated recently by earthquake, and descended at Jirgital. Here a green, flat plain is surrounded by hills and one can already see the Pamir snows. At 5000 ft the air was cool and fresh. We sat chatting with the pilots over tea, on this and that and world problems in general. Someone asked if it was true that the young of Russia were

295

browned off at having the Revolution still rammed down their throats. The answer was no, for they realise what they have escaped and are grateful for that. The pilots in turn asked us why we allowed German troops to train on British soil. And so on.

At 10 a.m. two brown dots against the red hillside indicated the helicopters. Seven to each, we clambered into these powerful-looking machines and took off. For me at any rate there began a fascinating flight. The huge white peaks were clearly visible ahead, but to reach our side of them, it was necessary to fly over two 13,000-ft passes, wheeling south and west, before we could strike due east up our Garmo valley. Up, then, we spiralled, passing close beside a village of waving figures and then seeing it, minutes later, far below; over the pass and across green plateaux on which horses ran and where great birds, perhaps Lammergeier vultures, swooped. A deep gorge appeared below, while on our left, looking very close indeed, there towered walls of rock backed by glaciers and high white snow saddles.

The Garmo river was a brown thread hemmed by hillsides. The storms, which had threatened ominously from the west and northeast, eased away and a weak sun shone. The helicopter pursued the river beyond the last village, the valley became stonier and the dominating peaks higher. Suddenly there it was – a grey caterpillar of a glacier, and the helicopter descended fast; a final whirr and a great thump as we hit the stones of the river bed. We had arrived.

The second helicopter landed a little higher on a shelf above the river. Boxes and bags were bundled out. Over the grey, broad river bed, between surprisingly green hillsides, the snows of Mt Garmo, over 21,000 ft high, glittered in the far distance between shreds of mist.

However there was little time for admiring the view. First, it appeared we were lower down the valley than originally intended: 10,000 ft we first thought, but in reality only 9500. Should we try to move higher at once? This did not appear practicable, particularly as more helicopter loads had still to come. It was agreed that Base Camp should be here, in a nearby walnut, willow and birch wood, and we set about carrying the necessary tents and stores across. For the rest of the day we sorted ourselves out and looked around. Ted Wrangham even went out after the local game – bear, deer, a type of ibex, many birds and small animals.

Malcolm Slesser (morning of July 8th):

I was awoken by a friendly diaphragmatic belch. Before me was Robin Smith, one of the duty cooks, all grin and raindrops, enquiring if we would like breakfast in the tent. For one whose role was that of a rebel it was a startling metamorphosis. We complimented him on his charity and accepted.

Wilf Noyce:

July 8: The first necessity, clearly, is to get as much as we can farther up the glacier; for we are still below the snout of the Garmo, 17 miles as the crow flies from the summit of Communism Peak and 15,000 ft below it. With this laudable intention eight of us plodded up today, with 35 lb sacks, up moraine and the boulder-strewn glacier to a site called 'Avodara', a tiny meadow between moraine and hillside about five long miles on. It was a toilsome, ankle-straining tramp, with no enlivening views since mist covered the higher peaks. It had rained hard yesterday evening, after thunder, and it rained most of the night. The Garmo glacier round here looks much as London might look after an H-Bomb: a chaotic brown waste. We dumped ration boxes and returned, very hot and thirsty. Avodara is about 11,500 ft and we were probably feeling the effect of hard work around the 11,000 ft level after the sudden rise in altitude from Dushanbe, where temperatures had been in the hundreds.

It looks as if 'tomorrow and tomorrow and tomorrow' the same dose will be repeated. Just possibly the helicopters may cooperate, by dropping ropes and other unbreakables at Avodara, but it is unlikely that they can land there, so near to steep rocks. The Russians who came up today showed that they were very fit and can move fast. They are also very helpful, and it is a pleasure to share tents. Nikolai, my tent-companion, has about as much English as I have Russian, and we get along well in a mixture, with frequent references to the dictionary.

Life in the wood is pleasant, apart from the flies. But it is obvious that there is a lot of very hard and hot work ahead, before ever a mountain can be climbed.

John Hunt (recording how he felt portering 30-lb loads):

9th July: Leaving Graeme, Ted, Derek and Robin in camp, the rest of us have carried food boxes up to Avodara, which is normally used by the Russians as base. For all of us, and especially myself, it has been a gruelling day. We plodded over deadly stone slopes beside the glacier for four and a half hours, feeling the weight and the altitude abominably. The Russians made light of the journey, but I became more and more exhausted on the way back; George kindly stayed with me. Graeme, Derek and Ted came out to meet us half a mile from camp. I am very disappointed with this poor showing. It is probably a combination of acclimatisation and years. I hope to improve but cannot go very high at present.

The prospect of humping thousands of pounds of gear, day after day for about a week, to that higher place was a depressing thought. In our state of unfitness the daily corvees proved to be as back-breaking a labour as we had feared. The Russians had the edge on us, for they had trained assiduously for the expedition and, with the exception of Robin Smith, were much fitter than we were at that stage.

John Hunt (a few days later):

By now I was really fit; even carrying those enormous loads was no longer unbearable; they made a tremendous difference to my own outlook on life. In my sleeping bag at Avodara, on our way up the glacier, I wrote: 'Lying out under the stars, in a half-moon, life takes on a new perspective.'

Anatoli Ovchinnikov:

Portering supplies to a higher camp showed that we had a different approach not only in climbing tactics but in our relationships within the group. When we were climbing in Britain the difference was not noticeable, as the time involved in rock-climbing is shorter. For example we even went along a path in groups and therefore our pace was slow. The British set a time for starting out but would leave as they were ready, that is before and after the appointed time. Moreover, if somebody for some reason fell behind we would wait for that person when we were resting. We usually chose a place to rest in the shade or by a stream. While we rested we would discuss various problems.

Tolia Sevastianov and I were surprised by, for us, Slesser's strange behaviour. We were going along a small path to Avodara and in front of us was Lowe, followed about 200 metres behind by Slesser. Lowe stopped by a stream, took off his rucksack and sat down to rest. Immediately Slesser also took his off and sat down on the dusty path under the burning rays of the sun. We went up to him and said he should go as far as Lowe and stop by the stream. There were some small saplings growing there and it would be more pleasant to rest. He replied that he did not wish to prevent Lowe from enjoying the mountain scenery. Since we were used to acting as a group we couldn't understand at that time the idea of taking into account the wishes of the individual. As for Robin he loved to walk with us and even enjoyed, or seemed to enjoy, our semolina and buckwheat porridge. It was the case, though, that his rucksack was lighter than ours.

Malcolm Slesser:

'Been pretty soft up to now. Thought it would have been much harder,' confided Robin, as he drank copious draughts of tea. He was dressed in his usual attire: boots, underpants, shirt and battered trilby hat.

John Hunt:

What a dull plod this is: and how we begin to realise the difference between this and the Himalayas, having to do all our own porterage! I am so impressed by the time consumed, the effort and the depressing effect that I have decided to experiment in air-dropping the balance of our food for the higher camps, when the helicopters are ready to help us. Malcolm and I are busy with calculations to this effect now.

Anatoli Ovchinnikov:

Sir John and I flew over the upper reaches of the glacier and agreed upon areas for the air-drop. At that time our pilots did not have experience of that and losses were therefore great. Boxes smashed open.

Robin (in a letter back home):

13th July (Base Camp): Things are going well though not as planned. We left the very pleasant neighbourhood of Dushanbe early on Saturday 7th, & flew to a village Tapbi [also known as Miraza or Jirgital] about 50 miles (at a guess) NE of Tavil Dara, which (our very helpful comrades have been obliged to tell us) is out of bounds for reasons into which it would not be tactful to inquire. The weather on this first 2-hr flight by plain plane looked quite ominous ahead, & we expected to be grounded for a day, but the helicopters arrived as scheduled & flew us for another hour over the gorges & grassy foothills to the foot of the Garmo glacier. However, recent rain has muddied the site planned for Base Camp, so that the helicopters couldn't land, and we find ourselves in trees 2000 ft & 8 miles lower down, below the snout of the Garmo Glacier. Since then we have been ferrying loads up the unsightly moraine which covers all of these 8 miles, to dump them on the island of grass which changes its name to Camp 1 [or 'Avodara']. A very back-breaking but fittening business. To make up for this setback we arranged for the 'copters to dump a lot of less breakable equipment on the sites of Camps 2 & 3, which none of us have even been to yet. But 3 days of shaky weather (what you would call quite good in Edinburgh) kept the helicopters away, leaving the 12 of us to cohabit & fraternise with ourselves & the 6 Russians we are climbing with, their radio operator (in regular touch with Dushanbe) and an amiable charlatan whose function is cook-cum-hunter, but who has so far shot nothing, though he beat me twice at chess. We get on very well with the climbers, though I suspect that they are a little more in sympathy with our rougher element (which some of us try to identify with the character of Scotland, trodden under England's heel) than with the slightly smooth & knightly basis of the expedition. On the whole they are very pleasantly surprised to find that none of us, even the knight, is the model English gentleman. So far I am on friendly terms with everyone, even in our own party.

Today, however, dawned bright blue & cloudless, & early on the 2 helicopters made their first arrival, ferrying in a further 25 Russians in a separate party (the Spartak team) to camp beside us, led by Abalakov, the 50-yr-old frost-de-fingered Iron Man of Russian climbing; and one of the 'copters loaded with our gear, some of our party and George Lowe with his Cine Camera flew (quite dangerously) away up the glacier to dump the gear from about 15 ft about 60 mph on the snow at Camp 3. They bring back reports of very fine mountains – from here we can see only the beginnings of the big ones. With the weather set fair, we can hope to set off in the next day or two, through camps 1, 2 & 3, for the first & shorter part of our revised programme. This takes us into the Vavilova Glacier, to assault Peak Garmo & a nearby wall in 3 parties, each comprising 4 British & 2 Russians. The Glacier branches sort of S. Eastwards off the Garmo, which we leave at Camp 2, & in about a fortnight we come back to rest at Base Camp, then (assuming, largely enough, that all goes well) we go back to Camp 2 & on up the Garmo for a major assault on Peak of Communism.

We are all in good health & well-fed, browning in the sun. Here, around midday, we are just low enough for swarms of flies, but should lose them soon. Today, apart from a bit of loading & unloading of helicopters (they come whirling down to kick up phenomenal spurts of dust, down by the glacier-river) we have been lazing with tea, books, tape-recordings from jazz to Beethoven & occasional reception on a wireless from Moscow, India, Australia, even Britain. Relayed, maybe. It is turning pleasantly cool.

Ralph Jones:

I think it was noticeable that Robin was on his best behaviour. He'd obviously been given a 'going-over' by somebody to the effect that John Hunt was due a certain amount of deference, that the English weren't all totally bad and that some of them could climb a bit as well – and I suspect that he showed rather more sympathy to the English/Welsh part of the party than he did to his fellow Scots. I must say that, from our point of view, it was hard to see what they had in common except nationality. I shared a tent with Robin and I must say I found it a not unpleasant experience. He took care of what he was about and I liked his wit when it didn't persist in taking the mickey out of the English.

He was incredibly fit – as fit as, if not more fit, than members of the Russian part of the expedition. I think it amazing that the accident occurred when and how it did because I would have thought that with his fitness and strength it was something he could have avoided. My first reaction to his death was one of disbelief. John Hunt told me later that his plans were that Robin, Wilf and I would accompany three of the Russians to either Peak Moscow or Peak Leningrad to do a new route that the Russians had lined up, while the rest of the expedition went on to climb Mount Communism.

Sue Bradshaw (back in London):

Thank you all very much for all your letters and cables; I'm much enjoying being Home Base (at least most of the time!). We are all avidly devouring any bits of news that come, and of course Wilf's articles which are terribly interesting. I send out a sort of bulletin each week, with all the bits I've collected from all the families, to all the other families. There was a very nice photo of you all in the *Herald* the Monday after you left.

I'm so sorry you are having so many headaches over finance. Actually, for future reference it would be more economical in the long run if you sent more explicit and longer cables. George's first one saying the Federation was awaiting roubles and would I expedite, I took to mean the roubles that had been sent out in May, and I thought they had never arrived. So I got on to the bank, who checked all along the line, including telexing Moscow, and I was just going to cable you that the roubles had fallen into the North Sea and I was donning my mermaid's tail, when Derek's letter arrived, saying that it was a *further* 3000 roubles that were wanted. It's sad but true that I've acquired about six grey hairs in the last few weeks; when the expedition is in funds again, I'm thinking of being dyed at its expense! This is just a small rocket, George.

The cable about arriving in Base Camp came yesterday. As far as I could make out, it had taken five days. Actually, Reuters picked up a report on the 12th and it appeared in the papers as a news item on the 13th, about you having set up Base Camp, so please send me any splendid news about reaching the top of Peak Communism, as soon as it happens. Bit galling people ringing up and saying how interesting that Base Camp has been established, and the Home Base not knowing anything about it. There are hundreds of questions I want to ask you when you get back. I can't tell you how frantic life has been since you left. I keep thinking of Mac telling me that once you had left, life would be dead.

I had a letter from Robin's mother by the way. She was approached by the *Daily Herald* in Edinburgh, who wanted an article on 'The Woman Behind' by Robin's wife! I feel I'm getting to know all your families quite well. I much enjoy getting letters from them.

Everybody connected with the expedition has your interests at heart. Please give my best wishes to all the Russian members of the party. With love to you all.

Anatoli Ovchinnikov:

The glaciers in the Pamirs are equal in size to those of the Himalayas. They also have ice-falls and are crevassed. The glaciers Balaev and Vavilova are in the upper part of the Garmo ravine; these two glaciers meet below Pik Garmo. It takes one or two full days to reach the foot of Pik Kommunisma or Pik Garmo or any of the other mountains lying in the upper reaches. The time depends on the state of the glaciers and the level of acclimatisation of the participants. In discussions as to how to tackle the ascent it was discovered that British mountaineers are used to carrying rucksacks which weigh no more than 20 kilograms. We are used to 30 kilograms – this for us is considered normal. Thus it was expedient to set up camps at about 5000 metres. In these camps food supplies, fuel and all the other necessities for the ascent would be stored. In line with Soviet practice at the time, acclimatisation sorties to 5000 and then 6000 metres were planned. These would take place successively. Thus, after approximately 15 days in the mountains, the mountaineer would be acclimatised and capable of climbing to 7000 metres.

John Hunt (to Home Base, July 14th):

We are about to set off on a strenuous 14-day trip, with some horribly difficult-looking climbs to do. This is going to prove a severe test of our relations with the Russians, for their outlook on mountaineering is so very different from ours. But they are a nice friendly lot and intentions are good on both sides.

I fear you won't hear, except possibly by cable, again until we come back! The last helicopter flight leaves at 12 noon, and I'm hastening to scribble this in time. One machine is just on its way back from dropping loads up the glacier. I had a most exciting flight yesterday, doing this! One food box was smashed, but so far we've dropped others successfully. A large group of Russian climbers of the Spartak organisation has arrived, and we are discussing plans with them, in order not to clash. Our groups leave this afternoon on their way to attempt Pik Garmo and other summits up the Vavilova glacier – they look formidable from the air. Love from us all to you.

The letter was signed by most of the group including Robin, that signature being the last memento of his own hand.

Anatoli Ovchinnikov:

The first acclimatisation sortie went as far as the old and new marmot clearings which lay on the right and left lateral moraines of the Vavilova glacier where it meets the Balaev glacier [Camp 3 was on the right, ascending the glacier]. Freight had already been air-dropped there. We began to gather it and take an inventory. Robin suggested to me that we should climb Pik Shcherbakeva but I had to refuse since Sir John and I were to discuss our subsequent plan of action, so Robin set off up the nearest ridge to the summit. A little later others, including Joe Brown and Ted Wrangham, were also attracted there. Thus, on July 16th, the British opened their climbing account in the Pamirs.

Joe Brown:

Only Robin reached the top. The remainder, including myself, sat down completely debilitated halfway up and shouted after him that he was foolhardy to continue on his own. The Russians took a dim view of our take-it-or-leave-it attitude and must have thought that we were a bunch of old women.

Anatoli Ovchinnikov:

> Sir John liked the Patriot and Garmo summits which were visible from here and between them, in the crest, there rose up another beautiful summit, which also caught his attention. When he discovered that it had no name and that no man had ever set foot on its summit, he expressed the thought that it would be a worthwhile climb. As the first to reach the top, he would have the right to give the mountain a name. This name, he decided, would honour the friendship between British and Soviet mountaineers.[2]

Assault teams for these three preparatory climbs were selected – to be led by Malcolm Slesser, John Hunt and Wilfrid Noyce:

Pik Patriot: 20,961 ft or 6389 m	*Unnamed Pik: 18,504 ft or 5640 m*	*Pik Garmo: 21,637 ft or 6595 m*
Malcolm Slesser	John Hunt	Wilfrid Noyce
Nikolai Alchutov	Eugene Gippenreiter	Derek Bull
Joe Brown	Ralph Jones	Anatoli Ovchinnikov
Kenny Bryan	George Lowe	Anatoli Sevastianov
Vladimir Malachov	Graeme Nicol	Robin Smith
Ian McNaught-Davis	Nikolai Shalaev	Ted Wrangham

The peaks were on a (west of) north–south axis, Pik Garmo to the south. The other peaks lay three and seven miles to the north of Garmo.

42

PIK GARMO

John Hunt's central team had the easiest assignment. He considered it the support team for the others in the event of problems and, for this reason, it included team doctor Graeme Nicol. Garmo was by far the toughest of the three and a few members of the other groups, in particular the two youngest Russians, were disappointed that it was not their own objective. Four of the strongest climbers were in it – Noyce, Ovchinnikov, Sevastianov and Smith (with Bull and Wrangham in support).

Ovchinnikov's party returned to Base Camp and rested for about two days. Before leaving for his own climb, John Hunt discussed with Noyce the need not to push too hard for the southwest face of Garmo which was heavily snow-covered and looked formidable. These were to be the last words they spoke together, John Hunt later realised.

Anatoli Ovchinnikov:

On July 20th we set out for our acclimatisation ascent and by that evening our group was in the new marmot camp [Camp 3]. We had agreed that by July 25th everyone would have returned to the camp, whether or not they had climbed the mountain. At that time we had very few long-distance portable radio transmitters, thus there was no radio link between the groups as we climbed. Each group had flares: red as a distress signal, green everything in order.

On the morning of the 21st July, we went up the Vavilova glacier, crossed the ice-fall and pitched camp on the moraine below the slopes of Pik Garmo. Robin was in the tent with us. Wilf, Derek and Ted were in the other. From our point of view, the English had settled in with comfort – they had pyjamas and read English translations of Tolstoy and Dostoyevsky before they went to sleep. We made the supper and, in the morning, breakfast. The weather was cloudy, visibility inadequate. On the slope the snow was deep. I went first. Towards the end of the day I had to ask Anatoli Sevastianov to take over the lead before we came out onto the ridge. Everyone was tired and, once on the ridge, nobody wished to go any further. Again we put up the tents, drank tea and had supper. The following day the weather hadn't improved, rather it had worsened. There was no visibility. In the hope that the weather would improve, we took down the tents and went along the ridge. However, our hope was not justified. As soon as the ridge ended we would have had to go across the snow fields but we decided to stop in case we got lost or came out onto a slope where there was danger of avalanche. We virtually had a day's rest. Towards evening on the 23rd the sky cleared and it became cold. We were at a height of approximately 5500 metres, about 1000 metres lower than the summit. In principle it was possible to reach the summit and come back down in a day.

Ralph Jones:

We thought it a good idea on the morning of the 24th to go to see how things were proceeding on Garmo, so we trudged up the glacier. There followed a series of quite unusual incidents. For example, Eugene Gippenreiter fell into a crevasse in which, luckily, a river was flowing. At least that was better than landing on ice. We saved him from drowning and, in fact, managed to pull him out uninjured – however, it did necessitate an enforced camp.

Anatoli Ovchinnikov:

On the morning of 24th July we got up quite early, had breakfast and put food supplies in our pockets. However, our boots hadn't dried and we were afraid of getting frostbite. The British had felt-lined boots, therefore they were not in danger of frostbite. We asked Wilf to wait till the sun appeared, which it did at about 6 o'clock. We set off on two ropes; first Anatoli Sevastianov and I at the ends of the rope with Wilf in the middle. On the second rope there was Robin, Ted and Derek. The snow was thickly packed and we climbed quite quickly. The second rope was a little behind – we stopped to rest and to wait for it. Suddenly Robin appeared and said that Ted and Derek didn't feel particularly well and had decided to return to the tent, but he wanted to go to the summit. Wilf undid one of his ropes and threw the end to Robin. Thus Sevastianov and Noyce were linked together and I was with Robin Smith. Tolia (Anatoli) and I began to climb up the snowy icy slope. As we got higher the layer of snow decreased. The snow had been frozen together since morning so we had put on crampons. The slope was not steep. Therefore there were no problems but we felt that Robin and

Wilf were not acclimatised sufficiently. However we couldn't slow down the pace as it was still a long way to the summit. At last the snowy icy slope came to an end and we reached the upper snow-covered rock faces. Here Anatoli and I took off our crampons as our boots had tricounis, that is studs, on the soles and for us there was no problem on snow-covered rocks. Wilf and Robin had Vibram boots, and therefore had to go up the rock face with crampons, as Vibram boots slip on such surfaces. The rocks were not difficult, but if you consider we were above 6000 metres, that gives one food for thought. I suggested to Robin that he went first and he agreed with pleasure. He coped normally with the rock parts, due to his talent, but it became obvious that insufficient acclimatisation and the altitude were telling on him. As a result, the speed of our ascent slowed whereas time was moving quickly on. I asked Robin if I could go first and he agreed. We then moved a bit more quickly. Just before the summit, I suggested to Robin that he took over the lead again so that he would be first up. This was his first 6000-metre summit. We got there about 3 o'clock. Looking at the photo of Robin and Wilf at Garmo's summit cairn it is obvious that they were exhausted.

Anatoli Sevastianov:

There was no time left for a serious planned assault that would allow us to stay at intermediate camps and one of our British friends (I don't remember who in particular) suggested that we should try to do the climb in one day. Ovchinnikov and I agreed to this suggestion as, by our calculations, it was only about 700 metres to the summit and the climb did not seem technically complicated. Much later we discovered that Pik Garmo was not 6200 metres as we thought at the time, but 6595 metres, which is significantly higher. This being the case, two intermediate camps would have been required on the climb from 5500 metres.

So, we set off early in the morning and kept moving at quite a good pace. Wrangham and Bull obviously did not feel totally confident and after about an hour they indicated they were going back and that they would wait for us at the tents.

About 3 p.m. or 4 p.m. we were at the summit and I remember well that we all realised there just how very tired we all were.

Ralph Jones:

At one point that day we had an incredible premonition of disaster, which everybody in the party, including the Russians, remarked upon.

I think the feeling of disaster was that something was going to happen to us, but it never occurred that it might be happening to another group. We discovered later that the premonition coincided precisely with the time of the accident on Garmo.

Anatoli Ovchinnikov:

The descent began in the following order: the first rope Wilf, then Anatoli Sevastianov; the second Robin, then myself. As we descended Robin became livelier and livelier as the altitude decreased. When I came down off the rock face onto the snow and ice slope, Anatoli Sevastianov was putting on his crampons. Robin untied himself from me. He remarked that we – that is, the Soviet side – would descend quickly and would catch them up. He gave the end of his rope, which had been attached to me, to Sevastianov. Robin then took the end of Sevastianov's rope, which was attached to Wilf, who had already begun the descent and had gone down the snowy icy slope almost to the full extent of the rope. I was putting on my crampons. Anatoli had done this before me and suddenly said that they had slipped. We didn't worry because, even though we couldn't see them beyond the crest, the slope wasn't steep. We were already used to the British using the fifth spot [their backsides] to go down snow slopes. However, having gone down a little further and not seeing anybody we became afraid and began to protect each other carefully, although usually on such slopes we would simply run. When we got to the foot of this slope everything became clear. Wilf and Robin had begun to slide. They had gathered a high speed. At the foot there was a mound of snow across the slope. They hit this, were deflected to the left and there, a few metres away, was a steep 70-degree slope. They fell about a further 800 metres. Ted and Derek had been watching our descent from the tent. When we got a little nearer they recognised our red jackets and realised that it was Wilf and Robin who had perished. Anatoli Sevastianov suggested that we should begin the descent, but Ted and Derek replied that it was now dark and that Wilf and Robin were definitely dead. It wouldn't be sensible to go down. It would even be dangerous in the dark.

That night was terrible. I shivered, sometimes from the cold, sometimes from the tragedy. There was no peace of mind for the thought that Robin and Wilf were lying down there, almost on the floor of the glacier. The following day we climbed down to a more northerly, lower level of the glacier and met Sir John and his group, who had come to look for us. We told them all that had happened. On seeing the condition we were in, Sir John suggested putting up the tents and resting till morning and only going to the bodies of Wilf and Robin the next day. We expressed our readiness to take part in transporting work even that day.

Anatoli Sevastianov:

We set off down on the same two ropes as we had ascended. When we reached the start of that tragic slope everyone was basically in the same state. We were very tired, but pleased that the peak had been conquered and that there was not far to go. Below, we could already see our tents. Just before the descent of the fatal slope, Ovchinnikov and I began to put on our crampons and Wilf and Robin, who had done this earlier, decided not to wait for us but to go down together. Although they had a good pretext to rest a little neither Robin nor Wilf wanted to. On the contrary they were experiencing a significant upturn in strength and spirit.

Robin and Wilf attached their karabiners to one rope and set off downwards. I had put on my crampons before Ovchinnikov and, as I stood there, I watched Robin and Wilf descend. The slope gradually became steeper and steeper and first of all one of them (I couldn't say who it was) disappeared over a crest on the slope and then the second one began to move out of sight. When I could only see the upper part of his body, something strange happened. If before the figure had been moving slowly and at an even pace, then now he disappeared almost in a flash from my field of vision. I can't say what happened. I can only say that I saw the figure hurtling downwards. Either he fell himself or he was sharply jerked by the rope. I don't know for sure. But, rerunning that scene through my mind again and again, I am more inclined to think that the upper figure was jerked down sharply from below.

I told Ovchinnikov that obviously something had happened with their rope. We came closer to the slope and looked about trying to see Robin and Wilf. They weren't there. Continuing to look around we noticed two small figures standing by the tents and one of them indicated to us a spot further down the glacier to the left of the slope we had been coming down. We understood that was where Robin and Wilf had fallen.

When Ovchinnikov and I were descending, we were immediately forced to move a little to the right from the path of our ascent as there was a solid mound of hard layered snow there and, to the right of it, soft snow in which deep safe footholds could be made. Robin and Wilf did not take advantage of this option but went straight down the ascent route along the mound, which was easier to slide off and harder to keep a good footing on. Perhaps this explains why one of them fell. However, this is only a suggestion. It is impossible to be certain.

When we got to the tents Derek and Ted told us that they had seen the fall from beginning to end. We suggested that we quickly break camp and that we climb down to Robin and Wilf, as there may have been a miracle and they might well be alive. But Derek and Ted said that, judging by what they had seen, they were convinced that they couldn't possibly be alive and that, in the approaching darkness, it would be an unnecessary and unjustified risk. Perhaps because we were incredibly tired their view made sense and we stayed in the tents until morning.

John Hunt:

From their camp some 1500 ft below on the West ridge Derek and Ted had been watching the four climbers, having heard a yodel [a Robin 'trademark'] which doubtless was meant to encourage them to start cooking. They saw Robin and Wilf fall, first into a snow couloir, then down a rock gully, moving now at terrific pace. Horror-struck, they hoped against hope that the fall might bring them out to the true right, onto less steep ground, but it was not to be. They fell to the left, over the edge of the ridge towards the upper basin of the Garmo glacier, down a huge ice slope which borders the west (rock) face; it is terrifically steep. The two men fell first over an upper Bergschrund and then over the edge of an ice cliff marking the upper lip of a second, much bigger one. To Derek it seemed that the fall was arrested at that place, on an ice terrace below that 60-ft ice cliff, about 800 ft above the glacier basin.

Ted Wrangham:

We arrived with little difficulty at a campsite from which the summit of Pik Garmo was just within reach, though the 3500 ft still to go would mean a long day. The next day was fine and in due course we came to a long steep snow slope, 12 to 18 inches of soft snow lying on hard ice. Derek and I were not confident enough to move together up such ground, and to have climbed it in pitches would have delayed the party too much. So the other four went on, while Derek and I returned to the camp to prepare for their return. Derek went out of the tent later to check their progress and I heard his voice, 'Ted, Ted, there is something terribly wrong; I think they've fallen.' He had seen what he feared were two bodies flash past down a great gulley of which a short section was visible to us. Hoping against hope that he was wrong, we scrambled across to a point from which we could just see the two bodies lying some 3000 ft below. At the time we did not know which two it was. They had fallen some 4000 ft, including several long rocky sections. We could see no movement where they lay.

John Hunt:

The time was 6.20 p.m. So died two outstanding British mountaineers.

Ted Wrangham:

Some time later, as it was getting dark, the two Anatolis returned, shocked and very tired. Any attempt to descend that night was clearly out of the question. During our descent next day, and later when we were trying to come to terms with the tragedy, the two Anatolis were most supportive; true friends.

Graeme Nicol:

I was with John Hunt in what was really meant to be a support team and therefore we had a less ambitious objective, although it did turn out to be a first ascent. This concept of support was, however, rather nullified by the absence of effective communication between the teams. I rather think that we had originally been promised radios. After we had climbed our peak, we set off to find the Noyce team. I can't now remember why, but we definitely had some logical or rational cause of misgivings. It might be that someone from the other team was meant to meet us or simply that we had seen no activity on the glacier below us which was the route to Garmo. At any rate, and whatever the logical or rational basis for concern, only on one other occasion can I ever remember such grim personal forebodings and the absolute conviction that something had gone wrong. I do have – or certainly did have when younger – a bit of 'second sight' which is, I think, a very mixed blessing.

John Hunt:

We, of course, knew nothing of all this tragedy on the evening of the 24th, although we had been scanning the face at about that time and had been puzzled by the absence of visible tracks; a small ice avalanche fell down the rock face at about 6.15 p.m. Something seemed to be wrong, but we could not place the reason for our disquiet; we even debated whether some or all should go down to Camp 3. In the end we decided, providentially, that we must press on next morning and clear up the mystery.

On the 25th we moved rapidly up the glacier on the hard frozen snow as far as the lower ice fall, then quickly up the true right edge to the lower of two high glacier basins beneath the peak, at a height of about 16,000 ft. There, at 9.00 a.m. we were at once greatly relieved to sight one Russian tent. A few moments later our worries seemed to be dispelled when we spotted two tiny figures on the west ridge of Pik Garmo; evidently they had abandoned the notion of attempting the unclimbed and fearsome-looking west face and were climbing (or more probably, had already climbed) by the ridge on its left.

We had a meal, for we started out without breakfast, then Graeme and I went up the higher ice fall, towards the upper basin. Both of us wanted to reach the ridge if possible, as well as making early contact with our friends. It was very hot in the seracs, and route-finding would have been difficult but for faint traces of the footsteps of Wilf's party, evidently made several days ago.

We could now see at least two people descending the steep snow slopes from a col on the left of the main ridge, going so slowly that we suspected an injury to one of them – nor would they respond to our shouts. Graeme and I were clearly going to wait, so we found shade and coolness in a huge ice grotto beneath a Bergschrund which terminated the slope they were descending; it was a welcome relief from the glare and fierce heat outside. After a time, not seeing any signs of the others, we decided to start up a rock rib which the other party appeared to have used when going up; we still had ideas of reaching the ridge if the descending climbers were, in fact, all right. Looking down from this vantage point, we suddenly saw two of them below us, on the glacier. A few shouted words from Derek broke the awful news.

Robin's mother (writing to Sue Bradshaw that same day):

It was very good of you to phone about the TV report on the climbers. I hastily made my way up the road to the friends who have a TV & who are keenly interested . . . but alas! . . . nothing of the climbers on the 6-o'clock news. Mr Hendry [the neighbour, not Archie] phoned the Scottish BBC TV House & was assured that it would be shown on the 9.15 news – at 6 p.m. a lot of local news is shown after the main general news. So I returned to their house again at 9 p.m. & the two dears sat again through the 'news', but nothing of the climbers. Mr. Hendry is going to write a letter of wrath to TV House in London, saying that since there are four Scottish climbers, any such news should be shown in Scotland.

However your telling me Robin looked – what was the word? . . . 'splendid' . . . & my thoughts flew to health! – have comforted me. Thank you again.

Wilfrid Noyce's wife (also writing to Sue Bradshaw on that same day):

Thank you so much for your letter and enclosures. It really was very good of you to take the trouble to circulate all the news.

Wilf has been wonderful about writing & has sent something out with every possible helicopter. I have had 6 letters, 3 postcards and a cable since they left England. I feel very lucky. The last letter was sent on 14th July and Wilf seemed to think it would be the last – have you had that impression from anyone? Wilf said he would send a cable when they get back from 'Phase I' at the end of the month. He did send one out by helicopter pilot to Dushanbe but I never had that.

I am being bombarded with letters & phone calls from people who have received those expedition stamp collection covers and who think their letters have been pinched by sabotaging Soviets! Are you having the same trouble? Hundreds of the beastly things have arrived here, much to the postman's horror. Am I to do anything with them?

Our various school terms are just ending and from 2nd August we shall be wandering about rather. Lady Noyce [her mother-in-law] will mostly be here so in an emergency will you please contact her & I will send you various addresses as I move about.

Something I forgot to mention is that they may come home on 2nd Sept. instead of 3rd. Apparently a drinking orgy is to be held when they get back to Moscow and that was what Wilf was dreading above everything. So if passages can be arranged, maybe the drinkers will stay for the orgy and non-drinkers will return home!

John Hunt:

Yet unwilling to believe and cheering each other with unlikely explanations of some mistake, we went carefully down to the level ground. Both parties now moved towards one another and I took a photo; the two Anatolis were, I now noticed, there as well.

There was little to say just then – the truth hadn't sunk in fully. It was suggested we might go at once to look for the bodies, but I decided that we must all return to our camp, for it was too late for safety and all were tired. A sad and silent party, with myself in front, roped with the Anatolis, descended through the seracs. Ralph and the others saw us from below and shouted greetings but we didn't reply. Shortly after, I broke the awful news to them in their turn. What to do? We debated this at length. At first we decided to bring the bodies to Camp 3, sending Derek and Ted in haste to call up Malcolm's group for more food, ladders and, not least, men. But I had doubts. Apart from the uncertainty and delay of being able to get in touch with Malcolm and his collecting the food and gear, we have only 24 hours' food left here and the nearest dump is at Camp 2.

I slept little, thinking specially of Wilf, of Rosemary and the two boys; of poor Mrs Smith who so wanted Robin to give up climbing. And the expedition? Whether it should go on, and what I ought to do personally? I told the others we would come to no hasty conclusions on these matters, but I could not switch them out of my mind.

6.00 a.m. on the 26th, and a clear cold morning. I asked Derek and Ted to stay in camp and prepare for our return; eight of us set off on our sad and difficult mission. In one hour we were back in the upper basin, moving to the foot of the great ice slope and the Bergschrund where we believed our friends to be. George had lost sensation in his feet and I did not feel Eugene capable of the difficult ice climbing ahead; so I left them below to collect the gear thrown down from the ridge by Derek two days before, and to be ready to help when we brought the bodies down. This left six of us to go up. We roped on two ropes: the Anatolis with Graeme, Ralph and I with Nikolai.

The climbing was difficult, including some feet of really steep ice, which we ascended on the two front crampon points. At last we reached a short ice wall below the big 'schrund which proved less of a problem than we had feared. We stepped onto the terrace, and there they lay. Wilf and Robin lay closely side by side, almost as though they had laid down to sleep. Wilf, stretched on his back, had his anorak pulled up over his head, doubtless by the rope. Robin was curled up with his back to Wilf, lying across the latter's right arm; his head, badly injured, was in the snow. We searched them, but there was very little; I took only a lighter inscribed 'Karakorum 1960' from Wilf's trouser pocket – I already had his pipe and diary from Derek.

Graeme Nicol:

They were loosely entangled in the rope as though one or both had rolled it up during the fall, and had either been mutually trying to ward off blows, or one had landed spreadeagled and the other on top of him. Whatever the mechanism, they essentially appeared to be lying in or near each other's arms. I cannot now remember details such as whether their crampons were on, but they both had extensive injuries.

Ralph Jones:

It happened to be my lead which took us to the shelf where Wilf and Robin lay. As suspected, it was too dangerous to remove them and I said this to John with a gesture towards a crevasse. It was a harrowing experience for us all, more so for John than for any of us, I think. Apart from the loss of two of his men, one of them a good friend and the other so young, without a doubt it cut across his ethos to leave fatalities on the mountain. But we had no realistic option.

John Hunt:

We quickly decided not to bring them down; it would have been necessary, in that event, to throw them down the ice slope. What would be the point of prolonging the agony and sorrow over several days, in order to bury our friends in the soil at Camp 3? Why not, as at sea, bury them where they lay, in the glacier? There was a deep crevasse at the lip of the terrace and we put them in there; it was a painful little act, which was too much for my composure as I helped with Wilf.

Anatoli Ovchinnikov:

Sir John said prayers and we saluted with three volleys from three signal pistols. We set off for Base Camp, sad and in mourning.

43

SO DOWN AGAIN

John Hunt:

So down again, mercifully preoccupied with the technical problems of descending the steep ice, fixing a piton belay, etc, etc. Lower down, as Ralph and I unroped and went ahead, a big stone – forerunner of many others – came humming and whining off the cliffs, and passed neatly between us. It was a near-miss and a timely warning that we had completed our task only just in time.

The rest of the day was spent resting at the camp, preparing for an early start next morning. It was time for reflection and decision about the future.

Should the expedition continue or not? What should I do personally? These questions went round and round in my head, till at last I was clear about them.

I must personally go back; to see Rosemary and Mrs Smith; to ensure that the events were properly told and understood; to help clear up many problems resulting from the tragedy. The expedition must go on, if there are enough of us willing to stay on; I am counting on Malcolm's group as the nucleus, as they have not been directly involved.

Anatoli Ovchinnikov:

In our expeditions, if a similar tragedy happens, then the expedition stops immediately. Everybody returns to Moscow and there the mountaineering community begins to analyse what has happened and of course find the reasons and come to suitable organisational conclusions. So it is usually the case with British expeditions. However, in my opinion Sir John took the correct decision, that is to go to Britain to inform the nearest and dearest of Wilf and Robin and to inform the leadership of the Sports Committee in Moscow, leaving in the mountains those who wished to continue the expedition. Anatoli Sevastianov and I fully shared the bitterness of loss which Sir John felt and supported his decision.

So Down Again

John Hunt:

27th July: Down the ice fall, starting very early while the snow crust still held. Down the glacier to our dump beneath Camp 4, where we breakfasted. Then still on down, all keeping together, to Camp 3; the Russians very considerately joined and stayed with us, probably so that I might break the news to Malcolm's group – they have been simply marvellous over all this sad business.

On arrival at about 5.00 p.m. we found a note from Malcolm explaining that they were over on the opposite moraine. Two of the group have reached the top of Pik Patriot by the west ridge.

So after 2? hours' rest, Graeme and I set off again, planning to spend the night with Malcolm's party. They were delighted to see us and all in good heart but they seemed by no means happy about the climb, which had been carried through in conditions of great objective danger. Joe and Mac, in particular, were not pleased with the attitude of Vladimir and Nicolai, who went to the top; they seemed only concerned about getting there personally, because they needed two more peaks to qualify as Master of Sport. Even Joe Brown, with his worldwide reputation for climbs requiring exceptional skill and daring, had found the mountain so dangerous that he felt it unjustifiable to continue beyond a certain point.

I talked of my decision and hope for the future. They were immediately in agreement and willing to carry on; in fact, they took this splendidly. So, with Graeme and (I hope) Ralph as well, this would make six to stay; the reasons for the remainder in deciding to go home are completely understood.

28th July: It rained in the night and was still dull this morning. Graeme and I returned across the glacier for breakfast with our party. We then set off for Camp 2, lifting huge loads which made balance very difficult on the steep hillsides. We fixed a rope for the descent of the steep rock gully and arranged all the gear for the second period, in a Russian tent at Camp 2. Long hours of descent down the glacier to Avodara, where we met Malcolm's group. Then on, in the evening, weary and footsore, to Base.

On arrival, what a meal awaited us, prepared by Vassili our hunter-chef. Later we sat round our fire to drink whisky and tea in the dark; Anatoli and I each said a few words about the events of the past fortnight; conversation then continued till about 11.00 p.m. At Anatoli's suggestion we stood for a few moments in silence, paying tribute to

Wilf and Robin. Tomorrow the important messages are to be sent, conveying the news and asking for a helicopter to take us out.

29th July: I sent a cable to the ambassador this morning, breaking the news of the accident and asking him to inform London. At the same time Anatoli cabled Moscow and Frunze, reporting events and asking for a helicopter. We now wait on events.

It has been a day spent cleaning up and resting; the weather has been very bad. My mind has been full of the news on its way to Joy [his wife], and through her to Rosemary [Noyce]; it will be almost a relief to be sure she knows. I went through Wilf's kit – a sad business; difficult to know what to take back.

The message in John Hunt's cable reached Sue Bradshaw via Moscow:

PERSONAL FOR AMBASSADOR FROM SIR JOHN HUNT.

DEEPLY REGRET INFORM YOU NOYCE AND SMITH KILLED DESCENDING PEAK GARMO 24TH. REQUEST YOU PASS INFORMATION QUICKEST BRADSHAW 2 OLD QUEEN STREET LONDON ADDING FOLLOWING. INFORM NEXT KIN. ASK LADY HUNT SEE ROSEMARY AND MRS CHARLESON SEE MRS SMITH. REASSURE ALL OTHER NEXT KIN ALL WELL INCLUDING MRS SLESSER GLASGOW WEST 2579. INFORM HERALD NEWSPAPER AFTER REPEAT AFTER NEXT KIN. TRYING ARRANGE RETURN TO REPORT PERSONALLY NEAR FUTURE. EXPEDITION CONTINUES. HUNT.

Sue Bradshaw:

I was visiting my parents in Lewes when the Foreign Office phoned on July 29th. It was a Sunday evening, I remember, and I was getting ready for bed. All I can say about that moment was the appalling sense of shock at the waste of two such different but valuable lives.

John Hunt:

30th July: In reply to my cable I received a sympathetic message from the ambassador this morning, confirming that he had sent the message on to London. So the pain of waiting is passing to the pain of receiving. Indeed, Rosemary and Mrs Smith must already have the news. This is the worst moment, and I pray that I may not be kept waiting long before going to see them both.

It has been a brighter day of weather, with consequent effect on our spirits. I was told of a Spartak deputation wishing to see me, but I elected to go myself to their camp at 11.00 a.m. Abalakov received me in some state, surrounded by his cronies and, with three movie cameras trained on us at point-blank range, proceeded to criticise my decision to leave the expedition. I stated my reasons and received some approval from some of those present; but Abalakov was adamant in his viewpoint. He seemed to imply that the expedition would not be in safe hands and that those who mourned at home needed me less than those who were here to tackle the climb ahead etc, etc.; relatives of climbers were ready for accidents and accepted them when they happened etc, etc. I felt somewhat upset, but was gratified by the incensed reactions of my own party. Later, Anatoli came up to say that he and all our Russian group disagreed with Abalakov.

31st July: I was daydreaming of the need for sending a 'hastener' message to the Russian authorities and to our ambassador when, at 8.00 a.m., the well-known sound of a helicopter woke me up. Everyone leapt up, astonished by this fantastically quick arrival. The four of us who were to leave hastened to get ready and before 10.00 a.m. we were off, in two lifts, to a lower point down the valley at first, because of the weight.

The wheels had really been set in motion, for at Jirgital a special aircraft waited for us. We were given a meal and then sped on our way to Dushanbe, where we arrived at 3.30 p.m. Ever since that moment it seems that the ears of the world have been trained on us: Reuters, Associated Press, United Press, Tass, the *Herald*, the *Mail*, the embassy, Sue Bradshaw: then Reuters again, then the Herald, then the embassy, etc, etc. The phone continued incessantly until midnight. If ever my return needed justifying, this seems to provide the answer, in part.

It was a great comfort to have a cable read from the embassy, stating Rosemary's and Mrs Smith's express wishes that the bodies should be left in the glacier, where we found them.

1st August: The magic-carpet treatment has continued all day; the kindness of everyone has been wonderful and most moving.

We were away from Dushanbe at 8.40 a.m. and arrived in Moscow (5 hours behind Dushanbe) at 11.30, to be met by representatives of the Central Council, the Mountaineering Federation, our embassy and the press. A press conference, and then we were taken to the Leningradskaya Hotel, to change and have lunch with Soviet officials. I was dragged off to telephone the BBC for a recorded interview, then went to see the Ambassador, who handed me a cable from Lord Home [Secretary of State for Foreign Affairs]. BEA offered to hold their evening Comet flight for half an hour but we had time enough to prevent a delay and we got away at 7.00 p.m.

Ever since the accident, our Russian comrades had shown themselves as towers of strength and support to us, sensitive to our sorrow and sharing our sense of loss. I will never forget Anatoli Ovchinnikov's personal consideration for me during that sad climb up 800 ft of steep ice to find Wilf and Robin. Moreover, from the moment the news was sent back to Dushanbe and Moscow the Russian authorities gave us wonderful assistance at every stage of our journey home.

So here we are, near the end of our journey and our part in the expedition, passing over Heligoland in the Comet on a fine summer evening. There are more poignant moments ahead and many problems to be solved. But I feel that good will follow the tragedy of Wilf and Robin; it may help to make us, their friends, a little less selfish, a trifle less intolerant; more concerned for, and understanding of others than we were before. There may be no point in linking the loss of personal friends with the theme of wider friendship; but I know that Wilfrid and Robin supported this theme and were beginning to share the satisfaction of it.

Anatoli Ovchinnikov:

After Sir John, George Lowe, Derek Bull and Ted Wrangham went back to Britain, those remaining and we, the Soviets, climbed Pik Kommunisma by the Georgian Variation. The ascent was dedicated to our dead friends.

While we were climbing Kommunisma, mountaineers of the Sports Society Spartak, led by Vitali Abalakov, built a memorial of stones on a hillock at the tongue of the Garmo glacier. The summit of Garmo is visible from the memorial which mountaineers from multilingual Russia and from abroad visit. Carved in stone are the names Wilfrid Noyce and Robin Smith.

Pik Sodruzhstvo [Concord, the peak first climbed and named by John Hunt], and the memorial to Wilf and Robin, were, are, and will remain in the future, I hope, symbols of friendship between British mountaineers and those from former Soviet countries, particularly ourselves, the Russians.

EPILOGUE

It took six days for news of Robin's death to reach his mother. The president of the Scottish Mountaineering Club and his wife informed her on July 30th, 1962, as well as letting her know that events in the Pamirs would be reported on television. Consequently, Mrs Smith visited a neighbour's house that evening and saw pictures of her son on the news. Less than twenty-four hours had passed since receipt at Home Base of John Hunt's telegram. Marion, Robin's sister, was on Voluntary Service Overseas work in Mackenzie, British Guiana, as it then was. News of the accident came over the radio before her mother's cable arrived, though Marion did not hear it herself: 'I happened to be in Georgetown at the time, and someone came to break the devastating news to me.' She at once returned to Britain to be with her family.

The expedition coincided with Robin's brother's marriage in Paris on July 12th to his French fiancée, Claudie Paulicand. Claudie still has the note she and Charlie received in Paris from her new brother-in-law, posted in Dushanbe on July 6th:

> I dare not write in French. We are sporting in the merciless sun. Cool only when swimming. Tomorrow we fly to Base Camp, and all goes very well.
>
> I wish you all the best in your forthcoming ceremonies, & happiness together ever after.
> Robin.

Charlie and Claudie returned from honeymoon unaware of the accident. Claudie recalls sitting with Charlie at the rear of a Glasgow bus opposite a person reading a newspaper. Although the paper was folded over, and was for them upside down, they managed to discern headlines of a mountaineering tragedy. Their fellow passenger folded up the paper and alighted before they could glean any detail. Charlie and Claudie also got off. They bought their own.

Mrs Smith to the expedition secretary, Sue Bradshaw, on September 2nd, 1962:

> . . . I saw Sir John too soon after the shock and of course the aftermath of thinking has raised a lot of questions which should have answers before I can expect any peace of mind. All Robin's friends – experienced climbing friends here – are so astounded as to how it could have happened. George Ritchie, who was very often in our house with Robin, came last night. He says he is a personal friend of Wrangham and will bring him to see us soon.
>
> I suppose Sir John will have access to the film at present with the *Daily Herald* – two of these seem very fine photos. I have not yet had the print you said the BBC were preparing of Robin peeling potatoes. I hope they will not forget. This month's *Scottish Field*, I have been told today, has some sort of hymn of praise to Robin in it . . . Funny how bits & pieces of information blow in.
>
> I am taking on half-day teaching – Senior English in a tutoring school, starting work on the 18th Sept. I think Marion and I will manage to run the house between us. The Festival and its visitors are keeping us busy meanwhile, thank goodness.

Many did their best to comfort the family, Marion recalls: 'It was a truly terrible time. But we were helped over the ensuing weeks by the very many letters and visits we received from Robin's friends and fellow climbers.' Indeed Ovchinnikov and Sevastianov were to keep in touch annually from Moscow. On December 25th, 1962 Ovchinnikov looked back, in Russian custom, to the fading year's most striking events. 'I recall the days spent together in a tent with your son, my climbing friend Robin,' he wrote. 'With him I shared the difficulties and dangers of the ascent of the Garmo Pik. Together with him I shared the joy of our victory over the summit. And in these hours once again it is so painful to think that Robin is no longer with us. My friends, Soviet mountaineers, and myself share your inconsolable grief. It is difficult for me to find adequate words to express my thoughts and feelings on the occasion of your grave loss. Please, accept from all of us, friends of your son, a splendid climber and wonderful man, our most profound condolence.' Ovchinnikov wrote again the following summer:

> On 24th July it was exactly a year since you lost your son and we lost a comrade and friend. On this day we, the two Anatolis, who were

with your Robin at that time, wish to send you our best wishes for your health and happiness. The image of your son lives in our hearts and blithe Robin could not fail to be a good son and comrade. Therefore we understand how heavy is your loss. We want you to know that we shall never forget Robin.

He sent their warmest words of greeting, encouraging kindly – 'May you be brave, healthy and happy.' However, that in total was scarcely possible, Eugene Gippenreiter recalls, citing an incident at an informal lunch in post-Cold-War Moscow at the office of one of Robin's former classmates, Alasdair Forrest. The two Anatolis were also present. 'Let's have *a bowl of soup*,' Forrest proposed, words that immediately struck a chord with Gippenreiter: 'Robin's mother once wrote to us that she did not believe that he was dead and that one day he would enter their house, unshaven and hungry, and would ask – as usual – for . . . "a hot bath and *a bowl of soup*".'

Robin's cousins remain conscious of the dreadful impact Robin's death had within the family. Alan Reid, for example, now deeply regrets that he saw so little of Robin – 'Indeed I was unaware of the full extent of his climbing prowess until he went off to the Pamirs. I remember the terrific family pride channelled through the communication-arteries of our clan: as a cousin I was so proud. And then the stunning, terrible news.' Reid, a minister, who nonetheless respected Mrs Smith's and Robin's integrity in holding opposing views about religion, remembers in later years the change in his Aunt Mary's face. 'She had a grave, sweet, infinitely brave look of deep engagement with something that would not win its victory over her. That impressed me beyond words,' he felt. 'And Charlie – on his deathbed (in 1991) he talked to me a lot about Robin. I comforted him for his grief and for a feeling of guilt which, for some reason as the elder brother, he had unspokenly borne. For all of us Robin was *alive*. His vitality, while physically alive, had an extraordinary quality. I now realise that it is completely *untouchable by death*.'

Robin's other cousin, Peter Lothian, is still a little discomfited by his initial reaction to the news of the accident. As he was tidying up the garden, his mother came out of the house to announce of her nephew: 'Robin's gone!' Not connecting the words with death he replied: 'You mean he's defected?' His unintended black humour was

elicited by the political Cold War and by Robin's somewhat revolu-
tionary views as expressed in his school mock election speeches.

Lothian well recalls the entirely different way in which Robin's
death was regarded by his mother and her generation, compared with
himself and friends in his own age group: 'My mother's immediate
reaction was "What a wasted life!". Mine was that Robin had died the
way he would have chosen, having packed more into his tragically short
life, than in a comparatively dull existence to ripe old age. Interestingly
now, over thirty years later and being, I suppose, roughly the same age
as she was then, I find it hard not to agree with her view!'

The competing claims of men's interests versus family responsibilities propel themselves to the fore. Rosemary Noyce received the
news about her husband from John Hunt's wife, Joy. Left on her own
with two young sons, aged ten and eight, she kept in correspondence
with Sue Bradshaw:

> I am so sorry to have apparently 'gone off the air' for so long, but I
> have had to make a determined effort during the last couple of weeks
> to tackle the mountains of correspondence which have accumulated.
> We had 500 cards printed acknowledging people's letters and kindness
> but there are still many which one can only answer by letter.
>
> I do want to thank you Sue for being such a tower of strength during
> that first ghastly week – do you find, as I do that it seems even more
> appalling in retrospect than it did at the time? I just don't know how
> we all got through it, except that it proves beyond doubt that one is
> given special strength to cope on these dreadful occasions. One can only
> hope that none of us may be called on to endure such an ordeal again.
>
> Also I was so very grateful for your thoughtful and comforting letter,
> which helped a lot – really it did. It may well be that some good may
> come of Wilf's and Robin's deaths in the end, though it is hard to see
> how and what it may be. I do think, though, that it will have been a
> bitter blow to other mountaineers with dependents who trust them to
> come home safely.
>
> I am so sorry that your work for the expedition has been added to
> by letters from people who should have written to me and ought to
> have been more considerate than to bother John and you. It is strange
> how people react – most of them so wonderfully thoughtful and consid-
> erate, but a few have been so inept, eg the ones who write 'Wilf would
> have wanted to go like this' – such utter nonsense.

I really do feel I am coming out on the other side. Though I feel I may have many setbacks and I think that, with the rest of Wilf's family, the boys and I will be able to make a new life for ourselves. It is so lucky that in any case I was starting a new job in September and that will help a lot. The best thing for me is to be forward-looking, and to forget the immediate past as quickly as possible – there are so many *happy* memories to treasure.

Moving forward to the 1990s, John Inglis, aged thirty-one, became another climber at the sharp edge of this family-versus-risk sports tussle. John, whose wife appreciated his need to climb, died as this book was being compiled, but not before he had had a chance to read contributors' letters, press cuttings and old correspondence, much of it now part of the text. Fascinated by the 1950s climbing scene generally and by Robin Smith in particular, his article 'Smith's Routes – a Short History', published in the 2002 *SMC Journal*, has provided several quotes for this book. I discussed Mrs Noyce's letter with him and we concluded that climbers are unlikely ever to take too seriously imaginings of their not coming 'home safely'. However, it all went wrong for John Inglis on February 19th, 1994, whilst climbing Lochnagar's Parallel Buttress. Another good man gone, another widow; two more fatherless children, daughters aged four and two.

Both of John's parents and Wilfrid Noyce's mother were also alive when their sons died, and there have been passing references in the book to other fatalities, each undoubtedly with its own tragic aftermath. Some will ask themselves if the risks of climbing are worthwhile, begging the perennial question of why climbers do it. Robin disclosed at least part of his own feelings on that question in the letter to his grand-uncle in April 1958: 'I find a very deep and healthy force in the mountains.'

Knowing what they now do, however, there will be those who feel inclined to keep well away from mountains. Others, conversely, perhaps inspired by Robin's moving and simply stated sentiments, will set out in search of this 'deep and healthy force'.

Many knew how Robin felt about climbing and were delighted with his selection for the Pamirs expedition. 'As with his Alpine trips with Haston, I looked forward to the postcard reports with relish,' reminisces Jimmy Marshall, one of any number who could tell their own tale of those days' events. 'The first and only one had all the subtle humour expected. The next communication came via banner headlines on a billboard in Hanover Street. I couldn't believe it: killed falling down an ice slope. Never! I thought of the cat-like reactions on the winter Ben. This could not happen. But of course it did . . .and we had lost a very fine friend and a great mountaineer.' Not long after the accident, Marshall wrote Robin's obituary for the 1963 *SMC Journal*:

City-wise, he was to be found clad in short Italian jacket, with trousered legs arrogantly bowed and tapering dynamically into once-pointed mangled suedes. Banana-fingered hands, a quizzical smile and 'What line today?' and the odd scar or two, and you had Smith. Ready for anything, an extended 'jar'; a feast of jazz; a midnight slog over the Pentlands or the all-night study. Being truly nocturnal, most of his studies were done at night, and for that matter, a great percentage of his climbing.

On the hills he was a tramp, and lived on the lower plane of impoverished interdependence with his friends or associates; tented or dossing he lived on a heap of hopelessly abused good gear, in a confusion of tortured pitons, jam pieces, slings, melons and the inevitable absence of spoon and cup.

He entered the climbing scene as a quiet, inordinately shy boy, climbing with a school friend. He chose to ignore the reigning 'tigers', shocking them by his boldness in attempting some of the most difficult climbs in any conditions. Experienced climbers were known to scuttle off the mountain, fearful of exposing themselves to some rescue, but always the smiling-faced youth would return, often stumbling through the darkness, bubbling enthusiasm; whereupon the old men waited – 'it would happen sooner than later'.

It never did, he developed a masterly ability as a cragsman second to none. Mind you, he had his lucky days; there was his 90-ft 'jump' off Whiteghyll, just to tear his newly purchased Alpine breeches. Then the time he got a faceful of avalanche on 'peeking ower' the top of the rimaye on the Ryan-Lochmatter; when he hung, semi-conscious, from a hastily contrived belay through the buttonhole of his anorak pocket. He was a bit 'cut up' by this and his face filled out with character.

In maturity, he was one of the hardest climbers I have known. His strength and perseverance were shattering. On one climb, he hung on a problem, spending five or six hours to gain some 10 ft, whilst using a towel to swab the wet weep from the rock. On his winter ascent of

Gardyloo, he cut for six hours to overcome the near-vertical 150-ft prow of the ice-plated buttress. Or his ascent, almost under winter conditions, of the Fiescherwand, with several unpremeditated bivouacs, frostbite, darkness, enormous cornices, and hunger; in fact, a typical Smith outing. He delighted in impromptu, unexpected incidents which would carry the adventure far into the night, to impress one's memory indelibly with a sense of satisfying fulfilment and a wild belonging to the mountain world.

Within a year or two of his arrival, he pushed the message home to the resident degenerates and injected newcomers to the group with his virile approach. His was no doctrine of rules or codes, but simply an unbounded enthusiasm at being born into an age of climbing when the overhanging corners, bulging walls and seeping black crags remained untouched. Couple this with a never-ending effort to improve his technical ability and a climbing history of inordinate experience and the result was the power-packed, agreeable Smith.

But now Smith's gone, killed unbelievably on some Russian mountain. He is, and always shall be, greatly missed by his friends and can certainly never be forgotten by the climbing world.

His long list of first ascents, both summer and winter, encompass some of the finest climbs ever to be made in this country. Abroad, his seasons, ill-planned and shambolic, naturally accounted for most of the great routes in both the Dolomites and Western Alps.

Undoubtedly the greatest climber of our generation to join the club, he was possibly the most outstanding mountaineer throughout the long and varied history of the SMC. It is hard to avoid the pitfall of remorse and endless eulogies; but he himself would reject these, and we are best to remember him by his wild whoops, the tuneless ballads wailing from some fearful dank wall, the hair-raising climbs far into the night and his wanderings about the moonlit snows of the Highland summits.

We have gained immeasurably from his living among us. He has left us a legacy of great climbs and fine climbers eager to express and extend his climbing ideals.

ACKNOWLEDGEMENTS

I offer sincere thanks to all contributors without whom a book along these lines would not have been possible: Davie Agnew, Kenny Allan, Howard Andrew, Sandy Bannerman, Martin Boysen, Sue Temple-Richards (née Bradshaw), Les Brown, Val Brown, Vic Burton, Marion Caldwell (Robin's sister), John Cheesmond (helped by Keith Bancroft), Willie Clark, Jim Curran, Geoff Dutton, Andrew Fraser, Jimmy Gardner, Eugene Gippenreiter, Goofy, Dennis Gray, Gordon Greig, June Hamilton, Archie Hendry, Janet Holt, David Hughes, Lord Hunt of Llanfair Waterdine (John Hunt), John Inglis, Ralph Jones, Trevor Jones, Ben Lyon, Jean Thomson (now Lawrence), Mona Tennent (now Lewis), Peter Lothian, Elizabeth 'Bee' MacNeill, Jimmy Marshall, Alan Mathieson, WH (Bill) Murray, Graeme Nicol, Rosemary Noyce (now Ballard), Geoff Oliver, Anatoli Ovchinnikov, Steve Read, Georgio Redaelli, Alan Reid, Sheila Samuelson (now Larsen), Donald Scott, Anatoli Sevastianov, Robin Shaw, Joe 'Morty' Smith, Lord Steel of Aikwood (David Steel), Willie Stewart, Brian Thompson, Brian Wakefield, Andrew Wightman and Ted Wrangham.

Sadly some contributors died during the course of the book's compilation: Elizabeth 'Bee' Macneill (d. 1993); John Inglis, killed in a fall on Parallel Buttress, Lochnagar (1994); Willie Stewart (1995); WH (Bill) Murray (1996); Trevor Jones (1996); Ralph Jones (1997); John Hunt (1998); Sue Temple-Richards (2001); Willie Clark (2002); Kenny Allan (2003) and Andrew Wightman (2002). Of all those deaths that of the thirty-one-year-old John Inglis is perhaps the most poignant. Married with two daughters, he had an intense interest in Robin Smith and for nearly two years we met regularly. Several quotes from John's informative commentary, 'Smith's Routes – a Short History', are included in the book. His piece was passed to the Scottish Mountaineering Club and later published in its journal. I remember him particularly warmly, as I do Lloyd Caldwell (Robin's brother-in-law), who died in 2000, and Kenny Allan, a life-long friend.

Acknowledgements

My appreciation and sympathy go to to the relatives of these people. These sentiments apply too in respect of climbers whose lives were lost before I started work on the book and whose material is quoted: Gunn Clark (1970), Jim Clarkson (1968), Dougal Haston (1977), Donald Mill, Wilfrid Noyce (1962), Tom Patey (1970) and Norman Tennent (1992).

Mountaineering clubs have been most helpful – the Alpine Club, the Creagh Dhu Mountaineering Club, the Fell and Rock Climbing Club and the Scottish Mountaineering Club. The National Library of Scotland kindly allowed me access to the Thomas Graham Brown material whilst the *Scotsman* (and Tom Weir, the writer and climber, who also helped by supplying photographs) have also been most amenable. I thank others whose correspondence or articles have been quoted: Donald Bennet, Sir Chris Bonington, Robin Campbell, John Porteous, Malcolm Slesser, Iain Smart.

I am particularly indebted to my 'editors' for criticisms and suggestions since the earliest drafts: Robin's sister and brother-in-law, Marion and Lloyd Caldwell, Gordon Greig, Robin's former Logic lecturer, and Jimmy Marshall. Jimmy's knowledge of mountaineering and mountaineers, and of Robin and his contemporaries, has been of special value. In addition Jimmy has allowed me to select from his many vivid and appealing photographs to help illustrate the book and its cover. Howard Andrew, Jill McClure, Jamie Thin and Andrew Wightman chipped in spiritedly. Brian Wakefield then worked painstakingly with me on three drafts. His input was truly enormous. Finally, Robin's niece Laura Doulton (Marion and Lloyd's daughter) read the draft through fresh eyes: a major help. My editor at Canongate, Helen Bleck, was immensely constructive and helpful, not just with matters of text but with the wider issue of what goes into the development of a book. I hope that one way or another the book will be seen as a 'good read'. If not after all that help, the fault rests with myself, perhaps for having gone my own way here and there.

Elizabeth White, Head of Russian at George Watson's College, Edinburgh, bore the brunt of translation work (twenty-five pages from one Russian alone!) and I thank her greatly. Olga Thujolay and Carol Decker are also thanked for translations, from Russian and Italian respectively. Olga too was of great help in Moscow where the temporary residence of another of Robin's former classmates – Alasdair Forrest – was fortuitous and invaluable in enabling me to make contact with the Russians who climbed with Robin in the Pamirs.

I would like to thank others too, for a variety of reasons: Joe Brown, Ken Crocket, Peter Hodgkiss, Hamish MacInnes, Charlie Orr, Tom Pentice, Kenny Spence, Ken Wilson.

Special thanks are due to Robin's sister, Marion, and sister-in-law, Claudie, for entrusting me with the family's memorabilia box. And I am grateful to the late Lord Hunt of Llanfair Waterdine for sending me a carbon copy of his Pamirs expedition diary and for permission to quote from expedition files held in London at the Royal Geographical Society, whom I also thank. It is at the late Lord Hunt's own suggestion that he is referred to as 'John Hunt' in the book.

NOTES

Chapter 2 – First Scrambles, First Hopes

1. Written retrospectively, Robin's 'diary' is not a diary as such. Twenty-four pages of rough jottings headed 'Climbing Memoirs' cover his climbing activities until September 1956, a few weeks before he enrolled at Edinburgh University.

2. Nails used in traditional climbing boots were: tooth-edged 'tricounis' around the edges of soles, 'clinkers' on heels, and 'studs' in the middle of soles.

3. Modern grades of climbs in the order in which they appear. See Appendix I and Chapter 12, 'Climbing – Then, Now, Why', for more information on the grading of climbs.

   Lagangarbh Chimney [Diff], Pyramid [Diff], Crack Climb [Diff], Hangman's [Hard Severe], Shackle [Mild Severe then, now Severe], Agag's Groove [VDiff], Tower Ridge by Douglas Direct [VDiff], Archer Ridge [VDiff], Rowan Tree Wall [VDiff], Church Door Buttress [VDiff], Deep Cut Chimney [VDiff], Slacks [Severe, on the Cobbler's South Peak], Eastern Buttress [VDiff], Cioch Direct [Severe], Cioch West [VDiff], White Slab [VDiff or Severe by the direct start].

Chapter 3 – Upping the Grade

1. The background to the Creagh Dhu Mountaineering Club has been gleaned from Jeff Connor's book, *Creagh Dhu Climber: The Life and Times of John Cunningham* (Ernest Press, 1999).

2. Six years after being helped up Gardyloo Gully Robin listed this climb on his Pamirs Expedition 'Previous Mountaineering Experience' form, noting that their leader was Andrew (Corky) MacCorquodale. A message of respect and thanks?

3. Modern grades of rock climbs in the order in which they appear

   Red Slab [VS], Satan's Slit [now VS], January Jigsaw [Severe], Shackle [Mild Severe, now Severe], Recess Route [VDiff], Nimlin's Direct [VDiff], Crowberry Direct [Severe], Agag's Groove [VDiff], Red Slab [VS], Crowberry Direct [Severe], Fracture [Mild Severe then, now Severe], Raven's Gully [VS], January Jigsaw [Severe], Satan's Slit [VS 4c], Lagangarbh Chimney [Diff], Lagangarbh Buttress East Face [Severe], Staircase Buttress [VDiff], Route 1 [VDiff], Bottleneck [Hard Severe], Slanting Groove [VDiff], Hangman's [Hard Severe], Harrow Wall [Severe], Slabs West [Severe], Old North [VDiff], Rib and Slab [Severe], New West [Diff, now VDiff], Punster's [Hard Severe], Chimney Arete [VS], Cat Crawl [Severe], Ardgartan Wall [various routes, all Severe or harder], Ardgartan Arete [no hard climbs].

4. Information has been gleaned from Donald Mill's diary.

Chapter 4 – Cracks of Doom

1. The others on Arran with Robin and myself were Stewart Robb and Alasdair Forrest.

2. Modern grades of rock climbs in this chapter: Agag's [VDiff], Shackle [then Mild Severe, now Severe], Cioch Direct [Severe], Inaccessible Pinnacle [Diff], Crack of Doom [Severe].

Chapter 5 – Nowt Doing

1. Robin's report of experiences on the Crack is a reprint of an article first published in the 1956–57 *Edinburgh University Mountaineering Club Journal* under the title 'Twenty Four Hours'. Upon receipt of his copy the club's Vice President Graham Brown sent this note to Robin:

   The journal is very good and I think your bit is excellent. I have read yours three times, each time with more pleasure than the last, and it is the very best story of a rock-climb which I have ever read. I hope that you are going to write many such articles in future, and I want to give you a piece of advice: You have got a style, or a knack, or whatever it is, which *exactly* suits the subject. It is a natural one, so for goodness sake *don't* try to 'improve' it. In most climbing stories you can't see the climb for the ancient jokes and/or the soulful uplift – you have got it just right. The ideal is to make the reader feel he is sharing the climb, or is in your own shoes. Keep it up!

2. Ted Wise and Ian Douglas were later killed in separate mountaineering accidents.

Chapter 6 – Studious Climbers

1. Logic and Metaphysics and both Ancient and Moral Philosophy formed Robin's philosophy programme. Psychology was his Science option, while his remaining three subjects – seven areas of study in all were then required for any Arts degree – were British History, English Literature and French.

2. Modern grades of rock climbs in this chapter: Blockhead [E1 5b], Labyrinth Direct [Severe], Serpentine [Moderate], Greig's Ledge [Diff], Observatory Ridge [Moderate], Tower Ridge [VDiff], Revelation [VS], Chasm Left Edge [VS 4c], Ladders [VS 4c], Cunieform Buttress [Winter IV], Cemetery Gates [E2 5b], Cenotaph Corner [E1 5c].

3. Janet Holt's experiences on the Labyrinth are extracted from her article, 'A Gregarious Ascent', published in the 1957–58 *EUMC Journal*. Reprinted with thanks to Janet and the *EUMC Journal*.

4. A few lines on Graham Brown have been taken from an obituary for the 1966 *SMC Journal*. (With thanks to its author, Robin Campbell.)

5. Quotes from Dougal Haston (throughout) are generally from his 1972 book *In High Places*. This chapter, however, includes several excerpts from a boyhood diary kindly provided by his brother Alex.

Chapter 7 – Alpine and Currie Seasoning

1. The M is the full name of a peak close to Chamonix, so called because it resembles that letter's shape when viewed from the town.

2. Jim Clarkson died in March 1968 when he was blown off Càrn Mòr Dearg. He was married with a young son.

Chapter 8 – Scholarly Reflections

1. After a spell teaching at the University of St Andrews, Greig in 1964 forsook Scotland for the Rockies, going on to become an Emeritus Professor at Calgary. Logic in turn was put to one side in 1985 when he became a full-time international chess player at Master level.

Chapter 9 – Robin as Student

1. Gordon Greig has provided some explanatory notes:

Hume's main philosophical thrust was that all sound belief was grounded in sense experience and justified on the basis of extrapolation from such experience. That extrapolation had its basis in the sheerly natural functioning of the mind through a host of mechanisms. These beliefs, rationally ordered, constituted our knowable world and, in sophisticated, quantified form yielded Science. All truths were truths of fact (Science as expanded common sense), or truths of reason which *au fond* were merely the tautologies of Logic and Mathematics. Beliefs allegedly founded on 'other' truths were but Superstition. Reason had no creative role or privileged objects of knowledge; it could only sort and shuffle what came from sense experience.

The Absolute Idealists disagreed with Hume's views on nearly every point. They endorsed or indulged in speculation on quasi-factual questions divorced from observation or experiment; they maintained that Mind and Spiritual Values were fundamental, neither emerging from, nor reducible to, material objects, events and processes. The finite world of sense-experience was inherently incoherent and contradictory. Such contradictions could be resolved only by transcending finitude. Reason, by transforming our conventional categories of thought could achieve this goal, positing in the process a single harmonious whole on a different plane of existence culminating in the *Absolute Idea*.

Chapter 10 – Spirit of Adventure

1. Robin's compilation of 'Climbs Round About Edinburgh' in the 1957–58 *EUMC Journal* had this to say of Castle Rock:

   The climbing here is pretty well restricted to one day in the year. Perched around the cliff are a few of the vilest of bivouac sites for camping out the night before, and when Charities' Day comes round the hordes of the peasants gather in Princes Street and the Gardens to gape at great strings of colourful noise beetling about on the annual storming of the Castle Rock. By the time we get up most of the colour has gone all black, for the whole place is sozzled in Waverley smoke, but things begin to look up again when they give us the free beer.

   The route more or less follows the broken line of rocks to the right of the overhanging mass facing Princes Street, and gives a lot of very pleasant V. Diff climbing to the foot of the Castle Wall. This last barrier is climbed in a corner, which gives quite a hard pitch of severe and delicate bridging.

   That natural line up Castle Rock – Closet Climb (S) – was first climbed in May 1958 by Robin and Andrew Fraser. 'Climbs Round About Edinburgh' also lists routes on Blackford Hill in Edinburgh's southern suburbs, on Caerketton (the Pentlands' hill closest to the city) and in Holyrood Park, the site of Salisbury Crags and other outcrops such as Samson's Ribs. Robin forged new routes on all these crags as well as on Traprain Law near Haddington, 20 miles to the east of the city.

2. Mention of 'Charities' Day' reminds Kenny Allan that it was not just the people of Edinburgh who fell prey to the students' fund raising:

   Mostly we all dressed up and waved collecting cans in front of hapless passers-by although some did take part in more risky ventures. Saturday was the highlight when Princes Street was closed for a procession, but funds were also raised in the days leading up to that by way of visits to sleepy little Border or Fife towns.

   On one such outing to Galashiels Robin disappeared and was still missing at departure time. The driver eventually decided to head home since no one knew if he was still there, or if he had hitched back earlier without telling anyone, or had even set off for the Lake District. Then as the bus started to leave, up pulled a police car from which Robin was escorted. He climbed on accompanied by advice from a Sergeant along the lines that he needn't bother coming back. He was being run out of town not just for having stuck a flag atop an apparently unreachable chimney on a public building but also, this easily accomplished, for a more ambitious encore on a church spire!

3.   Haston was twenty months younger than Robin.

4.   Boggle, climbed in October 1961, is graded E1 5b.

Chapter 11 – Yo-Yo

1.   For a while Robin was known as 'The Man with the Golden Trowel', a corny joke based on Eddie Calvert, a musician often in the pop charts as 'The Man with the Golden Trumpet'.

2.   Yo-Yo is now graded E1 5b.

Chapter 12 – Climbing Then, Now, Why

1.   Quotes from John Inglis come from his article 'Smith's Routes – A Short History', published posthumously in the 2002 *SMC Journal* on the initiative of Jimmy Cruickshank, who worked closely with John on the 'Robin Smith' theme.

Chapter 13 – Rash Enough to Break a Leg

1.   Andrew Fraser's account of 'Shibboleth' was published in the 1958–59 *EUMC Journal* and reprinted in Hamish MacInnes' book *The Price of Adventure* (1987). The introduction written by Fraser for that book has been used in abridged form in the introduction and here, supplemented by a few words from the start of his article.

2.   Bertrand Russell, a philosopher admired by Robin, used the words 'shibboleth' and 'taboo' as near synonyms in certain contexts – Gordon Greig explains, 'both words are equivalent to a state or condition under which something is regarded as inviolable, sacrosanct, jealously guarded as its own by some particular group.' The dictionary definition is 'a word or custom or principle regarded as

testing a person's nationality or social class or orthodoxy, the criterion or password of a group'.

3. Robin's piece was extracted from 'Slow Times on Slime Wall', a few notes in the 1959 *SMC Journal*.

4. Martin Boysen's ascent of Shibboleth was with Mike Yates in May 1967. His account of that ascent appeared in Ken Wilson's book, *Hard Rock* (1974).

5. Shibboleth is now graded E2 5c.

Chapter 14 – A Nightingale Ascending

1. Trevor Jones relished with amusement the thought that Robin '. . . hated all Englishmen'. The well documented anti-English reputation which Robin attracted after appointment to the SMC committee was largely because it was he who thwarted Englishman Ian Clough's membership application. However, it turns out that Robin was implementing the wishes of the Edinburgh group he represented, all of whom objected to Clough's intensive use of artificial aids. As it happened, most of Robin's Alpine climbing was done with Englishmen, and he corresponded with several, with much Scotland v. England banter. Robin was undeniably proud of Scotland's mountains and noted in letters home that he held them in higher esteem than even those of Norway and the Alps.

2. Robin's two big climbs that 1958 Alpine season had this said of them in the *SMC Journal*, presumably at the initiative of Robin himself: 'The Blaitière climb was much harder technically; but the Dru was more magnificent and serious, spoiled only by a vast excess of pitons. The party used none of their own.'

Chapter 15 – Near Canterbury Tales

1. Edward's Effort is now graded 6a, Niblick 5b, Birchden Wall 5c, and Unclimbed Wall 5b.

Chapter 16 – Walkering in the Alps

1. The obituary of Nea Morin (1905–86) appeared in the 1986 *Alpine Journal* – 'a brilliant climber and a rare person'. This chapter includes a few points of detail from that source.

2. Gunn Clark's piece was first published in the 1960 *Fell and Rock Journal* under the title 'The North Face of the Grandes Jorasses'. He died in 1970 in an avalanche in Glencoe.

3. Robin also wrote an article about the ascent – 'Walkering in the Alps', first published in the 1959–60 *EUMC Journal*. It is reprinted in Appendix III.

4. In her book, *A Woman's Reach* (Nea Morin, published by Eyre & Spottiswoode, 1968).

Chapter 17 – Dolomitic Dosses

1. Robin left Courmayeur for Chamonix with hopes of achieving a 'first ascent of the distant pillar in sunshine' en route. The weather was good but that did not last and ideas of tackling the Central Pillar of Freney had to be abandoned. Its first ascent was accomplished two years later by the predominantly British party of Bonington, Whillans, Clough and Duglosz. Not long before that a continental team was caught in a storm and four lives were lost.

2. Haston claimed that his money had been stolen, later adding in his book *In High Places* that Robin 'barely seemed to believe this'. Some of his companions believe that Haston might have taken his decision to return directly home on the assumption that the weather around Grindelwald and the Eiger would be as foul as at Chamonix. On the other hand, it was his first Alpine season and he was recovering after a tough time on the Marmolada. In an article published in the *Scotsman* weekend magazine in February 1967, Haston, in the context of energies jointly directed by himself and Robin towards the Eiger and the Matterhorn, said that their over-confidence was almost foolhardy: 'We had this primitive urge for big routes, but we just didn't understand big mountains . . .' Whether or not Robin did understand 'big mountains', it is

338

nonetheless a fact that in 1959, blessed with good weather, aided by foresight, graced with youthful optimism and determination but without acclimatisation or decent boots, he had comfortably made the first British ascent of the Walker Spur, leaving in the Western Alps only the Eiger as a route of greater prestige and difficulty. He was in good form, and so was the weather. It is not hard to imagine what was running through his mind.

3. Robin recounted in the *SMC Journal* that 'after a series of misadventures, I found myself at the Rifugio Vassoler. I climbed the Torre Venezia twice – by the Via Cassin, with Giorgio Redaelli from Como, and solo by the Via Tissi.' After reference to his diary, however, Giorgio Redaelli reckons that it was the Via Ratti they climbed together.

Chapter 18 – The Bat and the Wicked

1. Dick Holt shared the first ascent of the Grade V Orion Face with Robin in January 1959.

2. The renowned mountaineer and writer WH (Bill) Murray wrote to Robin shortly after 'The Bat and the Wicked' was published:

> It would begin to seem that I am destined to spend my life sending you short notes of congratulation about one thing or another – even though I have controlled myself on several occasions and not sent them when I wanted to.
>
> This time it's your SMCJ articles. As a literary gent, I am professionally impressed. Given a background of orthodox reading, as you are bound to have from Edin. University, it's very hard to hit off that beatnik vein in your Bat and make it sound natural, wholly free of affectation – unless one has real talent plus an ear. Anyhow, you have done it with complete success on top of which the style is peculiarly suited to rock-work – it makes everything graphic.
>
> I don't know if your talent (literary) is natural, or a product of hard work. I reckon from all the reports about you that it must be natural. If so, please don't let is perish from non-use.
>
> Your Bat blew thro' the pages of the SMCJ like a wind off a high mountain. It came to me like a dose of oxygen when I was on the point of collapse – recently I had been unable to read the SMCJ right through.

Chapter 19 – Old Man James and I

1. The modern grades of climbs referred to by John Inglis are:

   The Great Chimney (IV5), Minus Three Gully (IV5), Smith's Route on Gardyloo Buttress (V5), Observatory Buttress (Ordinary Route) (V4), Point Five Gully (V), Pigott's Route on the Comb (V6), Orion Direct (V5).

2. WH Murray's words that 'history is made...' came from an article, 'The History of Scottish Mountaineering', written for the *SMC Journal* in 1964 when he was the SMC's president. In the same piece he looked back to the 1930s amused that when Mackenzie, Dunn, MacAlpine and himself took on new ice climbs like *Garrick's Shelf* they were 'damned in official letters from the JMCS for bringing Scottish climbing into disrepute – that is, by trying climbs that were not justifiable'. Murray went on to emphasise the impact made by Jimmy Marshall when he 'rose out of Auld Reekie' onto the national stage in the early 1950s, adding that:

   . . . from 1955 onwards, the Edinburgh school had been emerging strongly as a dominant force in Scottish climbing. Their most important product was Robin Smith . . . Among the great winter climbs done by this group were the *Orion Face*, and the Tower Face of the *Comb*, both by Smith and Holt; *Minus 2 Gully* by Marshall, Stenhouse and Haston; and then, in one tremendous burst in the winter of 1960, Robin Smith and Marshall did *Gardyloo Buttress*, *The Comb*, *Orion Direct* and, finally, the second ascent of *Point 5 Gully*. When I wrote *Mountaineering in Scotland* in the innocent days of 1944, I had said: 'The ascent of this gully will be the most brilliant feat in the history of Scottish mountaineering.' The second ascent by Marshall and Smith in seven hours was a most astonishing demonstration of technique and pace.

3. Jimmy Marshall and Robin stayed at the CIC Hut where the log book was written up in through-lead style – by Marshall on the 6th, 9th, 11th (in part) and 12th; by Smith on the 7th, 8th, 10th, 11th (in part) and 13th.

4. Shortly after the 'domino' incident an SMC member contacted his legal counterpart in Fort William to ensure no misunderstanding

of the defendants' cases. There was no need for a trial after all. Robin's (and Jimmy Marshall's) reputation remains unblemished.

Chapter 20 – Jimmy Marshall Looks Back

1. Only 'bona fide' travellers – those who had travelled at least three miles from home – were then entitled to consume alcohol in a pub or hotel on the Scottish Sabbath.

Chapter 21 – The Mostest Fantabulous

1. This article, 'The Orion Face', by Jimmy Marshall, was first published in the 1961 *SMC Journal*. The route itself is called Orion Direct.

Chapter 22 – Nightshift in Zero

1. Dougal Haston's contribution was first published as 'Nightshift in Zero' in the 1960–61 *EUMC Journal*. Its first few lines are now part of the chapter's introduction. The remainder of the piece appears in slightly edited form. The journal was scheduled for publication in June 1961, although its editor – Robin himself – had to concede that 'we emerge with dark and furtive significance, 6 months late, on the longest night of the year. At long last Graham Brown has taken up his quill and set us down a historic document of that heroic age when a climb was ended on the day it was begun . . . But the rest is but a sorry tale of the literally and literarily benighted and blundering nineteen sixties. Sheila Samuelson's "Evolution" lends these pages their only feminine touch and it goes, of course, hand in hand with "Nightshift in Zero" to show that Mountaineering, for all its rough and tumble, has its moments of pastoral charm and metaphysical vision.'

Robin wrote two articles of his own, 'chronic chronicles of recent nights errant in the Oberland and Dolomites' ('Goofy's Last Climb' and 'Snakes and Ladders' – see Chapters 27 and 31), whilst the magazine's subtitle 'Nocturnal' reflected the growing trend to complete climbs after hours of daylight. His formal assessment of the year's activities was that 'the season was well met and the meets well seasoned, with lots of wet and lots of eats and just a little sweat. Some people said it was sweet and others said it was swell, and others, well. Scattered throughout the year there were several miss-haps, a lot of near misses and a lot of near Mrs. But nothing final.'

Chapter 23 – A Man Amongst Men

1. Talks to mountaineering clubs were supplementing Robin's income marginally after approaches like this from the Cambridge University Mountaineering Club: 'Having just read your two fabulous articles in the *SMCJ* ['The Bat and the Wicked'] and 'Mountaineering' ['The Old Man and the Mountain'], the club is most keen to entice you down south to give a lecture on what ever you would like . . .' And the Western District branch of the SMC wrote to Robin that 'having had our appetites whetted by your excellent article in the Journal, we are looking forward to a stimulating evening'. An invitation to speak in Dundee was also found, but it is unknown if these or any other requests were fulfilled.

2. The last sentence of Dougal Haston's quote from *In High Places* (1972) at the end of the chapter – 'This was the way he played the game' – has been repositioned slightly without any change of meaning.

Chapter 24 – An Odium Meeter Hikes to Kintail

1. Written in the *EUMC Journal* (1957–58) by JG Adamson, Bothy Secretary.

Chapter 25 – I Know a Wee Line Somewhere

1. Modern grades of climbs in this chapter are: Stook [VS 4c], Carnivore [E2 5c], The Big Top [E1 5a].

Chapter 26 – Rebel without a Cause?

1. Gordon Greig is presenting explanatory information, not excuses, on the subject of 'sodality'.

2. Smith may have influenced Haston to study Philosophy, but it was little more than an escape for Haston. He was originally set to go to Jordanhill College to train as a PE teacher, but a shoulder damaged in a motorbike accident soon after leaving school forced him to abandon that ambition. Desperately disappointed, he took a temporary job in an insurance office where, for him, the work was futile, soul-destroying drudgery. He started at Edinburgh University as a Philosophy student in around 1959, by which time he had known Robin for two years, but lost interest in his studies.

Chapter 27 – Tales of the Fiescherwand

1. Robin's account of the ascent of the North Spur of the Fiescherwand was first published in the 1960–61 *EUMC Journal* under the title 'Goofy's Last Climb'. Robin told Goofy that the Fiescherwand struck him rather like three of Nevis's Observatory Ridges piled one on top of the other, adding that he would not have minded soloing it. The climb was in fact tackled as if it was on Scotland's Ben. They carried neither route description nor map and for nutrition had only a handful of chocolate and some sugar lumps. After the adventure, Geoff Oliver recalls that Robin 'showed signs of having been in a battle but was thirsty for more', although Andrew Wightman's version of events is less laconic:

    We were waiting in the hut and when they were two days late we decided we'd better look for them. They were on their way down when we found them, absolutely exhausted and with no food. Even Goofy, who is the most stoical person I have ever known, was showing suffering. His feet were raw from ill-fitting boots. We later learned that two Dutchmen had been killed on the mountain at this time.

Chapter 28 – Fiescherwand: The Truth

1. The article that forms most of this chapter is an abridged version of one that appeared in the *EUMC Journal* in 2002.

2. The seven characters introduced by Goofy at the beginning of the piece are, in order of appearance: Dougal Haston, Jimmy Marshall,

Graham Brown, Ronnie Marshall, Eley Moriarty, Graham Tiso, Robin Smith.

Chapter 31 – Snakes and Ladders on the Cima Ovest de Lavaredo

1. Most of Robin's contribution to this chapter comes from an article 'Snakes and Ladders', first published in the 1960–61 *EUMC Journal*. The final quote is from a letter he wrote home.

Chapter 32 – Threading the Needle

1. The Aberdonians' comments appeared in the SMC's *Cairngorms Guide*.

2. The Needle's modern grade is E1 5a.

Chapter 33 – Wilfrid Noyce

1. Extracted from John Hunt's tribute to Wilfrid Noyce, jointly written with David Cox for the 1992 *Alpine Club Journal*.

2. John Hunt's words about Wilfrid Noyce were compiled with his approval and are taken in the main from the December 1962 issue of the *Geographical Journal*.

Chapter 34 – Russians on Our Hills

1. Robin's article, 'A Week in the Hills', was first published in the 1961 *SMC Journal*. Of those at whom Robin poked fun, Malcolm Slesser, Kenny Bryan, Ralph Jones and John Hunt (as leader) were to become companions in the Pamirs along with the Russians Anatoli Ovchinnikov and Eugene Gippenreiter, who were also in Scotland that week. Robin also referred to George Ritchie, and his propensity to hear noises from his car, Tom Weir (Tommie), who became an SMC president, and Alpine Club member Alan Blackshaw, who climbed in the Caucasus in 1958 with John Hunt and whose film of that expedition also attracted remarks.

2. Sir Fitzroy Maclean, a former British Ambassador in Moscow.

Chapter 35 – Invitations

1. Much of the contemporary correspondence in chapters 35–38 is taken from expedition files at the Royal Geographical Society, London.

Chapter 37 – Wilf's Hesitation

1. This was published in *The Times* (date unknown). It appears in abridged form here.

Chapter 39 – Preparations

1. All quotes by Joe Brown are taken from his book *The Hard Years* (1967).

2. Dennis Gray went on to become the first Secretary of the British Mountaineering Council (BMC) between 1974 and 1989.

3. Robin's most notable new climb between December 1961 and May 1962 was the April ascent of Girdle Traverse, an E2 5b route on Aonach Dubh with Robin Campbell, Dougal Haston and Neil Macniven.

Chapter 40 – Lowland USSR

1. Quotes throughout this chapter from John Hunt are largely from a typed version of his expedition diary and, to a small extent, from his 1978 book *Life is Meeting*.

2. Malcolm Slesser's quotes come from his book *Red Peak* (1964), his personal account of the expedition.

Chapter 41 – In the Mountains

1. The party's gear was initially dropped at an altitude of 9500 ft, leaving the climbers with a hike of three to four hours to the expected site 2000 ft higher. Thus developed the idea of helicopter drops at Camps 2 and 3. As the loaded helicopters were not able to hover let alone land at that altitude, however, drops had to be made at speed. There were many breakages, particularly to soft

goods like food. However, the risks were known in advance and had to be offset against the implications of portering, not just by way of its exacting physical effort but in terms of time which would ultimately have been at the expense of climbing.

2. John Hunt was left with the problem of what to call the unnamed mountain after its successful first ascent: '"Friendship", "Fraternity"? Something must be found to accord with Soviet principles in nomenclature. It will not be easy to find something appropriate.' The name Sodruzhstvo, meaning 'concord', was finally agreed with the Russians.

SELECT BIBLIOGRAPHY

Books:

Alvarez, A., *The Savage God: A Study in Suicide* (London: Weidenfeld & Nicolson, 1971)

Bonington, Chris, *The Climbers: A History of Mountaineering* (London: BBC Books/Hodder and Stoughton 1992)

Brown, Joe, *The Hard Years* (London: Gollancz, 1967)

Buhl, Herman, *Nanga Parbat Pilgrimage*, translated by Hugh Merrick (London: Hodder and Stoughton, 1956)

Connor, Jeff, *Creagh Dhu Climber: The Life and Times of John Cunningham* (Anglesey: Ernest Press, 1999)

Haston, Dougal, *In High Places* (London: Cassell, 1972)

Hunt, John, *Life is Meeting* (Sevenoaks: Hodder and Stoughton, 1978)

Jones, C. Trevor and Milburn, Geoff, *Welsh Rock* (Leicester : PIC, 1986)

MacInnes, Hamish, *The Price of Adventure* (London: Hodder and Stoughton, 1987)

Morin, Nea, *A Woman's Reach* (London: Eyre & Spottiswoode, 1968)

Rébuffat, Gaston, *Starlight and Storm*, translated by Wilfrid Noyce and Sir John Hunt (London: E. P. Dutton & Co., 1956)

Slesser, Malcolm, *Red Peak* (London: Hodder and Stoughton, 1964)

Smith, Malcolm, *SMC Climbers' Guide to the Cairngorms*, vols 1 and 2 (Glasgow: SMC, 1961)

Watson, Adam, *The Cairngorms: The Cairngorms, Lochnagar and the Mounth (SMC District Guidebook)* (Glasgow: SMC & Trust, 1992)

Wilson, Ken, ed., *Hard Rock: Great British Rock Climbs* (London: Granada, 1974, and Bâton Wicks: Diadem)

Climbing articles :

Campbell, Robin, 'Obituary of Graham Brown' (*SMC Journal*, 1966)

Clark, Gunn, 'The North Face of the Grandes Jorasses' (*Fell and Rock Journal*, 1960)

Fraser, Andrew , 'Shibboleth' (*SMC Journal*, 1958–59)

Haston, Dougal, 'Nightshift in Zero' (*EUMC Journal* 'Nocturnal', 1960–61)

Holt, Janet, 'A Gregarious Ascent' (*EUMC Journal*, 1957–58)

Hunt, John and Cox, David, 'Tribute to Wilfrid Noyce' (*Alpine Club Journal*, 1992)

Hunt, John, article on Wilfrid Noyce (*Geographical Journal*, 1962)

Inglis, John, 'Smith's Routes – A Short History' (*SMC Journal*, 2002)

Marshall, Jimmy, 'The Orion Face' (*SMC Journal*, 1961)

Murray, W.H., 'The History of Scottish Mountaineering' (*SMC Journal*, 1964)

Noyce, Wilfrid, *The Times* (date unknown, abridged)

Smith, Robin, 'Twenty Four Hours' (*EUMC Journal*, 1956–57)

Smith, Robin, 'Climbs Round About Edinburgh' (*EUMC Journal*, 1957–58)

Smith, Robin, 'Slow Times on Slime Wall' (*SMC Journal*, 1959)

Smith, Robin, 'Walkering in the Alps' (*EUMC Journal*, 1959–60)

Smith, Robin, 'The Bat and the Wicked' (*SMC Journal*, 1960)

Smith, Robin, 'Memoirs of an Odium Meeter' (written in visitors' book at the Hadden-Woodburn Memorial Hut in 1959, found in c. 1964 by David Hughes)

Smith, Robin, 'The Old Man and the Mountain' (*SMC Journal*, 1960)

Smith, Robin, 'A Week in the Hills' (*SMC Journal*, 1961)

Smith, Robin, 'Goofy's Last Climb' (*EUMC Journal* 'Nocturnal', 1960–61)

Smith, Robin, 'Snakes and Ladders' (*EUMC Journal* 'Nocturnal', 1960–61)

Smith, Robin, ed. 'Nocturnal' edition of *EUMC Journal*, 1960–61

Weir, Tom, 'Soviet Climbers on Scottish Peaks' (*Scotsman*, 20th June 1960)

GLOSSARY

Abseil A means of sliding down a rope in a controlled fashion.

AC Alpine Club (based in London).

Aid climbing Using equipment which directly assists progress.

Anchor Point of attachment of ropes or slings to rock, snow or ice.

Arête Narrow ridge of rock, snow or ice.

Artificial climbing See **Aid climbing**.

Ascende(u)r A mechanical device used to help climbers ascend a rope (see also **Jumar**).

Backing up (or **Bridging**) A method of climbing a wide crack with the back pressed against one wall and feet on the other.

Belay A means of tying oneself to the face in order to be able to protect one's partner by paying out or taking in the rope. The 'stance' where this occurs is sometimes referred to as a 'belay'.

Bergschrund The gap or crevasse between a glacier and an adjacent face (German).

'Biner An abbreviation used for **karabiner**.

Bivouac or **Bivvie** A small tent or basic shelter. (Often applied by climbers to an overnight stop in the open.)

Brocken Spectre An occasional occurrence in mountains, whereby a person's shadow is cast in huge form on mist or clouds.

Carabiner or **Crab** See **Karabiner**.

CC Climbers' Club.

CDMC Creagh Dhu Mountaineering Club.

Chimney A fissure in ice or rock wide enough to ascend within it.

Chimneying Using back and feet to climb a fissure or 'chimney'.

Chockstone A stone wedged between rocks. They may be the size of buses or mere pebbles placed there to facilitate a belay.

Choss An expression coined by Robin meaning shambolic, useless or chaotic (it based on 'chaos').

CIC Hut Charles Inglis Clark Hut on Ben Nevis

Classic route A climb of outstanding merit due to such as its location, elegance or history. Standard of difficulty is invariably not a factor.

Col A dip in a ridge, or a pass.

Commit To make a move from which retreat for the climber is invariably impossible.

Cornice Overhanging snow on a ridge or plateau formed by the action of the wind.

Couloir An open gully.

Crampons Metal spiked frames fitted to boots to provide grip on snow and ice.

Crack A (usually) vertical narrow fault in rock, narrow enough to accommodate an arm or hand or foot or fingers, or perhaps only a small pebble to make an artificial chockstone.

Creagh Dhu See **CDMC**.

Crevasse A split in the surface of a glacier, often concealed by overlying snow.

Crux The most difficult part of a climb.

Dièdre The Continental equivalent of the British 'crack', though sometimes wider.

Direttissima Continental term for the most natural line up a face.

Étriers Short rope and metal portable ladders used in artificial climbing.

Exposure Where a climber can see that he/she would fall a long way should a mishap occur.

Face Steep or vertical aspects of a boulder, cliff, hill or mountain to which climbers are attracted.

Flake Thin piece of protruding rock.

Free climbing Climbing without using pitons, étriers etc as direct aids, but using ropes and running belays for protection (cf **Aid climbing**).

Front pointing The use of sharp points at the front of crampons to ascend steep snow or ice.

Gear A general name for climbing equipment or, equally, for protection equipment in isolation.

Gendarme A rock pinnacle obtruding from a ridge.

Glissade Controlled descent of frozen snow, whilst sliding in a sitting, squatting or standing position

Grade The level of difficulty of a climb gauged from a consensual scale. See Appendix I and Chapter 12.

Gully A fault that separates, and lies below, two large rock faces.

GUMC Glasgow University Mountaineering Club.

Hand jam See **Jammed holds**.

Headwall Steep rock barrier at the head of a glen or valley.

Ice-axe Shaped like the letter 'T' in Robin's day, they were used for cutting steps in snow and ice. One end of the head had a small blade (the 'adze') while the other was pointed like that of a pick-axe. This end of the axe doubled up as an emergency-stop mechanism to climbers sliding down frozen snow, while the shaft provided belays when pressed deep into snow.

Icefall Frozen waterfall.

Ice-picks Modern ice-climbing tools, used in pairs by climbers to hack into ice above their heads. Ascent is achieved by pulling on the picks from above while pushing upwards on feet clad in front-pointed crampons. This technique evolved in the late 1970s.

Ice screw Metal screw hammered or screwed into ice for protection (not available in Robin's day).

Jammed holds Whereby a climber's jammed-in finger, hand or fist attains grip.

Jammed knot runner A running belay derived from a knotted rope jammed into a narrow crack.

JMCS Junior Mountaineering Club of Scotland.

Jug handle A large hand-hold.

Jumar The original make of **Ascende(u)r**.

Karabiner or **krab** Oval metal snap-link devices used for connecting gear together, such as the rope to an anchor point.

Kletterschühe Lightweight continental rock-climbing boots used in the 1950s.

Knitting A mess of tangled rope.

Layback Method of climbing an edge of rock where hands pull and legs push to provide counter-balance.

Leader The first person on the rope.

Moraine Accumulated debris carried down by a glacier.

Nails Nailed climbing boots: three types of nails tended to be used, serated-edged tricounis round the edge of soles providing grip.

Neve An expanse of granular snow not yet compressed into solid snow or ice.

Nose Protruding mass of rock.

Objective danger Events beyond the control of a climber, like rock-fall or avalanche.

PAs Tight-fitting, rubber-soled rock-climbing boots of the late 1950s, named after developer, Pierre Allain.

Peel To fall or jump off a climb.

Peg See **Piton**.

Pitch A section of a climb between main belay points.

Piton (or **peg**) A metal spike, with an eye for a karabiner, hammered into a crack in the rock to facilitate a belay.

Protection A system of running belays which make climbs safer (physically) and easier (psychologically) for lead climbers.

Prus(s)iking Climbing a rope with the aid of prussik knots (friction hitches) and foot loops.

Ramp Slab of rock running diagonally across a face.

Refuge Mountain hut.

Rib A minor protruding (vertically directed) bit of rock.

Ridge The (often sharp) terrain that connects peaks or other high parts of mountains.

Rimaye The gap or crevasse that naturally forms between a glacier and an adjacent face (French).

Roof Large horizontal overhang.

Route Alternative word for a climb.

Runner (or **running belay**) A sling and karabiner used in tandem to provide a leader with protection.

'Schrund See **Bergschrund**

Second The one who climbs a pitch after the leader, having earlier provided protection for the leader via running belays.

Serac A block of ice found where a glacier falls steeply.

Siege-style The use of fixed ropes and large resources.

Slab An inclining sheet of rock often devoid of significant holds.

Slack Loose rope between the two climbers.

Sling A small loop of rope to assist with belays and abseiling.

SMC Scottish Mountaineering Club.

Spindrift Powdered snow falling in small avalanches or carried by the wind.

Spur Rock or snow protrusion on the side of a mountain.

Stance A place on a climb that separates pitches, from which climbers can (in reasonable comfort if possible) provide protection for their partners.

Step A short steep rise in a gully or upon a ridge.

Sustained Said of a route with a continuous level of difficulty.

Téléférique Cable car.

Thrutching Inelegant efforts, often seen in chimneys, using knees, elbows, etc.

Tie on When a climber attaches the rope to him/herself, nowadays usually via a harness.

Top-rope A rope from above, providing protection.

Traverse To move across snow or rock or ice.

Undercut A low horizontal crack or hole on which a climber can either pull or can get a grip by pinching fingers and thumb.

Verglas A thin coating of ice on rock (from sleet or rain).

Vibrams Solid climbing boots with deep-cut soles like modern walking boots (a postwar development).

Voie normales The most regularly climbed routes.

Wall A steep, large mountain face.

Wand German for wall, as in 'Fiescherwand'.

White-out Where driving snow or mist in front of a white (snow) background debars sound judgement on distances whilst making the appearance of solid ground and space indistinguishable.

APPENDIX I

ROCK-CLIMBING TECHNICAL GRADES

These notes have been largely taken from the Scottish Mountaineering Club's guides. Reprinted with kind permission of the Scottish Mountaineering Trust (Publications) Ltd and the Scottish Mountaineering Club.

Summer Grades

A system of grading has been standardised throughout Britain since Robin Smith's day.

Grades of rock climbs now range from Easy, Moderate, Difficult (Diff), Very Difficult (VDiff), Severe, Hard Severe, Very Severe (VS) and Hard Very Severe (HVS), to Extremely Severe (E). In Robin's time the hardest category in Scotland was VS; this category thus contained climbs of variable levels of difficulty, ranging from those still considered VS to others now classed as Extremely Severe E2 routes.

The HVS grade was introduced in Scotland in the late 1960s and the E grade was introduced in the late 1970s. This latter overall assessment of a climb's difficulty is further subdivided into E1, E2, E3, E4 and so on up to E9.

Additionally, technical grades, indicating the level of athletic skill required, are given for routes of VS and above. The normal technical grades to be expected on routes are as follows (from 4a up to a maximum of 7c):

VS – 4b, 4c, 5a
HVS – 4c, 5a, 5b
E1 – 5a, 5b, 5c
E2 – 5b, 5c, 6a
E3 – 5c, 6a
E4 – 5c, 6a, 6b
E5 – 6a, 6b

Routes with a technical grade at the lower end of the range are likely to have shorter and generally well-protected cruxes. Those at the upper end are likely to present sustained levels of difficulty and/or be poorly protected. Shibboleth on the Buachaille, first climbed by Robin in 1958, has a modern grading of E2 5c.

Winter Grades

Climbs are graded in two ways, similar to the method used for E grade rock routes. Both parts of the grading system are open-ended. A Roman numeral indicates the overall difficulty of a climb, whilst the additional technical indicator (as an ordinary number) relates to the hardest move of a route. Overall difficulties are assessed as follows:

Grade I – Uncomplicated, average-angled snow climbs normally having no pitches. They may, however, have cornice difficulties or long run-outs.

Grade II – Gullies which contain either individual or minor pitches, or high-angled snow with difficult cornice exits. The easiest buttresses under winter conditions.

Grade III – Gullies which contain ice in quantity. There will normally be at least one substantial pitch and possibly several lesser ones. Sustained buttress climbs, but only technical in short sections.

Grade IV – Steeper and more technical with vertical sections found on ice climbs. Mixed routes will require a good repertoire of techniques.

Grade V – Climbs which are difficult, sustained and serious. If on ice, long sustained ice pitches are to be expected; mixed routes will require a degree of rock climbing ability and the use of axe torquing and hooking and similar winter techniques.

Grade VI – Thin and tenuous ice routes or those with long vertical sections. Mixed routes will include all that has gone before but more of it.

Grades VII and **VIII** are yet harder routes.

SMC guidebooks advise that 'a V,4 route is normally a serious ice route and V,5 would be a classic ice route with adequate protection, V,6 would be a classic mixed route and V,7 would indicate a technically difficult but well-protected mixed route. Each route has the same overall difficulty (Grade V) but with differing degrees of seriousness and technical difficulty.' Orion Direct on Nevis, Robin's and Jimmy Marshall's new route in February 1960, when winter climbing was a different sport in view of the equipment available, is today classified as V,5.

Readers can find more information on the SMC website: www.smc.org.uk.

APPENDIX II

ROBIN SMITH'S FIRST ASCENTS – MOUNTAIN ROUTES

The table below shows modern grades. The symbol (W) after a route name signifies a Winter route.

Route	Grade	Location	Date	With
Blockhead	E1 5b	Garbh Beinn, Ardgour	April 1957	Victor Burton (EUMC)
The Rosetta Stone	HVS 5a	Rosetta Pinnacle, Cir Mhor	May 1957	Solo
Glueless Groove	E2 5b	The Cobbler, Arrochar	June 1957	Crux unseconded?
Chasm Left Edge	VS 4c	Sgurr nan Eag, Skye	Sept 1957	Hugh Kindness (EUMC)
Ladders	VS 4c	Sgurr nan Eag	Sept 1957	Crux unseconded?
Cuneiform Buttress (W)	IV	Buachaille Etive Mor, Glencoe	Dec 1957	Derek Leaver (JMCS)
Chartreuse	E1 5a	Scafell East Buttress, Lakes	May 1958	Derek Leaver
Leverage	E1 5a	Scafell East Buttress	May 1958	Crux unseconded?
July Crack	HVS 5a	Great Gully Buttress, Buachaille	June 1958	Andrew Fraser (EUMC)
Dwindle Wall	HVS 5a	Creag na Tulaich, Buachaille	June 1958	Andrew Fraser
Halfway (see Yo-Yo)	n/a	North Face of Aonach Dubh, Glencoe	June 1958	David Hughes (EUMC)
Shibboleth	E2 5c	Slime Wall, Buachaille	June 1958	Andrew Fraser
Tower Face, the Comb (W)	VI 6	Ben Nevis	Jan 1959	Richard Holt (EUMC)

Route	Grade	Location	Date	With
Orion Face (W)	V 5	Ben Nevis	Jan 1959	Richard Holt
Stook	VS 4c	North Face of Aonach Dubh	April 1959	Dougal Haston (JMCS)
Yo-Yo	E1 5b	North Face of Aonach Dubh	May 1959	David Hughes
Shibboleth (True Finish)	E2 5c	Slime Wall	June 1959	John McLean (CDMC)
The Bat	E2 5b	Càrn Dearg Buttress, Ben Nevis	Sept 1959	Dougal Haston
The Long Wait	E2 5b	Trilleachan Slabs, Glen Etive	Sept 1959	John Cunningham (CDMC)
The Great Chimney (W)	IV 5	Tower Ridge, Ben Nevis	Feb 1960	Jimmy Marshall (SMC)
Minus Three Gully (W)	IV 5	North-East Buttress, Ben Nevis	Feb 1960	Jimmy Marshall
Smith's Route (W)	V 5	Gardyloo Buttress, Ben Nevis	Feb 1960	Jimmy Marshall
Ordinary Route (W)	V 4	Observatory Buttress, Ben Nevis	Feb 1960	Jimmy Marshall
Pigott's Route (W)	V 6	The Comb, Ben Nevis	Feb 1960	Jimmy Marshall
Orion Direct (W)	V 5	North-East Buttress, Ben Nevis	Feb 1960	Jimmy Marshall
Thunder Rib	HVS	Sgurr a' Mhadaidh, Skye	April 1960	Geoff Milne (EUMC)
Gob	HVS 5a	Carnmore, Wester Ross	April 1960	Dougal Haston
Yo-Yo (continuation)	VS 4c	North Face of Aonach Dubh	May 1960	James Moriarty (SMC)
Dan	E1	Trilleachan Slabs	date uncertain	James Moriarty

Robin Smith's First Ascents

Route	Grade	Location	Date	With
Central Route	HVS	Minus Two Buttress, Ben Nevis	May 1960	John Hawkshaw (EUMC)
Marshall's Wall	E2 5b	Gearr Aonach, Glencoe	June 1960	George Ritchie (SMC)
Jubilee Climb (W)	II	Trident Buttress, Ben Nevis	1961	Dougal Haston
The Peeler	HVS 5b	Garbh Beinn	June 1961	James Moriarty
The Big Top	E1 5a	West Face of Aonach Dubh	Aug 1961	James Gardner (GUMC)
The Clean Sweep	VS 4c	Hell's Lum, Cairngorms	Sept 1961	Graham Tiso (SMC)
Hellfire Corner (Direct)	VS 4b	Hell's Lum	Sept 1961	Graham Tiso
Turnspit	VS 4c	North East Nose of Aonach Dubh	Oct 1961	Dougal Haston
Boggle	E1 5b	Beinn Eighe, Torridon	Oct 1961	Andrew Wightman (EUMC)
Kipling Groove (Variation)	5b	Gimmer Crag, Langdale	Oct 1961	James Moriarty
GeeGee	VS	Gimmer Crag	Oct 1961	James Moriarty
Girdle Traverse	E2 5b	North Face of Aonach Dubh	April 1962	Robin Campbell (EUMC) Dougal Haston Neil McNiven (EUMC)
The Needle	E1 5a	Shelter Stone Crag, Cairngorms	June 1962	David Agnew (CDMC)

P.T.O.

CDMC – Creagh Dhu Mountaineering Club
EUMC – Edinburgh University Mountaineering Club
GUMC – Glasgow Uninversity Mountaineering Club
JMCS – Junior Mountaineering Club of Scotland
SMC – Scottish Mountaineering Club

APPENDIX III

WALKERING IN THE ALPS

This was Robin's own account of the first British ascent of the Walker Spur by himself and Gunn Clark in 1959 – see Chapter 16. First published in the 1959–60 *EUMC Journal*, and reprinted here with kind permission.

The day we came into Chamonix looking like a storm we packed our sacks with two great steaks and climbed to the ruins of the Leschaux hut. Avalanche echoes and ghosts of heroes and the smell of Nordwand hung in the black rafters. Two Poles came breathing upon our beds, hot from the Caucasus. Three gutteral Teutons were squatting in the shadows round a glittering heap of gear. Two French were talking fast and rushing out and in to look at the cloud on the Walker; then they looked everyone up and down and set off back to Chamonix. Gunn and I sat and scowled in a corner and cooked a meal as it went dark, and we burnt our steaks so badly that Gunn had eaten his before we realised they were rotten and hurled the other one into the night. And then the Jorasses came floating out of the clouds and a big moon came up and all the Walker Spur was black as pitch. Three or four hours of trying to sleep drifted away, then we were up and trying to eat and stumbling out of the hut, and by three o'clock Gunn and I and the two Poles had gathered under the chaos where the Glacier split into vast crevasses and reared into 4000 ft of North Wall hunched black above us.

The Poles found the start and disappeared over the Bergschrund into a rotten couloir. The first step was desperate, a dirty crack with cold wet Polish snow on the holds and barely enough light to see and Polish stones whistling round our ears. We hid in a hole to let the Poles get out of the way, then followed the couloir up and right to the neck behind the first little shoulder of the Spur. From here a heap of easy shelves shambled away up round to the left, and Gunn was full of rotten steak and began to go very badly and soon he was moaning and doubling up and horribly retching and the Poles were forging ahead. But then while I was blindly chasing the Poles, Gunn saw straight ahead the twin corners of the Thirty Metre Crack. Resurrected he led off along a series of steps on the right and we zigzagged up to the big ledge at the bottom of the crack.

Here we came into the sun, and the clean, rough, free rock of the Crack was sheer joy. The Poles appeared below from a long detour over on the left, muttering about a 'grande système' – we could only communicate in bits of French and Rock 'n' Roll. They seemed to want a top-rope, and indeed they didn't bother with the rock and more or less climbed our rope. Down on the Glacier we saw the Teutons prowling round the bottom of the Spur; we sent off a volley of stones and they retreated to the Hut. Gunn and I seized a start and turned to the traverse of the Ice Bands, four or five pitches over to the right curving up to the Ninety Metre Corner. But before we got halfway over, Lechec the dashing Pole came past, without belays, trailing a protesting Stachec, old man of the expedition. And next to our dismay we came to Stachec, belayed from above, standing under an easy crack and wanting us to climb his rope. We turned a cold shoulder and forced a fearful icy wall just to the side, and by the time we were up the Poles had gone off in a huff. And then we stepped round an edge to find Stachec firmly placed across the foot of the Ninety Metre Corner, with Lechec beaming down at us from the top of the first pitch and a great twisted double rope burying the corner crack and the corner the only feasible line. They said this was the 'grande système Alpège', seemingly universal through the Alps; but it seemed very complicated and maybe we couldn't understand and no doubt they were only trying to help, but we couldn't see what you save by swarming up a hairy rope when you could be floating over the rocks! We said it was unscrupulous and they doubled up cackling, so we jeered like crows whenever we saw them using holds on the rock instead of the rope. We submitted as far as the top of the corner, three really good pitches. There we stood out for our principles, only they managed to move off first and kept the lead for the rest of the day.

Iced rocks led to the bulging base of the Grey Tower – 1000 ft of soaring slabs, like a cigar, the backbone of the Walker Spur. We spiralled rightwards under the bulge: a tapering shelf to a ring-spike and an old fixed rope, an abseil and a gentle swing to a sloping ledge on the right, and then rising slab, a chimney choked with ice and chockstones, and up and right by cracks and blocks to a balcony stuck like a limpet right out on the edge of the Spur overhanging the vast sweep of the rattling Central Couloir. The sun had turned right round behind the summit ridge of the Grandes Jorasses, and now it was pouring round from the

West all over the Dalles Noires making them look not at all black or repulsive. But we found the next few pitches the technical crux of the climb: there was no one definite line and finding a route was hard, and now that we had finished the long traverses the Poles were straight above, and still trundling stones with furious purpose, and here there weren't any holes to hide in. A big stone rumbled over Gunn and a little one hit him on the head, and we shrank up under a scanty bulge till the Poles disappeared to the right, and from there we trailed as close as we dared pulling sickly face and beetling off to one side or other side as soon as the boulders came down in a beeline. It was going gloomy and the sun went off into clouds. Then I pulled off a great sharp rock and it fell on the rope and cut it in two. We doubled the longer bit, which let us run out about 100 ft, and we stuffed the rest away, feeling for the first time what a big Wall it was, like ants running up a long tree out of a forest fire. One last volley just to the right and then there was peace, and we scuttled away to the right, too low down in the darkness, and back up left on holds we could hardly see, to the ledge the Poles had cleared for the night.

We took a sack of ice to the bottom end of the ledge, flattened the rubble and pegged ourselves to the wall. Gunn dangled over the edge and I curled up in a ball, and we brewed up coffee and shivered and crooned and fried bits of bacon and gravel to keep ourselves warm. Far away down we could see a light in the Leschaux Hut. Some or other time Gunn fell asleep on top of the candle and set his duvet on fire, and suddenly the air was full of oaths and feathers. And around four in the morning we were shaken out of a doze to the sound of the Poles getting ready to go.

We made a sly move by having nothing to eat and rushed off up the ledge into the lead. We ham-fisted over bitter jugs on the first frozen wall of V, but we soon broke out on the left right on to the crest of the Spur into the morning sun, and the rest of the Grey Tower was fantabulous, never more than Severe, pitch after pitch of clean rough rock all free and always out in the open . We came out on a shoulder of snow and took a fiendish delight in sending lumps of ice thundering down on to our friends the Poles. The thing was to go up and left until we could traverse the slab on the right to the foot of a steep couloir. But in the joy of swinging an axe I charged off too far up the ice, and by the time we got sorted out the Poles had slipped through with glee and crossed into the couloir. Whereupon ensued the greatest shamble of all the expedition.

Lechec led the first pitch and belayed at the side, and Stachec led through heaving down fantastic heaps of snow and stones and icicles that piled up on our rucksacks and stotted off our heads as we dodged and scrabbled our way to Lechec's belay. Then they had an evil habit of sack-hauling, only Stachec had forgotten to take the sack rope, so Lechec followed with one sack on, trailing the sack rope, and we were to launch the remaining sack so that they could pull it up. So then it jammed in the couloir about 20 ft up. So I led off wearing my sack, clipped on with a sling to the bottom of their sack, and battled on with their sack sitting on my head, butting it over the bulges, with the sack-rope taking most of the weight and sweeping off all that was loose that was left and Gunn squatting at the bottom like an ostrich. Then I came to a peg 100 ft up and the end of our rope and tether. Stachec was 30 ft away up on the left, so I belayed on the peg to bring up Gunn and unclipped from the Polish sack and let it swing over to the left, and so it swung away down with a squeal of delight and spiked itself under a bulge as stuck as a pig. So I got Stachec to throw me the other end of the sackrope, tied on 30 ft from the end, untied from our rope, tied the ends of the two ropes in a vast knot that couldn't slip through a karabiner, clipped our rope into the karabiner on the peg so the knot was on the same side as the rest of the sackrope, and with Stachec holding me on his miserable little sack-rope I skated across the iced wall on the left and yanked their wretched sack over the bulge. And then with Stachec hauling in both ends of the sack-rope twanging like a Spanish guitar the sack and I moved slowly upwards flailing at the verglas until finally like a sinker and a haddock on a hook we slid up and over and on to the ledge at the top. Gunn followed as soon as I was fit to take in the rope, still relying on the sack-rope for the first 30 ft; then the Poles took their rope back and pressed on with the climb while Gunn floundered in the couloir with all the old holds in the ice demolished. By the time we got ourselves organised and rolled our eyes upwards over all the quantity of Spur above, the Poles had disappeared into the blue.

As from here both of us were shattered, lurching around and just rolling off into sleep at the stances. We went up and curled away to the right and up a corner and over little walls and breaks and back to the left in a chimney, and we came out on the final crest of the Spur running up into the Pointe Walker. It cut like a knife down either side, and clouds were blowing out above us over the summit ridge. Sometimes it looked like 100 ft, sometimes like 1000, then we were into and over the cornice, wallowing in soft snow and out of France into Italy. And then there was only the pain of descent down the other side, dirty rock and wet snow and on to the glacier just at dark and crawling around without a light into holes and over humps and Gunn fancied a spidery snow-bridge and I wanted to go down a crevasse and we sat on our haunches fuming and shouting the odds. In the end we got through to screes and into the moonlight and prowled around looking for a hut, and we found it at two in the morning hidden under a stone with consummate skill and bawled the Guardian out of his miserable pit to let us in.

INDEX

Index

Index

High Endeavours

Jimmy Cruickshank was a contemporary and schoolfriend of Robin Smith's, and was his climbing partner during their last two years at school together. Jimmy is now a sixty-six-year-old grandfather of two. This is his first book.